Between People

A New Analysis of Interpersonal Communication

Between People

Gerald R. Miller

Mark Steinberg

Michigan State University

A New Analysis of Interpersonal Communication

SCIENCE RESEARCH ASSOCIATES, INC.
Chicago, Palo Alto, Toronto
Henley-on-Thames, Sydney, Paris

A Subsidiary of IBM

We wish to acknowledge the following for permission
to reprint or adapt material.

Page 4: Alvin Toffler, *Future Shock*. Copyright © 1970 by Alvin Toffler. Reprinted by
permission of Random House, Inc.

Pages 32, 233–34, 238: Reprinted from *Pragmatics of Human Communication* by Paul
Watzlawick, Ph.D., Janet Helmick Beavin, B.A., and Don D. Jackson, M.D. with the
permission of W. W. Norton & Company, Inc. Copyright © 1967 by W. W. Norton &
Company, Inc.

Page 168: Reprinted from *Empathy: Its Nature and Uses* by Robert L. Katz. Copyright
© 1963 by The Free Press of Glencoe, a Division in the United States of America. Used
by permission of Macmillan Publishing Co., Inc.

Pages 142, 148–49, 149–50: Two Dogmatism Scale items from Chapter 4, "The Measurement of Open and Closed Systems," Quotation from "Introduction," and para-
phrased material from Chapter 3, "A Fundamental Distinction Between Open and Closed
Systems," by Milton Rokeach and Frank Restle, in THE OPEN AND CLOSED
MIND, by Milton Rokeach, © 1960 by Basic Books, Inc., Publishers, New York.

Pages 147–48: Reprinted from "The Approach of the Authoritarian Personality," by
Nevitt Sanford in James L. McCary (ed.), *Psychology of Personality*: *Six Modern
Approaches*. Copyright © 1956 by Logos Press, Inc. Used by permission of the author.

Page 198: BETWEEN MAN AND MAN by Martin Buber. Copyright © Macmillan
Publishing Co., Inc. 1965.

Page 224: R. D. Laing, *The Politics of Experience*. Copyright © R. D. Laing, 1967. Used
by permission of Penguin Books Ltd, London, England.

Pages 310–11, 320: Reproduced by special permission from *Interpersonal Process of
Self-Disclosure: It Takes Two to See One*, by Samuel A. Culbert, p. 2, 1967, N.T.L.
Institute for Applied Behavioral Science.

Page 329: Selection reprinted from COMMUNICATION; The Social Matrix of Psychiatry, by Jurgen Ruesch, M.D., and Gregory Bateson with the permission of W. W.
Norton & Company, Inc. Copyright © 1968, 1951 by W. W. Norton & Company, Inc.

Page 342: From "The Sounds of Silence" by Paul Simon. © 1964 Paul Simon. Used with
the permission of the publisher.

Contents

Preface

Unquestionably there is keen interest in interpersonal communication. It is reflected by the dramatic increase in courses with "interpersonal communication" (or some variant thereof) in their titles, and by the spate of new trade and textbooks that ostensibly deal with interpersonal communication or interpersonal relationships. At a broader societal level, there is evidence of this interest in the continuing concern about the psychologically debilitating effects of anomie, alienation, and relational superficiality, as well as the individual quest for greater sensitivity and authenticity.

Despite this deep concern, few (if any) introductory texts provide clear conceptual boundaries for delineating interpersonal from noninterpersonal communication transactions. Indeed, it is sometimes hard to understand why the term *interpersonal* is used at all (as when interpersonal communication is defined as any communication occurring between persons) or what the rationale is for ascribing certain characteristics to the process (as when interpersonal communication is restricted to face-to-face transactions). In fact, a cynic could argue persuasively that the defining characteristics of interpersonal communication often seem to matter less than the inclusion of the phrase in a book's title.

In *Between People* we attempt to rectify this shortcoming and to achieve certain goals. Perhaps the best way to introduce you to this book is to acquaint you with some of our goals and to indicate how we tried to accomplish them.

As we have already said, we wanted to develop a clear, useful conceptual distinction between interpersonal and noninterpersonal communication. The first chapter of part I, "Conceptual Foundations," articulates that distinction. It provides an organizational signpost for the entire book. In addition, we thought it important to define other key concepts such as communication and communication relationship and to present our position concerning the functions of interpersonal communication. Chapters 2 and 3 deal with these important conceptual matters.

We also wanted to emphasize the importance of analyzing interpersonal communication from a relational perspective. Given the inherent linearity of ordinary language, this is no mean task, and we are not entirely satisfied with our efforts. Still, we feel the book does reflect a reasonably consistent commitment to a relational viewpoint. Besides the material on communication relationships found in chapter 2, the three chapters that comprise part III, "Communication Relationships," deal with the initiation and development of interpersonal relationships and their structural dynamics, and specific problems that may arise within relational contexts.

While believing that a relational vantage point affords the richest opportunity for analyzing interpersonal communication, we realize that the emergence of particular relational patterns is partially determined by characteristics of the individual communicators. Consequently, we wanted to consider some of the important factors that may influence an individual's ability to communicate interpersonally. Part II, "Individual Communicators," was written with this goal in mind. In chapter 4, we discuss some of the strategies that communicators use to exert control over their environments, and we introduce a new concept, patterns of

communicative control. Chapter 5 examines the influence of cognitive style on interpersonal communication effectiveness, while chapter 6 deals with the process of empathy and presents a relational analysis of this important communicative skill that differs from previous treatments of the topic.

Like most students of communication, we have a lively interest in message-making. We wanted to write a relationally-oriented discussion of message-making, focusing on problems of import to the interpersonal communicator. Although part IV, "Making Messages," consists of only one chapter, each of the four topics covered could have been granted chapter status had we not felt that the relational perspective would be strengthened by combining them. We first introduce the concept of communicative energy and examine its relation to interpersonal effectiveness. Then we take a relational look at self-disclosure, arguing that it is not the unqualified interpersonal panacea that some writers have painted it to be. Next we consider the role of conversation in developing interpersonal relationships; there can be many interpersonal rewards in "talking about the weather." Then we identify some of the pitfalls in the ways that communicators use language: interpersonal effectiveness demands recognition of the misunderstandings and conflicts that can arise from careless language usage or from overreliance on language as a medium of communication.

There is one final thing we wanted to do. Even though our primary concern in this book is with interpersonal communication, we sought to develop a new way of conceptualizing the entire field of communication. Typically, students of communication have subdivided the field according to the contexts, or settings, in which communication occurs: mass media, organizational, small group, dyadic, and the like. Our conceptualization divides the field according to *how*, not where, people communicate; we are interested in the kinds of data people use to make predictions about message outcomes, regardless of the settings. We believe that our fresh vantage point has potential payoffs for the communication practitioner and researcher alike.

Now that we have told you what we wanted to do in this book, we want to tell you for whom it is written. Primarily, this is a book for those in introductory interpersonal communication classes who wish to understand the subject and improve their own effectiveness in practice. We have tried to write in a style that will be clear and interesting for such readers without sacrificing the integrity of our ideas, using examples, illustrations, and dialogues to clarify and to amplify our main points. Although we think we have been successful in reaching the members of our primary audience, they must remain the final arbiters.

Also, we think the book has something to say to more advanced students of interpersonal communication. Many of the concepts and ideas that are introduced suggest research possibilities; and, as we indicated earlier, our overall conceptualization provides a new way of looking at the entire field of communication.

Of course, this is not a book for everyone. We take a definite stand about the nature and functions of interpersonal communication and about the major factors influencing interpersonal effectiveness. To a large extent, the book is a bilateral labor of love; it is our personal statement about interpersonal communication. Certainly, we will be chagrined and disappointed if it does not excite controversy and disagreement. We hope that many instructors will view our committed stance both as an opportunity to stimulate discussion among readers and as a springboard for introducing competing views. But for the teacher who seeks a summary of all the divergent views about interpersonal communication or a sampling of currently "popular" research topics, this book, at the very best, can serve only as a supplement.

Taken as a whole, we are pleased with our final product. Naturally, even today, if given an opportunity for yet another rewrite, we would probably do certain things different-ly. Still, we feel that the major shortcoming among introductory texts (alluded to at the beginning of this preface) has been elimin-ated, or at least lessened, by our efforts.

More accurately, of course, we should say, "by our efforts and by the efforts of many others." Countless students and col-leagues have participated in the honing and refining of our ideas; sometimes we have argued, sometimes we have acquiesced, but always we have benefitted from their com-ments. In particular, Michael Roloff, who authored the study guide accompanying the book, and Kenneth Villard endured the travails of teaching with an early copy of the manuscript and offered many useful ideas for changes. The reviewers engaged by SRA criticized early drafts of the manuscript profusely and perceptively; as a result of their suggestions, the final product was im-mensely improved. Frank Geddes, Karl Schmidt, Gretchen Hargis, and others at SRA not only did what publishers tra-ditionally do, but also encouraged us to write the book we wanted to write and con-tributed generously of their own resources to make it as good a book as possible. The Department of Communication at Michi-gan State University not only provided us with an environment ideally suited for reflection and writing; it also gave us Edna Seeley, who, besides typing the entire man-uscript diligently and expertly, discovered numerous instances of gruesome grammar and perfidious punctuation. Gerry thanks Pearl Ann, Patricia Anne, Greg, Caleb, Louie, and the numerous teachers, students, and colleagues who have shaped and sharp-ened his thinking about human communi-cation. In addition, Mark wants to thank especially Norm, Jean, Marsha, Sue, Josep, Akiba, and Martin, as well as the many other interpersonal and noninterpersonal communicators who have offered sugges-tions and support. These people receive our thanks: some interpersonally, some nonin-terpersonally, but all sincerely!

Gerry and Mark
East Lansing, Michigan

Communicating Interpersonally:

Conceptual Foundations

While you are walking down a street in your hometown, a stranger stops to ask you directions to the public library.

You arrive at a professor's office to talk about a paper you are writing for his course.

A close friend asks you for advice on how to handle some problems she is having with her boyfriend.

Think about the information available to you for making communicative predictions in each of these situations. In the first one you are likely to know only as much about the other party as you would know about any stranger who asks for directions. You know that he speaks English, and that he wants to go to a library, and this knowledge is usually enough to enable you to fulfill his request. You have little additional information and do not need more.

In the second situation you not only have more information than if you were dealing with a stranger but also need more in order to arrive at accurate communicative predictions. Obviously, you should communicate with your professor differently than you would with just any person you meet on the street. Moreover, you have the opportunity to do so. You know that he is a teacher, that he holds an advanced academic degree, and that he has certain expectations about his behavior toward students and their behavior toward him. Your message-making efforts can profit from your knowledge that professors usually expect interest in their classes, anticipate some deference from their students, and reward quality academic performance among their students.

What about the third situation? What information must you have to make accurate predictions about your communicative exchanges with a friend who needs advice? Certainly you require more information than in the first two situations. You probably would not advise this particular friend in the same way you would advise other friends you have. You probably know specific things about this friend that will enable you to "fit" your messages to her immediate needs and to anticipate her responses to your messages.

In these brief sketches we have described the principal distinction between three levels of analysis and prediction-making: the cultural level, the sociological level, and the psychological level. The first two levels involve noninterpersonal communication while the third level involves interpersonal communication. Chapter 1 sets forth this key distinction between these two types of communication. We discuss the necessary conditions for each type, the uses to which each can be put, and the advantages and disadvantages of each. The distinctions established in chapter 1 provide the foundation for most of what we say throughout the rest of the book.

We have chosen to emphasize initially some key differences in communication situations because of their crucial consequences for communicators. But we do not want to overlook the many similarities in all communication situations. Chapter 2 focuses on these similarities. We suggest that communication, whether interpersonal 'or noninterpersonal, is a complex process involving symbolic transactions by two or more people. The terms *process, transactions,* and *symbolic* are crucial to our definition of communication. In chapter 2 we also introduce the concept of communication relationship. We discuss the importance of adopting a relational view of all communication situations, and we describe some differences between interpersonal and noninterpersonal communication relationships.

In chapter 3 we examine the functions of communication, both interpersonal and noninterpersonal. We propose that the primary function of all communication is the achievement of some degree of environmental control by the communicator. In other words, people communicate primarily to influence the natural and social processes going on around them. Furthermore, their relative success or failure shapes their self-concepts; hence, we argue that self-concept development is a consequence rather than a function of communication. Our position about the functions of communication permeates this book; it is an essential element of the foundations of interpersonal and noninterpersonal communication.

1

All of us seem to need some totalistic relationships in our lives.
But to decry the fact that we cannot have *only*
such relationships is nonsense.

Alvin Toffler, *Future Shock*

Conceptualizing the Interpersonal Communication Process

Communication is as much a part of today's world as the air we breathe. We are born into an environment in which the exchange of messages between people is as constant and prevalent as the exchange of oxygen and carbon dioxide in our lungs. Communication is by far our most important medium for personal development and social contact. Through it we learn and grow; we discover ourselves and other people; we govern nations, wage war, and make peace; we hurt one another; and we fall in love. Without it our friendships, families, and societies could not survive. Communication, like breathing, is necessary for our continued existence.

Communication is a symbolic activity. We often manipulate symbols rather than things; our livelihoods hinge on our ability to influence the actions of others by communicative means. Television dominates our leisure hours. Even the satisfaction of basic sexual needs and, ultimately, species survival depend upon mastery of an intricate set of communication rules and behaviors. "The chief problem with *Playboy*," proclaims an acquaintance, "is that a whole generation of American males has grown up believing that women are born with staples in their navels." This view, though whimsical, underscores the dominance of the symbol in our society.

Many scientists and laymen have become concerned that our complex, symbol-oriented society is plagued as much by communication pollution as by air pollution. When our privacy is invaded by sophisticated electronic devices and mammoth data banks, our right to communicate freely is challenged. When deceptions and half-truths are commonplace among the most trusted and gifted members of our society, we find it hard to depend on the information they transmit to manage our daily lives. When people cry for help all around us and we seem not to listen; when we reach out and get no response; when the accelerated pace of modern life seems to minimize opportunities for sustained, meaningful contact; and when communication style becomes more important than communication substance, we must urge ourselves to develop rational and effective techniques for combating this pollution.

Man can be viewed as a social animal whose existence is largely defined by his symbolic commerce with his fellowmen. Moreover, survival in a communication-free environment would be hazardous at best and impossible at worst, as studies on the effects of social isolation and sensory deprivation have shown. Think for a moment of the consequences of being deprived of the opportunity to interact with others. The sole survivor of a nuclear attack (a fictional character widely exploited in recent years) experiences fear, anxiety, and helplessness. He is doomed to social disintegration, for he cannot function as a communicating animal.

Just as people exist in many ways, so they communicate in a myriad of physical settings and social contexts, in different numbers, and through a variety of channels. The mass media spew messages to large, heterogeneous audiences; classrooms drone with lectures directed at eager and not-so-eager students; and couples join together, exchanging verbal and nonverbal messages. The opportunities for communication seem almost infinite.

Our concerns in this book

This book deals with only part of the communication within our society: interpersonal communication. Many writers have stressed the importance of interpersonal communication (e.g., Katz and Lazarsfeld, 1955; Barnlund, 1968; Keltner, 1970; Giffin and Patton, 1971; McCroskey, Larson, and Knapp, 1971); but careful attempts to delineate the kinds of communication transactions that qualify for the label *interpersonal* are few.

The dominant concept of interpersonal communication holds that it occurs when two or three persons interact face-to-face. Given such circumstances, it follows that feedback (the reaction of one communicator to another) is immediately available, that most of the senses (seeing, hearing, touching, smelling, tasting) can be used, and that no mechanical devices (public address system, telephone, television camera) separate the communicators.

This concept of interpersonal communication is both too broad and too restrictive. It includes every situation in which two or three people are engaged in face-to-face communication and, conceivably, excludes all situations in which four or more people are interacting. It includes face-to-face interaction between two strangers but excludes a telephone conversation between a wife and her husband. It implies that a chat between a waitress and a customer shares equal interpersonal status with an intimate interchange between two lovers. In short, the dominant concept of interpersonal communication strikes us as wanting in clarity, common sense, and usefulness.

Our first major task, therefore, is to develop a conceptual framework that will provide the foundation for this book, and that will enable the reader to distinguish interpersonal from noninterpersonal communication. We hope that our viewpoint also will square with common sense and appeal intuitively to the reader so that he can identify communication transactions that deserve the label *interpersonal.* Finally, and most important, we will seek to develop a concept of interpersonal communication that is useful. We believe that most readers of this book want to become better communicators. To accomplish this goal, they must know what they are doing when they communicate interpersonally and what abilities and skills they need.

A crucial assumption for distinguishing between noninterpersonal and interpersonal communication

Our concept of interpersonal communication rests on this fundamental assumption: *when people communicate, they make predictions about the effects, or outcomes, of their communication behavior*; that is, they choose among various communicative strategies on the basis of predictions about how the person receiving the message may respond.

Suppose you need to ask your parents for the money to buy a car. You consider various communication strategies for achieving your objective. You are fairly certain that you will be unsuccessful if you ask for the money after your father has paid the bill for a dent you put in the family car or shortly after your mother has gotten angry at you because the dog got out when you left the door open. Conversely, making the dean's list may create an environment conducive to loosened purse strings. Thus, the timing of your request depends on your assessment of the communication climate.

Once you have chosen the ideal time to ask for the money, you must decide on the best tactics to use. Should you ask only your father or only your mother or the two of them together? When pleading your case, should you remind them of your accomplishments, or is such a strategy likely to provoke a negative response? What are some probable initial responses of your parents ("But we gave you $100 for clothes

last month!"), and how can these responses be met? While pondering each of these questions, you make numerous predictions about the results of communication strategies. If when you finally ask for the money, the interaction does not go as you expected, you must make new predictions rapidly and spontaneously and choose appropriate communication behaviors.

Consider a second communication problem of interest to most persons: creating a favorable initial impression on someone of the opposite sex. This objective is seldom achieved by random, haphazard communication probes; rather, you must carefully assess the specific situation and make predictions about the probable outcomes of various communication strategies. You may, for example, sometimes be an intellectual, at other times an athlete, music lover, or concerned activist. All people have many different selves, from which they can choose the one most appropriate to the situation, the other person, and their own goals. Once interaction has begun, you may discover that many of your preliminary predictions are wrong, in which case you make new predictions and devise different communicative strategies to conform with these predictions.

Each time we communicate with others, we engage in a predictive process. Consider the kind of questions we ask when we size up a stranger. What is this person like? How is this person like me, and how is he different? Can I trust this person? How is this person likely to react if I do this or that or some other thing? Will this person follow the same rules my acquaintances and I do? Often we do not consciously ask these questions: our perceptions of another person may provide immediate answers. Nevertheless, even with people we already know, we may try to predict their responses to our communication efforts. Will she understand what I mean by a particular word or statement? Does he expect me to respond to his last statement? What kind of responses does she desire? . . . will she accept? . . . will make her angry?

Predictions are made at conscious and nonconscious levels

Prediction requires knowledge of past events and expectations about future events. Our perceptions and attitudes about present situations are constrained by what we have learned about similar past situations and by what we expect to happen. Similarly, when we predict the best communication strategy to use in a particular situation, we are influenced by our past experiences and by the extent to which we perceive the present situation as similar to previous ones.

An essential ingredient in prediction-making is the possibility of change in our environment. Without it, the concept of prediction is meaningless. Our experience of the present and our expectations about the future must indicate the possibility of more than one future. If the only possible future impression we can make on others is negative, for example, prediction is to no avail and it makes little difference how we communicate. Thus, when we predict the outcome of communication situations, we note the similarities between present and past situations, and on the basis of these, project responses to our communication efforts.

Whenever we are strongly aware of the possibility of alternative outcomes of communication, we tend to be conscious of making predictions about them. For example, the debaters in a tournament know that one side will win and one side will lose; they are therefore likely to be highly conscious of making predictions about how the judges will react to their messages. In many communication situations, however, our predictions occur quickly and at a low level of awareness. When we transmit a simple message such as "How are you?" we seldom doubt that the other person will understand it. Moreover, we are confident of his response. Still, if we ask, "Could he possibly respond in some unexpected way or not at all?" we must acknowledge the possibility of alternative responses. Whenever the possibility for change exists, prediction is a latent feature of communication. Therefore, we cannot be absolutely sure that someone will understand our greeting and respond in the expected way. Even this simple communication situation involves prediction, although in most such situations the probability of understanding is extremely high.

We can see, then, that prediction is a part of even the most trivial communication situations, and that the degree to which we are conscious or nonconscious of prediction-making depends on our awareness of alternative outcome possibilities. When we are open to the availability of different outcomes, and hence to predictions, we become open to the possibility of various strategies for bringing about one outcome or another.

We make these points about levels of consciousness, prediction, and strategies to underscore *the fundamentally creative element in all communication*. When we realize that all symbolic interchanges—from the trivial to the significant, the simple to the complex—are open to our own personal influence, our social environments become more exciting and rewarding, more directly colored by individual expression.

When we feel certain of the outcomes of communication, we usually make no attempt to intervene. When we are not so sure of ourselves or of other people, however, as when we interview for a job, we usually try to calculate the effects of forming our messages in a certain way. We rehearse answers to questions we might be asked. (Recently, Mark worked with a contestant in the Miss Michigan contest to increase her awareness of the general types of questions that might be asked and to encourage her to weigh the likely impact of various answers she might give.) When one rehearses possible answers to questions, whatever their source, he is developing a scenario of the interaction before it actually begins.

A necessary condition for sanity is the ability to anticipate fairly consistently the unfolding of events around us. The behavior of other human beings is probably the most significant class of events with which we must deal. Where we have meager experience with the other communicators, we may initiate communication in order to establish expectations about how they are likely to behave and how we "ought" to behave. Try to imagine yourself in a very unfamiliar situation. Quite likely, you would say or do very little until you could take a reading of what other people are doing and saying, especially if you wished to avoid appearing ignorant or peculiar. Fortunately, few situations provide absolutely no grounds for prediction. Almost all people have at least something in common, and even minimal similarities provide a starting point for generating further data.

For example, upon boarding an airline flight on which seats have not been assigned, you begin checking out your fellow passengers to pick a seatmate. If you want to sit next to someone who is friendly, you may look for a smiling face. Based on your experience, you are predicting that the person who smiles will be friendly. If seclusion is your goal, you may look for someone who is gazing out the window, or who is deeply involved in a magazine, or who is scowling. Such cues often indicate that the person prefers to be left alone. If you are a businessman and you want the company of another businessman, you may look for someone who is wearing a business suit or who is reading the *Wall Street Journal*. If you are tired and wish to nap, you will probably avoid sitting next to a person with a baby.

Two sets of factors strongly influence one's predictions. One set may be called *situational*: the given, unalterable features of a communication setting. In the airplane example, the length of the flight and the number and location of available seats will influence your predictions. Greater concern about the accuracy of your prediction is likely if you are embarking on a long trip; while you may be able to endure one hour with an unfriendly person, eight hours might be unbearable. Similarly, if there are few empty seats, you may have to predict who is likely to be least unfriendly rather than who is likely to be most friendly.

The other set of factors may be called *dispositional*. Our past experience and our expectations dispose us to look for certain behaviors and to interpret them in certain ways. For instance, the businessman boarding the plane is more disposed to see business suits than is someone not looking for a businessman. Moreover, he is likely to evaluate the person wearing a business suit differently than would someone who sees business suits as a negative cue and so looks for them to avoid sitting next to a businessman.

Summary

We have discussed a crucial assumption of this book: when people communicate, they make predictions about the effects, or outcomes, of their communication behaviors. As our examples have underscored, people use different data to make their predictions. We will distinguish between interpersonal and noninterpersonal communication on the basis of the major kind of data used in making predictions. Since this distinction is central to our thesis, we turn next to its development.

Three levels of analysis used in making predictions

Three levels of analysis are used in making predictions: cultural, sociological, and psychological. Each level is distinguished by the kind of data that provide a basis for predictions. By data we mean the characteristics of a person (for example, brown hair, American, doctor, selfish, or a Ford owner) or situation (for example, competitive, informal, or familiar) as perceived by another person and the ways these characteristics are interpreted.

The levels of analysis are related to the amount of information available at each level. As an individual moves from the cultural to the sociological to the psychological level of analysis, he both has and needs to have more information if he is to communicate effectively. Furthermore, at each successive level the number of people to whom his information applies decreases. In other words, communicators generally know a little about a great number of people and a lot about very few people.

Cultural level of analysis

As defined by many anthropologists and sociologists, a culture is the sum of characteristics, beliefs, habits, practices, and language shared by a large group of people, usually living in a definable geographic area. People in a culture are united through their norms and values.

Norms may be revealed through patterns of expectations and behaviors. We usually find, therefore, that people of a certain culture behave in similar ways. People's values predispose them to perceive certain institutions, situations, or persons either favorably or unfavorably. Cultures exert a great deal of control over their members, influencing not only everyday behavior but also perceptions of good and bad, just and unjust, and right and wrong.

The members of a culture transmit their norms and values from one generation to another. Each child learns acceptable behaviors and desirable values from his parents, neighbors, and teachers. Although not all people in a culture always act the same way, it is possible to discover certain cultural patterns of behaving and valuing. In the United States, for example, most people eat three meals a day, and they label these meals *breakfast, lunch,* and *dinner.* They also tend to value similar things. At the concrete level, there is some status attached to owning a color television set or two automobiles. At a more abstract level, such notions as free will and capitalism are regarded positively and their abstract counterparts—determinism and communism—are valued negatively.

If people in a culture generally behave similarly and value the same things, the culture is said to be *homogeneous.* Conversely, differences in behavioral patterns and values reflect the *heterogeneity* of the culture. A culture may be homogeneous in some respects, and yet it may be considered heterogeneous as a whole, and vice versa. The relative homogeneity or heterogeneity of a culture is influenced by the degree to which (1) norms and values are enforced, (2) the culture is exposed to outside influences, (3) it is threatened by hostile external forces, and (4) people from other cultures have been assimilated into it. Obviously, if all these factors favor cultural homogeneity, predictions based on cultural data will be more accurate than they would be for culturally heterogeneous societies. In either case, however, some predictive error is unavoidable.

Cultural norms and predictions
The concept of norm implies a recurrent, observable pattern; a behavior occurring at one point in time will be repeated at another. This regularity provides the basis for predicting from cultural data. After observing the car-driving behavior of many members of our culture, for example, we begin to expect that all drivers in this culture drive on the right side of the road. Once our initial observation has been repeatedly confirmed, we are very surprised if we see someone deviating from our expectations; and we would probably make other predictions about him—he is drunk, inexperienced, or ignorant of the culture's traffic laws.

Often, the behavioral patterns of a culture are considerably more complex. In our own culture, for instance, there are several sets of norms governing people's dining habits, some of which apply in some situations but not in others. If we base predictions about eating behavior solely on observations of people dining at exclusive restaurants, we will probably make many erroneous predictions about the eating behavior of picnickers. Despite the complexities of many patterns, we usually begin to make some sense of them. As our cultural experiences increase, our predictive accuracy improves.

Many communication situations are governed by cultural norms. We can find numerous examples of behaviors that are regularly accompanied by certain words or sentences. When acquaintances meet, they say hello or some equivalent greeting such as hi or how are you. Each can predict what the other will say as well as what the other expects him to say. Having several interchangeable responses to choose from, however, allows the communicator some latitude and flexibility. Furthermore, greater precision is not necessary in such communication situations; a culture holds together very well when a range of communication behaviors is allowed.

In many cultures, certain rituals and customs have established communication patterns that permit accurate prediction. Examples include marriage ceremonies, funerals and burials, governmental functions, and religious pageantry.

Ideology and predictions
Knowledge of a society's dominant values and beliefs—its prevailing ideology—allows one to predict probable responses to certain messages. Frequently, Gerry begins his communication theory course by attacking the notion of free will and arguing that all behavior is determined by genetic and environmental circumstances over which the individual has no control. Most students oppose this deterministic position, for they are certain they have freedom of choice. Usually, they are somewhat taken aback when told that their responses are causally determined by the cultural emphasis placed on freedom and responsibility, that their opposition to determinism was predictable. By contrast, a Marxist has no trouble accepting the proposition that people live in a deterministic universe, even though he is likely to take the position that the important determinants of behavior are exclusively economic.

No doubt the reader can supply other examples of the ways in which a culture's ideology influences responses to certain messages. If one wishes to be elected to public office in the United States, he does not extol the virtues of communism, nor does he find it advantageous to embrace religious tenets alien to Judeo-Christian doctrine. Some

writers have gone so far as to derive god-words and devil-words from
our ideology. For instance, Weaver (1953) has argued that such terms
as *progress* and *science* are ultimate god-words in our society, while
epithets such as *un-American* and *communist* are of the devil. He
suggests that communications linking a particular proposal with progress and ostensibly grounding it in scientific evidence will be favorably received by most Americans. Conversely, an opponent's cause can
be seriously harmed by labeling it un-American or tying it to a murky
communist plot.

Gathering cultural data
Communication makes it possible to learn a great deal about a culture
without actually living in it. If you were planning to visit India or
Brazil, for example, you would probably read books about the
country, watch televised programs concerning it, and discuss its customs with acquaintances who had visited there. By the time you
actually arrived for your visit, you would have amassed considerable
information about the country's culture and would be able to make a
number of predictions about the probable effects of certain communication behaviors. Still, there are some things that can be learned only
by direct experience with a culture. After living in the new culture for a
while, you would probably increase your store of cultural data and
would be able to predict more accurately.

Suppose you had absolutely no information about a culture—a
far fetched supposition in this era of rapid communication, but imaginable. Considerable anxiety and uncertainty would accompany
attempts to initiate and carry on communication. In addition, hostility
and suspicion would probably dominate early contacts. Part of our
anxiety and concern over UFOs reflects uncertainty and suspicion; we
realize that if contact with persons from other planets is eventually
established, we may have no cultural grounds for predicting appropriate communication behavior. The only thing we can do, therefore,
is to predict behavior of creatures from outer space on the basis of our
own culture. An example of this was actually reported recently: a
community tried to lure flying saucers to earth so that their occupants
would buy goods and services from local businessmen!

Errors in prediction at the cultural level
When our predictions fail, it is often because we are ignorant of the
other's experiences or because we try to predict his behavior in terms
of experiences different from his own. We may use words for which he
has no meaning or words for which his meanings differ from ours.
These problems are especially acute when we try to communicate with
someone from another culture. For instance, we may have learned that

Mexicans are lazy and that they spend most of their time sleeping under huge sombreros, while their burros wait peacefully nearby. If we base predictions of a Mexican's behavior on these data, we are likely not only to be incorrect but also offensive. Our stereotype is more a product of United States culture than of Mexican, and using it may cause serious breakdowns in communication—breakdowns that in turn have calamitous social, political, or economic consequences. Some students of the Vietnam War have argued that both the French and the Americans failed to achieve victory because they imposed their own cultural values on a situation where they did not apply: both expected the enemy to acquiesce after suffering heavy casualties, but the enemy endured and continued fighting.

Many situations can be cited as examples of errors in predictions at the cultural level. When Gerry uses the determinism argument in his classes as described earlier, there are always some students who respond favorably to it. Similarly, in a political campaign, some voters do not automatically accept or reject candidates who embrace Judeo-Christian religious tenets. Several years ago, the Seattle Chamber of Commerce launched a Greater Seattle campaign based on the proposition that an influx of new industry would be a sign of community progress. Opponents organized a Lesser Seattle movement, arguing that progress—at least when defined as industrial expansion—should not be Seattle's most important product.

A communicator who bases his predictions solely on cultural data will often err. As a society attains greater cultural diversity, he will err more frequently. Most often, the communicator knows his predictions are not entirely accurate, but he is willing to accept a margin of error that still permits effective communication with a majority of his intended receivers. If it is extremely important to communicate effectively with a certain person, it could be unwise to rely on the cultural level of prediction.

Summary
Some acquaintance with cultural norms and values allows predictions to be made about the behavior of individuals in a given culture—even when we have learned nothing about them per se. If we have previously communicated with people like them, we can generalize—cautiously—from these experiences.

Predictions based on cultural data, while often useful to communicators, suffer from serious limitations. There are realms of behavior for which cultural norms and values are ambiguous and inadequate, requiring the communicator to use a different level of analysis for predictive accuracy. For instance, predicting the behavior of workers in a factory, students on a campus, or shoppers in a supermarket on the basis of cultural data can be only marginally successful. In such cases, the communicator simply does not have enough information. To make sense of these situations, a different set of experiences must be tapped. Let us turn to a level of prediction that embraces some of these experiences.

Sociological level of analysis

When a communicator's predictions about a receiver's responses to his messages are based on the receiver's membership in certain social groups, the communicator is predicting at the sociological level. A membership group is a class of people who share certain common characteristics, either by their own volition or because of some criteria imposed by the predictor. Groups resemble cultures, for their members exhibit patterns of behaving and valuing that distinguish them from other groups. Groups also enforce certain norms and values and may be classed according to the relative homogeneity or heterogeneity of their members.

Despite these similarities, groups and cultures differ in many respects. Groups generally contain fewer members than are in the entire culture. Moreover, members of a particular culture may belong to many groups; conversely, within a given society, persons from numerous cultures may form membership groups. In many universities, for example, students from various cultures join together in a foreign student group. While the same cultural norms and values usually apply to specific groups within the culture, many group norms and values are more specific. In some groups, norms and values are clearly articulated for all members, and adopting them is a prerequisite for group membership. Group membership is not necessarily restricted to geographic boundaries. Catholics have similar religious norms and beliefs whether they live in Cleveland, Dublin, or Rome; and university professors demonstrate many behavioral similarities whether they teach at the University of Washington, Harvard, or Tientsin.

People may actively seek out group membership, or certain characteristics may cause them to be classified as part of a particular group. Thus, people usually choose a particular religious denomination, political party, professional society, or social club. By contrast, persons do not choose to be teenagers, females, or senior citizens; rather, membership in these groups results naturally. While people usually experience more pressure to conform to the norms and values of voluntarily selected groups, involuntary membership can also produce strong conformity pressures—witness, for example, the conformity of many members of the heterogeneous group labeled *teenagers*.

No matter how people become members of groups, they have similar interests and perceptual patterns, which engender common group norms and values and allow predictions to be made about certain behaviors of group members. Sociological as well as cultural predictions are based on familiarity with a few "typical" group members.

Predictions based on knowing people's group memberships
Suppose you are discussing family planning and population control with several Catholics. You can be fairly certain that they will respond unfavorably to numerous methods of contraception and that they will oppose abortion as a means of population control. Conversely, they will endorse family planning programs founded on the rhythm method. If you discuss the same topic with a group of Unitarian-Universalists, you will alter your predictions dramatically.

Examples of predictions based on sociological data abound. When a student initially interacts with an unfamiliar teacher, he probably tailors his messages to fit his conception of the teacher role position; that is, he bases his predictions on prior observations of other teachers. Unfamiliarity is not, however, a necessary condition for basing predictions on sociological data. Marriage partners may construct their messages to conform with sociological expectations. Rather than viewing each other as individuals, each bases communication predictions on experiences with, or expectations about, the membership groups labeled *husbands* and *wives*. A friend of one of the authors, for example, recently attributed his broken marriage to the fact that his former spouse performed her wifely duties because she enjoyed them, rather than because she understood that these role behaviors were required of her. Incredible and chauvinistic as his attitude may sound, the husband obviously perceived his wife as a set of sociological roles, not as an individual.

Sometimes the line between sociological and cultural prediction is blurred. In his novel *One Hundred Dollar Misunderstanding*, Gover (1961) creates a monument to communication breakdown: a weekend confrontation between a white, upper-socioeconomic-class college sophomore named JC and a black, teenaged prostitute named Kitten. With rare exceptions, JC and Kitten cannot relate to each other as individuals. They tend to base predictions on sociological and cultural stereotypes. JC expects prostitutes to feel and behave in certain ways (sociological stereotype) and believes that blacks have certain sexual attitudes and appetites (cultural stereotype). Kitten, while considerably more perceptive than JC, is hampered by erroneous preconceptions about a somewhat hazy group that she labels "invessments"—wealthy males capable of providing, and willing to provide, semiperma-

nent economic support for rootless prostitutes. The two bumble
through a weekend crammed with inaccurate cultural and sociological predictions that ensure a minimum of effective communication.

Dangers in making predictions at the sociological level
A person may at the same time be a teenager, a high school student, a
female, an honor student, and a sister. When we make predictions
about her behavior, we cannot always be sure which group's values
will guide it. Often, these values are contradictory, or even mutually
exclusive. People may be members of one group because they agree
with some of the group's values, while rejecting others. How are we to
know the particular values to which the individual subscribes and at
which times these values will guide and direct his or her behavior? For
example, some Catholics do not oppose the use of contraceptive devices and some do not reject abortion—and their numbers are probably growing. If we base predictions about these people's responses
solely on their membership in the Catholic Church, we will miss
the communication target by a wide margin.

   Given these shortcomings of sociological data, what alternatives are
available? It seems unlikely that we will refuse to make predictions
about people's behavior simply because we do not have enough data.
We may try to delay prediction until we have more data, but sometimes this is not feasible. We may go ahead and make predictions
anyway, clearly telling ourselves what we expect to find and closing
our minds to any deviations from our predictions, thus ensuring that
they will be "correct." A more satisfactory solution would be to collect
data of a very different sort for those situations where cultural and
sociological data do not suffice. This requires another level of prediction, the psychological.

Psychological level of analysis

Suppose that as a salesman for a machine parts firm, you are dealing
with the vice-president in charge of purchasing for a manufacturing
corporation. You know that he is a U.S. citizen, is forty years old, has a
wife and two children, drives a convertible, attends the Presbyterian
Church, and belongs to the Rotary Club. These membership groups
provide the sociological basis for choosing your message strategies;
you are uncertain how strongly he is affiliated with them and to what
extent he will deviate from their norms and values.

   Since your information is inadequate, you may seek the answers to
other questions about the executive. Will he consider my firm and me
more credible if I wear a navy blue suit or a plaid sportcoat? Will he
be more influenced by the quality and price of my product or by the

rapid delivery I can offer him? Should I push him for a decision? Should I spice up my sales pitch with a few off-color jokes?

Suppose that you are trying to console a friend who has just had an unhappy experience. Should you say, "I know just how you feel; it's a terrible thing" or "Buck up, these things always work out in the end" or "Tell me all about it"? Should you adopt your friend's frame of reference and display the appropriate emotions, or should you maintain your own perspective but encourage him to talk about his problem? These questions are important, for depending upon how accurately you assess your friend's needs, you may either bolster his spirits or reinforce his sadness and loneliness.

In neither of these two situations can you base your communication behavior exclusively on cultural or sociological data. As we have all discovered, there are many situations where people react quite differently. Furthermore, when placed in what appear to be similar situations, the same people will sometimes react differently at different times.

We have discussed some of the characteristics of cultures and groups and have demonstrated how a culture or a group imposes similarities on the behavioral patterns of its members. What, however, are the sources of individual behavior, of behavior that deviates from cultural or group expectations?

Sources of behavioral differences

It is commonplace to note that when an individual's learning experiences differ from other people's, his behavior also differs. (Conversely, behavioral consistency is to be expected when there is overlap in prior learning experiences.) People's learning experiences may vary in as many ways as there are stimuli to influence people. Consider the number of groups to which a person might belong: people with black hair, members of the Elk's club, veterans, part-time workers, and so on. Each group, both alone and in concert with other groups, provides varied learning experiences. Each book one reads, each movie one sees, and each new person one meets provides a fresh set of experiences. Just as people learn some similar norms and values, they also learn some different ones.

Another source of variety can be found in the many ways people react to what might seem to be identical experiences. Ten new members of a group will each have some unique reactions to the experience of group membership. Some will conform to all the major norms and values of the group, while others will not. A few may even rebel against group constraints but may still find individual membership personally attractive. These differences cannot be anticipated and predicted by using only cultural and sociological data.

A final source of individual differences is the varying perceptions by observers of behavior. When we communicate with others, we may attribute our own peculiar norms and values to them. Often when one laments "Doesn't he know what's good for him?" this kind of attributional process is at work: the person making the lament has imposed his own norms and values—his perceptions of what is good for people—on the other person. Thus, in many cases, behavioral disparities may result from differences imposed by others.

Predicting from psychological data
When predictions of others' responses to our communication behaviors are based on analysis of unique individual learning experiences, they are grounded in a psychological level of analysis. Two or more people who interact frequently and base their predictions about each other primarily on psychological data typically assert that they "know" each other as individuals. This assertion means that they have gained insights into the unique characteristics of each other's personalities, rather than merely defining one another as a set of cultural attributes or sociological roles. Although such insights are hard to acquire, their acquisition fosters a depth of communication not found in superficial contacts governed by cultural or sociological predictions.

Often, interactions based on psychological predictions strike outsiders as strange or even bizarre. In Albee's (1962) powerful drama *Who's Afraid of Virginia Woolf?*, the protagonists, George and Martha, play what appears to be a very destructive game in which the moves are rooted in psychological predictions. Each understands the other's personal needs and knows how to wound the other deep inside. To outsiders—in this case, the young faculty couple who have dropped by for an evening of "fun and games"—George's and Martha's communication behaviors defy explanation. But for George and Martha, the relationship apparently satisfies compelling psychological needs.

The case of George and Martha illustrates another point of general communicative importance. For almost any interaction situation, a set of rules emerges that governs communication. When exchanges have cultural or sociological roots, these rules are usually widely understood. For example, in the simple greeting situations discussed earlier, most members of a culture understand the communication latitude at their disposal. To respond to a casual "How are you?" with "None of your damned business!" suggests either ignorance of the rules or a relationship very different from the typical greeting situation.

By contrast, exchanges with psychological roots are frequently governed by an "idiosyncratic rule structure": the rules are known only to the participants and seem ambiguous, perhaps even inexplicable, to outsiders. So complex and peculiar are the rules governing George and Martha's interaction that one team of authors (Watzlawick, Beavin, and Jackson, 1967) has devoted an entire chapter to analyzing them. Obviously, such rules are not initial givens but grow out of the interaction itself. Of course, lengthy contact does not guarantee that the communicators will move to the psychological level of analysis, a must for developing a unique rule structure. The reader can probably think of some instances when he has established a psychological relationship with someone as well as instances when such a relationship did not evolve, even though a great deal of communication transpired. More will be said about the rule structure of communication in later chapters.

Barriers to accurate predictions at the psychological level
Accurate predictions at the psychological level are not easily made. They must be based on direct experience with an individual, not impressions generalized from contact with others. Another barrier to accurate prediction lies in the tendency to see others in terms of patterns we ourselves have learned; when predictions at the psychological level are based on such patterns, they will often be wrong. Prediction at this level requires careful analysis of the other's behavior in terms of the behavior itself; the communicator must resist the allure of cultural and sociological evidence and must avoid overreliance upon his own prior learning.

The fundamental distinction between noninterpersonal and interpersonal communication

We can now state the conceptual distinction between interpersonal and noninterpersonal communication that serves as a foundation for this book: *when predictions about communication outcomes are based primarily on a cultural or sociological level of analysis, the communicators are engaged in noninterpersonal communication; when predictions are based primarily on a psychological level of analysis, the communicators are engaged in interpersonal communication.* Throughout this volume, the term *interpersonal communication* is reserved for situations in which the communicators base their predictions primarily on psychological data.

Stimulus generalization and stimulus discrimination

At the noninterpersonal cultural and sociological levels, predictions about communication outcomes can be likened to stimulus generali-

zation: the person making predictions looks for samenesses among other communicators. We have discussed numerous situations in which people can make fairly accurate predictions from cultural and sociological data, and we have also mentioned some of the shortcomings of these methods of prediction. Stimulus generalization is closely akin to abstraction: one observes a group of objects and notes aspects they have in common. For instance, on the basis of knowledge about one professor, a person could generalize that all college professors have advanced degrees, are committed to scholarship, and control certain rewards of importance to most students. But suppose a particular professor has not earned an advanced degree, and moreover, he is touchy about this fact. To address him as "doctor" may cause him to assume an intended slight and to react negatively. Another professor may have earned an advanced degree but may have an aversion to the status barriers erected by the title "doctor." In either case, continued use of the formal title may produce undesirable communication outcomes for the student. While a professor may sometimes reveal his prejudices, there may be times when the student will have to ferret them out himself.

Stimulus generalization necessarily ignores the characteristics on which objects and events differ. The preceding examples illustrate the predictive problems that lack of concern for differences creates. Even though in most cases better than chance predictions are possible, predictions based on stimulus generalization are fraught with error and should not be relied upon.

By contrast, at the interpersonal level, psychologically based predictions about communication outcomes can be likened to stimulus discrimination; that is, the person making predictions seeks relevant differences in other communicators. If predictions are based on stimulus discrimination, the amount of predictive error can be greatly reduced. Were you to rely on stimulus discrimination rather than on stimulus generalization in dealing with a particular professor, you might ask yourself how he is different from other professors with whom you have studied. Some professors encourage disagreement with their positions, while others abhor it; some professors encourage out-of-class contact, while others avoid it. How does this one feel? In what ways will he behave like other professors? Most importantly, does he vary in ways you cannot now predict?

Sometimes, of course, if we waited for answers to questions like these, we would not be able to communicate with people. Still, it is possible to use stimulus discrimination in predicting even without having all the necessary data. We can make predictions of others' behavior on incomplete data and at the same time remain open to the possibility that our predictions or our data are not accurate. This

approach enables us to refine our predictions and adapt them to actual circumstances. Over time we can considerably reduce our predictive errors. By the end of a few weeks, you should be able to list a number of ways in which one professor differs from other professors.

When used to make predictions, stimulus generalization and stimulus discrimination are often closely related. Suppose, for instance, you wish to predict how certain members of a group are likely to respond to your messages. A noninterpersonal approach would involve identifying some of the group's important norms and values and then tailoring messages to them, on the assumption that all group members subscribe equally to these norms and values. But suppose you reject the validity of this assumption and attempt to discern differences in each member's relative acceptance or rejection of the group's norms and values. For members who wholeheartedly embrace the group's position, your message decisions will be quite similar, if not identical, to the strategies you would have arrived at noninterpersonally. For the remaining members, however, your reliance upon stimulus discrimination permits you to construct messages better calculated to elicit the responses you are seeking.

Some further implications
of our conceptualization

1. Seldom, if ever, are initial interactions interpersonal.
The first time people meet they rarely base predictions about each other on psychological data. Not only are they disinclined to make such predictions, but also they often find it impossible to do so.

Most people are not disposed toward interpersonal communication during initial encounters. Attempting to predict responses to one's message on the basis of stimulus discrimination is usually much more physically and psychologically taxing than are attempts grounded in stimulus generalization. We enter communication situations prepared to assign others' behavior to previously formulated categories; we have developed considerable skill in this process and can perform the activities involved fairly spontaneously. It is far easier to plug the behaviors of others into existing categories than to try to discern how their behaviors depart from those of persons with whom we have prior experience.

A second reason why people prefer to base initial predictions on cultural and sociological data is that these levels of analysis often provide all the information needed. All of us quickly assign others to general, broad categories (for example, safe/unsafe, potential friend/potential enemy, or similar to me/different from me). Each of these categories has components such as clothing, language style, and manners. Normally, an initial interaction requires and allows only that a person assign others to these general categories and discover cues that verify or modify the assignments. Since eliciting and accurately interpreting psychological cues consumes much time and energy, we settle for less precise, though still useful, cultural and sociological analyses. If we find that a person falls into a favorable category, we may seek to move to the level of interpersonal communication but often find it impossible to do so during initial interactions.

Dominant cultural and sociological norms dictate that initial interactions are not the time to present psychological information. Thus, even if one individual attempts to communicate interpersonally during an initial interaction, the other persons may foil him by behaving according to cultural and sociological dictates for the situation. Moreover, people hesitate to reveal personal information until they are certain they can trust the other communicators. Such trust and self-disclosure rarely occur during a first encounter.

Although certain factors argue against the rapid development of interpersonal communication, it can occasionally happen. In psychiatric interviews and contact groups, for example, there is considerable pressure to achieve interpersonal communication, as well as a

frequent desire to do so. Participants in barroom conversations sometimes move quickly to the interpersonal level because fewer restraints
and inhibitions intrude.

Some people in certain situations may progress toward the interpersonal level during their initial encounter. More common, however,
is failure to ever achieve the interpersonal level. Some people may
never communicate interpersonally with anyone. In many cases, people interact for years without getting to "know" one another; they base
their mutual predictions on sociological and cultural data. Typical
examples are the husband and wife who have been married for twenty
years and have never achieved the psychological prerequisites for
interpersonal communication, or the father and teenaged son who
cannot talk to each other. Instances of interpersonal alienation are
frequently encountered in popular literature and motion pictures.
Each of us can probably recall sudden divorces occurring after years of
an apparently good marriage. Or we may know of cases (perhaps we
have even experienced this feeling) where children have finished
school and left home, and the parents and children suddenly realize
that they know little about each other as individuals. People in such
circumstances have never reached the interpersonal level of communication or have simply stopped trying. They have never come to
know each other as psychological beings, but only as cultural and
sociological beings.

*2. Very little communication in our society can be
characterized as interpersonal.*
To determine the amount of interpersonal communication within our
society, one might consider both the communication situations that are
now interpersonal and those that have at some time reached the interpersonal level. Application of either of these measures would probably
show that a relatively small amount of the total communication in the
United States qualifies as interpersonal. Some of the reasons for this
have been mentioned. Yet another reason is that the economic structure of our society (and of any modern industrialized society) is largely
incompatible with the development of interpersonal relationships.
Most Americans work for organizations that impose highly stylized,
complicated role behaviors. Whether this is good or bad, it has generally been considered a necessary condition for the management of a
successful organization.

Should communication always aim for the interpersonal level?
There are at least two possible views. Many people, including some
scientists and philosophers, believe the interpersonal level represents
the ultimate form of communication. Proponents of this *teleological
view* contend that each human relationship should gravitate toward

the interpersonal level. This view sees man as naturally free and open and holds that from childhood he is blocked from developing his true self. Thus, while each human relationship has the potential of becoming interpersonal, socially imposed defense mechanisms counteract this process. Supporters of the teleological view argue that people need to overcome these defense mechanisms so that they may attain the interpersonal level. Destruction of harmful defense mechanisms is the underlying theme of many encounter and sensitivity groups.

A second reaction to the relative infrequency of interpersonal communication in our society—a reaction captured by the quotation from *Future Shock* that began this chapter—can be labeled the *pragmatic view*. People who subscribe to it doubt that all relationships should be interpersonal. They argue that while human beings should have the facility to develop interpersonally, it makes no sense to assume that every interaction should move to the interpersonal level. Attaining this level is hard work. Just as one cannot be a universal parent or a friend to the world, so it is impossible to develop interpersonal relationships with all people. To do so would take too much time and would distract our attention from those who depend on us most heavily, such as our immediate families or our closest friends. Consequently, one should strive for a limited number of highly meaningful interpersonal relationships with the people of paramount importance in one's life.

At first glance, the pragmatic view may seem elitist or isolationist: one should draw a circle around oneself including a few, excluding the many. Such a reaction is founded on the notion that noninterpersonal relationships are necessarily unfulfilling, barren, or hostile, that they are characterized by snobbishness, ethnocentrism, or racism. Of course, noninterpersonal relationships need not manifest these characteristics. Lack of an interpersonal relationship with someone does not necessarily imply that we remain unconcerned about his problems, dehumanize him, reject him, or do not love him. Neither does noninterpersonal communication necessarily imply disdain, distrust, or dislike. Rather, reliance on noninterpersonal communication simply recognizes that in most communication situations it is unnecessary, perhaps even harmful, to strive to reach the interpersonal level. Many communication relationships can be carried out perfectly well at the cultural or sociological levels. Finally, as the case of George and Martha illustrates, interpersonal communication is not a panacea for the world's human problems. To be able to predict accurately at the psychological level permits one to inflict harm and make unreasonable demands as well as to provide support and understanding.

3. People vary in their ability to communicate interpersonally.
Not all persons have the same ability to communicate interpersonally.

Some people move very quickly to the interpersonal level, while others seem unable to move beyond sociological prediction. Consideration of the difficulties involved reveals why people cannot easily reach the psychological level. To do so, one must be able first to pick up meaningful cues from another, then to interpret them accurately, and finally to translate the knowledge gained from these cues into actual communication. The complexity of these three steps ensures that interpersonal communication will remain relatively rare.

One possible explanation for differences in ability rests in psychological makeup. If a person sees similar characteristics in most other people, he cannot discriminate among cue stimuli—that is, his perceptions are based primarily on stimulus generalization. Considerable research has dealt with this psychological perspective and suggests that people who are high in assumed similarity of opposites and people who are highly dogmatic (characteristics that will be discussed more fully in chapter 5) will be relatively poor at basing predictions about other people on psychological data. Furthermore, the greater the amount of selective perception, the lower the ability to communicate interpersonally.

Still, we assume that people can improve their interpersonal communication effectiveness by expanding their understanding of the communication variables facilitating movement to the psychological level of prediction. The following chapters are devoted to discussing some of these potentially important variables.

4. There is a difference between interpersonal communication and interpersonal relationships.
We have said that interpersonal communication occurs when one person bases predictions about another person's responses on psychological data. When two people are interacting, only one may be communicating at the interpersonal level, while the other is communicating at the cultural or sociological level. Therefore, it is useful to distinguish between interpersonal communication, as we have defined it, and an interpersonal relationship, which requires that at least two people must be communicating interpersonally. The significant implications of this distinction are dealt with in the next chapter.

Summary

We have now completed much of the groundwork for our approach to interpersonal communication. At the beginning of this chapter, we discussed some of the shortcomings we see in other approaches. Because *interpersonal* is so commonly and so variously used, we wanted to direct you away from these other views before we discussed our own, and we wanted to give you an opportunity to make critical comparisons. Our approach is more narrow than many others, but we believe that its greater precision, coherence, and suggestiveness make it preferable to more global conceptions.

Communication may be regarded as an information-sharing process. Communicative information ranges from that which is applicable to most people within a culture, through that which is applicable to groups of people, to information applicable only to single individuals. Our three levels of predictive analysis (cultural, sociological, and psychological) refer to classes of communication behavior that use certain kinds of information along this range. They are not always easily distinguishable, but the implications of our tri-level perspective for communicative accuracy and understanding, and for personal freedom of action and expression, are important and widespread.

Our emphasis thus far has been on the differences among various kinds of communication. In the next chapter, we discuss the primary features that all levels of communication have in common.

Probes

1. Do you know people who seem to move quickly to the level of interpersonal communication? Are you acquainted with others who seldom communicate interpersonally? How do the two types of people differ in their personal characteristics? In their communication behaviors?

2. Probably you are familiar with the process of stereotyping. On the basis of our discussion here, do you think we would regard it as a positive good, a definite evil, or a mixed blessing?

3. Read Robert Gover's *One Hundred Dollar Misunderstanding*. Try to analyze when cultural and sociological data are used to make predictions about communicative outcomes. In what specific ways might JC and Kitten have improved their chances of moving to the interpersonal level?

4. Think of some recent communication transactions you have had. As best you can determine, did you make predictions about the probable outcomes of various message strategies available to you? What do you think of the authors' assumption that prediction-making is an inherent dimension of the communication process?

5. Attack or defend this statement: Accurate predictions about communicative outcomes based on cultural data are more likely in the People's Republic of China than in the United States.

6. Do you belong to some groups but wish you didn't? Are there some groups you would like to belong to but don't? How would such circumstances influence other people's predictions about you based on sociological data?

7. What is your position regarding the relative merits of the teleological and pragmatic views of interpersonal communication?

2

Even man's awareness of himself is essentially
an awareness of functions, of relationships in which
he is involved.

Watzlawick, Beavin, and Jackson,
Pragmatics of Human Communication

Communication and Communication Relationships

e have discussed two kinds of communication, noninterpersonal and interpersonal, and the differences between them. In chapter 1 we proposed that the fundamental distinction lies in the data used for predicting outcomes of communication behaviors. In noninterpersonal communication, predictions are based on cultural and sociological levels of analysis; whereas in interpersonal communication, predictions are based on the psychological level of analysis. The first part of this chapter will deal with elements that these levels of communication have in common: we will discuss the nature of communication per se.

In the second part of this chapter, we will explore some newer territory: communication relationships. One of our central propositions holds that it is often useful to regard the communication process as a series of relationships among individuals and groups. This thesis suggests an approach to the study and practice of communication that is radically different from some approaches currently in vogue. In developing a notion of communication relationships, we will focus on important differences between communication relationships that are interpersonal and those that are noninterpersonal.

On defining communication

We will delineate some of the characteristics of the genus *communication* in order to enhance our understanding of the species *interpersonal.* By roughly defining the context of our inquiry, we set boundaries on our discourse and specify some criteria for deciding which aspects of our environment we will call "communication" and which "not communication."

If these are our goals, we need a definition not *of* communication, but *for* communication (Newman, 1960). When someone says, "Here is a definition of communication," he implies that he has "found" the one true definition, that no other can be tolerated, and that his definition will stand for all time. When a person says, however, "Here is a definition for communication," he implies that he is offering a definition that he hopes people will find useful and will at least temporarily agree upon, but he makes no claim that it is perfect or should be universally accepted. The definition we will suggest is not the only satisfactory definition for communication; it is, however, the one best suited to our purposes.

We will impose two general boundaries on our definition. First, we will confine it to human communication—a widely imposed, but by no means universal boundary. The September 1972 issue of *Scientific American* contained articles on cellular, man-machine, and machine-machine communication. People have also argued that we can communicate with dogs, horses, porpoises, and toads. Others say it is a shame people cannot communicate with mountains, rivers, and clouds. Years ago, a songwriter wrote, "I talk to the trees." Whether we can or should communicate with these environmental objects (beings?) is not an issue we will take up in this book. We will deal only with communication behaviors among human beings.

A second boundary is that our definition must be broad enough to encompass a variety of conceptions of communication, without being so broad as to set no limits on the kinds of human behaviors we call communicative. Numerous definitions of communication have been offered to fit the needs of various academic disciplines, schools of thought, and the personal convictions of individual authors. Some of these definitions are very broad. S. S. Stevens (1950), for instance, defines communication as "the discriminatory response of an organism to a stimulus." This conception may be too flexible. Miller (1966) argues that "in its scope, this definition lumps every human interaction—and, indeed, some nonhuman interactions—under the rubric of communication" (p. 92).

We believe that we must restrict our definition of communication to something smaller than the entire realm of human behavior, and yet we want our definition to be useful for a broad range of communicative purposes. Therefore, we will stipulate that *communication involves an intentional, transactional, symbolic process.*

While this definition is fairly concise, it is power-packed. Each word in the statement is important, and from all of them we can derive a set of assertions about communication. Our assertions do not say all that might be said about it, but they do comprise our response to the perennial question: "If you were to list the most important things about communication, what would you include?" Here is our answer in some detail.

Communication behaviors are intentional

People have argued inconclusively about whether behaviors must be intentional (i.e., performed for the purpose of bringing about some desired outcome) to qualify as communication. In one sense, suggested by Stevens's definition cited earlier, almost any behavior—or for that matter, the absence of any behavior—communicates something, assuming there are others in the environment to observe the behavior. From this perspective, Watzlawick, Beavin, and Jackson (1967) are right in asserting that "we cannot not communicate."

We have chosen to restrict our discussion of communication to intentional symbolic transactions: those in which at least one of the parties transmits a message to another with the purpose of modifying the other's behavior (such as getting him to do or not to do something or to believe or not to believe something). By our definition, intent to communicate and intent to influence are synonymous. If there is no intent, there is no message.

Problems may arise in determining whether intent is involved in a particular transaction. Intent may be perceived by any of the following: the person or persons who receive the message, outside observers of the transaction, and the person or persons who may or may not have sent the message. We can conceive of several instances in which sender, receiver, and observer may not agree on the intentionality of a "message." For example, in 1775 when the American patriots agreed to use lights—"one if by land, two if by sea"—to signal Paul Revere on his famous midnight ride, they knew that no outside observer (least of all the British) would attribute any symbolic intent to them. Sometimes communicators disguise the symbolic intent of their behaviors when they want to give outsiders the illusion that no messages are being exchanged. It should be obvious that such camouflage is more likely at the interpersonal level where the transactants can rely on idiosyncratic communication rules.

Sometimes the sender and receiver of a message do not themselves agree on the intentionality issue. The intended receiver of a message may fail to attribute symbolic meaning to the behavior of the sender. When Mark was younger, his father once put the family lawnmower on the front lawn as a reminder that he wanted the lawn mowed. Mark, thinking someone had carelessly left the mower outdoors, returned it to the garage, having failed to recognize its role as a com-

municative message. Musclemen and bathing beauties who promenade along the water's edge at a crowded beach sometimes have a problem similar to that encountered by Mark's father: their intended receivers fail to recognize that these vain strutters are trying to communicate their sexuality.

There are also occasions when a person intends no symbolic significance at all for a particular behavior, but someone else reads intent into the behavior. Returning again to Mark's younger days, when he discovered that his father sometimes communicated through the placement of objects, he attributed similar intent to his mother when she left the vacuum cleaner in his room one day. Recalling that she had frequently expressed dismay at his lack of tidiness, Mark proceeded to vacuum the room. When his mother heard the noise of the machine, she was surprised, for she had intended to do the job herself.

Although such mistakes may often have pleasant consequences, the erroneous attribution of communicative intent can sometimes strain people's relationships. When some people fail to receive a Christmas card from a friend or acquaintance, they interpret this behavior (or lack of it) as a deliberate snub. Similarly, many students recall experiences with suspicious professors who, prepared to believe that their students are likely to cheat on exams, perceived every cough, pencil tap, or wink of the eye as a symbol of dishonest intent.

How, then, shall we decide whether or not a given behavior was intended as a communicative act? We might ask the suspected communicator, "Did you intend to communicate with that person?" Or we could query of the receiver, "Do you think he was trying to communicate with you?" Finally, we might also ask a third party, "Do you think that behavior was intentional?" Each of these perspectives has distinct advantages and limitations, and each is a valid approach to assessing intentionality.

However, most communicators are not terribly concerned with the theoretical issues of defining communication and would probably do best simply to remember that *people—yourself included—may mistakenly attribute or fail to attribute intentional symbolism to the behavior of their companions.* This approach is not completely satisfying, since it does not tell us when to define behavior as intentional. However, it seems to be the most reasonable approach to daily communication activities. It reduces the probability of communicative error and sharpens one's ability to communicate with other people.

Another point concerning our intentionality restriction is this: to say that someone intended to influence someone's behavior by communicating does not imply that he was successful. Quite the contrary, his messages may have little apparent effect, or their effects may be the opposite of what he intended. Indeed, this book is largely devoted to considering factors that contribute to successful communication (i.e., communication that results in outcomes consistent with the communicator's intent) as opposed to factors that contribute to unsuccessful communication (i.e., communication that results in outcomes inconsistent with the communicator's intent).

Finally, *it is one thing to determine that a particular behavior was intentional and quite another to determine what, specifically, was intended.* For example, if you were walking down a sidewalk and saw a friend waving to you from across the street, you might not immediately discern whether he was transmitting a greeting, motioning you to cross the street, or signalling that you were in danger of being hit by a branch falling from a nearby tree. Although we shall later be interested in the interpretation of symbolic behaviors, we are concerned here with "Are people communicating?" not with "What are they communicating?"

Much more could be said about the intent issue; but since much of chapter 3 touches upon it, we will turn now to the second important characteristic of our definition for communication.

Communication behaviors are transactional

Two of the oldest and most profound questions asked by philosophers and scientists are: How do we come to know something? Of what is our knowledge composed? If we believe that a fundamental aspect of the communication process is making predictions about the outcomes of our communicative acts, and if we base our predictions on things that we know (data), then these questions are important to us as students of communication behavior.

Two contemporary schools of communication theory have hypothesized about the origin and composition of people's knowledge of their communicative acts. One school, the *behaviorist* school, says that knowledge comes from objects and events in the external environment. Behaviorists argue that the impact an object has on a person can be measured according to the characteristics of the object itself. For example, if behaviorists wanted to know what kind of data an individual was collecting in order to predict communication outcomes, they would observe certain objective features of his social environment—such as other people's facial expressions and the number of rewarding messages they send to the individual—and not concern themselves with the mental activities of the person collecting the data.

The second school, which we call the *mentalist* school, focuses on the workings of people's minds in order to understand the origins and composition of communication knowledge. Mentalists argue that to determine the nature of the data an individual collects, we have to examine the internal thought processes of the individual himself. They contend that it is not very useful to focus on objective features of the environment, because people impose their own conceptions on these features.

In short, behaviorists say that the data we use to make communication predictions come from the external environment; reality is in the world. Mentalists assert that our data come from our own perceptions; pointing to their heads, they say, "Reality is in here."

We think both of these schools are too extreme and too simplistic. We prefer a transactional perspective of communication, which contends that the nature of the data we collect is a product of both environmental objects (or stimuli) and internal mental states. That is, our reality is construed partially from the objective characteristics of external stimuli and partially by the way we perceive them.

There are some important implications of this position for us as students and practitioners of communication. Suppose, for instance, you have developed an intimate relationship with someone, but find that the sexual aspect of your relationship is less than satisfying. Two common responses to this state are: "Boy, are you a lousy lover!" and "Boy, I must be a lousy lover!" In the former case you cast all blame on your partner; your data are composed only of your partner's behavior, with the implication that all you have to do is change your companion (external stimulus) and your sex life will improve. In the latter case, you place all blame on yourself (a mentalist position). Your data are mainly subjective, and you imply that you will not be happy, no matter who your companion is. Except for instances of frigidity or impotence (which are indeed "real" behaviors), both of these responses indicate poor management of your communication relationships. You have failed to consider that the frustration you are experiencing may be a

product of the transaction, that it could stem from the way you respond to each other. Had your response been, "My friend, something isn't working right; let's figure out what it is," you would have kept yourself open to the possibility that your problem originates in the way both of you react to each other.

This example illustrates a key implication of transactional behavior: when we communicate, we have an impact on other people, and they have an impact on us. The term *transaction* is appropriate in describing communication behaviors because it refers not only to the data collection aspect of communication but also to its aspect of mutual impact. When you send a message to another person, the content of your message and the manner in which you present it will vary according to your perceptions of yourself and your receiver and the actual behavior of the other person.

Communication behaviors are processual

Since the publication of Berlo's *The Process of Communication* (1960), the term *process* has been widely used by students of communication, and has been considered fundamental to an understanding of communication. Miller writes in *Speech Communication: A Behavioral Approach* (1966, p. 33), that the term "implies a continuous interaction of an indefinitely large number of variables with a concomitant, continuous change in the values taken by these variables." If we conceive of communication as a process, then we must approach our study and practice of it with some idea of its complexity, one aspect of which is the large number of variables that affect our communication behaviors. A variable is any phenomenon that may take on more than one value; for example, communicator credibility is a variable, since a communicator may be perceived as having little, some, or much credibility. Consider for a moment all the variables that might influence a conversation between two friends: their experiences, clothing, health, topic of conversation, the weather—but a tiny fraction of all the variables that could be relevant.

Aside from the number of relevant variables in a process are the interrelationships of these variables. For example, if you feel your vocabulary is inadequate in communicating with someone of higher status than yourself, your self-esteem may be lowered; whereas if you use the same vocabulary in a conversation with someone of status equal to your own, self-esteem may be scarcely affected. Of course, there are other possible interrelationships among these three variables (vocabulary, status, and self-esteem), and we have considered only three of the variables that might have an impact on communication.

Another aspect that adds to the complexity of processes is time. In viewing a fantastically large number of interrelating variables, can we ever determine where a particular process began or ended? Think of the most recent argument you had with a friend. When did the argument start? When you first spoke angry words? When you first realized you had something to be angry about? Or did it start when you first met? We could go back further, all the way to when your parents taught you how to speak. A similar train of thought could be applied to the ramifications of your argument for the future: when will its effects cease? Although this reasoning sounds like a children's game, it is nevertheless an essential component of a process view of communication. Though we can, and very often do, put arbitrary boundaries on processes ("The argument started when she was late to pick me up"), we can never certify where communication processes begin or end.

A final implication of process is *change*. The variables in a process, and their relationships to each other, change continuously. Nothing is ever quite the same from one moment to the next. Some changes are significant, and some are trivial, but to be aware of the inevitability of change is to be prepared to act as a more effective communicator. Significant change can be discovered in the relationship of two old friends who have not met for many years. Neither should expect his once accurate predictions of the other's behavior to have eternal validity. Even during a few hours a person's mood can change enough to warrant his companion's maintaining predictive flexibility.

In adopting a process point of view toward communication, we accept the following beliefs as guides to our communication behavior.

1. Since communication events are very complex and constantly changing, I cannot have the ultimate answers to questions; I cannot see the totality of a communication situation.
2. When I collect data and make predictions about communication, I omit many data, and so the predictions I make should be tentative.
3. Even though errors are always possible, I am less likely to blunder if I am aware of change and of the interrelationships among variables in communication situations.
4. Things were happening long before I entered a communication situation and will be happening long after I leave it.

It is unrealistic and perhaps even impossible to act in all communication situations according to these four beliefs. To consider fully every message that you send or receive would drastically cripple, if not paralyze, your capacity for decisive action—especially since all communication transactions are inherently uncertain and ambiguous.

And yet a simpleminded approach to a complex, ever-changing environment will ultimately lead to communication errors, breakdowns, and failures. Frank Herbert, writing in *Harper's Magazine* (December, 1973), warns us of the "dangerous business of wishing for absolutes in a relativistic universe" (p. 92). He cites several examples of how simplistic, comfortable thinking has caused or aggravated world crises. There are no easy formulas for either a peaceful world or successful communication.

Improved communication through taking a process orientation is within the grasp of any communicator willing to reflect periodically upon his patterns of thought and action. Taking a process view does not obligate a communicator to deliberate every move he makes, nor does it doom him to paralysis of action. Rather, a process view suggests a method of thinking about how you think, a way of adopting and holding your beliefs, and some criteria for evaluating and guiding your communication behavior.

We can illustrate some consequences of process and non-process views of communication through a problem that a girl named Janet faces with a guy named Herb. They had their first date yesterday. Herb was friendly and outgoing and appeared interested in developing a serious interpersonal relationship. Today he seems aloof, disinterested, and just plain unfriendly. Janet now feels that Herb is outrageously inconsistent, that he doesn't like her anymore, that she's done something wrong, and that something in their relationship has gone amiss.

Adoption of a process viewpoint enables one to point out quickly some possible errors in Janet's assumptions. For one thing, she assumes that Herb's responses are products of the immediate communication situation, rather than of past situations (Herb may have been jilted several times, and he's now afraid of getting too hooked on Janet) or future situations (Herb may fear that if he gets seriously involved with Janet, he will have less time for schoolwork and his grades will suffer). Janet has also neglected to consider that factors other than herself may have influenced Herb's behavior: he may be pressured by schoolwork or worried about his increasing baldness. Moreover, Janet thinks consistency rather than change should be the rule of human behavior—she is surprised and upset that Herb's behavior today differs from his behavior of yesterday. She implicitly assumes that Herb is on a course of unfriendliness, whereas tomorrow he could very well revert to his attentive self.

All of Janet's assumptions could, however, be correct. Herb could be a roguish playboy who encouraged her affection by feigning interest in her and, having accomplished his objective, has grown bored with her. Nevertheless, Janet's static viewpoint hinders her efforts to confirm her assumptions about Herb, for it lessens her awareness of alternative assumptions that are relevant to the present situation. Confirmation involves testing these assumptions, seeking more information than is immediately available, and temporarily delaying action on her initial assumptions. If it is true that we define "the truth" as what we found the last time we looked for it, we are all encouraged to develop and pursue a process frame of mind when making decisions that affect our communication relationships.

Communication behaviors are symbolic

A symbol is anything that, by convention, is used to stand for, or represent, something else. Almost anything can be a symbol. Written or spoken words, of course, are the most commonly used symbols; but facial expressions, gestures, flags, decals, and a host of other items can also be used symbolically. In turn, almost anything can be a *referent*, the thing a symbol stands for. The word *source*, for instance, is a symbol, and its referent often is "someone who sends a message." Actions, objects, and ideas can all be referents of symbols. Generally, there is a two-way relationship between symbols and their referents: when you are presented with a symbol, you recall its referent, and vice versa.

The usefulness of symbols in human affairs is sometimes thought of in terms of their potential for freeing us from temporal and spatial restrictions. It is usually much easier to deal with people on the symbolic rather than the nonsymbolic level. Consider the difficulties, for example, of having to carry with you a ladder, or Japan, or your mother whenever you wanted someone to know what each is like. Symbols permit us to talk of things that were or will be but are not now, of things far removed from us on earth, or of entirely imaginary things. Because of our capacity for using symbols, we can overcome physical restrictions, and speak and think of whatever we wish.

Symbols are symbols only by convention. That is, people can say that a particular flag stands for the United States simply because they have agreed that it does. This makes it difficult for us to determine in advance which behaviors are symbolic and which are not: a minimum of two people must agree to give referential quality to a behavior. If we observe one person make a gesture to another, we cannot necessarily define the behavior as communication. For some people, the words "Hit the beach!" have referential meaning, while for others they do not.

If people can make a symbol of any word, gesture, or object they wish, then we must conclude that the relationship between symbols and their referents is arbitrary; that is, there is no natural connection between a symbol and the thing it is taken to represent. You can demonstrate this point for yourself by collecting some common objects (such as a pen, a glass, a marble, and a book) and listing the name (symbol) for each object (referent). Present this list and the collection of objects to someone whose only language is very different from English or to a young child, and ask him or her to correctly match each name with each object. You will find that in almost all cases it is impossible to deduce which name should be matched with which object. If there are only arbitrary relationships between symbols and their referents, then the only way to know these relationships is to be taught them. In other words, *if we are going to communicate with other people, we have to learn how.*

This is an important and fairly difficult notion for us to grasp as communicators. It means that communication is *inherently social.* Throughout this book, we emphasize the social nature of communication. Just as it takes two to tango, to wrestle, and to make love, it takes two to communicate. Most of us place too much emphasis on our own communicative selves, even though usually when we communicate, the other person must hear us, understand us, and respond to us. His job is as crucial as ours. We learn to communicate from other people, and all our communication is carried out through, for, and with them. This point is especially important for interpersonal communicators.

To communicate at the cultural level it is necessary to learn the connections between symbols and referents commonly used in the culture. Similarly, to interact with members of a particular group, one must learn and use the symbols that the group uses, in the ways the group uses them. At the psychological level, one person must recognize how another is using particular symbols, for quite often individuals have meanings for symbols that differ from those of both their culture and their membership groups. At each successive level, from the cultural to the psychological, conventions that relate symbols to referents become narrower: fewer people share the same meanings for given symbols. This may suggest that interpersonal meanings are "more arbitrary" than noninterpersonal meanings, for we often have greater trouble understanding meanings that are unique to an individual than understanding meanings that are widely shared. Nevertheless, the process by which symbols become connected with referents—by association through experience—is the same.

Our approach to communication does not include *intra*personal communication, or communication "with yourself." Although it seems reasonable to "give yourself a pep talk" or "talk yourself into doing something," these internal thought processes vary considerably from the message-sending and message-receiving processes that

transpire between two or more people. We do not agree with Dance and Larson that, since in intrapersonal communication the "sender and receiver are one in the same," we necessarily have "common-sense evidence that communication . . . does not require two persons" (1972, p. 51). Their argument is based on an arbitrary definitional maneuver. We are not saying that intrapersonal communication does not happen, but only that we find it more useful to emphasize the transactional nature of communication, the interdependence of behavior among people.

Summary

By offering a definition for communication and discussing some fundamental aspects of human communication behavior, we have discussed the twin species of noninterpersonal and interpersonal communication and the genus communication. You should have some means of distinguishing between and recognizing these two kinds of communication and some notion of how they are alike.

Up to this point, we have intentionally ignored (or slurred over) one of the essential elements of the communication process. You may have noticed that our description of all forms of communication has been mainly from the standpoint of the individual communicator. We have described three processes by which individuals make predictions about the effects of their communication behaviors. While it is important to understand communication from the point of view of the individual, we do not get into the fundamentals of communication until we develop a perspective of communication that accounts for the transactions of a minimum of two people. In fact, given the implicit nature of communication—revolving around the sharing of meanings for symbols—we cannot meaningfully deal with communication unless we learn to think of communication situations as *relational*.

We will now develop a further set of criteria for distinguishing between noninterpersonal and interpersonal communication and extend our concept of communication to take in communication relationships.

Communication relationships: parts and wholes

While writing this book, we had an opportunity to converse with a student from Thailand. Since we had just met, we asked him a stock, cultural level question: "What has most impressed you about the

United States?" We expected to hear about our marvelous highway systems or the amount of time we spend watching television, but the young man said: "Americans are most unusual in this respect; everybody has to be an individual. You need to think of yourselves as separated from the things around you. You try to separate individuals from their environments, even from other people." This reply echoed some of our own thoughts on American culture, particularly about the way many Americans tend to view communication.

When our Thai friend suggested that Americans are inordinately concerned with individuality, he may also have been implying that Americans (and here we might include members of most Western cultures) tend to be preoccupied with parts rather than wholes, with factors that make people distinct rather than with factors that bind them together. Another way of saying this is that Americans have tended to ignore their natural and their social environments. For decades we assumed that we could dump our wastes in any convenient spot without ever suffering the consequences of being directly related to our ecosystem. Lack of concern for our social environments can be seen in our recently developed understanding that blacks and other minority groups may appear less intelligent than the larger white population, not because they are mentally inferior, but because of the social and economic climate in which they live. We have viewed ourselves and our fellowmen as separate entities, forgetting to note our relationships to larger systems.

This tendency to reduce wholes into parts is evident in the way we focus on individual performers, the "stars." We take them out of the context of the athletic team, the band, or the acting cast, and examine how and why they stand out rather than how and why they blend effectively with their fellow performers. In another context, a father is likely to ask his two sons who have just had a fight, "All right, who started it?" as if one boy or the other were solely responsible.

Focusing on individuals can be contrasted with focusing on relationships between individuals. For instance, rather than heap awards on a football quarterback who completed a record number of passes, why not create awards for quarterback-receiver combinations? After all, a quarterback can be no better than the receivers who catch his passes, nor for that matter, than the offensive linemen who protect him. Another good move would be to create awards for students and teachers who interact successfully. We give awards to outstanding teachers and to outstanding students, but more often than not, each cannot be successful without collaboration with the other. For us to talk about passers without receivers, or students without teachers, or leaders without followers is to attempt to reduce social wholes to their parts—and parts have little meaning outside of their relationships to other parts and to the larger environment. In fact, from a role theory perspective, positions such as "father," "coach," or "wife" have meaning only insofar as there exist the relational counterparts "child," "players," or "husband."

Just as our preoccupation with individuals gives some people more praise than they deserve alone, it also lays unwarranted blame in the laps of others. Researchers at the University of Michigan (Caplan and Nelson, 1972) have expressed concern that our individualistic bias may be counterproductive in solving a number of social problems, such as drug addiction, alcoholism, and crime. Our tendency in examining individual problem behavior is to look within the individual for causes of and cures for the behavior. In trying to solve our nation's drug problem, we try to "get inside" addicts to find out why they turned to drugs, and in trying to get them to stop using drugs we again focus almost exclusively on the addicts themselves. Of course, this perspective leads to blaming problem individuals for their own undesirable behavior. We recognize that, in the short run, it is easier and less expensive (and less threatening to many vested interests) to concentrate on individual deviants than to look for causes and cures in broader social relationships; but until we do so we cannot expect widespread success.

Adopting a relational perspective on communication

The preceding comments bear directly on the way we view communication processes. When people talk about communication, they often refer to two or more individuals who are transmitting and receiving messages. They give you a picture of two persons, *A* and *B*, sequentially alternating speaker and listener functions. Many persons in the field of communication accept this picture. In fact, to people who began their communication studies twenty or thirty years ago, this concept of communication seems quite an improvement over Aristotle's view, which focused almost entirely on the source of the message. Only in recent years have we begun to give much attention to such communication variables as receivers, feedback, or message channels, and these additions are welcome and beneficial. Unfortunately, we have not advanced far enough. We need to conceive of these variables as comprising whole communication systems; we need to adopt a relational perspective on communication; we need to focus on communication relationships.

Any time two or more people communicate, they form a communication relationship. Our major reason for considering any two communicators as being in a communication relationship is that *in order for any two people to communicate, they must form a mutual system.*

The very act of communication places two people in a system. This fact provides the basis for a relational view of communication.

A system, as we define it, is a collection of components that are interdependent by virtue of a set of rules governing their interrelationships. In a communication system, the principal components are human communicators. We need not elaborate on these human components at this point; however, we should go into more detail on the notions of interdependence and rules.

People in a communication system are interdependent because of the kinds of rules that govern communication processes. One elementary rule states that in order for communication to occur, there must be someone to send a message and someone to receive it. This rule seems trite and self-evident, and yet it establishes the groundwork for a relational view of communication. Save for instances of intrapersonal communication, we are dependent on others if we wish to communicate, and they are dependent on us.

Another rule of communication systems holds that in order for communication to occur, people must first share meanings for some symbols. Again the communicators are interdependent. People cannot make just any gestures or sounds if they wish to communicate; instead, they must tap the collection of symbols which other people have previously learned.

A large number of terms that are used to describe individuals (e.g., strong, popular, skilled, beautiful) are comparative. "Strength" is a more-or-less notion. If we observed someone lifting a boulder, we could not describe him as strong unless we also observed someone trying, and failing, to lift the same boulder. In communication situations, such comparative concepts are meaningless outside the context of at least a pair of people: *these notions, and the people who use them, are dependent on communication relationships for their meaning.* Moreover, individual communicators often have little capacity for self-assessment unless other communicators provide feedback for them. We cannot call ourselves strong or popular or intelligent or beautiful or sensitive unless we have seen at least one other person fail where we have succeeded, or succeed where we have failed. We are inextricably bound to other people for information about who we are.

The whole is different from the sum of its parts

From a relational perspective, communicators are members of a communication system, not isolated individuals. Patterns of individual communication behavior are ultimately meaningful only in the larger context of the more complex patterns of transactional behavior. We might aptly regard a communicator, then, as *a set of*

communication relationships, since people learn, carry out, and evaluate their communication acts in social contexts.

It might be useful to go one step further. Rather than saying that people can better understand themselves and their fellow communicators through relational perspectives, we can conceive of communication relationships as distinct entities, as something different from the two or more individuals who comprise them. In the terminology of general systems theory, *the whole is different from the sum of its parts*. When people develop a communication relationship, they "create" something that did not exist before—a unique, functioning, behavioral unit.

How can a relationship be considered apart from its members? If we can assign some characteristics (even intangible) to a relationship at all, we must first admit that we cannot account for these characteristics solely by accounting for the characteristics of either member of the relationship. A relationship is not person *A* nor person *B*; rather, it emerges from the transactions of person *A and* person *B*.

Suppose we list several characteristics of each person. Some of their values, attitudes, expectations, and general patterns of behavior will be similar, while some will be different. For example, person *A* and person *B* may both have a high propensity for self-disclosure, in which case their relationship will probably also be characterized by self-disclosure. Or suppose person *A* tends to be very dominant in his communication behaviors, while person *B* leans toward submissiveness; their relationship might then be characterized by unequal interpersonal influence. It is important to note that these relational characteristics stem not from the individual characteristics of either individual, but from the mutual similarities and differences between the two, i.e., from the way their characteristics *interact*.

When people form an interpersonal relationship, they must coordinate their mutual behaviors and adapt to one another. In the give and take of a communication transaction, neither can operate solely according to his own idiosyncratic dispositions. The relationship they form is the product of the interdependence of their communication behaviors. Therefore, any characteristic of an individual that is relevant to his relationship with another person is likely to become part of the relationship, though often in a form modified by the very fact of interdependence. Although neither person loses his identity (not all characteristics are necessarily relevant to a given relationship), each contributes to the structure and quality of the relationship. Their contributions give it a distinct flavor. Relationships that may be characterized as strikingly different from either individual involved clearly illustrate this point. You can probably think of relationships that are restrictive, while each individual enjoys considerable freedom. Some relationships are highly sociable, whereas their members are generally isolates. In other relationships, there is very little communication, but each of the relationship's members tends to be highly vocal.

From a pragmatic viewpoint, the notion that a relationship can have a distinct identity is useful in assessing the potential success of a continued transaction between two people. You cannot predict how well the two people will get along by looking at each individually; instead, you must look at the kind of relationship they are likely to form. Furthermore, when evaluating one of your own interpersonal relationships, it is not enough to look at your companion as an isolated individual. Whatever characteristics he or she may have, they are most important in the light of their contributions (for better or for worse) to the relationship.

Summary

Whenever two or more people are involved in a communication system they are in a communication relationship. A relational view of communication assumes that all communication questions ultimately involve consideration of at least two people; in communication, the individual cannot be considered apart from other individuals. Therefore, communication should be analyzed in terms of at least a two-person system, rather than using the individual as the unit of analysis.

If you have followed our argument to this point, you should understand why people often prefer to look at communication from the individual's perspective: such an approach is much less complex and much more likely to give persons the illusion that they understand communication.

In chapter 3 we will discuss the notion of environmental control as a paramount function of both noninterpersonal and interpersonal communication. As you read the rest of this chapter on anticipating and predicting other people's communication behavior, ask yourself whether environmental control is possible without the direct participation of other communicators. Is communicative control possible without someone with whom to communicate?

Noninterpersonal communication relationships

When two or more people base their communicative predictions mostly on cultural data, sociological data, or both, their communication relationship is noninterpersonal—even though they may not rely exclusively on these types of data. Two people who communicate noninterpersonally must observe certain mutually shared rules that regulate message exchanges.

Cultural level communication relationships

Generally, communication relationships at the cultural level serve as stepping stones to sociological level relationships; hence, they are short-lived. In cultural relationships, we base our communicative predictions on knowledge shared by the culture as a whole. This knowledge allows us to predict the remarks of people we have just met. It also guides our ways of speaking to them. Two people communicating for the first time need some common ground. Being able to join in a conversation and anticipate the behaviors of the other makes further transactions possible.

Cultural level relationships are founded on a set of rules governing how a person should communicate. Some rules govern the content of communication messages; for example, both parties should talk about things with which the other is familiar (such as the weather, food, or sports). Usually, no personal discussions occur in a cultural level, noninterpersonal relationship. Other rules govern the structure of the interaction—e.g., there should be short exchanges, not too many questions, and each participant should be allowed to speak.

At the cultural level, there is generally little that can be said and very few ways to say it. These are two reasons why such relationships tend to be short-lived. They provide little information and their maintenance requires considerable energy. For instance, do you find it easy to talk with a stranger during an elevator ride? In the main, cultural level communication relationships are used for brief encounters with strangers or as a necessary preliminary to sociological level relationships.

Sociological level communication relationships

Most of us spend the majority of our communication time in sociological level relationships. They are similar to cultural relationships except that people base their predictions primarily on the group membership of the other person. There are two kinds of sociological relationships, *formal* and *informal.*

Formal sociological relationships usually provide a very narrow range of communication alternatives, and these alternatives are usually carefully specified for the communicators. To engage in a formal relationship, people must learn the behaviors that are permitted, as well as those that are forbidden.

One common formal communication relationship system can be seen in the task-oriented communication of the military service. All communicators in the military are taught their specific relationships to other members of the military, and they are warned of the punishments that result from deviating from them. For instance, enlisted men must salute officers; they must say "Yes, sir!" and not "Okay, buddy," when issued an order.

Writing bank checks involves a formal sociological relationship between the check writer, the bank, and the receiver of the check. Clearly, writing a check is a communication act involving the intentional exchange of written symbolic information. Every check writer learns the rules for filling out the blanks on his checks, and any deviations to fit individual styles are highly restricted.

Other formal sociological level communication relationships occur when filling out applications for employment or dealing with clerks at grocery checkout counters. In these relationships fairly rigid rules restrict the ways in which people may communicate with one another.

Informal sociological relationships embody many of the same characteristics as formal relationships, but to a lesser degree. The manner in which people relate to one another is also governed by preordained constraints, but more communication behaviors are available. For example, most student-teacher relationships operate according to informal relationship patterns. Certain limits are placed on the times, places, and ways that students and teachers may communicate, but within these limits a fair degree of latitude is allowed.

Informal sociological relationships usually dominate the flow of conversation in bars. Barroom communication generally is open and unfettered by the restraints governing other communication situations, even though people may be communicating at the sociological level. In fact, communication is so uninhibited that persons may move to the interpersonal level rather rapidly.

Interpersonal communication relationships

In interpersonal communication relationships, communicators make predictions about each other's behavior on the basis of psychological data. Each tries to understand how the other operates as an individual, not how he or she may act when constrained by sociological or cultural standards. The range of permissible communication behaviors may thus be quite different from the range permitted in noninterpersonal situations, and personal choice can be liberally exercised in the development of relationships. Some individuals condone swearing, for instance, in private, interpersonal contexts, but not in public, noninterpersonal contexts. Other individuals may place even greater restrictions on interpersonal contexts than on noninterpersonal contexts: they may feel that swearing is tolerable for the general public, but not for members of their families.

Examples of interpersonal communication relationships include close friendships and many marriages. In these situations, the communicators have a great deal of information about each other's personal wants, needs, and values, and can develop communication styles accordingly.

Comparing noninterpersonal and interpersonal relationships

We devote part III of this book to describing communication relationships, both noninterpersonal and interpersonal. In that section, we will discuss the development and maintenance of relationships and consider some of their major characteristics such as trust, love, and power. Our remarks here are meant as a brief introduction to the primary dimensions of various kinds of communication relationships. Perhaps we can highlight these dimensions by comparing and contrasting some of them at the noninterpersonal and interpersonal levels. We have selected three dimensions: the generation of rules governing the relationship, the criteria by which the relationship becomes defined, and the degree of individual choice in the relationship.

Generation of relational rules

Where do rules come from? Who makes them up? In noninterpersonal relationships, most rules are articulated by a group of people who impose them on others. For instance, even the highest ranking military officers have little say about the nature of the rules governing their relationships with enlisted men; these rules have evolved historically. In the same vein, when a student and a teacher discuss a homework assignment, the ways they communicate with each other are largely dictated by years of tradition and custom. Both are generally acquainted with the rules, and they have little choice but to accept them. The only way effective communication can occur in such situations is for all parties to know the rules ahead of time or be willing to follow the lead of one who already knows them.

In interpersonal communication relationships the situation is very different. No one else, no other group of people, directly influences the rules that develop. The communicators are free to set up patterns that suit their own needs. For instance, two friends may agree that each is free to call at the other's home without invitiation. No one told them to make such an agreement. Not only is the decision theirs, it conflicts with typical cultural expectations.

Criteria for defining relationships

By criteria for defining relationships, we mean the factors that determine the position of communicators in relation to one another. In noninterpersonal communication relationships, these criteria are generally dictated by the goals of the groups to which people belong. For example, in a business enterprise, certain people are designated as managers and others as clerks; some people are hired as salesmen and others as executives. For a business enterprise to survive, managers, clerks, salesmen, and executives must have particular capabilities; they must meet certain criteria in order to occupy their positions. A manager, for instance, must be able to take charge and to supervise other employees in the company. Usually it matters little whether he plays chess well or has a happy marriage. The personal aspects of his life are not used as criteria for defining a manager's relationships to the rest of the company's employees, as long as they do not seriously influence the way he carries out his assigned duties.

Criteria for defining positions in interpersonal communication relationships are very different. For instance, while you may not care whether a friend is a good manager, you may be concerned with his ability to help you through personal problems or to accept your style of behavior. If you and your friend develop a trusting relationship in which both of you are considered equals, the roles you play in the sociological realm will probably not be considered. In less "healthy" interpersonal relationships, one of the parties may assume a "one-up" relationship because of his ability to evoke guilty feelings in the other. Such a criterion for deciding relational positions is not often found at the sociological or cultural levels.

Degree of individual choice

When compared to interpersonal communication relationships, personal choice in noninterpersonal relationships is relatively restricted. In noninterpersonal relationships, individual expression is discouraged, since it detracts from the stability of the relationship. Emphasis is placed on similarities, on how well people can follow previously established rules. Conversely, in interpersonal relationships, the emphasis is on expression of individual differences. Not only is personal freedom accepted, it is encouraged and nurtured.

The mixed levels problem

Up to this point, we have referred to relationships in which all the participants were communicating at the same predictive level. As you can imagine, this similarity provides some regularity and consistency to the communication behaviors of the people involved. But what about situations in which the communicators are operating at different levels of prediction (e.g., one person is communicating at the sociological level and another at the psychological level)? We cannot call such a relationship either interpersonal or noninterpersonal. Rather, it is a mixed relationship, and particular problems can arise as a result.

Suppose a friend invites you to a party at a stranger's house. You have never met anyone else at the party. After arriving, you hear another guest shout to the host, "Hey, fat boy, bring me a whiskey sour!" Hearing yet another guest call for a drink in the same manner, you call out, "Hey, fat boy, bring me a gin and tonic!" Next you see a man approach an attractive woman who is talking with some other men, squeeze her on the arm, and ask whether he can see her later. She laughs and declines his invitiation. Sensing an opportunity to score, you begin to move in her direction. On your way over, however, you stop to chat with some people who are apparently discussing the personality quirks of one of the conversationalists; as an "in" you say, "Would you repeat that please, I didn't quite hear what you were saying?" How long would it be before someone asked you to find yourself another party?

Of course, this example is rather extreme, but it does illustrate some of the difficulties involved in mixed level communication relationships. Probably the men shouting to the host for drinks were his good friends and had established precedents for using insulting language with him. Since you had not established such precedents, you should not have followed their lead. They were communicating interpersonally, whereas you were communicating sociologically—and rudely, from their point of view. Similarly, the man who approached the woman may have been her husband playing a friendly game of seduction with her. Again, they may have been communicating interpersonally, and you should not have assumed you could get away with the same behavior. Finally, when you approached the group talking about one of its members, you may have assumed that everybody at the party was free to join in discussions of that sort, whereas they may have felt you were boorishly intruding on a matter of no concern to you.

As a general rule, when entering any communication situation, you should ascertain whether all communicators are at the same level. If you do not, there may very well be a communication breakdown, or worse, some hard feelings.

Summary

This chapter has covered considerable ground. It has introduced several concepts and terms, some perhaps that you have not come across before. We have discussed some basic propositions about communication and offered some advice on how better to understand and manage your communication transactions. Thus, we have been both descriptive (relaying some information about communication) and prescriptive (suggesting how you ought to behave on the basis of this information). The discussion applies to both interpersonal and noninterpersonal communication: at both levels, communication is an intentional, transactional, symbolic process, and at both levels, a relational view of communication is important.

Probes

1. On the matter of defining the terms you use:
   a. How does defining the key terms you use help you in your inquiry into an area like interpersonal communication?
   b. How do definitions help you to communicate with other people?
   c. In your daily transactions with others, how can you estimate the degree of overlap between your meanings and theirs? What general indications do you have that you and others are using words differently? Under what conditions will you be sure to check on the similarity of definitions?

2. In a general sense, how do you know whether you are communicating with someone? Can you cite certain behaviors or feelings that indicate successful communication is taking place, or do you just get a vague "gut impression"? Many people believe that they have communicated with another person when they use the same words as he does, or when he responds appropriately to a message (they tell him to close a door, and he closes it). What are some drawbacks to each of these indicators?

3. In this book, we have limited our definition for communication to intentional symbolic transactions that occur among human beings. Certainly there are other forms of behavior and relationships, involving both humans and nonhumans, that are excluded from our definition. Can you think of some important noncommunicative transactions?

4. As the sources of messages in this book, we have never met you, the receiver of our messages. Look over these first two chapters and examine the communication strategies you think we used to increase the probability of successful communication between us.

5. Make a careful study of how some national or international agency is handling a current crisis. From what you can gather, how closely does the agency's handling of the crisis conform to a process orientation? How might they use process-thinking to improve their problem-solving techniques?

6. What proportion of your communication relationships are interpersonal? Would you prefer to have more or fewer interpersonal relationships? How would you go about increasing or decreasing your present number?

3

"It's not a pose, I really *do* like him. You see,
I have to like him, otherwise I'd never
get to know him. And if I don't get to know him
I won't beat him."

Boris Spassky, speaking of Bobby Fischer,
Harper's Magazine, December 1973

Functions of
Interpersonal Communication

t is difficult to talk about human communication apart from the functions it serves. To be sure, some very general observations are possible: we can say that message transmission is central to communication or that communication is an ongoing process. But when we begin to consider the nature of message transmission, how messages are transmitted, the specific kinds of transactants for whom they are intended, or the ways in which the ongoing process can be altered, we are confronting questions of communicative function. Obviously, the intended function of a communication transaction determines its message content and the specific behavioral changes sought.

An example

Suppose Gerry and Mark are spending an evening working on this book, and to lighten their burden, they buy a bottle of wine to share. Both have drunk several glasses, and only one glassful remains in the bottle. Since their thirsts are not yet sated and their tongues are loosened by the alcohol, a conflict ensues over who should have the last glass. Finally Mark exclaims, "I've got an idea! Let's split it," and Gerry accepts this solution.

In this example, Mark's suggestion serves the function of resolving conflict. Moreover, an observer would probably say it was his intent to defuse the quarrel. His precise motives for seeking de-escalation may remain a mystery, and while they make for interesting speculation, a thorough understanding of them is not essential in order to deal with the question of communicative function. Mark may have sought to resolve conflict because he generally feels anxious and tense in conflict situations, because he values Gerry's friendship and does not wish to

risk it by further controversy, because Gerry has the power to punish him for continued intransigence, or for numerous other reasons. Whatever his motivation, his communication behavior aims at resolving conflict.

Obviously, Gerry could have disagreed with Mark's solution. Had he chosen to do so, their communication behaviors would have continued to serve different ends: while Mark's communication aims at conflict resolution, Gerry's response seeks Mark's compliance with his demand for the entire glass of wine. Such situations are not unusual; just as we may have mixed interpersonal-noninterpersonal transactions, we may have transactions in which the communication of the various participants is intended to serve different ends.

Defining function

We shall define *function* as the purpose for which communication is used. It follows, then, that communicative functions are intimately linked with the intentions of the communicators, as can be seen in our hypothetical example. Two further points concerning this example merit consideration.

First, both Gerry's and Mark's major concern lies in gaining certain tangible rewards from their environment. More specifically, one glass of wine remains in the bottle, and both want the pleasure of consuming it. Since each stands in the way of the other's achievement of this objective, both must devise communication strategies that attempt to control the other's responses. We argue that *the basic function of all communication is to control the environment so as to realize certain physical, economic, or social rewards from it.* This contention is central to our entire discussion of communicative functions.

A second important consideration is that nothing in our hypothetical example implies that interpersonal and noninterpersonal communication serve uniquely different functions. Quite the contrary, when arriving at predictions about the outcomes of their communication behaviors, Gerry and Mark might have been functioning at either the noninterpersonal or the interpersonal level. Suppose, for instance, Gerry pursues this line of noninterpersonal reasoning: I am a full professor and Mark is a graduate student; graduate students are intimidated by professors and are fearful of the power they exercise over students; because of my favorable position in this relationship, Mark will yield if I press my demands; therefore, I will hold out for the whole glass. Armed with this sociological analysis, Gerry responds in a way calculated to force Mark's compliance. Much to his surprise, Mark refuses to acquiesce, and the conflict intensifies.

But suppose Gerry's analysis takes the following interpersonal form: most graduate students yield quickly to professorial demands: however, in this respect, Mark is not a typical graduate student. He is blessed with considerable independence and a fair amount of ego-strength, both of which I have seen him exercise in the past. If I try to use my status and power to impose an inequitable settlement, he will resist. Since my chances of success are slim and since nothing is to be gained from further conflict (after all, we share a desire to complete our book), I shall reconcile myself to the fact that half a glass is better than none. This psychological analysis results in a conciliatory response.

The preceding discussion underscores a fundamental point in our treatment of the functions of interpersonal communication: we hold that *the functions served by interpersonal and noninterpersonal communication differ not in kind, but only in degree.* Our position appears to be at odds with that of certain other writers (e.g., Giffin and Patton, 1971), who imply that the major functions served by interpersonal communication are personal growth and the development of self-concept. We believe that the development of self-identity is an important by-product of communication, but that it is a consequence of one's success or failure in controlling the environment, rather than a communicative function. Even when attempts at environmental control are clearly linked with the communicator's self-identity, they are often noninterpersonally grounded. For example, a person who uses boasting as a communicative tool for gaining the admiration of others seems to assume that most people are impressed by individuals who speak well of themselves—inaccurate though this cultural or sociological generalization may be. Conversely, while noninterpersonal communication often is used in crassly economic, marketplace settings (witness the barrage of advertising emanating from the mass media), the skilled entrepreneur can maximize his economic gains by using interpersonally based strategies. Most of us have been confronted by salesmen with the ability to reach the interpersonal level quickly, and we realize how hard it is to resist their blandishments.

Interpersonal and noninterpersonal communication differ not in the functions they serve, but in the levels at which predictions about communicative outcomes are grounded. Given this perspective, our major thrust in this chapter is to delineate the principal functions served by both interpersonal and noninterpersonal communication and to discuss differences between interpersonal and noninterpersonal approaches to these functions. We begin this task by considering what we believe to be the basic function of all human communication.

The basic function: environmental control

A popular song of a few years ago asks the plaintive question, "What's it all about, Alfie?" As we have already emphasized, human communication—both noninterpersonal and interpersonal—is "all about" controlling the environment so as to realize certain physical, economic, or social rewards from it. Relative success in achieving environmental control through communication enhances the likelihood of a happy, personally productive life; relative failure leads to unhappiness and, eventually, to a self-identity crisis. In fact, when one hears such laments as, "I can't find anything meaningful or useful about my life!" he is usually safe in assuming that the person has rather consistently failed in his communicative efforts to control certain important dimensions of his environment.

What we are saying echoes the words of other recent communication theorists. In his pioneering work *The Process of Communication*, Berlo (1960) stresses the centrality of environmental control to human communication, asserting that *"we communicate to influence—to affect with intent"* (p. 12). More recently, Mortensen (1972) recognizes the extent to which our position is shared by contemporary writers, stating that "few would have qualms about saying that it [communication] occurs whenever people attempt to use the power of spoken or written words to influence others" (p. 13). Obviously, success in this venture of controlling the environment brings with it the physical, economic, and social rewards necessary to a meaningful existence.

Our position concerning the basic function of communication is likely to disturb and even antagonize readers for whom *control* conjures up images of naked coercion or of an insidious conspiracy to brainwash and manipulate. As we use it, however, the term has a much broader meaning. Specifically, one has successfully controlled his environment whenever there is at least some correspondence between his desired and his obtained outcomes. When Mark suggested to Gerry that they split the last glass of wine, he was attempting to control a relevant portion of his environment; when Gerry agreed with his suggestion, the distribution of the wine provided Mark with a physical reward (pleasure in drinking the wine) and a social reward (success in persuading Gerry to accept his solution). Furthermore, had his initial communicative effort failed, Mark would have probably made further attempts to exert control—e.g., "I think it's only fair we split it, since we each paid half the cost," or "If you won't give me half of the wine, I'll go someplace where I can get a drink."

As we define it, control is a basic staple of all communication transactions. Examples of successful control range from the jubilant, post-election party of a victorious political candidate to a son's enthusiastic, "Gee, Mom, you're great!" *When used in this sense, control per se can be viewed as bad only if one believes there is something wrong with people preferring one set of outcomes to another.* What we often rebel against, and rightly so, is not control itself, but rather the use of certain means for achieving it. Thus, if the son's, "Gee, Mom, you're great!" results from an encouraging word or a deed of kindness, we applaud the successful control exercised by the mother. If the same words stem from a threat of punishment by the mother, we abhor her means of imposing control. But in either case, control has been exercised, and since we applaud one instance and abhor the other, it seems that Skinner (1971) must be right when he asserts that "the problem is to free man, not from control, but from certain kinds of control" (p. 41).

Reward is another word that makes many wince because it smacks of the marketplace. Again, however, we use the term in a much broader sense: *a reward is any positively perceived physical, economic, or social consequence.* Certainly, money is a positively perceived economic consequence of some communication transactions. If an employee succeeds in controlling the behaviors of his boss, he receives a raise in pay; if a salesman controls the responses of his customers, he earns a commission; if an industrialist controls the behaviors of his associates, he completes a profitable merger. But rewards can also be pleasant consequences that have little or no material value: the smile on a loved one's face, a thank you from a student, the satisfaction realized from giving directions to a stranger (to better grasp the rewarding features of this last situation, recall how you have felt on occasions when you were unable to supply the needed directions; your embarrassed feelings of inadequacy flowed directly from your inability to exert control over that particular aspect of your environment), or the joy of being told by a friend that he has relished a conversation with you. These are moments we all treasure, and they result from the success of our communicative efforts at environmental control.

The transactional nature of the preceding examples should be readily apparent. Thus, the boss uses pay raises (and his communication about them) as one means of controlling his employees' behavior, and the salesman's behavior is largely shaped by the way his customers respond. A loved one's smile is a powerful instrument of control, while a thank you from a student exerts a definite influence on a professor's future behavior. In short, *control is a reciprocal, transactional concept.*

Our definitions of the terms *control* and *reward* now permit us to state the basic function of human communication in somewhat different language. *Communication originates with a set of desired outcomes; if it is successful, the transactants' obtained outcomes at least partially correspond with their original desires. Moreover, their success carries with it certain positive physical, economic, or social consequences.* When stated in this way, the proposition captures what we believe to be a basic aspect of human existence, and its scope far transcends a manipulative, marketplace view of communication.

Much of the time, we are not totally triumphant in our communicative efforts at environmental control, and success must be measured relatively. To be completely successful, our desired and our obtained outcomes would have to correspond perfectly. In some instances, negotiation and compromise are necessary. Originally, both Gerry and Mark desired the entire glass of wine. To refuse to compromise their original positions might have produced unfortunate consequences for both of them. Obviously, the "loser" would have had to forego the wine; in addition, his self-esteem would have been bruised. But in all likelihood, the "winner" would not have emerged unscathed, for while the remaining wine would have been his, he would have incurred the resentment and hostility of his colleague. This negative social consequence probably more than offsets the physical rewards and leads to negotiation and compromise.

We distinguish between two levels of environmental control: one in which the desired and obtained outcomes correspond exactly—a level we shall call *compliance*—and a second in which the obtained outcomes reflect some compromise of the original desires of the involved parties—a level we shall call *conflict resolution*. Attempts to exert control at each of these levels may be grounded in either noninterpersonal or interpersonal communication. Let us next consider how noninterpersonal and interpersonal approaches to the communicative functions of compliance and conflict resolution differ.

Achieving environmental control through compliance

Compliance occurs when the behavior of one or more individuals corresponds with the desires of another. In a communication situation, compliance represents the level of environmental control at which the desired and obtained outcomes of the communicator correspond exactly. Since our ability to control many features of our external environment depends largely on the willingness of others to comply with our message requests, compliance is an extremely important communicative function.

Reflect for a moment on how many of your daily communication transactions are compliance-oriented. While taking a shower, you find there is no soap and ask someone to bring you some. You remember that you left some important class notes at a friend's house, and so you call and ask your friend to bring them to class. When you arrive on campus, you go to your history professor's office and request a week's extension on a paper because the necessary references are not in the library. You spend an hour urging fellow students to vote for a student representative whose candidacy you strongly support. During lunch one of your friends balks at your request to pick up your tickets for Saturday's football game; however, when you threaten to quit loaning him your chemistry notes, he agrees to stop by the box office.

Our expectations about the probable success of a compliance attempt will vary from one communicative situation to another. You may be almost certain that your friend will bring you your notes but entertain considerable skepticism about your history professor's willingness to grant an extension on your term paper. Some compliance-oriented messages are so socially routinized that the probability of success is high, even if one knows little about the person to whom they are directed. Consider, for example, a request to someone sitting on the next stool at a lunch counter to pass the salt. Such transactions are usually noninterpersonal. But if the outcome is seriously in doubt, a much more careful analysis is necessary. We suggest that, as a rule of thumb, *the greater the difficulty of achieving compliance, the more important the ability to move to the interpersonal level.*

Your hypothetical luncheon argument underscores another aspect of the compliance function as we conceive of it. Some writers have used the term *compliance* in a more restricted sense. Kelman (1961) identifies three processes of social influence, one of which he labels compliance. For Kelman, compliance occurs when a source has means-control over a receiver; i.e., when he has the power to dispense rewards or punishments. Given just the information contained in the sample situations, your threat to withhold lecture notes from your friend constitutes the only case of compliance in Kelman's sense; in no other instance is means-control invoked to ensure behavioral conformity with message requests. As we have indicated, we view the compliance function more broadly, and we will use the term *forced compliance* to refer to the special case where behavioral conformity results largely from the coercive power of the communicator.

In some of the sample communicative transactions, success or failure in securing compliance is the only meaningful outcome that can result; while in others, the transaction may begin at the compliance level but shift into a situation involving conflict resolution. Thus, when you ask someone to bring a bar of soap, your desired and obtained outcomes may correspond (i.e., he brings it) or they may be totally at odds (i.e., he may refuse to bring it). In the same vein, your friend either will bring the class notes with him or will not, and your fellow students either will or will not vote for your preferred candidate. By contrast, you may initially ask for a week's extension on your term paper, but through negotiation and compromise with your professor, settle for three days. In short, some compliance-oriented communication transactions are best viewed from a dichotomous success or failure perspective; others provide greater flexibility for moving from one level of environmental control to another.

Noninterpersonal approaches to compliance

Among the most obvious examples of noninterpersonal communication approaches aimed at securing compliance are mass media advertising appeals and political campaigns. Geared as they are to large, heterogeneous audiences, messages transmitted via the mass media must be based on cultural and sociological predictions. Some error is therefore inevitably built into the prediction. For while many American males may seek to identify with athletic heroes and will therefore buy a breakfast cereal endorsed by a football star, others are disinterested or even dislike sports. The latter group is unlikely to comply with requests grounded in the attractiveness of a skilled quarterback or a hard-hitting outfielder.

This illustration suggests a potential ambiguity that merits clarification. Many writers label the process of identifying with sports stars a psychological phenomenon. While we believe it can as easily be interpreted from a sociological perspective—i.e., people who aspire to some reference groups identify with athletes, while those who aspire to others do not—we would not quarrel with those who wish to call identification a psychological process. But as used in mass media advertising appeals, it is grounded in behavioral similarities, rather than in a thorough consideration of individual differences. By the same token, the so-called motivational researchers (as described by Packard in *The Hidden Persuaders*), who purport to gear media sales campaigns to deep-seated psychological motivations, are also catering to behavioral consistencies among some members of our society; hence, messages based on the dicta of motivational researchers are noninterpersonal. For the fact remains that many American males are not driven to Freudian ecstasies by a sleek, powerful sports car—the fabled "surrogate mistress" of the motivational researcher. Moreover, the used car salesman who bases his noninterpersonal pitch on the assumption that all male customers are motivated by such considerations will probably lose a number of sales.

While the prevalence of noninterpersonal communication in mass media compliance attempts is readily apparent, it can also be observed in numerous face-to-face communicative situations. For example, many door-to-door salesmen operate almost exclusively at the noninterpersonal level. During their training period, these salesmen learn a standard set of messages constructed on the basis of predictions derived from cultural and sociological data associated with potential purchasers. Thus, when the salesman knocks at your door to peddle his magazines, encyclopedias, dancing lessons, brushes, or life insurance, he communicates with you not as a person, but as a set of cultural stereotypes or sociological roles. In many instances, this may be enough; the intended customer may comply with the salesman's request to purchase the product. But if you are not like most customers and you resist the blandishments of the salesman's noninterpersonal messages, he may try to salvage the sale by moving to the interpersonal level. More will be said about this transition from noninterpersonal to interpersonal communication later in this chapter.

Face-to-face attempts to secure compliance through noninterpersonal means are often observed in relations between the sexes. The chauvinistic "pickup" has become an institution in our society, one with potential social and physical rewards. The social rewards are particularly great when competition is involved, as reflected in the term *scoring*. At large gatherings such as student meetings or scholarly conventions, where men usually far outnumber women, the social rewards derived from a successful pickup often stem more from the joy of competitive victory than from the woman's company; by achieving compliance the winner has succeeded in exercising environmental control while the losers have not.

That such social battles are frequently fought with noninterpersonal weapons is attested to by such phrases as "the line," or, in a more contemporary vein, "dealing chicks." The combatants may choose from a large arsenal of potential noninterpersonal weapons, including the "big man" line, the "intellectual snow job," or the "no one understands or appreciates me" line. Obviously, each of these communicative commonplaces is rooted in cultural or sociological expectations. Even when one of the combatants engages in the formality of deciding which line best fits a particular female, his eventual choice will probably be dictated by cultural or sociological considerations. For example, frequent use of the intellectual snow job at scholarly conventions seems to rest on the assumption that female members of such groups attach great importance to certain intellectual role behaviors.

One interesting aspect of such lines is that they attempt to create the illusion of interpersonal communication, even though message transactions remain at the noninterpersonal level. This is particularly true of the "I've never met anyone like you" line, which is grounded in the cultural assumption that people in our society are taught to value their uniqueness and individual identity. Unquestionably, some persons are very skillful in creating the interpersonal illusion; in Goffman's (1959, 1963) terms, they manage their behavior effectively. Still, if their predictions about communicative outcomes are based on cultural or sociological (rather than psychological) data, they are communicating noninterpersonally.

As with door-to-door selling, these noninterpersonal gambits often secure compliance. The woman may fall for the interpersonal illusion; more likely, she may fully understand the noninterpersonal nature of the communication transaction, but still comply because of potential rewards. In many cases, the woman may even maneuver the man into initiating a line—a maneuver itself often based on cultural or sociological predictions about male behavior. Still, such exchanges are based on assumed similarities among persons and, as such, are subject to considerable error and subsequent failure to achieve compliance. When viewed in this light, the meaning of a statement such as "My batting average hasn't been too good at this meeting" is readily apparent.

Interpersonal approaches to compliance

Put yourself in the shoes of our hypothetical salesman for a moment. Of necessity, his initial communication with a potential customer takes place at the cultural or sociological level, for these are his only bases for prediction. But if he is aware that his selling success may sometimes be enhanced by moving to the interpersonal level, the salesman will immediately ask himself, consciously or unconsciously, such questions as: How is this person responding to my messages? In what ways does he differ from my typical customer? How can I alter my communication strategy to accommodate, or to take advantage of, these differences? Are the differences so marked and so at odds with my purpose that compliance is an unrealistic goal? After all, another advantage of communicating interpersonally is that one can determine when further communication is futile. Since time wasted with an intractable customer cuts down the salesman's potential economic rewards, this advantage should not be taken lightly.

A personal experience of Gerry's illustrates the difference between noninterpersonal and interpersonal sales pitches. Within a month, two encyclopedia salesmen called at his door. In both cases, their sales pitch emphasized the educational benefits for children who have a set of encyclopedia in the home. This widely used pitch is, of course, grounded in sociological data concerning appropriate role behaviors for parents: specifically, parents should seize upon all available ways to facilitate their children's educational growth. But in this particular instance, Gerry had a strong bias against excessive use of the encyclopedia, feeling that this practice promotes superficial habits of inquiry. The first salesman was incapable of grasping this fact; in the face of numerous contradictory cues, he continued to stress that an encyclopedia was indispensable to a good education. Turning him away from the door was, therefore, an easy task.

By contrast, the second salesman, after a few brief probes, said, "I know a couple of people who use the encyclopedia to play a game with their children. They get them to read particular entries and then encourage them to go to other sources to find inaccuracies and inadequacies in the encyclopedia account." Since Gerry had not stated any reservations about encyclopedias, the salesman must have detected resistance from Gerry's nonverbal behaviors, predicted accurately the source of the resistance, and adjusted his messages to accommodate it. While the sale was not made, it was much more difficult to resist complying with the second salesman's request.

One point should be made concerning this experience. Some readers may argue that the second salesman based his message on a sociological prediction: he redefined the appropriate membership group from "parents" to "parents who are members of a university community." One can accept this argument and still maintain that the crucial first predictive step requires identification of the relevant differences between these particular parents and parents in general— i.e., that the salesman's initial task is to move to the interpersonal level. That the resultant message will be based on stimulus generalization is often the case, though this fact may become less and less obvious as interaction develops.

Summary

The compliance function aims at inducing someone to behave consistently with the desires of the communicator; it seeks an exact match between the communicator's desired and obtained outcomes. A compliance attempt may be either noninterpersonally or interpersonally grounded. If the attempt occurs interpersonally, the communicator bases predictions about his message outcomes primarily on psychological data; he seeks to identify differences that may influence the response of a particular receiver, or receivers, to his message decisions.

Achieving environmental control through conflict resolution

Conflict resolution occurs when two or more competing parties reach a solution about the allocation of some physical, economic, or social resource, and the solution is perceived as relatively equitable by the competing parties. Obviously, such situations require that the communicators accept something less than a perfect fit between their desired and obtained outcomes. Neither party is absolutely successful in exerting environmental control; however, the resultant compromise leaves each feeling partially successful.

Conflict resolution versus conflict management

Unless the parties in conflict agree that a solution is relatively equitable, the conflict has not been resolved, but rather dampened or managed. In these cases forced compliance may be used as an instrument for conflict management. Seldom, if ever, does a party who is forced to comply perceive the solution as equitable. Although the conflict may be temporarily dampened or managed, it will probably flare up again; if this is impossible, the injured party will probably stimulate conflict about other matters.

Consider the case of the father who consistently dampens conflict by imposing his solution on his young son. While the son considers many of these solutions grossly inequitable, his father holds all the trump cards: he is physically stronger and, more importantly, he controls many physical, economic, and social resources that are vital to the son's well-being. Because of the father's power, the son may angrily endure an imposed solution to a particular conflict. But out of hostility and resentment, he will stimulate conflict about other matters. Eventually, the balance of power will shift. In rare cases, the son may repay the father's despotism with a sound thrashing. More frequently, the son, no longer economically and socially dependent on his father, leaves home. In the end, the father's reliance on forced compliance to manage conflict spawns a perpetually antagonistic relationship.

Probably it is true, as certain writers have suggested, that some conflicts can never be resolved. In the *Communist Manifesto* Marx argued that the interests of labor and capital are so diametrically opposed that conflict resolution is possible only by the overthrow of one of the competing parties. A few contemporary social critics seem to identify a host of conflicts as irresolvable: children's interests are diametrically opposed to parents', women's to men's, students' to faculties', faculties' to administrations', and so on. We are not so pessimistic. While recognizing that in some cases the ends of the contesting parties may preclude any mutually satisfactory resolution, we believe that persons often share common aspirations and ends that offer the potential for compatible solutions. Moreover, success in achieving a solution depends largely on the communicative sensitivity of the parties in conflict.

Sources of conflict

A resource may be in such short supply that the parties in conflict are unable to obtain what they define as an ideal quantity of it. Consider the dramatic cliché in which two men and a woman are shipwrecked on an island or remain as the sole survivors of a nuclear attack. Under such circumstances, female companionship becomes a scarce human resource, and because of prior learning experiences, both men may initially seek to lay total claim to this resource—i.e., each may try to achieve the compliance of the other. If the woman does not like either of the men, there may be a three-way conflict, further complicating attempts to reach a solution perceived as relatively equitable by all parties. Tempting though it may be to treat the conflict as insoluble and to resolve it by the death of one of the male antagonists, the common objective of continued survival may be greatly enhanced by the presence of both males. If so, the parties will probably communicate extensively in search of an acceptable solution, and if they are persistent and relatively sensitive, a somewhat equitable compromise will eventually emerge.

Most conflicts over scarce resources are considerably less dramatic. Mundane conflicts such as Mark and Gerry's disagreement over the remaining glass of wine may become far more important than would seem appropriate to an observer. How many times in the midst of a heated conflict have you heard a third party remark, "What a silly thing to quarrel over!"

A second source of conflict between individuals stems from inherent restrictions on the number of resources that can be used at one time. Since people cannot be in two places at once, they must frequently choose between two or more attractive alternatives. Many such conflicts can be easily resolved. If several men often eat lunch together and each has a favorite restaurant, a trade-off usually develops without too much disagreement, particularly if the parties enjoy each other's company at lunch. Suppose, however, that on a given day two members of the group are adamant about their choice of a restaurant. Perhaps one of the men likes a drink with lunch, while the other does not. Because he has had a hard morning, the first man insists they must patronize a restaurant that serves liquor. Unfortunately, his abstaining companion has been keenly anticipating the mushroom soufflé at a restaurant where liquor is not served. These two people are in conflict because they cannot simultaneously avail themselves of these two attractive resources.

Noninterpersonal approaches to conflict resolution

Noninterpersonal approaches to the resolution of conflict are particularly tempting in formal settings where there are clearly defined role and status differences between the conflicting parties. When a student confronts a professor about receiving a low grade, for example, the latter's first inclination often is to base his communicative predictions on what he perceives as appropriate role behaviors for students. In addition, professors may assume a defensive posture behind socially expected, professional role behaviors; of course, the low grade did not result from his dislike for the student, for professors grade students on competency, not attractiveness. Because the professor has a good deal of power at his disposal, he may be able to impose his solution on the student. But if he wishes to resolve the conflict, not just dampen it, he may need to look for ways in which this particular student differs from other complaining peers. Moreover, he can explain the bases for his decision, trying to get the student to understand the reasons for the low grade. This approach can elicit compliance just as effectively as the more heavy-handed method, with the added advantage of perhaps resolving conflict rather than merely dampening it. This approach is less efficient, however: the professor has to exert more energy to achieve control. A communicator must decide what kind of control he wants, and how hard he wants to work to get it.

Clearly defined differences in status or roles are not a necessary condition for conflict to remain at the noninterpersonal level. As our examples have underscored, attempts to resolve conflict within families may often be limited to noninterpersonal means. What works for the eldest daughter of the family may prove ineffective for the youngest daughter. Unless the parents recognize this fact and base their communicative predictions on psychological data, their relationship with their youngest daughter may be troubled.

Interpersonal approaches to conflict resolution

One evening, a talented dance troupe was to perform in Cincinnati, and an important football game was to be televised at the same time. A conflict flared between a married couple: while the husband did not seriously object to dance programs in general, he much preferred to see this particular football game; while the wife was generally tolerant of her husband's mania for televised athletic events, she wanted him to accompany her to this dance program. Since she did not consider it an equitable solution for both to go their separate ways, one party would have to sacrifice his or her sole opportunity to take advantage of an attractive resource.

Fortunately, the husband was able to approach the problem interpersonally. He reasoned as follows: unlike some wives, my wife is not a demanding person. The fact she is so insistent on this occasion indicates that both the dance program and my company are very important to her. I should be willing to forego the game and attend the dance program with her. The husband's subsequent "Dear, I think I'd like to go to the dance program tonight" not only pleased the wife a great deal, but in turn, her pleasure was rewarding to the husband. Conflict was resolved. The dance program was excellent; and the couple even returned home in time for the husband to catch the last quarter of the game—a reward he had not anticipated. (Whether the same analysis would have worked on Super Bowl Sunday is a moot question.)

Admittedly, a noninterpersonal approach to the conflict was initially attractive to the husband. This approach, grounded in chauvinistic, sociological reasoning about appropriate wifely role behaviors, goes as follows: I am the breadwinner in this household, and my wife should try to please me. In this instance, she should be willing either to stay home with me, or to attend the dance program by herself. Therefore, I'll tell her that she has those two choices. In all likelihood, this strategy would have dampened the conflict, with the wife acquiescing to her husband's demands. As we have already indicated, however, it would not have resolved the conflict, since there would have been residual hostility and resentment on the wife's part. In order for conflict resolution to take place, an interpersonal, rather than a noninterpersonal, analysis was necessary.

Although we have little proof, we suspect that if genuine conflict resolution is to occur, interpersonal communication is usually a necessary precursor. While some management of conflict can take place at the noninterpersonal level, shared perceptions of an equitable solution hinge upon an understanding of the individuals involved and upon the ability to communicate with them as individuals—abilities that can be possessed only by the skilled interpersonal communicator.

The role of information exchange in achieving environmental control

Many communicative transactions are marked by extensive exchanges of information between the participants; in fact, such exchanges often seem to be the central feature of these transactions.

Generally speaking, acquisition of information enhances a person's potential for exercising environmental control. To a certain extent, we tend to equate information with understanding, and we view understanding as a necessary precursor of control. In a broader sense, however, availability of information affects one's chances of exercising environmental control in several ways. Let us examine some of these ways briefly.

First, information fosters greater control because most people tend to confer credibility on highly informed individuals. Many researchers (e.g., Andersen, 1961; McCroskey, 1966; Berlo, Lemert, and Mertz, 1970) have studied the dimensions of communicator credibility, and all of them agree that competence is an important component of one's image. We respect individuals who know what they are talking about, who consistently "have the dope" about problems, people, and situations. Thus, information is power in the sense that being perceived as highly knowledgeable makes others more susceptible to communicative attempts at control.

Moreover, possession of information also increases the possibility of control if others who do not have the information believe that it is important to have it. Small children quickly grasp the potential efficacy of this controlling technique. How many times have you heard a child say, "If you do something, then I'll tell you a secret that you don't know"? In almost any organization, such as an academic department within a university, there are certain individuals who seem to know everything that is going on. They are abreast with all of the scuttlebutt, and they share this information with ignorant colleagues in ways calculated to increase their control of the environment. In particular, they barter information for social rewards; their fellow workers bestow a certain grudging deference on them in exchange for their information. Reliance upon this technique for achieving control does have certain disadvantages, for in order to keep on top of current happenings, the individual must monitor the organization constantly. Eventually, this may seriously restrict his freedom of movement and cause him to spend as much time as possible in his office.

Using information in this way may justifiably be regarded as highly manipulative. There are, however, more defensible means of using information to enhance control possibilities. As we have already indicated, information enriches our understanding of the environment. By adding to our understanding, we are more capable of identifying available alternatives for exercising control. In particular, *information is a necessary prerequisite for moving from the level of noninterpersonal communication to the interpersonal level.* The ability to make relevant discriminations between individuals rests on the acquisition of information: as we gain more information about a person, we are more likely to discover ways in which he differs from other members of his particular culture or specific group. Since we have taken the position that interpersonal communication enlarges one's potential span of control by improving his predictive accuracy, it follows that information is a vital ingredient of success.

Effects of lack of information

Just as the availability of information confers certain powers, ignorance of important information carries with it a feeling of powerlessness. "Why don't I ever get the word?" queries a dissatisfied worker, and the question itself captures the anxiety he is experiencing. Usually when we lack relevant information, our attempts at environmental control are, at best, only partially successful; and in turn, our opportunity for physical, economic, or social rewards is severely curtailed.

Consider a recent occurrence in the Department of Communication at Michigan State University. An important midterm examination was imminent, and the first-year graduate students were studying feverishly for it. The environmental control dimensions of test-taking are readily apparent, for in imparting information to an instructor, students are striving to control certain of his behaviors. Specifically, they hope to persuade the instructor to respond with a high grade; for if they do, certain social rewards are immediately forthcoming, and the likelihood of long-term physical and economic gains is enhanced. Moreover, the outcomes are sufficiently important to cause many students to aim at the interpersonal level of analysis; they try to identify the idiosyncrasies of the particular instructor and to predict how his test will differ from those of other instructors.

In this particular instance, the students spent considerable time identifying the biases of the instructor, as well as itemizing the things he emphasized in class. Furthermore, one of the students ferreted out (entirely legally) a copy of the midterm given in the course the previous year, and a number of students scrutinized it. Each of them noted that the test provided several options: in the first section, students were asked to write about any two of three essay questions; while in its second section, students were instructed to respond to any five of ten short-answer, identification items. Armed with this information, the students predicted that similar options would be available on the forthcoming test and tailored their study sessions accordingly. As it turned out, they were right and most of them performed well on the examination.

Several days later, we were conversing with a first-year graduate student. When asked how things were going, the student expressed concern that certain information was not reaching him. He went on to use the test as an example, indicating that he had not known options would be provided on the test. As a result, he felt he had studied for the test differently than had most of the students and that his performance had suffered somewhat from his ignorance about the likelihood of examination options. He concluded the conversation by reassuring us that he was not upset about this particular event, but that he was concerned about finding ways to obtain such important information in the future.

Noninterpersonal and interpersonal approaches to information acquisition

The communicative tasks of acquiring and exchanging information can be approached either noninterpersonally or interpersonally. Formal education encompasses a vast institutional system dedicated primarily to information exchange. Students enter the system with the assumption that the information gained will be a valuable asset in their later attempts to control a variety of social and professional environments. Recently, however, students have objected to the noninterpersonal ways in which information is exchanged. They berate the impersonal atmosphere of the university campus, the tendency of faculty and administrators to view them as student numbers rather than as individuals, and the remoteness and relative anonymity of faculty members. To a large extent, these student complaints are legitimate; for with the advent of the huge, teeming university, opportunities for interpersonal communication between students and faculty have decreased. What we are witnessing in some schools is an effort to create conditions where the potential for interpersonal communication, as we have defined it, at least exists. Without smaller classes and more extensive opportunities for faculty and student interaction outside the classroom, predictions about the probable outcomes of educational messages will probably remain largely rooted in cultural or sociological data.

One need not look at a vast university to contrast noninterpersonal and interpersonal approaches to information exchange. The parent who demands that every child process and retain information because it is the child's role to do so, or because all children "ought to learn," has fallen victim to a noninterpersonal view of information acquisition. While this role-prescriptive formula may work for some children, it will fail for others. Likewise, the employer who assumes that all of his employees will attend to and understand the information disseminated to them because of their subordinate role positions risks serious morale problems or production breakdowns within the organization. In cases where accurate exchange of information is important, efforts aimed at moving to the interpersonal level may well be worth the time and trouble.

Information exchange is a crucial ingredient in the control process. Given its importance, a skilled communicator can increase his potential for control by developing the ability to exchange information interpersonally. While a noninterpersonal approach may sometimes suffice, there are times when accurate transmission of information must be insured, and the best insurance of all lies in the ability to move to the interpersonal level.

The development of self-identity as a consequence of success or failure in achieving environmental control

From success or failure in exercising control over the environment—particularly the other people in it—a person develops a picture of himself or herself. Self-identity provides a barometer of a person's relative effectiveness as a communicator. If a man usually succeeds in realizing physical, economic, and social rewards from the environment, he is likely to perceive himself favorably; if his efforts go largely unrewarded, he will probably view himself unfavorably. As we see it, *the development of self-identity is not primarily a function of communication, but rather a consequence of the outcomes of a person's communicative efforts to achieve environmental control.*

Developing self-identity is, of course, a gradual process. Feelings of failure and social alienation do not spring into full bloom overnight.

Both of us have talked with numerous college students who have low self-concepts when it comes to communicating with others. Such students, who manifest a great deal of anxiety about communicating and a tendency to withdraw from communication situations, usually have a long history of failure in exercising environmental control. Often, they come from a home where conversation is discouraged; their parents are taciturn and expect similar behavior from their children. They have probably been told many times that "children should be seen and not heard." By the time they enter school, they are apprehensive in communication situations. This apprehension not only prevents them from making friends, but also hinders them in assignments involving communication with others. Under such circumstances, a negative self-concept rapidly develops, and it is constantly reinforced by further information indicating they are unsuccessful in realizing social rewards from the environment. By the time they reach college, many are convinced they are social misfits; moreover, they behave in ways consistent with this self-image. The only way the vicious process can be arrested is by providing them with a great deal of contradictory, positive information—a strategy

calculated to enhance their communicative self-concepts.

Just as success or failure in achieving environmental control influences judgments about the self, one's self-judgments affect his transactions with his environment. Failure to exercise environmental control manifests itself in a negative self-concept; in turn, development of a negative self-concept reduces the likelihood that future attempts at environmental control will meet with success. In communication, there is considerable truth to the adage about "the rich getting richer and the poor getting poorer." Success in exercising environmental control begets success, whereas failure begets failure.

Some examples

Consider physical aggression, which ranges from warfare among nations to combat between individuals. While perhaps only tangentially related to communication, physical aggression is often used to realize physical, economic, or social rewards from the environment. In particular, young boys often resort to fighting to impose their will upon their peers and to extract material or social gains from them.

Suppose that while playing marbles with some friends, Fred and Jack dispute ownership of a particular marble. Unable to resolve the argument verbally, Fred shoves Jack, who hits him back and gives him a bloody nose. Fred gives up the fight, and some of the other boys jeer at him.

Not only has Fred's effort to realize the economic reward of the marble failed, but also his perception of himself has been altered by the defeat: where previously he thought himself to be as good or better than Jack, he now sees himself in a subordinate position. The taunts of his peers seriously bruise his self-esteem; in fact, contrary to the ancient cliché, their words are probably much more destructive than the "sticks and stones" represented by Jack's fists. Fred's reassessment of himself will almost certainly affect his future dealings with the environment. He will probably become less assertive and less eager to use physical aggression as a means of resolving disputes over material rewards.

Consider a second example where communication plays a more central role. During the last year of college, job interviews become crucial to future planning. They are, of course, communication transactions; for the applicant, success in obtaining a position ensures numerous physical, economic, and social rewards. Mary Smith, brimming with confidence and enthusiasm, enters eagerly into interaction with her initial prospective employer. After the interview, Mary is certain she has created a favorable impression and that she has a good chance of landing the job.

Unfortunately, Mary is later told that the position has been offered to another applicant. At first, she is likely to speculate about where she went wrong. Her speculation, in turn, will probably produce changes in her self-concept: she may feel less confident about the impression she makes on others, about her qualifications for a good job, or about her skill in communicating during job interviews. Since a job is essential to Mary's economic and social well-being, she will probably continue to interview for desirable positions. But the next time she interviews, she will be less exuberant and less confident of the outcome. Moreover, as we have emphasized, her uncertainty increases the likelihood that she will be unsuccessful. And so the destructive pattern continues, with each successive failure to realize the desired environmental rewards exercising a negative impact on Mary's self-identity and each unfavorable change in her self-identity increasing the probability of further interview failures.

Communication about one's self-identity

Critics of our decision to view self-identity development as a consequence of communication, rather than as a function of it, may point to instances where people consciously solicit information about their self-identities. The little girl who frequently queries, "Mother, do you think I'm pretty?" raises a question that is intimately linked to her self-esteem. In a similar vein, consider the following interchange between father and son, related by Rodney Dangerfield in one of his comedy routines:

RODNEY: Gee, dad, I don't know what I'm going to do. Everyone I know seems to dislike me. I haven't got any friends. I'm rejected by all the people around me.

FATHER: Don't worry about it, son; you haven't met *everyone* yet.

Obviously, Rodney is crying out for reassurance. He perceives that others dislike him, and he is asking his father to invalidate his perception, or at least, to suggest ways for Rodney to improve his social standing. Instead, his father confirms Rodney's low opinion of his social skills and offers only the vague, unsubstantial hope that there exists somewhere in the world a person who may be able to tolerate Rodney. What began as an attempt by Rodney to buttress his self-concept ends as yet another negation of his personal worth.

But what is the communicative end sought by both the inquisitive little girl and Rodney? They are trying to affect the behavior of others so as to realize certain social rewards. If the mother responds, "Yes, you're a lovely little girl!" the attempt to exert control has been successful; if she ignores the child, and snaps, "Don't bother me!" or

"Why are you always asking that same stupid question?" the little girl's efforts to obtain social approval have been thwarted. By the same token, had his father chosen to praise Rodney's social skills or to show some concern about Rodney's problems, Rodney would have had some evidence of his ability to control his social environment. That the father failed to respond in an understanding way only increases Rodney's sense of social powerlessness and reinforces his belief that he is an inept controlling agent.

Sometimes, communicative attempts that ostensibly seek to solicit information about the communicator's self-identity are readily shown to be compliance-oriented. In his youth, Gerry competed keenly with a peer for the title of top pool shooter at a local pool hall. Every time Gerry's adversary would miss an easy shot or play poor position on the next ball, he would angrily deprecate his pool-playing skills. Invariably, one of the spectators would assure him that he was an expert player. Having tired of this ploy, Gerry one day parried his opponent's outburst by responding, "Come to think of it, you don't shoot very well!" Immediately, the other player launched a vehement defense of himself, heatedly announcing to Gerry, "I can shoot better pool than you ever could!" What at first glance appeared to be a self-criticism, or at most a plea for reassurance, was actually a calculated attempt to reap the social rewards of spectator praise. Transactions in which people consciously solicit information about their self-identities are still within the purview of environmental control.

Self-identity, environmental control, and social norms

At times, people may try to control their environments in ways that initially strike others as strange and inexplicable. Such incongruities occur because people's needs and motives do not always correspond with prevailing social norms of what constitutes a healthy personality. Some people thrive on ridicule; some prefer to be dominated; still others conform unswervingly to the mandates of authority. When communicating interpersonally with such persons, one can identify these varying dimensions of self-concept; in other words, one can specify the kinds of control the other person is attempting to exert. Armed with these discriminations, one may choose to reinforce the other's self-concept or attempt to change it. This decision transcends the acquisition of interpersonal communication skills; it rests instead upon certain value judgments concerning the ways people ought to communicate with each other and the kinds of behaviors that reflect healthy self-identities.

For instance, in *Who's Afraid of Virginia Woolf?*, George and Martha's communication, while unquestionably interpersonal, focuses on areas of environmental control calculated to reinforce self-concepts that would be judged by many as exceedingly unhealthy. In the unlikely event that George and Martha should choose to enter therapy, their therapist might eventually move to the interpersonal level in communicating with them. If so, he would probably use his interpersonal insights to fashion changes in their self-concepts; i.e., he would deliberately foil George and Martha's efforts to exercise control over his behavior. Thus, from George and Martha's perspective, their communicative efforts at environmental control have failed; while from the therapist's viewpoint, George and Martha's failure to control represents a needed first step in their development of more healthy self-concepts.

Sometimes there is a marked disparity between the extent to which a communicator seems to perceive control over his environment and the degree of control that others concede to him. Most of us know people who act as if the world is at their beck-and-call while others snicker at their ineptness. The self-styled "big shot" may be regarded as a buffoon by his colleagues; the intellectual merits of the "know-it-all" student may be suspect by his peers; the "ladies' man" may be held in contempt by members of the opposite sex. Such perceptual aberrations are not uncommon and frequently persist in the face of much conflicting evidence. Still, these defense mechanisms may eventually fall upon hard times; they spell trouble for the person who continues to cling to them. We will have more to say about this situation in chapter 4 when we consider fairyland methods of control.

A seeming contradiction

What of the individual who is apparently very successful in realizing many physical, economic, and social rewards from the environment, and yet lives a miserable existence? Each of us has known the Richard Cory of Edwin Arlington Robinson's poem, a man who achieved all the "good things" of life except personal fulfillment. Although not all the Richard Corys of the world "go home and put bullets through their heads," their unhappy lives remind us that personal fulfillment is an elusive commodity. In fact, do their lives not testify to the fact that mere environmental control does not ensure a stable, healthy self-concept?

We would answer the preceding question negatively. What is required when analyzing such paradoxes is a more comprehensive definition of the relevant environment. To be sure, certain individuals are able to amass huge physical and economic returns from the environment; in commercial transactions, their communicative attempts at exercising control meet with unqualified success. Moreover, the achievement of these material rewards brings with it certain social benefits: others confer status upon the individual and treat him with deference.

Still, there remain broad dimensions of the environment over which the individual may perceive he has little control. In particular, he may feel incapable of developing meaningful relationships with others, of exercising control at the individual, interpersonal level. Or he may be dissatisfied with his perceived means of control, feeling that people comply because of his economic power rather than because of his personal attractiveness. In such cases, the importance of interpersonal communication can hardly be overstated. For if the individual could move to the psychological level and establish interpersonal relationships with others, his perceived span of environmental control would be vastly expanded and would culminate in a more healthy, positive self-concept, one that is consistent with a sense of personal fulfillment.

Summary

The basic function of all communication, both interpersonal and noninterpersonal, is to control the environment so as to realize certain physical, economic, and social rewards from it. When communicating with others, we may aim for one of two levels of control: compliance, which occurs when there is an exact correspondence between one's desired and obtained outcomes; or conflict resolution, which occurs when the obtained outcomes reflect some compromise of the competing parties' originally desired outcomes. In our communicative transactions with others, we use information as a means of enhancing the possibilities of environmental control; consequently, information exchange serves as a communicative means rather than as an end in itself. Moreover, we hold that self-identity develops as a result of our relative success or failure in achieving environmental control; instead of treating development of self-identity as a communicative function, we view it as a consequence of communication.

Throughout this chapter, we have contrasted noninterpersonal and interpersonal approaches to the achievement of this basic communicative function. By now, our message should be clear: *ability to communicate interpersonally increases the potential for environmental control.* Consequently, while noninterpersonal and interpersonal communication do not differ in the function they serve, they can be distinguished in terms of their relative effectiveness in achieving this function. In the next chapter we begin to examine specific variables that influence one's ability to move to the more effective of the two levels, the level of interpersonal communication.

Probes

1. What we often rebel against, and rightly so, is not control itself but rather the use of certain means for achieving it. Think about this statement in terms of people you know. Can you identify differences in their typical strategies for achieving environmental control? What kinds of controlling techniques do you especially dislike? Why?

2. In some communication relationships one person consistently complies with the other's demands. Taking a transactional approach to environmental control, consider how compliance may itself be used as a control mechanism. Might the complying party assume an equal or greater amount of control? How could this happen?

3. Consider the act of doing a favor for someone. How does the person who performs the favor enhance his potential for environmental control? Relate your thoughts on this question to research demonstrating that people feel psychologically uncomfortable about accepting favors from others.

4. Conflict resolution, as we have defined it, is inconsistent with our view of communication as a process. Attack or support this argument.

5. Read Skinner's *Beyond Freedom and Dignity*. What relationships, if any, do you see between his argument that behavior is a function of its consequences and ours that self-identity is a consequence, rather than a function, of communication?

6. Under what conditions might the exchange of information detract from one's attempts to achieve environmental control, rather than furthering them? In what ways does the seeker of information establish control over the behavior of the information giver?

7. People differ in the things that they perceive as rewarding. How does this proposition influence our efforts to analyze the control dimension of a communication transaction? How might our own reward preferences produce a faulty analysis of a particular transaction?

8. We have indicated that some writers would take issue with our assertion that the development of self-identity is not a communicative function. How would you develop an argument refuting our position; i.e., how would you defend the contention that development of self-identity is an important communicative function?

Communicating Interpersonally:

Individual Communicators

In this part we discuss selected characteristics of the individual communicator: who he is, what makes him tick, and, most important, what skills he needs to become an effective interpersonal communicator. Chapter 4 introduces the concept of *pattern of communicative control*, a concept that bears heavily on the development of communicative identity. We describe several techniques of communicative control, placing special emphasis on how these techniques relate to interpersonal effectiveness.

Chapter 5 focuses on some ways in which cognitive styles—habitual ways of perceiving and thinking about communication transactions—may add to or detract from an individual's ability to communicate interpersonally. Some people are frequently unable to arrive at psychological level analyses because they see the world as black and white, whereas other persons are acutely sensitive to subtle individual differences among their fellow communicators. We suggest several methods for "interpersonalizing" people's cognitive styles.

Chapter 6 focuses on a fundamental interpersonal skill: a communicator's ability to *respond empathically*. Empathy has traditionally been a slippery concept to define, let alone a difficult skill to practice. Our approach removes empathy from the fuzzy fields of emotional mysticism to the sounder grounds of a behavioral process. We think our approach will prove useful in helping communicators with their empathic endeavors.

Why should we single out the individual communicator, especially since we have argued that we can fully understand communication transactions only in terms of the relationships formed by the participants? Particularly, what about the individual interests us as interpersonal communicators? First of all, the creature we call the "individual communicator" clearly does exist. She and he—whether big or small, old or young, smart or stupid, effective or ineffective—are active participants in any communication transaction. Not only do they behave, but they behave with some consistency over time, and this consistency gives stability and form to their communication relationships. Second, the individual "who" that each of us is becomes especially active in interpersonal situations. Because interpersonal situations are relatively free of externally imposed rules, the individual has greater opportunity to communicate in his own style; in interpersonal situations individual characteristics come to the fore.

Finally, the individual communicator, by virtue of his active involvement in interpersonal transactions, strongly influences the development of interpersonal relationships. Since individual behavior patterns often constrain the development of interpersonal relationships, they are the raw materials of interpersonal relationships. Just as the raw materials you have on hand for cooking limit the number and kinds of dishes you can prepare, so do the available raw materials of interpersonal relationships limit the number and kinds of relationships that can develop. In order to understand interpersonal behavior, it is necessary to understand the mechanisms of individual behavior and how the individual is influential in interpersonal settings.

4 The basic assumption running through our analysis is
that every individual voluntarily enters and stays
in any relationship only as long as it is adequately satisfactory
in terms of his rewards and costs.

John Thibaut and Harold Kelley,
The Social Psychology of Groups

Patterns of
Communicative Control

n Chapter 3 we talked about environmental control. We said that all people need to have some control over the events around them. People exercise control every day, in many ways. Someone who goes on a low-calorie diet seeks to exert some control over his or her weight. Someone who gets a job to earn money seeks to exert some control over the flow of material goods—namely, to ensure that some of the goods flow in his or her direction. If people do not take steps to achieve environmental control, they are sure to be bounced about by whatever the environment offers them. With some luck they manage to stay alive, but their lives are likely to be barren and chaotic.

Environmental control is the primary function of communication. The most frequent use we make of communication is to exert control over our social environments: to elicit desirable and predictable responses from other people. Control is a social skill. Our message-response patterns involve interdependent relationships among people.

Similarities and differences among communicators

There are a number of things common to the efforts of all people to exert environmental control in communication settings. For one thing, just as we all have to learn how to communicate, we also have to learn how to use our communicative skills for the purposes of control. It takes time and what we might even call practice to develop useful control behaviors. For another thing, some of us use these skills more effectively than others. Some usually succeed; some usually fail; and most of us do a little of both.

One of the more striking aspects of control is that people go about it so differently. Their styles vary. Some people are very blatant about trying to exert control: they come right out and say, "I need ten bucks; hand it over." Others are more subtle: you find yourself handing over the money without ever quite realizing that they asked you for it. One communicator may come across as very offensive to you, whereas another, trying to achieve the same goal, may seem entirely lovable.

People's basic control strategies also differ. One person may typically depend on logical argumentation to exert control: "I think we should go to bed together because (a) with the pill, we don't have to worry about pregnancy; (b) psychologists have proven that variety in bed partners is emotionally healthy; (c) our relationship will stagnate if we don't." Another will rely on emotional outbursts: "If you don't go to bed with me I'll kill myself." For some people, handing out rewards underlies their basic approach to control: "Let me borrow your notes for today's class, and you can borrow mine next time." Others basically rely on punishments: "If you don't let me borrow your notes, you'll never get mine again."

Of course, people differ in their abilities to exercise control for specific purposes. There are numerous purposes to which we can apply our communicative control skills, from getting ahead in our business and professional endeavors to making and maintaining close friendships, from settling disputes to advancing particular self-images, from entertaining people at a party to getting them to donate to a charity. Most of us are adept at achieving some purposes, but fall flat on our faces when we move to situations with other purposes.

These differences help make up the basic stuff of interpersonal communication. As interpersonal communicators, we need to recognize these differences and make use of them in our daily transactions. One of the things we might recognize about people's control behavior is that, despite the enormous variety of control behaviors, each individual has a characteristic, predictable approach to control. If you observe someone on several occasions, you will probably find that he or she typically transmits certain kinds of messages in certain situations and seems to find certain kinds of responses desirable. Each individual has a *personal repertory of control messages, a personal way of transmitting these messages, and a personal way of reacting to the responses he or she gets from other communicators.* We call the combination of these things the individual's *pattern of communicative control* (PCC). This concept implies that individuals develop special preferences for, and skills at, particular control strategies. Most people are able to weave many strategies into their repertories, but still rely on certain control methods in interpersonal settings. It is largely through the repetition and uniqueness of these patterns that we come to know one another as individual communicators. In interpersonal transactions, the "who" that you are to the rest of us largely involves the ways you try to elicit desirable responses from us.

Overview of the chapter

The interpersonal "who" that each of us is will be the primary focus of this chapter. We have just suggested that one of the major attributes of each individual communicator is his or her pattern of communicative control. Our initial discussion will elaborate on this notion, describing how we come across to one another as individual persons.

Next we will describe the growth and development of people's patterns of communicative control. Learning these control patterns is related very strongly to learning about other people and to coming to understand oneself. As people acquire and modify their methods for eliciting desirable responses from those they meet, they develop a picture of where they fit into broad social and interpersonal processes; they learn to adapt to their environments; and they discover how to adapt their environments to themselves.

We also deem it useful to consider what control is all about. What does it mean to "exercise control" in a social transaction? How can the ways people elicit desirable responses indicate whether they generally succeed at communicative control? The answers to these questions are important to understanding a wide range of interpersonal behaviors, and we will try to provide some tentative answers in this chapter.

The fourth section of this chapter describes five common strategies of communicative control. We will try to identify the special advantages and disadvantages of each strategy, and to indicate how an interpersonal approach to each can significantly enhance your communicative effectiveness.

Finally, we will place our assertion about the centrality of the communicative control function in an ethical context. We will raise the issues of one communicator's responsibility for another, of egocentric orientations toward communication, and of con games and philanthropic societies. We do this primarily to underscore our assertion that *there is nothing immoral or devious about the concept of control, nor is it unethical for communicators to strive to increase their potential for exercising environmental control.*

Who is the individual communicator?
Or, how do you know one when you transact with one?

To describe the individual communicator, we might begin by asking, "What is an individual?" People have answered this question with reference to blood cells, genetic traits, broad-scale social forces, and abstract philosophical speculations on the nature of humankind. These topics, while certainly important to many perspectives of the individual, are not very relevant for us. We are more interested in developing a transactional, interpersonal perspective of the individual communicator. We want to portray him as much as possible as he appears to other communicating individuals in his natural habitat, exchanging messages in social settings. Our perspective of the individual communicator will evolve as we respond to the question, "How do you know one when you transact with one?"

Well, how do you know chocolate cake? You know it because it tastes like chocolate cake, not like banana nut cake, roast beef, or pineapple. You also know it by its appearance, its texture, and perhaps by its caloric content or its ingredients. For most cake-eaters the primary attribute of chocolate cake, and the primary means by which they come to know it, is its taste.

How do you come to know someone as an individual communicator? What information do you have at your disposal? First, there is the person's behavior, what he says and does in transacting with fellow communicators. Much of an individual's social performance is in the form of messages, ranging from an exchange of greetings to small talk at social gatherings to complex dissertations on the modern political scene. If we observe these messages for some time, we can usually find some regular patterns, some particular styles, some recurrent sets of purposes that characterize an individual's communication behavior. The individual will say and do things that we can say are "like" him, that we come to recognize as characteristic of him as a communicator. Moreover, he will treat us in certain ways. To the extent that his behavior is consistent, we develop a coherent picture of who he is.

To be sure, no individual behaves in a completely predictable, consistent pattern; he can occasionally be expected to do the unexpected. But the behavioral regularities that individuals exhibit make up what has been labeled as the individual's social identity, personality, or what we call his pattern of communicative control.

Effects of your own behavior

You make a significant contribution to who another person is for you. Your own behavior is an important influence in developing your conceptions of other people. When you transmit messages to an individual, you act as a stimulus for him; his messages are likely to be somewhat different because you are there. Your PCC will activate certain dimensions of his PCC. In a sense, your experience of someone else is an indirect experience of yourself.

Your behavior toward another person has further implications: it influences how you conceive of him. Some portion of your behavior toward someone else is planned; i.e., you decide in advance what you will do and say with him. But much of what you say and do is spontaneous. It happens on the spot as a function of his attempts to elicit desirable responses from you. Or you may find yourself "behaving" toward him without really thinking about it before-hand. Suppose you catch yourself smiling a lot when you are around someone else. You may conclude that "He is the kind of person who makes me happy." Or suppose you find yourself treating him with deference and respect. You may conclude that "He is someone I look up to." These conclusions do not come from some abstract idea about the nature of happiness and respect: they come from the concrete behaviors you perform in another person's company. You can learn how you feel about someone by observing what you do when you are with him.

The notion that your perceptions of another person arise in part from your behavior toward that person is an extension of Daryl Bem's (1965) theory of self-perception. According to Bem, people's attitudes toward things around them are often influenced by their behavior toward those things. How you behave toward someone can create a self-impression of your attitude toward him. Your behavior becomes an observable "data point," which you use to infer what is going on in your mind. How do you know whether you like someone? If your behavior toward that person is friendly, you probably do. How do you know whether you are afraid of someone? If you are usually nervous and uptight in that person's company, you probably are.

Behavior is the key element of your conception of another person. We have focused on mutual behavior, directly involving the two of you, but your observations of a person's performances with other people are also important. Your perceptions of how he treats others and of how they treat him contribute to your perception of him.

Creating a conceptual framework

We cannot rely on behavior alone to understand how people come to know one another as individuals. Behavior is too complex and there is too much of it for us to say that an individual "is" a set of behaviors. We cannot keep track of every verbal and nonverbal message in every transaction. Our minds would boggle. We somehow have to organize our perceptions of individual communicators: we have to develop a framework for interpreting, evaluating, and predicting these message behaviors. We also must develop a framework for organizing our own responses to particular individuals. It would excessively tax our energies if we were forced to plan carefully every message for every individual with whom we communicate.

People seem to organize both their conceptual and behavioral responses to one another by sorting raw behavior into abstract category systems. For example, it would not be economical to deal with an individual as someone who frowns a lot, keeps his mouth in a down-turned position, rarely laughs, and says things such as "I don't think I'll have any fun at the party," "I'm sure I'll flunk the exam," and "I wonder if I'll ever be happy in my life?" It is impossible to respond to each discrete message an individual transmits. Instead, we look for behaviors that form consistent patterns and categorize them accordingly. In the above example we might categorize the person as pessimistic or as having a low self-concept. When we have been able to categorize a wide range of a person's behaviors, we can predict his future behavior on the basis of these categories, rather than basing predictions upon numerous separate behaviors.

Our conceptions of other communicating individuals emerge out of complex, interrelated processes. It is difficult to separate and isolate the contributions of any single component to these conceptions. Moreover, it is hard to say how much our impression is based on the individual's behavior and how much it results from our interpretation of his behavior. People's conceptions of one another are created by their mutual transactions. In a behavioral sense, an individual communicator is the messages he sends and the ways other people respond to these messages.

How our approach differs from some others

We have structured our perspective of the individual communicator to emphasize certain aspects of interpersonal behavior. We wanted to focus on how people come to know one another as individuals; i.e., how other people perceive you and how you perceive them. This is a transactional approach, and, as such, ignores some aspects of the individual that are emphasized by other approaches.

We differ from many "personality" approaches, for instance, since we do not see the boundaries of the individual as extending only so far as his skin. Individuals actively participate in their social environments, and we sought to recognize this fact in our perspective. We have also avoided looking at individuals from an introspective approach; i.e., we have not asked, "How do you know who you are?" The "who" you see yourself to be is certainly important to you. You have observed yourself in more situations than any other person; you have had considerable time to reflect on important patterns in your own behavior of which most others are not aware.

In the final analysis, others' reactions to you are determined by what you do and how it is interpreted. Others can never know (though they surely may guess at) what you think and feel. Moreover, you are similarly limited in what you can comprehend about them. Therefore, we have emphasized people's behavior, as opposed to their thoughts and feelings. We have not tried to rob you of your individuality—only to expand your self-conception, to situate it in a transactional, interpersonal context.

Learning patterns of communicative control

The methods we use to control other people's responses must be learned: effective controllers are made, not born. Nevertheless, we are born with some of the basic equipment necessary for control, albeit in a rudimentary, unpolished form. We will begin our discussion of PCC growth and development by describing how one of our innate capacities for control evolves into more sophisticated control methods.

A human infant is born with the capacity for making noise. This capacity, while at times burdensome to his parents, serves a useful function: by crying, he lets other people know that something is wrong in his tiny world. When his parents hear him, they may not know exactly what is wrong; but they usually check to see what the problem is and do whatever is necessary to eliminate it.

An infant is, in most respects, helpless. About all he can do to influence his environment is cry, and the success of his crying behavior is dependent on the good intentions and sensitivity of his parents. Time after time, however, the infant cries and his parents generally respond. As he grows older, he may begin to see an action-reaction relationship between the two behaviors: when he does one thing, his parents do another. This realization is a first step in the growth and development of his PCC, for *he begins to feel that he can participate in, and influence, his own need fulfillment.*

This action-reaction sequence is not always perfect. The infant's parents may be busy when he cries, or too far away to hear him, and so he may have to cry longer and louder to get their attention. His brother or sister or his grandmother may not respond the same way to his crying as his parents normally do. As the infant grows older, then, he moves to a second important stage in his PCC development: he learns that he may have to vary his behavior according to different situations and according to the characteristics of different people, that he will not achieve the same response from all people in all situations.

This realization is not very clear or precise at first. But as the infant grows and his crying becomes speech, he learns about social behavior and begins to see better how the sounds and gestures he makes relate to the ways other people respond. He learns to prefer some of these behaviors to others and to associate certain of his behaviors with undesirable responses and certain others with desirable responses.

There are many ways for a child to learn these relationships. He can learn them through direct experience, as when he discovers that people tend to be nicer to him when he smiles. He may learn them when his parents instruct him as to how he should behave, as when they tell him to eat his vegetables. The child may also learn through various social models; he may observe what other people do to elicit desirable responses or to avoid undesirable responses, and follow their examples. An older brother or sister or a fictional person in a book or television program can contribute a good deal to a child's understanding of control behavior. Yet another method of learning is trial and error, an experimental way of checking how his behaviors can be associated with responses from other people, of trying out various combinations of behavior to assess their effectiveness. As the child becomes more sensitive to the relationships between his own behavior and the behavior of those around him through the use of all of these methods, he learns to scrutinize other people's responses in various situations and to decide what kinds of behaviors will be most effective for him.

These are some of the learning processes involved in developing our patterns of communicative control. We discover early in life that we can elicit favorable responses from other people through particular combinations of verbal and nonverbal behaviors. As we learn to speak, these behaviors become more refined and complex. We should emphasize, however, the active role that other people play in this process, that communicative control is a social event. When an infant's parents react to his crying, they are not only interested in providing the child with a desirable response: they also want to elicit a desirable response from the child. If they can get him to stop crying and to express some sign of satisfaction, they can participate with him in a transaction of mutual satisfaction in which they, too, achieve some control.

Now that we have an idea how specific methods of control are learned, we can examine how these methods are integrated into an overall pattern of communicative control.

Fixed and variable elements in a PCC

When we say that a person develops a pattern of behavior, we mean that his behavior is consistent and predictable, that he tends to repeat characteristic sequences of speech and gesture. Although the variety of PCCs is extremely large—some researchers say as large as the number of individual people—all people acquire behavior patterns similarly. Rather than enumerate the many varieties of pattern, we will deal with the commonalities of all patterns.

A PCC consists of a specifiable set of fixed and variable elements. The fixed elements are captured in the following assertions.

1. All people need to elicit desirable responses from others.

2. Communicators are dependent upon one another for achieving these responses.

3. The control procedures for eliciting desirable responses are learned in social situations, their adoption depending upon their success in eliciting desirable responses.

4. The behaviors of the controlling and responding persons form a transactionally interdependent relationship.

This set of fixed elements gives us a general description of PCC evolution.

A more detailed picture of an individual's PCC can be gained by assessing values for each of the variable elements in the configuration. The elements that can vary are

1. the specific control procedures that are rewarded and incorporated

2. the types of people who are associated with the rewarded behaviors

3. the situations that call for certain behaviors and offer certain rewards

Given our fixed elements, these variables take on different values depending on the particular learning experiences of an individual.

The three variable elements become part of a PCC when an individual associates them all with one or more favorable responses. That is, PCC development evolves from a person's prediction that, by transmitting message-type x in situation-type y, he can elicit a desirable response from people of type z. Although the processes by which the variable elements are incorporated into an individual's PCC are complex, we can reasonably capture them in a brief illustration using one kind of communication problem, conflict resolution.

If a boy's parents favor rational-logical methods of conflict resolution, such as intelligently discussing conflicts rather than shrieking and yelling about them, he will quickly learn that he can assure both favorable settlement of conflicts and parental approval by adopting these methods, especially in family conflicts where the parents have considerable control over the adjudication of disputes. The boy says, in effect, "Here I am in conflict with my parents. I know I cannot get anywhere with them by crying or demanding to have my own way, so I have to send messages they want to hear."

Here we have the genesis of a portion of the child's PCC; when conflict situations involving his parents arise, he will be rewarded if he performs according to their expectations. Similar analyses are germane to other dimensions of his PCC. Such analyses are based on a stimulus-response model: given a situation in which desirable responses are possible and given the presence of people from whom these responses can be elicited, certain behaviors will be performed. *To the extent that the perception of the possibility of a desirable response, the situation, and the people recur together, the control behaviors will also recur.* This is the essence of the development of patterns of control behavior.

You probably are thinking, "But that's too simple!" Of course it is. For instance, there are many varieties of rational-logical conflict resolution, ranging from informal bargaining to formal debate, and so the pattern is not always identical nor clearly observable. A further complicating factor involves the degree to which an individual generalizes from the original learning situation to other situations—in other terms, the number of different referents he has for "conflict resolution situations" and "people like my parents." For some people all conflict situations are the same, and the same response is triggered by each conflict. For other people conflict situations vary widely, and each one requires a somewhat different control strategy. For some individuals all people are the same, being equally disposed to proffer rewarding responses to the same control strategy. Other individuals learn that different people respond differently to different strategies.

PCC and interpersonal communication

This brings us face-to-face with the crucial distinction between interpersonal and noninterpersonal communication discussed in chapter 1. An individual's PCC will vary considerably depending upon his ability to base his predictions of communication outcomes on psychological data. Suppose that the child in our illustration perceives that all people prefer rational-logical methods of conflict resolution. In a sense he is communicating at the cultural level of prediction, seeing only what he feels all people have in common and remaining unaware of their differences.

Sooner or later problems are bound to arise with the child's non-interpersonal approach to conflict resolution. If he continues to recognize only one general class of conflict situations and only a single kind of person whom he confronts in conflict situations, and if he has practiced only one set of communication methods for handling these situations and these people, he will find that there are many times when his particular PCC is ineffective. For example, when he meets a playmate who has learned to settle disputes with his fists, his failure to anticipate important differences in people may result in a bloody nose. To be more effective in the long run, he must integrate this new information into his PCC and learn to modify his control behaviors according to his experiences.

Suppose our child is now a young man and has become romantically involved with a young woman at college. Because of her jealousy toward two women with whom he works part-time, she wants him to quit the job, a move he feels he cannot afford to make. In this conflict situation he may find that his typically rewarded mode of conflict resolution fails: rational-logical methods often are not applicable to conflicts that have an emotional foundation. Again, our young man must modify his PCC if he is to deal successfully with this new situation. The more he adapts and refines his control procedures to accommodate various situations, the more complex and diversified his PCC is likely to become. Complex and diversified PCCs result from the emergence of control procedures based on stimulus discrimination, or psychological data. The prediction-making processes discussed briefly in the preceding paragraphs represent a first step in developing empathic skills, which we will discuss in detail in chapter 6.

Measuring your effectiveness at communicative control

In the next few pages we will suggest some rough guidelines for gauging your control effectiveness. In many respects, effectiveness entails personal judgment. Some people seem to be content with the quality and quantity of favorable responses they elicit even though most others would call them losers. We sometimes rate other people as highly effective, but they regard themselves as rather inept. What we will seek to do, then, is to account for the differing conceptions that communicators have concerning their effectiveness or ineffectiveness. We will begin by elaborating on the nature of the responses people strive to elicit by their control endeavors.

Eliciting responses: the minimal signs that you are in control

A response, very broadly, is a reflexive form of behavior. We call a particular behavior a response when we believe that some prior event triggered or caused it. Generally, we can say that behavior B, occurring at $time_2$, is a response to behavior A, occurring at $time_1$, if we have some logical, empirical, or intuitive basis for reasoning that the second behavior, B, was triggered by the first behavior, A.

$$behavior\ A\ (time_1) \rightarrow behavior\ B\ (time_2)$$

Sometimes it is difficult to determine whether one behavior constitutes a response to another. The two behaviors may be separated in time and space, and we may be unable to identify any kind of connection between them, as when one person "gets back at" another for some imagined slight that happened weeks ago. But most of the time we have little trouble determining whether or not another person has responded to us, and we can readily identify the nature of the particular response. We have even less trouble determining whether we ourselves have responded to people who have communicated with us. This is fortunate, for if we could not pinpoint our own and others' responses to messages, we could never evaluate people's effectiveness at control.

When performing a purposive activity, the performer must specify the goals of the activity with some clarity. The goal of communicative control is, at a minimum, to elicit responses from other people. Control presumes that one affects others in some way. Few of us, of course, are satisfied merely to elicit just any response. We put additional demands on ourselves; we believe that the responses we elicit must satisfy other criteria before we are willing to consider ourselves effective controllers. Among other things, we weigh the desirability of the responses we elicit, our responsibility for these responses, and our capacity to replicate them. As you read our remarks about each of these criteria, you might use these standards to assess your own effectiveness at control.

Desirability of responses

What makes a particular response favorable or desirable? Why should we prefer one response to another? These questions cannot always be answered clearly and simply. To make some sense of them we will break the concept of desirability into smaller, more understandable dimensions to try to grasp some reasons for the variability in individual control behaviors.

One dimension of desirability is the *specificity of our goals in any transaction involving a distinction between "desirable" and "desired" responses.* A desired response is one that we actively and consciously seek to elicit from other people. When we have as our goal a particular desired response, we transmit a message or combination of messages specifically designed to elicit this response. We think about the messages we send; we analyze the situations and people relevant to our goal; and we can usually determine success by the response we get. People develop strategies of communicative control when they seek to elicit desired responses, as when they apply for jobs, sell merchandise, settle disputes, or try to get good grades in a college course.

We are usually not so self-conscious about communication strategies when we have no clear-cut response goal. When we participate in informal communication situations, for instance, we are not generally inclined to construct our messages to elicit definite responses. In fact, we might even be unable to specify our exact goals in these situations. We might say that our goals include making the transaction relaxed, friendly, entertaining, civil, and informative. Although these transactional qualities are certainly desirable, we are not likely to plan carefully for them unless we have difficulty achieving them. Goal specificity, then, is important both in terms of whether we bother to develop particular communication strategies and in terms of our degree of consciousness of response desirability itself.

Whether or not we are actively aware of trying to elicit particular responses, we generally have some idea of the kinds of responses we can actually hope to trigger. The range of these responses helps fix the degree of relative desirability of any given response. For example, someone convicted of committing a felony might be faced with a prison sentence ranging from five to fifteen years. His attorney, then, is faced with the task of evoking the maximally desirable response from the judge or jury: a five-year sentence. If any other person, not faced with a felony conviction, were asked, "Would you find it desirable to spend five years in prison?" he would surely say no. But for the trial defendant, whose range of alternatives does not include freedom, the answer would be, "I'd find it highly desirable."

Suppose you are arguing the merits of multiple-choice exams with a small group of people. You might regard the responses to your arguments as ranging from totally rejecting to fully accepting, and then aim your control strategies at achieving full acceptance of your position—in other words, you might be satisfied only with compliance by the group. Another group member, however, might see a broader range of possibilities for himself. His experiences with people in groups may have included frequently being ignored by them and rarely achieving widespread acceptance of his arguments. His control strategies, therefore, will include getting the group's attention, and he will communicate accordingly. The group may perceive his attention-seeking tactics unfavorably—other people may regard their responses to him as undesirable—but he may feel rather successful in triggering any response at all.

A third factor that helps account for individual variations is the degree to which given responses are predictable. Some responses are so predictable they foster boredom, thus losing their desirability. Other responses become desirable because their very uncertainty makes them exciting. Desirability-as-predictability leaves considerable room for individual variation. Not only are the probabilities that certain responses will occur highly subjective, but also a person's assessment of the desirability of high and low predictability varies with his emotional state. When people feel secure, they seem to have greater preferences for uncertainty than when they feel relatively insecure. When a person feels generally ineffective at eliciting desirable responses, he may settle for familiarity as his criterion for control.

One final aspect of response desirability must be considered: the cost involved in eliciting a response. It is not uncommon for communicators to sacrifice more time, energy, or self-esteem than a response is worth to them. Effectiveness at control is partially a function of efficiency: there is no point in eliciting a response with a value of 10 if your control strategy costs you 12. In this respect, communicative control involves some purely economic considerations. Just as the success of a business cannot be measured solely in terms of its gross revenues, so must people audit their communicative expenses to calculate their control effectiveness.

Responsibility for responses

A second measure of our effectiveness at control is the degree to which we feel personally responsible for eliciting responses. We said earlier that we could define a particular behavior as a response if we could see a connection between it and some prior behavior. The concept of personal responsibility for responses will become more meaningful if we distinguish various kinds of connections between behaviors.

Some responses are almost automatically connected to particular triggering messages. When someone says hello to you, you automatically return the greeting. When someone asks you a question, you usually respond with some kind of answer. Automatic connections between messages, at least on a cultural level, are brought about by powerful socialization processes. They are common in every society, and often go under the heading of "good manners" or "social graces." All children learn them from the time they begin to talk. To elicit responses of this kind, all you need do is learn the appropriate triggering messages—and all that is required to learn them is minimal intelligence. There are similar sets of automatically connected messages at sociological levels of communication. Most groups have established rituals that all members learn.

In most cases, individuals do not feel personally responsible for eliciting desirable responses under conditions of automatic connection. The society or the norms of the group take the bulk of the responsibility, assuming the members have been well indoctrinated. When an individual triggers these responses, he is merely tapping into the response patterns of a collectivity of people, and these responses provide little evidence of his communicative control.

It is important to note, however, that one way to severely diminish a person's feelings of control is to deny him access to these seemingly natural responses. This phenomenon was observed in the near panic many automobile drivers experienced during the gasoline shortage in late 1973 and early 1974. In effect, they appeared to have lost their abilities to evoke what they felt should have been automatic responses from service station attendants. Similar uneasiness is induced in the would-be diner who has to wait an overly long time for a waitress to take his order in a restaurant (his mere presence at a table should be sufficient to ensure a service response from restaurant personnel), or in the person whose acquaintances do not respond to his greetings.

As a general rule, people feel more personally responsible for eliciting desirable responses, and hence more in control of communication situations, when they perceive the desirable response to be non-normal or unusual; i.e., when they feel that not everyone could have achieved the same response. For example, when you ask a cab driver to take you to your destination and he does, you deserve relatively little applause for your control effectiveness. However, if you have been picked up while hitchhiking and can persuade the driver to go ten miles out of his way to take you home, especially when the driver is in a hurry, you can count yourself among the effective communicative controllers.

We generally feel that an unusually desirable response must have required an unusually effective control message. If we have command over such messages, we feel more in control. People who are popular, who achieve coveted honors for themselves, who are famous or highly respected, or who have been elected to important positions generally have mastered unusually effective control behaviors. It may be an unfortunate reflection of our modern culture that even people who can boast of happy marriages must be ranked with these other more well-known successful controllers, according to this criterion: they have elicited what is more and more becoming an unusual desired response.

Of course, the mere fact that we elicit an unusual response does not ensure that we are personally responsible for it. For instance, lottery winners certainly "elicit" highly desirable and unusual responses, but they can claim no particular skill or expertise. Furthermore, certain people are prone to emitting unusual responses; i.e., they frequently say and do things that other people rarely say or do, thus giving would-be controllers an illusion of special effectiveness. Some professors refer to all their students as very bright students, but the student who does not know this may erroneously believe that he has been selected for a rare academic compliment. Many of us can imagine the chagrin of the self-styled Casanova who returns from a date and announces to his roommates that he has scored, only to find that his roommates' experiences with the same woman parallel his own.

Replicability of desirable responses

The extent of our personal responsibility for a desirable response is often hard to judge. Our third measure of control is the replicability of desirable responses, or our ability to achieve similar control successes in situation after situation. This measure can be used as a check on our perceptions of personal responsibility. If we can elicit a particular response across a variety of situations, it seems reasonable to conclude that we must be doing something to contribute to our success.

A young child sometimes enters a room filled with adults and makes some comment that the adults find uproariously amusing. Their laughter and favorable attention prompt the child to utter more comments aimed at triggering similar responses. But try as he might, the child's efforts are in vain, and the adults may quickly tire of the demands he makes on their attention, until his parents send him off to bed chagrined at the inconsistency of his elders' responses to his performances. In the same vein, professors are often disappointed when, on the first day of class, a student responds brilliantly to a difficult question, but on all successive questions misses the mark by a mile. And how many students have sat in rapt attention during a professor's opening-day lecture, only to find that this was the one high point of the course?

In these examples, a communicator was able to elicit a relatively unusual and desirable response, but woefully failed to replicate, or repeat, the feat on successive attempts. To be an effective controller you must be able to say of yourself, "I did it this time, and I can do it again." This measure of control is related to the responsibility measure. The more capable a communicator is of replicating his successes, the more likely it is that these successes are not dependent on chance events or on the strong disposition of certain individuals to emit desirable responses.

The capacity to replicate is also closely related to the concept of security. We have previously mentioned the fundamental importance of being able to anticipate future events. For instance, a simple walk across your living room floor would fill you with anxiety if you were continually uncertain whether the floor would support your weight. Similarly, in social transactions we would experience intolerable anxiety if we were continually uncertain that we could elicit desirable responses from other people. We must be able to predict our own probable success at controlling communication responses; if we could not, we might cease to function as normal human beings.

Summary

Our discussion of the three dimensions of communicative control emphasizes both the possibility and the difficulty of measuring effectiveness at control. Desirability is a highly subjective element of responses, since it depends on the specificity, range, and predictability of the responses people seek and obtain. These factors vary with a person's own goals and experiences. The responsibility dimension is no more objective. A communicator, his respondent, and their observers may all disagree on the communicator's responsibility for a response. Replicability is probably the most objective of the three, since it is defined according to sequences of usually observable response behaviors. Even here, however, there is a subjective element. A communicator may elicit a series of similar but ambiguous responses. For example, if a person smiles and then grimaces during a conversation, his companion may assess them both as favorable reactions, differing only in degree.

The more desirable a response, the more a person may want to take credit for it. He may also perceive that he can replicate it. The opposite, of course, is also true: if he can replicate the response, he may also come to find it more desirable. When asked why he smoked, a ballplayer once answered: "It's one thing I'm good at. I do it consistently, and I do it well." Despite these problems, our three dimensions do provide a basis for some assessment of a communicator's effectiveness at control. Although not foolproof, they are useful guidelines for the creation of a feedback system for any communicator.

Strategies of communicative control

PCCs are composed of numerous strategies of communicative control. Specific strategies become incorporated in a communicator's repertory through a relatively simple testing process: if a strategy works, he retains it for further use; if not, he discards it. Most communicators modify their PCCs over time. A strategy that works in one environment may become inoperative when the communicator moves to a different social setting, and therefore he may either permanently drop it from his repertory or store it for later use. New strategies become part of an individual's PCC when he acquires new information about more effective approaches to eliciting desirable responses.

We will discuss five broad categories of control strategies. (We cannot examine specific, individual strategies, for there are simply too many of them.) Each category represents a general approach to communicative control, and each suggests numerous strategic variations. You will probably see some resemblance between our sample strategies for each class and strategies that you yourself use.

No one of the five categories is meant to describe an individual communicator. Few people are so restricted that their repertories consist of only one kind of strategy. Nor are our classes intended as a composite of a "typical" communicator. Rather, most people probably use several kinds of strategies, some more than others.

We want to caution you that the following presentation is limited to an examination of the underlying principles of five different approaches to control. Except for purposes of illustration, we have tried to avoid detailing specific control messages or situations. We believe that an understanding of fundamental control principles will improve your capacity for eliciting desirable responses from your fellow communicators, but the task of assessing particular demands in particular transactions we must leave to you. As you read about the various strategies, you might pause periodically to consider how you would apply them in different situations and how the use of psychological level data might relate to your effectiveness at control.

Dangling carrot strategies

The dangling carrot is a reward one communicator bestows upon another. Dangling carrots come in many forms. They may be actual objects, such as precious gems or money, record albums or bottles of wine, athletic trophies or college diplomas. They may be services such as cooking a meal, doing a term paper, extending a social invitation, or giving a kiss. And many times carrots come in the form of intangible symbolic messages, such as "You did a fine job," "I think you're a wonderful person," or "I like the coat you have on."

Whatever form the carrot takes, all dangling carrot strategies assume that *you can increase the probability of eliciting a desirable response if you offer someone a reward for making it*. People are more likely to do things you want if they enjoy it, benefit from it, are entertained by it, or in any way get something they want in return.

Although carrot strategies, with their many variations, are among those most commonly used by communicators, they are also among the most complex and least understood. We will begin by highlighting some of the basic elements and procedures in carrot approaches to control to show the major tasks facing carrot strategists.

Goals of dangling carrot strategies
The primary goal of carrot strategies is *to change the rate and/or the direction of a person's behavior*. Rate is the frequency with which a person performs a particular behavior and may range from zero (no performance of the behavior) to some number smaller than 100 percent (nobody can do something all the time). To take a common example, parents sometimes want to increase the rate of their children's vegetable-eating behavior; the children may not be eating any vegetables at all, or they may not be eating enough of them. A wife might want to increase the rate of affection-giving behavior by her spouse, or a brother might wish to increase the rate of his older sister's helping-with-homework behavior.

The direction of a person's behavior might be toward the controller or toward some third person or persons. A communicator who recognizes that someone is already prone to perform a certain desirable behavior at a desirable rate might want to be the target of that behavior. Advertising campaigns for toothpaste, basic foodstuffs, and some medicines seem to assume that consumers are buying these products; the campaign is designed not to get consumers to buy but rather to get them to buy from a particular seller. Men tend to assume that women are generally disposed to engage in romantic relationships, but this assumption is not very satisfying to someone who cannot influence the direction of feminine romantic behavior.

Two secondary goals of carrot strategies are *to induce substantive changes in behavior* and *to reinforce existing behavioral rates, directions, and substances*. The substance of a person's behavior is what he does or how he does it rather than how often he does it or with whom.

An obvious example here is the attempt by professors to get their students to write substantively more scholarly papers. Golf pros try to influence the quality of their clients' putting, not the frequency with which they play golf. Friends try to improve the openness of their communication, but they might be content with how often they talk and with whom they talk.

When a communicator reinforces some dimension of another's behavior (its rate, direction, or substance), he increases the probability that that dimension will remain about the same. If you are pleased that someone is talking to you five times a week about work-related topics and you want this behavioral direction, rate, and substance to continue, your task is to reinforce his current behavior.

Strictly speaking, the distinctions among rate, direction, and substance are imprecise. A professor who improves the substantive quality of a student's writing might be said to increase the student's rate of high quality writing. A boxer who floors an opponent in the ring and then knocks out a companion in a tavern is performing two substantively different behaviors: one is a highly commendable feat of skill and the other may be a crime. The direction of his pugilistic activities bears strongly on definitions of their substance. However, these distinctions are relevant to the design and implementation of carrot strategies, for they suggest different areas of concentration with qualitatively different strategic emphases. Logical nuances aside, people tend to react differently to attempts to change each of these three behavioral dimensions, and this is the fact of paramount importance for would-be controllers.

Procedures for using dangling carrot strategies
The fundamental task of the carrot controller is to get someone to associate him with rewards and satisfaction. To accomplish this objective, the controller may use either or both of two basic procedures. The first procedure consists of establishing a stimulus-response-reward sequence in his transactions with another person. The strategist tries to "teach" his companion that when the controller presents stimulus x, if his companion emits response y, then he will receive reward z. If the controller is fortunate, he can tap into a stimulus-response-reward sequence that the other person has already learned; i.e., he can get the other person to direct the learned response to him if he presents the appropriate stimulus under the appropriate conditions.

This procedure operates at all three levels of prediction-making. At the cultural level, most young children automatically respond to an adult's request for help under reasonable circumstances. Children value adult approval and will generally behave in ways to get it. If you ask a child for help (stimulus), he will give it to you (response), because he expects a reward (your approval of his response). At the sociological level, members of the group "college students" can generally be expected to respond favorably to minor personal requests from their professors because they expect some academic reward in return. At the psychological level, of course, recognition of the triggering stimuli requires sensitivity to the past experiences of particular individuals. Suppose you want to increase someone's disposition to transact with you. You know that a skier will almost automatically respond favorably if you say, "I like skiing." He foresees some reward in skiing together, or at least in talking with you about skiing. Another person might think that skiers are elitist bums, however, and respond negatively.

Carrot controllers may not always be fortunate enough to discover preestablished stimulus-response-reward sequences. They may have to create the sequence specifically for a particular relationship. This process is very much akin to methods of training laboratory animals and household pets, but it can be useful and effective in eliciting desirable responses from fellow communicators. It involves a teaching task. You might say to someone, "Come over for dinner tonight." If your intended guest does not dislike you and is free for the evening, he will probably come. Getting him to come again involves making the evening rewarding for him. A pleasant evening conditions him to respond favorably to future invitations. Numerous examples of this procedure have probably occurred to you already; it is commonly used, successfully and unsuccessfully, by most communicators.

Note three things about this carrot procedure. First, the control stimulus is someone's cue to respond in a certain way, and he will do so upon its presentation by another communicator. Of course, the stimulus-response part of the sequence is not always automatic. The stimulus should be presented in transactional settings similar to the settings in which the respondent learned to expect a reward. If you approached even the most avid skier when he was running to catch a bus, he would probably respond negatively to your announcement that you too are a skier. In addition, the triggering stimuli are often multifaceted. Not only must you announce that you are a skier, but your respondent must perceive that you have attributes similar to the skiers from whom he has received skiing-related rewards in the past.

A second notable feature of this procedure is that the predictability, or strength, of the stimulus-response pairing depends on the degree to which the respondent has been rewarded for making the response. A response that is almost always followed by a high reward almost automatically follows the triggering stimulus. A response that is infrequently rewarded will appear less often. The child who almost automatically responds to an adult's request for help has probably been given approval very regularly. The skier who responds cautiously or unenthusiastically to someone's announcement that he too is a skier, has probably met several non-rewarding skiers.

This notion has an interesting corollary concerning the relationship between level of communication and the complexity of the triggering stimulus. As we move from the noninterpersonal to the interpersonal level, the triggering stimulus generally becomes more complex and multifaceted. At the cultural level anybody (a simple stimulus) can elicit rewarding cultural responses. At the sociological level, members of higher status can generally elicit desirable responses from members of lower status; thus, the stimulus becomes more complex since group membership plus rank are now necessary. At the psychological level, the complexity increases further. The facets of a stimulus that elicits friendship behavior are, for most people, numerous and varied.

Third, note that effectiveness ultimately depends on the controller's capacity to reward his respondent. If you have the opportunity to tap a previously established stimulus-response-reward sequence, mere presentation of the stimulus will be sufficient to elicit the response; you need not have access to the reward itself. This tactic will not last for long, however. If the respondent discovers that no reward is forthcoming, he will cease to make the response; i.e., he will no longer associate the stimulus with a reward. If you want to establish a new sequence or reinforce an old one, you must come up with the goods you "promised" when you presented the stimulus. Otherwise, you will weaken the person's tendency to respond and eventually, after enough disappointments, extinguish it altogether. For example, if you have enjoyed a highly satisfying interpersonal relationship with someone but the relationship has turned sour, a telephone call or a visit can act as a sufficient stimulus to elicit some kind of favorable response for quite a while because the response is strongly associated with the reward. But eventually, as the response-reward bond weakens, so does the stimulus-response bond.

The second basic procedure for implementing carrot strategies focuses on the behavior of the respondent rather than on the stimulus presented by the controller. The controller's task is to reward certain behaviors performed by the other person in hopes of getting him to behave similarly in the future. Effectiveness rests on teaching him that he can expect certain rewards if he performs in certain ways. In other words, rather than merely responding to a stimulus that you present, he guides his own behavior toward a goal: eliciting a desirable response from you.

The essence of this procedure lies in *developing a carrot strategy response in another person.* You want the person to say, "You have a reward to offer me, and I must figure out what I can do to get it." The two primary tactics for using this procedure are:

1. Establish for your respondent a link between his behavior and a reward from you.
2. Make certain he has a good idea of the strategy he can use to obtain the reward.

In regard to the second tactic, the world is full of communicators who have learned that particular individuals have certain rewards to offer them but who have never learned what tactics to use in getting the rewards. If you have any doubt as to whether your respondent is capable of determining just what rates, directions, and substances of behaviors you find desirable, it is best to make these factors explicit. Many communicators hesitate to do this. They seem to feel, "Well, if he doesn't already know what makes me happy, I'm certainly not going to tell him. That would be artificial and presumptuous. What right do I have to tell him how to behave?" Yes, it might be artificial, but only until both people get used to the new behavior. It may also be presumptuous, but hardly more so than expecting someone to understand you through subtle hints or no hints at all. If you want certain responses from someone and that person wants to provide them, then perhaps you are shirking an important interpersonal responsibility by not directing his behavior.

The goals of dangling carrot strategies are to change the rates, directions, and substances of behaviors and to reinforce these changes when they are desirable. The two basic procedures for implementing carrot strategies are establishing stimulus-response-reward sequences and engendering the development of carrot strategies in other people. Beyond understanding these goals and procedures, the effective carrot strategist must have several communicative skills.

Skills essential to effective implementation of carrot strategies
One necessary skill is the capacity to *recognize what a particular individual finds rewarding.* Most communicators can make accurate cultural level predictions of what many persons will find rewarding. Individuals in our culture generally value money, happiness, prestige, security, love, and a host of other material and symbolic commodities. Similarly, it is often not difficult to predict what members of certain sociological groups will find rewarding. Students value good grades. Soldiers value promotions and medals. Waitresses value tips. Many cultural and sociological rewards are relevant in interpersonal trans-actions, but beyond that all we can say is that people are different and tend to find different things rewarding. Some people, for instance, seem to find submissive responses rewarding, since they prefer to

dominate transactions. Others prefer dominating responses, since they would rather take a submissive role.

The wide variation in what people find rewarding underscores one of the major difficulties in understanding human behavior: no one has ever clearly and unambiguously specified what it is about a reward that is "rewarding." Operationally, rewards have been defined as stimuli which tend to increase rates of behavior, which someone will work hard to attain, and which reduce need or drive states. But these definitions are not very satisfying. They do not provide communicators with a basis for predicting the particular stimuli people will or will not find rewarding. In other words, as interpersonal communicators we are left to our own perceptiveness to discern how our fellow communicators will respond to particular stimuli. We will assume, however, that most communicators are capable of exercising such perceptiveness.

What, then, is the next skill required of the carrot strategist? Even if you perceive what commodities someone defines as rewarding, *you must have command over the symbolic or material resources that constitute the rewards.* It is not sufficient, for instance, to know that someone can be rewarded with money, status, and ego-boosts; you must also be able to dispense money, confer status, and boost his ego. Many commodities are rewarding simply because they are scarce, which indicates that all communicators are not equally capable of dispensing them. If you could offer someone happiness, you would indeed become the most successful of controllers.

Let us move on another step and assume that you can both recognize what someone finds rewarding and actually offer the reward to him. Several new skills then become relevant. By far the most important of these additional skills is the ability to *see the logic between particular rewards and responses.* We emphasize this skill because without it carrot control is a hit or miss affair and also because many communicators seem deficient in this skill. It is not enough simply to identify what an individual finds rewarding; you must also learn what he is prepared to offer for that reward. Nor is it enough to get a reward from someone else; you must also discover what he wants in return. For example, we can safely say that most professors value money, and we can just as safely say that most students value high grades. But very few professors would accept money as an inducement for offering a student a high grade. Professors define quality academic achievement as the appropriate, logical incentive to give high grades. Although some say our culture places overriding emphasis on the reward value of money, there are numerous responses that money cannot buy.

Consider a second example. Paul, a person we know, buys cigarettes by the carton and keeps them in his office. Consequently, when

his smoking acquaintances run out of cigarettes, they go to him for one. Frequently these people approach him with a one-down, apologetic expression in their voices and on their faces and humbly ask, "Hey, Paul, would you mind if I bum a cigarette from you?" Paul firmly believes that people should not demean themselves when asking such a small favor; he finds the semblance of groveling wholly undesirable. He would prefer to be rewarded with the tacit agreement that he could freely ask his acquaintances for cigarettes should he need them in the future. If Paul were asked, however, "Do you like to feel important and feel that people need you?" he would surely respond affirmatively.

The concept of a logical connection between pairs of rewards does not necessarily involve reward magnitude. Stated differently, failure at control need not involve an insufficient amount of reward but perhaps the wrong kind of a reward. Carrot strategists must discover the *premium of exchange* for a given transactional setting. As is the case when predicting most communicative outcomes, it is easier to predict logical reward pairs in noninterpersonal situations than in interpersonal situations. For example, our culture prescribes that politicians, policemen, and professors do not exchange favors for money. Even though this prescription apparently carries little weight among some of these individuals, most prospective controllers at least know enough to be "delicate" when suggesting money as the reward they have to offer and to try to keep news of an accomplished exchange from reaching the mass media. But as our example shows, there is much room for error in following noninterpersonal prescriptions of reward-reward logic.

Psychological predictions of appropriate and effective exchange premiums are indispensable to carrot control success. Support for this assertion abounds in men's and women's attempts to establish interpersonal relationships with each other. One common example involves the man who prepares for a date by getting his suit dry-cleaned and having his hair styled, who buys his date flowers and takes her to an expensive restaurant, and who is courteous and attentive the whole evening. In return for these rewards he may expect his date to spend the night with him. This strategy (and some more or less elaborate) sometimes works, but often it is unsuccessful. When the man realizes his failure, he may exclaim, "But look at all I went through for you! The least you could do is spend the night with me!" His chances of success would probably not have been improved if he had taken his date to a more exclusive restaurant and thrown in some diamonds for good measure. His date just did not define the rewards he offered as logically connected to the response he expected in return.

Sometimes failure results from factors other than a simple mismatch of rewards. The *timing, frequency*, and *magnitude* of rewards may also be relevant to considerations of reward-reward logic. Would-be controllers can extend rewards too soon or too late, too frequently or too infrequently. When the magnitudes of the rewards they exchange are either too little or too great, they have violated the *parity principle*: "I am giving x amount of what I have to offer. I expect you to extend to me a comparable amount of what you have to offer." As Gamson states it, it is a communicator's assumption that he "ought to get from an agreement an amount proportional to what he brings into it" (1964, p. 88).

People tend to want to receive as much as they give. This does not necessarily mean that if they give a dollar they want four quarters back. But if they give a dollar they generally expect, for instance, a dollar's worth of eggs, personal support, or love. If one party to a relationship is putting forth 50 percent of his capacity to maintain the relationship, the other should also put forth roughly 50 percent, even if one participant's absolute capacity is greater than the other's. When an individual feels that someone else is not upholding his share of a relational bargain, he may well become frustrated or angry, and curtail his own efforts.

Communicators should be careful, however, to avoid confusing parity problems with reward logic problems. The man on the date who failed to elicit a desired response may have become upset because he thought his companion was not upholding her part of the bargain. But his assessment was unfair if she did not define his reward as appropriate to elicit his intended response.

Many people approach carrot control situations as they would an economic investment situation. They perceive themselves to be investing so much time, energy, and emotion in eliciting a desired response, and they want a profitable return on their investment. They predict the outcomes of relationships in terms of short- and long-term profit potentials. The realization of relational profit is an important motivation for communicators. A good portion of our discussion of a second kind of control strategy, the hanging sword, will center around this concept.

Hanging sword strategies

Dangling carrot strategies are designed to increase the probability of desirable responses. They are based on the assumption that a communicator will repeat a behavior for which he is rewarded. Communicators who want to decrease the probability of undesirable responses have recourse to hanging sword strategies. Hanging swords are punishments. One communicator may punish another to get him to decrease or eliminate behaviors that the punisher does not like.

Three types of hanging swords
One type consists of *presenting a communicator with aversive stimuli.* An aversive stimulus is, by definition, one that a communicator finds hateful and will try to avoid. Cultures have used monetary fines, jail terms, execution, and banishment as aversive stimuli. Groups hang the swords of expulsion and ostracism over their members. Individuals can punish one another with verbal aggression, rejection, and physical assaults. The basic procedure for using aversive stimuli is to communicate a conditional prediction: if you do something I (or we) don't like, then I (or we) will punish you.

A second type of hanging sword is the *withdrawal of rewards.* Some communicators do not regard this behavior as a punishment. They conceive of messages as ranging from plus one for rewards to minus one for punishments, with a neutral zero point midway between. They reason that the withdrawal of rewards is a move from plus one to zero, and, since punishments are regarded as negative, rescinding rewards cannot be punishing per se. However, the effects of withdrawing rewards have much in common with the effects of aversive stimuli. The person deprived of expected rewards experiences discomfort and perhaps anxiety; the amount depends on how valuable the rewards were. Upon the withdrawal of some rewards, such as money or love, he may face serious deprivation (hunger, loneliness), which becomes aversive in itself. He is also less likely to repeat the behaviors that precipitated the reward loss.

Pieper and Marx (1963) have observed depression effects on laboratory subjects who were initially presented with highly rewarding stimuli that were then decreased. Although subjects continued to receive rewards, the relatively lower value of the rewards produced effects closely approximating those of punishments. This kind of hanging sword is typically used in the same way as aversive stimuli, through a conditional prediction procedure. One communicator might say to another, "I've been lending you money. If you don't become more prompt in your repayment, you'll never get another cent from me." It can be especially punishing to withdraw a reward that someone expects to get from you.

The third type of hanging sword is what we might call *profit loss*. Profit loss differs somewhat from aversive stimuli and reward withdrawal, both in the kind of punishment it is and in the strategies for its implementation. We can define *profit*, following Homans (1961), as the difference between the rewards accrued from a course of action and the costs of undertaking that action. One kind of cost is reflected in the amount of time, energy, material goods, and emotional well-being that must be sacrificed to obtain the reward. This cost must be subtracted from the value of the reward to compute the net profit of the course of action. People often talk about "punishing themselves" to achieve a goal. And one communicator may offer another a highly attractive reward but make it so difficult for him to obtain that the net effect of his offer is punishment. People can surely lose more than they gain from certain transactions.

Homans argues that another form of cost should also be considered. He says that "the costs, or *unavoidable punishment*, of any one activity include the withdrawn or foregone rewards of an alternative activity" (1961, p. 26, italics ours). For example, if your boss asks you to work late, you are likely to be rewarded with overtime pay or at least with your boss's gratitude. But if working late prevents you from spending time with your family or from engaging in some needed recreational activity, you must subtract the rewards you would have gotten out of these activities from the rewards for working late. If the value of the former is greater than the value of the latter, the effects can be similar to those of the other two types of hanging swords.

In other respects, however, loss of profit is somewhat different from the other hanging swords. A communicator may not be aware of or intend the punishment he inflicts on someone else. It is not uncommon for one person to complain about the behavior of another only to have the latter exclaim, "But I thought I was doing you a favor!" People sometimes bite the hand that feeds them because the feeder's charity makes them feel one-down or lacking in self-determination. The reward costs more than it is worth and therefore constitutes a punishment. As far as the second kind of cost is concerned, it may be very difficult for one communicator to predict how much reward another will lose by foregoing an alternative option. Suppose that a person has an opportunity to spend some time with one of two people, from each of whom he expects comparable rewards. If he decides to spend his time with one of them and for some reason does not get the rewards he anticipated, then he has missed out on the other reward possibility with a net loss to himself. He may then respond to his companion as if his companion had intentionally punished him: he may feel uncomfortable and less inclined to transact with his companion in the future. But if his companion was unaware of his second alternative, he would be unable to understand the negative reaction and could not compensate for it in the present or in future transactions.

Aversive stimuli, withdrawn rewards, and loss of profit are the three major kinds of hanging swords. Before we discuss key strategy elements in using punishment as an approach to communicative control, we will consider some of the predictable behavioral effects of punishments. There are significant differences among these effects, especially in terms of their desirability for the prospective controller. A well-designed hanging sword strategy should, of course, be directed toward eliciting favorable results, but it must also make provisions for avoiding those that are unfavorable.

Behavioral effects of punishments
All three hanging swords, when implemented through a control strategy, can have similar effects—with one important exception. The presentation of aversive stimuli produces sharper effects more quickly than does the withdrawal of rewards or loss of profit. According to D'Amato (1969), aversive stimuli that cause someone "immediate pain and discomfort" result in "very abrupt, practically instantaneous" behavior changes. Loss of rewards and profits is surely discomforting, but unless the lost rewards are extremely valuable or the profit losses immediately bring a communicator near "bankruptcy," they are less likely to result in behavior changes as dramatic as those brought about by aversive stimuli.

Among the many possible effects of hanging sword strategies, five seem common and important enough to be of interest to communicators:

1. *The reduction or elimination of the punished behavior.* This is usually an intended effect, one that a controller wants to bring about. Most sword strategies seem to have this effect as a primary goal.

2. Very often sword strategists try to influence people to discontinue one behavior and adopt a preferable substitute. A second effect of punishment, then, is the *replacement of the punished behavior by some other behavior.* This is a secondary

effect and can be considered desirable as long as the new behavior is more desirable to the controller than the behavior it replaced.

3. *Escape* by the punished person is a third effect. We can generally consider this an unintended effect of sword strategies. Rather than changing one or more particular behaviors as intended by the controller, the target person responds by ceasing all contact with the controller.

4. Another undesirable, unintended effect is possible when sword strategies are mismanaged. Punishment, whatever the reason for it, is an uncomfortable experience. Some people react by *returning punishment for punishment*. They may become angry and respond almost automatically by striking back at their would-be controller. Or they may be more level-headed and reason that one way to put an end to their punishment is to punish their punishers; i.e., to reduce or eliminate their punishers' undesirable behaviors. Their motive may also be revenge: hurting someone who has hurt you can be a pleasurable, if not always constructive, experience.

5. A final effect that controllers want to avoid deserves mention. When we say that someone's behavior is undesirable, we are also saying that it is deviant. This is not to say that the deviant behavior is objectively wrong, but that it diverges from our personal preferences and expectations. Sometimes the effect of punishment on undesirable, deviant behavior is *deviation amplification: it increases the rate or intensity of the target behavior*. For example, if you punish someone for being overly dependent on you, he may respond by becoming more dependent.

Of the five effects mentioned, we have assumed that the first two are intended and desirable, whereas the other three can be considered undesirable. We are sure some communicators occasionally intend their respondents to try to escape the punishment, fight back, or amplify their deviant behavior. However, we will propose strategy elements that raise the likelihood of the first two effects and lower the probability of the others.

Procedures for using hanging sword strategies
If you want to bring about the reduction or elimination of an undesirable behavior and perhaps replace it with a more desirable alternative, your first strategic procedure involves analyzing your relationship with your respondent. Several questions are relevant to your analysis. What degree of aversive stimuli can you reasonably

present? What degree of reward can you threaten to withdraw? To what extent are you capable of increasing the cost of the target behavior? You must also be able to compute the reward value of the target behavior for your respondent as well as his capacity to change it.

These questions have important implications for the design and utilization of your control strategy. For example, should you threaten to withdraw five units of reward if your respondent continues to behave in a way that brings him ten units of reward, you are not likely to meet with success. If you inflict ten units of punishment when your respondent can only expect five units of reward for maintaining your relationship together, he is more likely to escape or fight back than accede to your demands.

Many sword strategists fail in their control efforts because they do not analyze the function of the target behavior for their respondents. Most activities can be described as either consummatory or instrumental. *Consummatory activities are their own reward*; they are necessary and valuable in themselves because they are inextricably tied to the attainment of a goal. Eating when one is hungry is a consummatory behavior; if a person's goal is to stay alive he must eat, and eating in itself helps to keep him alive. Anxiety release is also consummatory. It is rewarding in and of itself and brings immediate goal attainment. By contrast, *instrumental behaviors are merely steps toward a goal*. Walking into a restaurant is instrumental to eating, but is satisfying only if it results in the acquisition of food. Getting into your car can be instrumental to going to a football game where you expect to release some anxiety. For some people doing a favor is instrumental to getting a favor in return, but it is not inherently satisfying.

How is this distinction relevant to strategy procedures? Consummatory behaviors are much more resistant to change than are instrumental behaviors. In punishing a consummatory behavior you are necessarily making it more difficult for someone to reach a goal. If the goal is valuable, you will cause your respondent considerable pain and probably precipitate an undesirable response to your control efforts. Your chances of success lie either in *threatening a goal that is more valuable to him than the goal you want him to replace or in creating such a goal as a replacement for the undesirable one.* In other words, your strategy should focus on alternative goals rather than on the undesirable behavior itself. For example, if smoking is a consummatory activity for someone, any attack you make on the smoking behavior itself is likely to be in vain. Your respondent may reply with, "Hey, I enjoy it, so leave me alone." However, if your friendship is valuable to him, you might threaten to terminate your relationship unless he stops smoking. Or you might try to establish health as a more valuable goal than smoking. If you suggest the benefits of health as an alternative to smoking, you can lower the profits of smoking, perhaps to a level where he will substitute another goal.

You would probably adopt a different strategy if the behavior is instrumental rather than consummatory. If you find that the goal of someone's behavior is desirable, but not his means of achieving it, the logical procedure is to *suggest more desirable ways to reach the goal*. In other words, one set of instrumental procedures is being substituted for another one. Suppose that someone's goal is to get you to like him (which you find desirable), but his basic strategy consists of ingratiation tactics (which you find undesirable): agreeing with whatever you say, endlessly complimenting you, and generally playing a one-down role toward you. Your task is to punish his strategy while rewarding his goal and, if possible, to create rewards for alternative strategies by which he can attain the goal.

Granted, it may be difficult to decide whether a behavior is consummatory or instrumental. Eating, for example, could be instrumental if a person wants to gain weight. Entering a restaurant may be more than a prelude to eating; it may serve an intrinsic socializing or status-seeking function as well. Obviously the advantages of psychological data here are great. To recognize what function a particular behavior serves for an individual, you must be able to see how he, as an individual, uses the behavior.

In a somewhat different respect, a functional analysis of behavior is necessary to avoid the deviation amplification effects of punishment. Consider Scheff's (1966) contention that *a function of deviant behavior may be to elicit a punishment response*. Some people deliberately transmit undesirable messages to fellow communicators because they find reward in the negative responses they get. In cases where punishment responses act as dangling carrots, they increase rather than decrease performance of the target behavior. The deviant person may be striving for attention or hoping to gain some recognition as an individual. He may also be trying to exert control for its own sake (a consummatory function). Appropriate punishment, therefore, should not take a form that is desirable to the respondent or it will be self-defeating.

Deviant behavior may also provide an *escape from punishment*. Certain punishments of escape behavior are likely to increase an individual's need to escape. Jones asks, "What happens when we punish . . . a response that has been established by punishment? Punishing a child for being shy by criticizing and ridiculing him may, if the shyness is the result of previous criticism and ridicule, produce only further withdrawal" (1967, p. 75). This kind of punishment reinforces the escape behavior by raising its perceived profit: the more the child is ridiculed, the more it is to his advantage to withdraw. A carrot strategy of offering the child rewards for more extroverted behaviors might prove more effective than punishing him for shyness.

The fundamental problem in using sword strategies is to minimize their undesirable effects while still exercising some degree of control. To accomplish this end, a communicator should avoid an egocentric orientation toward control. He should realize that people will behave as he wants only if they perceive that to do so is advantageous to them. His wanting them to do or not do something is not enough. We acknowledge that it is difficult to predict how an individual will respond to a particular stimulus, to determine whether he will find it rewarding or punishing, or to calculate how he will value a stimulus in his cost-benefit accounting system. Much of this behavior is idiosyncratic and not immediately measurable. But interpersonal communication is useful and necessary precisely for making such predictions. The sword strategist who focuses on the personal characteristics of his respondents rather than reflecting exclusively on his own needs is likely to meet with success fairly regularly.

Sword strategies are similar to carrot strategies, for their effectiveness depends on whether the respondent finds personal benefit in providing responses desirable to the controller. A major tactic of sword controllers is the triggering of complementary strategies from respondents. A controller says, "I am punishing you for doing something I don't like, but you will find it rewarding to change your behavior." Rewards may consist of a cessation of punishment, a reinstatement of rewards, or a recouping of lost profits. The controller wants his respondent to reply, "I don't like being punished, and I can best put a stop to it by finding out what he wants and acting accordingly." Armed with this line of reasoning, an individual can embark on a control strategy which, if successful, will bring both controller and respondent what they want.

These issues suggest some further tactical considerations for the sword strategist. One consideration certainly must be: when should I use sword strategies instead of carrot strategies? If the effectiveness of both strategies rests largely on getting my respondent to discover personal benefits in doing what I want, why should I punish someone instead of straightforwardly rewarding him? Resolution of this issue requires the answer to another question: can I command sufficient reward resources to take an effective carrot approach? Perhaps it is impossible to make a positive offer strong enough to induce the respondent to change his undesirable behavior. For example, if someone is already earning $15,000, it is unlikely that he can be hired at a salary of $10,000. Without adequate resources, carrot strategies cannot be effective. In an interpersonal relationship, if you have offered as much as you have to give and cannot exert further carrot control, you might then turn to a sword approach. Given that the other person wants to maintain the relationship, you can extend your control by threatening a withdrawal of current rewards. Furthermore, a person must often experience aversive reactions to a particular course of action before developing the motivation to change it. In other words, behavioral inertia should be considered: people sometimes find it more comfortable to sustain even an unprofitable course of action if that course is not made distinctly unpleasurable. Even if you could command infinite carrot resources, your success would not be guaranteed. Recall the concept of parity that we discussed earlier. Excessive rewards can be as counterproductive as lack of rewards. If the respondent becomes satiated with them, the prospect of additional benefits may not be very persuasive.

When you have decided to take a sword approach, you should still be careful to emphasize that your respondent can choose an alternative that is preferable to continued punishment and that does not involve escape, fighting back, or increasing the target behavior. Punishment that only punishes has little redeeming relational value. A communicator may find satisfaction in maliciously or vengefully inflicting punishment, but his partner is not likely to share the satisfaction. One tactic in using sword strategies, then, is to make conditional prediction statements ("if . . . then . . .") as clear as possible. Make it obvious to your respondent just what he is doing "wrong" (or not doing "right"), and indicate how you will attempt to influence the consequences of his behavior. Aimless punishment will only confuse, frustrate, and perhaps anger him. If you do not clarify what you want, as well as how he can restore your relationship to its previous equanimity, you are gambling on his ability to figure you out. This can be a losing gamble.

One final note: it makes good sense to measure, from time to time, the extent to which you may be unintentionally punishing your relational partners. When relational difficulties arise, communicators sometimes ask themselves, "Am I providing enough rewards? Maybe I'm not giving enough." While sometimes useful, this perspective is limited. We recommend that you also ask, "How can we decrease the costs in the relationship?" The relational reward value may be, in an absolute sense, entirely adequate. But if the reward exchange process you develop (the "meshing" of your PCCs) is inefficient, the exchange can be as burdensome as it is beneficial. How much do people have to give up for a given reward? How hard do they have to work for it? Maintaining and increasing mutual relational profits involves more than simply upping the gross reward rate. It also involves monitoring the net profit value and decreasing costs whenever possible.

Catalyst strategies

The following statements illustrate the use of catalyst control strategies:

> "When was the last time you told me you loved me?"

> "You can stay up late tonight if you want to, but you'll be tired tomorrow."

> "You should vote for our candidate because he has supported several pieces of legislation I know you favor."

In each of these statements a communicator tries to elicit a desirable response; but rather than offer a reward or threaten a punishment, he reminds his listener of a course of action that the listener would probably find desirable. This method relies for its effectiveness on getting the individual to behave in a self-reinforcing way without directly rewarding or punishing him. The controller must supply the stimulus message to trigger this process, but the listener is largely acting as his own change agent.

There are several kinds of catalyst strategies. The strategist may prompt his listener, implying that he knows the listener is already prepared to act in a certain way and suggesting that the present moment would be a good time. A subtle approach for prompting a desirable response is to say, for instance, "Boy, I'm depressed," thus inviting the listener to offer some form of consolation or encouragement. Although the controller hopes that the kind of response he desires will be obvious to his listener, this strategy gives him the advantage of not asking for it directly, a step that many communicators feel puts them in a one-down position.

Another catalyst strategy involves supplying your listener with new information that makes the response you desire seem more rewarding to him. Salesmen often inform their prospective customers of the strong points of their products. In other words, they try to point out to a prospective customer certain advantages of making a purchase, advantages that may not otherwise be apparent to him.

Yet another approach is to appeal to people's "rationality." All communicators have a set of values, acquired from their culture, their membership and reference groups, and their own experiences. Although they may or may not regularly act in accordance with these values, they generally think they should do so. The perceptive controller is able to discern a particular individual's values and use these values to suggest appropriate avenues of behavior.

Many variations of catalyst strategies of control have been studied and supported for years by motivational and cognitive psychologists.

Frequently, however, the methods they suggest are ineffective for many communicators. To be successful, the catalyst strategist must accomplish two things. First, he must be sensitive to the kinds of behaviors that particular individuals find personally rewarding. Communicators who are unable to make such psychological level assessments are rarely effective with catalyst methods. Second, he must recognize that there is often a wide gap between what someone thinks is right to do in a situation and what he feels compelled to do. Many people who think they should vote never enter a polling place; many people who think they should be more considerate of their neighbors never are. Therefore, the strategist must also concentrate on making it as easy as possible for his respondents to act in desirable ways. A salesman who wants his customers to make purchases encourages the use of credit cards or offers liberal credit terms. Someone who wants his friend to quit drinking does not invite him for an evening at the local tavern.

Personal involvement in control strategies

The major distinction between catalyst techniques and other control strategies lies in the relative unobtrusiveness of the controller. With carrot and sword strategies the controller emphasizes his own role in the process; e.g., "If you do as *I* would like, *I* will do such and such." With catalyst strategies, however, the controller attempts to elicit desirable responses by emphasizing the listener: "If *you* do such and such, wouldn't *you* find it personally rewarding?"

A communicator must decide how much to make himself a part of his strategy. A catalyst strategist minimizes the influence of the "I" in communicating with other people. However, a communicator may decide to supplement a catalyst strategy by implying his personal approval or disapproval of certain responses. For example, the parent who allows his child to choose between staying up late and going to bed at the usual time can intimate his preference for one course of action over the other. By implying his approval for one of the options, he hopes to enhance the probability that the child will choose that option. However, the child may react against the fact that the communicator is openly trying to influence his behavior, subtle though the strategy may be. He may directly oppose the option preferred by the would-be controller—even though he agrees with its merits—because he does not want to submit to control. Many people seem to operate this way. They respond, in effect, with "I'm going to *not* do it just because you want me to do it." They may even do things they would rather not do to avoid being placed in a one-down position.

Catalyst strategists may err in the opposite direction: they may fail to assert their own preferences when to do so would increase the probability of eliciting a desirable response. It often happens in large organizations, for instance, that managers who have been trained in human relations techniques distribute to their employees memos that say such things as "Wouldn't it be nice if everyone came to work on time in the morning?" or "We could get a lot more work done if people would restrict their coffee breaks to twenty minutes." These memos are intended as direct orders, but management thinks its way of communicating the orders is good for employee morale. However, employees tend to interpret these memos not as orders but as non-formal expressions of opinion and they respond accordingly.

The question of how much to emphasize your personal involvement in a control strategy also arises when you ask someone for help. Consider these two messages, both seeking the same response:

1. "I'm in a jam, and I'd like your help."

2. "I'm in a jam. Would you be a good person and help me out?"

Message 1 emphasizes the personal nature of the request; it focuses on the individual asking for help. Message 2 downplays the communicator and directs itself toward the proposed helper. If you needed help from someone, which message would you choose?

Each message implies a different reason why the respondent should help the communicator. In message 1, the communicator seems to assume that the respondent should help him because "*I* am the person asking for help." This assumption could be taken to mean that he and his respondent have a personal, friendly relationship that entails mutual support. It could also imply that, while the source and receiver are not particular friends, the source is in a position to offer a reward for the assistance. For example, a professor might emphasize his role when asking a student for help: their role relationship is such that the professor can return the favor with a good grade, a letter of recommendation, or his personal esteem. An employer might use a similar approach with an employee: the "I" asking for help is also the "I" who can promote or fire the employee. Similarly, people who believe they are physically attractive to members of the opposite sex may base their strategy on sex appeal. Message 1 further implies that the communicator perceives the respondent as someone who will agree to his request because of either the friendly relationship or the likelihood of a reward.

Message 2 does not assume a friendly relationship between speaker and listener; in fact, such a message exchanged between friends might indicate that the speaker perceives a strain in their relationship. Message 2 also gives no indication that the communicator will personally reward the proposed helper. Instead, it is based on the following reasoning: people in our culture have been taught to help others; I perceive you to be a person who has learned this value; the reward you get from helping me is the personal gratification of knowing that you have acted in accordance with an important cultural value. A person's choice of messages such as 1 and 2, then, should depend on the nature of the relationship he has with the respondent and his capacity to dispense rewards to him.

Siamese twin strategies

We have portrayed the successful carrot strategist as a person who can discern what another person wants and offer it to him in exchange for something he himself wants. The sword strategist knows what people do not want and he threatens them with these undesirable consequences unless they come through for him. Catalyst controllers elicit desirable responses with the aid of stimuli less conspicuous than rewards or punishments, but they can be no less effective. These three strategists seem to share the assumption that desirable communication relationships can be developed by the effective application of their respective strategies. The relationships they develop may involve a brief interchange or may last for several years. Whatever their duration, the relationships are to a great extent a reflection of the participating communicators' styles and skills at control.

There is a fourth strategy of control that, rather than aiming to create desired relations, is an outgrowth of a certain kind of established relationship. This strategy, called the Siamese twin strategy, can be implemented only after a relationship has been formed. In this sense, Siamese twins are people who place extreme importance on maintaining their mutual relationship. They seem to believe that their ultimate happiness is tied to staying together; therefore, they strongly depend on one another for personal satisfaction. Since relational maintenance is their highest communicative priority, they sometimes sacrifice more immediate personal goals. Given such a relational perspective, significant constraints are placed on the kinds of strategies people can use to elicit desirable responses. Variations of carrot, sword, or catalyst strategies may sometimes be appropriate and effective but only when modified according to the unique relational circumstances.

Two relational conditions engender the development of Siamese twin strategies. We have already suggested the first condition: *high dependence between the communicators*. Although there are many kinds of dependence, the general condition is typified by the proverbial couple stranded on the desert island or by the relationship between the last survivors of a nuclear attack. These people must make the best of their relationship, for they have only each other. The second condition is that *neither person be considerably more powerful than the other*. Even if two people are mutually dependent, one person can still dominate the relationship by using carrot or sword strategies. Siamese twin strategies arise when both communicators have roughly equal amounts of control.

Siamese twin strategies are found in several specific kinds of relationships. One such relationship is that between corporations and employee unions. Each participant is dependent on the other: one needs people to work at certain jobs and the other needs someone to pay them. In their relationships neither party can exercise complete control. Management is restricted, in some cases by law and in some cases by threat of a strike, in the kinds of control strategies it can use. Unions must operate under a complementary set of restrictions. Thus, the two groups of people are bound together. Neither is legally or financially free to terminate the relationship, and neither can exert singular control without the other's cooperation. When the two groups are successful, they learn that what is good for one must be good for the other.

Some marriages reveal similar characteristics. The partners feel they must maintain their marriage even if they are dissatisfied. Their reasons for staying together may stem from religious convictions, financial obligations, social pressure, or the presence of children. When a couple are generally unhappy together, they become acutely aware of their mutual dependence: each person's behavior is very important to the other's happiness. Since each person is an important source of desirable responses, they must somehow cooperate to make their relationship tolerable, if not highly satisfying. Not all unhappy marriages give rise to Siamese twin control strategies. One person may seek desirable responses outside of the marriage, thereby reducing the control of the marriage partner. Or both people may look elsewhere for desirable responses, thus decreasing their interdependence. It is when people are unwilling or unable to find alternative relationships that they tend to develop Siamese twin methods of control.

A third relationship that is prone to Siamese twin techniques is one where there is considerable one-sided investment. We mentioned earlier that many people tend to view their communicative interchanges economically. Sometimes one person backs another for a long time while getting little in return. People whose spouses are in medical, law, or graduate school often must act as the financial and emotional mainstays of the relationship while their mates further their education. Similarly, the families of drug addicts and alcoholics often endure severe difficulties while trying to rehabilitate their loved ones and yet survive themselves. People who make costly investments in another person for a long period of time often feel their investments (and a good chunk of their lives) have been wasted unless and until they can collect on them—perhaps even with interest. But people with this "you owe me something" attitude may become dependent on the other person, for their ultimate satisfaction rests on being repaid by the other person. Thus, they force themselves to maintain their relationship at least until they are repaid. If their partner recognizes this fact and feels guilty about it, he too is tied to the relationship until he can repay his debt. It may seem that one of the partners has more control in the short run—he is receiving more than he is giving—but in such relationships this is as much a fallacy as believing that the money you borrow from a bank is yours. The mutual basis for control can be measured only in the long run.

Development and utilization of Siamese twin control strategies
The three kinds of situations just described exhibit the two characteristic dimensions of Siamese twin relationships: strong mutual dependence and equality of power. These two relational dimensions have a strong impact on the development and utilization of control strategies. At a general level, the communicators form a tighter unit than do people in other kinds of relationships, since each person is the primary (if not the only) source of important desirable responses for the other and since their relationship is relatively long-lasting. This means that each person's relational environment is likely to reflect more extensively the effects of his own patterns of control. It would seem, then, that a Siamese twin would be highly concerned with developing control strategies that maximally abet mutual satisfaction; however, this is not always the case. Siamese twins adopt differing patterns, one potentially *destructive* and the other potentially *constructive*. Both patterns stem from the communicators' recognition that Siamese twin relationships offer greater freedom than other relationships in one respect: the communicators need not be immediately concerned about whether the relationship will endure. Rather, they are free to focus on the quality of their association.

A shortsighted communicator may abuse this freedom. He knows that his partner will tolerate behaviors which, under other relational conditions, would be completely unacceptable. For example, husbands and wives often complain that their mates changed considerably after their marriage. They may show less sensitivity, act less responsibly, and consistently violate mutual relational agreements. Relationships that manifest an "I know you'll never leave me" attitude are susceptible to these kinds of behaviors. Cycles may readily develop in which one person mistreats the other, feels guilty about it, becomes frustrated at the helplessness of experiencing a state of guilt, and lashes out again. His partner is forced to endure his abuse, and he is forced to continue feeling guilty because they are bound together in a Siamese twin relationship. Of course, people can extricate themselves from destructive cycles; but often, because they are so intensely involved in the circumstances, they cannot do so without outside help. Counseling psychologists frequently advise Siamese twins that before they can solve their problems they must seriously consider the possibility of terminating their relationship. Married couples, for instance, are urged to decrease their mutual dependence, at least conceptually, as a first step in altering their destructive control patterns.

Communicators who embark on mutually constructive control patterns interpret the freedom of a Siamese twin relationship as an opportunity to work together for mutual gain in a relatively secure environment. They "have" each other, and use this potential asset as a basis for commitment rather than as a license for abuse. They can take the time to develop control procedures that maximize mutually beneficial strategies of control. For example, roommates who are legally or financially committed to live together for a year may find that they are seriously incompatible on several levels; but because they are forced to remain together in the same dwelling, they make the effort to settle their differences in an agreeable manner. Such a resolution may take time, which they would not have if either were free to exit from the scene whenever he chose to. Similarly, married couples who choose to stay together for the sake of their young children may diligently strive to overcome their difficulties both for their own sanity and for the well-being of their offspring.

Fairyland strategies

All people try to elicit desirable responses from others, but some people are generally ineffective, if not in all situations, at least in numerous situations that are important to them. While successful controllers reap great rewards, those who are unsuccessful often endure painful anxiety. Sometimes prolonged anxiety can lead to serious mental disorders. In less severe cases the result may be the development of fairyland strategies of control.

Fairyland control strategies rely on illusions, on self-induced feelings of control. These illusions may offer some respite from anxiety, but they have little basis in reality and are hardly adequate substitutes for genuine control. Some fairyland strategists seem unable to accept the limits of their own capacities to elicit desirable responses. They prefer to live as total escapists, such as James Thurber's character Walter Mitty, who spent most of his time imagining himself as an ace fighter pilot, a baseball star, or a sex-object to the women of the world. For a Walter Mitty to be successful as a

fairylander, he must avoid contact with real people: he must dwell in an environment where the only constraints on his behavior are of his own creation. Of more interest to us are the fairyland strategists who seem unable to recognize their limitations, whose illusions have some basis in actual communication transactions and whose success at control depends more on misinterpreting actual events than on totally creating their own environments.

Recall that the three measures of control we discussed earlier—response desirability, responsibility, and replicability—are all open to considerable subjective interpretation. Fairyland strategists are generally unable or unwilling to use these measures objectively. They seem oblivious to strong environmental cues from their fellow communicators. Perhaps they have never learned effective communicative skills and seek to compensate by overrating their effectiveness. Or perhaps they never learned to interpret accurately other people's responses and are thus unable to modify their control strategies through experiences with success and failure. We can highlight some common fairyland strategies by showing how fairylanders apply overly subjective criteria to gauge their effectiveness at control.

One tactic of the fairylander is to *ignore undesirable responses*. A cocktail party comedian, for example, may ignore his audience's displeasure at a particularly crude joke and proceed to tell another. A young man out on a date may ignore subtle cues of rejection from his companion and continually press her to return his affections. Another tactic is to *distort undesirable responses* by giving them a positive interpretation. Some teachers interpret numerous sleepy student faces as a sign that the students have attended so diligently to their lectures that they are exhausted, when actually the students have been bored to drowsiness. Professional communicators such as salesmen or stage actors are unlikely to make these kinds of mistakes.

People's responses to their messages, as measured by sales receipts or applause, are clear-cut and usually easy to read. But in most informal day-to-day settings responses are open to various interpretations. Fairyland communicators consistently err in their own favor, reading success into responses most people would consider failures.

Fairylanders also tend to *overrate or deny their own responsibility* for eliciting responses. When the response is desirable, they quickly claim complete credit for it, as in the case of the pool player who claims to have "called" a tricky three-rail bank shot that falls into a pocket quite by accident. The desirable response could be attributed to luck, to a favorable predisposition on the part of the respondent, or to other related events. Moreover, fairyland strategists are equally prone to deny personal responsibility for undesirable responses. They dismiss calamitous responses by denying fault or by claiming the cards were stacked against them. Some people look for any reason but their own ineffectiveness to account for their lack of control.

People who resort to fairyland strategies are trying to convince both themselves and other people of their effectiveness at control. Some-times they may be conscious of these attempts, but more often they are unaware of their unrealistic assessments. In this respect fairy-land methods differ from deliberate lies. The fairyland strategist misperceives communication situations more than he purposely misrepresents them. In this respect, also, the fairyland approach can-not properly be called a strategy for eliciting desirable responses. Rather, it is a means for coping with undesirable responses, for mak-ing up the difference between the level of control effectiveness a communicator wants and the level he can actually attain.

Some comments on the moral implications of communicative control

Some people rebel at the word *control*. Or at least they think they should rebel. The term has many unpleasant connotations; it seems antithetical to cherished values relating to individual freedom, love, tolerance, cooperation, and quality of life. We are not about to de-nounce these values. We do not contend that it is a cruel world where everybody must be tough to survive, nor do we believe that we live in a ferociously hostile environment where every communicator must continuously struggle to keep afloat. Our emphasis on communicative control should not be construed as an unqualified endorsement of every imaginable kind of control strategy, nor should it give the impression that we believe all communicators spend all their time either engaged in control or thinking about control. If we have engendered any of these reactions, we want to take a few pages to clarify our position.

Communicative gangsters

It might be useful to pinpoint some of the clearly unpleasant dimensions of control-seeking behavior. We will characterize people who engage largely in odious control practices as "communicative gangsters." They are the con men, manipulators, demagogues, and archetypal used-car salesmen most people so strongly abhor. What is it about their behavior that gives control a bad name?

The intentions of such communicators certainly help to create an unfavorable impression. Gangsters operate selfishly; their communicative orientations are highly egocentric. Having no desire to maximize mutual rewards, they seek to become the sole possessors of whatever rewards may be squeezed from their relationships with other communicators.

Likewise, the gangster's strategies may generally be regarded as unsavory. Deception is sure to abound, for gangsters can hardly announce their intentions and expect to be effective very often. Since they tend to distrust people, gangsters prefer to disguise their basic strategies to prevent their companions from gangsterizing them. They may promise greater rewards than they know they can give, but they are often quick to administer severe punishments, frequently as a mere exercise in demonstrating control capacity.

We must also condemn the effects of a gangster's efforts at control. While they may or may not actually be harmful to other people, they are rarely helpful. Gangsters are good at taking but not at giving. They can leave their fellows despondent and less capable of functioning in further communication relationships.

We are sure you have encountered more than one communicative gangster, and there is probably little need to elaborate extensively on their intentions, strategies, or accomplishments. But perhaps you have encountered few communicative angels: people who find any form of control reprehensible. Let us next see what they contribute to our communicative environment.

Communicative angels

Angels express a "let it be" philosophy. It offends them when people try to elicit desirable responses from them; they do not wish to be "bought." An angel might reason that if he is going to provide someone with a desirable response, it will be because he finds it intrinsi-

cally pleasing to do so, not because another person offered something in exchange. Angels also believe that the deliberate and calculated design of a control strategy is ruthless and immoral. They prefer complete spontaneity, hoping for the best but doing nothing directly to bring it about. If their relationships progress smoothly, that is fine. If not, "That's the way things were meant to be. You can't force yourself on anybody."

Although we hardly condone gangster approaches to communication situations, we also believe that, for most communicators, an angel approach is unlikely to engender much satisfaction. Our position is essentially hedonistic. It centers around the notion that most people want to be happy and that happiness is generally a good thing. Considerable happiness can be attained by receiving material, behavioral, and symbolic rewards from other people. But our position is also based on the notion that good things do not come to people automatically. Nobody is naturally endowed with sufficient personal grace that he should expect rewards to flow his way solely through the goodness of other people. If you want the joy and pleasure that come from getting rewards from fellow communicators, you have to work for them; i.e., you have to engage in mutual exchanges of desirable items. If the maximization of the benefits of exchange requires forethought and planning, this does not seem to us to negate its value.

Let us be presumptuous enough to say that there are three kinds of people in the world. First, there are your friends. They are disposed to help you and generally want only the best for you. But even though they are your friends, they may not always know just how you want to be rewarded. Like all persons, their skills at sensitivity and reward dispensation are limited. You may sometimes have to let them know how they can most please you. Interpersonal behavior is highly complex, and even one's best friends have hangups and shortcomings. The exchange of mutual rewards, even given the best of intentions by the communicators, can often profit from careful planning. This does not seem ruthless to us; rather, it seems humane to avoid unnecessary conflicts and to increase the probability of mutual reward.

Second, there are your enemies, the people who are disposed to thwart your acquisition of rewards. Few people in our culture have deadly enemies, but most of us occasionally find that some people just do not like us. This is natural. But to the extent that they can control the flow of rewards toward us, we ought to be able to intervene in their strategies.

The third kind of people are those who are neither favorably nor unfavorably disposed toward us, by far the largest of the three groups. Most people in the world do not know we are alive. Since they do not perceive themselves to be interdependent with us, they take no steps to reward or to punish us. But they may have a great deal to offer, and we may have something to offer them. If neither of us makes a move to create awareness of this potential, no rewards can be exchanged. We are not suggesting that you make friends with everyone in the world, but if you find that your reward level is lower than you would like, we believe that you ought to develop the capacity for creating new sources of rewarding experiences.

When to control

We will turn now to a somewhat different aspect of communicative control. The question may be asked: do all communicators spend all their time exerting control or planning to exert control? This question can be answered with a qualified no. Many communication situations do seem to flow naturally, with no elaborate tactical planning nor much awareness of goal-seeking. It seems useful to examine some of the conditions under which communicators concentrate on the control dimensions of their transactions.

It seems that a communicator's certainty about the outcomes of a transaction relates to the degree that he will think about or engage in control behaviors. If someone is perfectly sure of what is going to happen, there is no point in striving to effect an alternative outcome. If he has some doubt about the outcomes of a transaction, however, he may be more disposed to take an active role in trying to bring about desirable outcomes.

The importance of the outcomes of a transaction also bears on this issue. If an individual is unsure of the outcomes of a trivial situation, he may not bother to exert any influence on them. Even if he is reasonably sure of obtaining a positive outcome in a highly significant situation, he may still do all he can to increase his certainty.

An individual's communicative skill represents another relevant factor. Someone who is not practiced in executing a particular control strategy deliberates more carefully than does an "expert." Beginners in any field of human activity rehearse their tactics ahead of time and are quite conscious of the relationship between their performance and the achievement of their goal.

In addition, the more effort an individual must put forth to obtain a particular goal, the more he is likely to be aware of what he is doing. The effort may be painful or he may want to improve the efficiency of his goal-seeking behavior. Communicators who need to expend considerable energy in achieving even low-level goals are probably more conscious of communicative control than people who have developed more efficient communicative practices.

Another factor contributing to an individual's consciousness of control is the probability of particular negative outcomes in a given transaction. If this probability is high, a person is likely to experience some anxiety or apprehension that may induce him to consider just what steps he must take to lower the probability of negative results. No one wants to incur costs unnecessarily.

A final consideration is the degree to which a communicator feels he can influence the outcomes of communication situations. Communicators sometimes find rainy days highly undesirable, but since there is nothing they can do to prevent the rain from coming down, they do not spend much time trying to figure out control strategies to accomplish this feat. Confidence is an important factor. If an individual's confidence level is zero, he may not attempt any form of control. If he has no expectations of success, there is no point in designing a control strategy.

All of these factors are interrelated. Skill, for example, is related to certainty about outcomes and to the amount of effort needed to undertake a particular course of action. The importance of transactional outcomes and the probability of negative outcomes also interact: the more crucial it is that a communicator avoid a certain negative outcome, the harder he is likely to work to develop preventative measures. All six factors are listed below in proposition form.

> People tend to be more conscious of strategy-making processes and these processes take longer when. . .
>
> . . . the outcomes of a communication situation are uncertain
>
> . . . it is important to them that particular outcomes occur
>
> . . . they are not skilled in behaviors that will lead to rewarding outcomes

... they need to expend more effort to achieve rewarding outcomes

... the probability of negative outcomes is great

... they feel that they can be influential in bringing about rewarding outcomes

One explanation for the existence of communicative gangsters and angels can be discovered in this list of propositions. Gangsters, perhaps, act the way they do because they place inordinate importance on eliciting desirable responses and avoiding undesirable responses, while at the same time being uncertain about the outcomes of communication situations and having little real confidence in their abilities to successfully engage in mutually rewarding behaviors. Perhaps angels are able to thumb their noses at control endeavors because they are generally highly successful at eliciting desirable responses. Their skill may be so great that they do not seem to try to exert influence over their fellow communicators.

This is not the only explanation for the gangster-angel distinction, but it does point out one of the major social benefits of effective control. People who are confident of their control abilities and who have successfully obtained a significant storehouse of interpersonal rewards are less prone to use gangster tactics. Julius Caesar is reputed to have said, "Let me have men about me who are fat." He preferred to be surrounded by confident, satisfied people who were not likely to stab him in the back. In more recent history, Will Rogers expressed this notion from a more positive perspective: "When somebody kicks you in the seat of your pants, don't get too upset about it. It only means that you're out ahead of him."

Summary

We have chosen to describe the individual communicator by looking at his or her efforts at environmental control. This perspective has three major advantages, which are compelling for our purposes.

First, it is essentially transactional: an individual's communication behaviors are strongly interwoven with those of his companions. Only in social, symbolic contexts can he become known as a communicating individual, develop his PCC, and seek to elicit and provide desirable responses. People get to know one another, we suggest, not by sitting back and observing, but by actively participating in communicative situations. Their PCCs grow out of social learning and not as things in themselves, unrelated to other people. The very concept of control is meaningless unless considered within the context of at least a sequence of messages and responses between two people.

Second, a control perspective helps one understand relational processes. The discussions in this chapter, particularly of the five control strategies, bear heavily on our treatment of communication relationships in part III. One of the primary dimensions of interpersonal relationships is that people expect to receive some reward in return for the energy they expend in communicating interpersonally. Providing mutually desirable responses forms the basis for satisfying relationships.

Third, a control perspective affirms both the self-determination of each individual and the fundamental brotherhood of all human beings. No person can achieve communicative success unless he works at it, and yet mutual cooperation is also necessary to the exchange of symbolic rewards. In emphasizing this exchange, our position is hedonistic without being decadent. It maintains that happiness is a good thing, but it warns against solitary, selfish efforts at pleasure-seeking and manipulation.

Probes

1. Think about the quotation at the beginning of this chapter. Does it assert a basic truth, or is it too mercenary to be representative of your own approach to communication relationships?

2. What is the basic composition of your PCC? What control strategies do you use most often? Which are the most effective for you? Can you characterize yourself as a particular kind of controller?

3. In your daily transactions how conscious are you of trying to exert control? At what times are you more conscious than usual? When are you least conscious? How do your answers to these questions reflect on your personal capacity to exercise control?

4. We suggested three measures of control: response desirability, responsibility, and replicability. Try using these measures to rate your own control effectiveness. Do they seem valid to you, or would you modify them to make them more appropriate for your own approach to communication?

5. To be effective in the long run, communicative control must be a sharing process; each participant must reap some benefit. Would it seem strange to ask yourself, in the midst of a transaction, "What am I doing for my co-participants? How am I maximizing their rewards?"

6. Try sitting down with a close friend and laying out for one another the major rewards each of you is seeking in your relationship. Also discuss the costs you want to avoid. Then try to use this information as the basis for mutually profitable control strategies.

7. Of the five kinds of control strategies we described (carrot, sword, catalyst, Siamese twin, and fairyland) which, if any, would you rate as having the highest probability of success for most communicators? Which might be the least effective?

8. It is easy to botch a control strategy if you do not have the right kind of information to design and implement it. Think of a kind of transaction in which you generally implement control strategies. What information do you have about your co-participants that improves your chances for success? What further information would you want to have?

How can you elicit the information you need? Have you ever had information about someone else that actually decreased your chances to elicit desirable responses from him, or her?

9. Examine the control messages of different groups of people, such as politicians, clergymen, professors, professional athletes, parents, or advertisers. Can you discern particular patterns of control across these groups? Does one group seem to specialize in one kind of control or another? Do you think any of these groups should specialize in a particular kind of control?

10. Think of someone with whom you communicate on a noninterpersonal but not an interpersonal level. How do you utilize noninterpersonal data to elicit desirable responses from this person? Imagine that you did not have some of this information. Do you think your effectiveness at control would decrease? Imagine that you have acquired considerable psychological information about this person. In what ways would you modify your current control strategies toward him, or her, on the basis of this information?

5

Of all the different philosophies which exist in the world
there is probably only one which is correct.

There are two kinds of people in this world:
those who are for the truth
and those who are against the truth.

items from Milton Rokeach's Dogmatism Scale,
The Open and Closed Mind

The Influence
of Cognitive Styles on
Interpersonal Communication

n chapter 4 we introduced the construct of *pattern of communicative control* (PCC). Our concern with control is consistent with our view that the basic function of all communication is to control the environment so as to realize certain physical, economic, and social rewards from it. As we have repeatedly emphasized, communicative attempts to control may occur at either the noninterpersonal or the interpersonal level. Our major aim in this chapter is to examine some of the ways that certain cognitive styles of communicators may help or hinder them in moving to the interpersonal level. Thus, we are again dealing with individual behavior patterns, the raw materials of interpersonal processes.

What is cognitive style?

To clarify our meaning for the term *cognitive style*, it may be best to begin with some statements people often make about other people.

> "He sees the whole world in black and white."

> "There are two ways of doing things: her way and the wrong way."

> "She may not agree with someone, but at least she tries to understand how that person feels about an issue."

> "He thinks there's a communist [or a fascist, or a sex fiend, or the like] under every bed."

> "Doesn't she ever think about anything but money [or clothes, or food, or some such thing]?"

> "He's a Republican, and he always has been, but if a Democrat comes out with a good idea, he'll buy it."

Each of these comments says something about cognitive style. The first three are concerned primarily with how individuals *structure*, or organize, their views of the world, while the latter three are more closely related to the manner in which *content*, or substance, is processed. Together, these two dimensions lead to the following definition: cognitive style refers to the *characteristic ways in which an individual structures his beliefs and attitudes about the world, and to the ways he processes and responds to incoming information*. In a sense, one's cognitive style is a relatively habitual way of reacting to people, acts, and situations.

Psychologists have devoted a great deal of attention to the study of cognitive styles. Our purpose is not to expand this psychological literature nor to examine cognitive styles as psychological constructs per se. Rather, this chapter rests on a single premise: *certain cognitive styles facilitate movement to the interpersonal level, while others inhibit such movement*. Armed with this premise, we shall discuss some cognitive styles that get in the way of interpersonal communication and consider some strategies for overcoming the injurious interpersonal effects of these styles. We feel that alteration or modification of one's cognitive style is possible, though difficult since it is the product of considerable prior learning and experience.

Ambiguity versus clarity: how simple can the world be?

People vary widely in their tolerance for ambiguity. Some seem compelled to organize the world into neat, mutually exclusive categories; others are comfortable in a universe where the dividing lines are fuzzy. Some constantly seek unequivocal, precise answers to ultimate (and our own bias would lead us to say usually unanswerable) questions, while others are willing to live in a state of uncertainty and suspended judgment. Consider this account of an actual exchange between Gerry and two students.

STUDENT A: Well, then what exactly is communication?

GERRY: Communication isn't *exactly* anything. When we ask, "What is communication?" we are posing an issue of definition, even though the language makes it sound like a factual question. And of course we can define a word in many different ways, depending on our purpose for defining it.

STUDENT A: Well, it seems to me that either something is communication, or it isn't. Suppose I stub my toe on a rock and hurt it. Has the rock communicated with my toe or hasn't it?

GERRY: It depends on how you define communication. If you define the term broadly enough—for example, if you say that communication is any response of an organism to a stimulus—then you can say your toe and the rock have communicated. Personally, for the kinds of things I'm interested in, I don't find that definition too useful, because it makes everything under the sun communication.

STUDENT B: I think I can see that it's useless to try to identify *the* definition of communication. What I've got to do is look at a variety of definitions and then decide which one best suits my purpose. If I'm an electrical engineer, I may choose one definition; if I'm a student of interpersonal communication, I may choose another; and if I'm a theologian interested in God's communication with the world, I may choose still another.

GERRY: Exactly!

STUDENT A: But what I want to know is, what exactly is communication?

The dialogue has now turned full circle, and student A is still uncomfortable. Whereas student B quickly accepted that there is no "correct" single answer to the original question, student A finds this position incomprehensible—for him, the world must be divided into two tidy compartments: "communication" and "not-communication." Moreover, we would probably expect student A to place many other aspects of the world on his cognitive carving block; for him, there are Good Guys and Bad Guys, Moral Acts and Immoral Acts, Geniuses and Idiots, and a host of other similar categories. By contrast, student B manifests a willingness to settle for less clear-cut categories, as well as an understanding of the fact that some ambiguity is inevitable. In short, student A thinks in black-and-white terms, while student B is aware of the many shades of gray that surround him.

We take the position that a rigid, simplistic cognitive style—the kind reflected in student A's thinking—constitutes a barrier to interpersonal communication. Initially, our stance may seem inconsistent, for it may appear that student A is more aware of the importance of sharp stimulus discrimination than is student B. Recall, however, that we said stimulus discrimination involves the ability to differentiate individuals from other members of particular cultural or social groupings. Thus, discrimination requires a communicator to identify ways that Brazilian C (or D, or E, and so on) differs from Brazilians in general, or to specify differences between Unitarian-Universalist F (or G, or H, and so on) and the entire class of churchgoers who call themselves Unitarian-Universalists.

Obviously, this process does not concern student A. In his case, the important question centers on the identification of airtight, unambiguous criteria for differentiating classes of people or events from other classes. In other words, student A would not much care how Brazilian C differs from Brazilian D, but he would be mightily curious about what Brazilians, in general, are and how they vary from Norwegians. Consequently, his typical level of discriminating is too gross; he focuses on differences between *classes*, rather than between *individuals*. As we shall see, his approach predisposes him to base communicative predictions on cultural or sociological data (which may often be erroneous), not psychological data.

Psychologists have investigated a number of cognitive styles that are characterized by a low tolerance for ambiguity and a tendency toward rigid, simplistic organization of beliefs and attitudes. We shall next discuss several of these for the purpose of illustrating how they inhibit movement to the interpersonal level. So as to avoid falling into the same trap as student A, we should underscore the fact that these cognitive styles share many common features, even though they can be differentiated on certain grounds.

Authoritarianism

After World War II, numerous social psychologists began to study the kinds of individuals who could espouse the Fascist ideology of Hitler's Germany and Mussolini's Italy. Allegiance to this ideology had fostered shocking, heinous crimes against mankind, and so it was not surprising that researchers sought to discover what motivated a "good" Nazi or a "good" Fascist.

The most extensive series of studies was conducted by Adorno, Frenkel-Brunswik, and their associates (1950). By using a number of clinical tests and experimental settings, these researchers tried to identify the main dimensions of a cognitive style that they labeled *authoritarianism*. Sanford summarizes the nine dimensions identified:

1. *Conventionalism*. Rigid adherence to conventional middle-class values.

2. *Authoritarian Submission*. Submissive, uncritical attitude toward idealized moral authorities of the in-group.

3. *Authoritarian Aggression*. Tendency to be on the lookout for, and to condemn, reject, and punish people who violate conventional values.

4. *Anti-intraception*. Opposition to the subjective, the imaginative, the tenderminded.

5. *Superstition and Stereotype.* Belief in mystical determinants of the individual's fate; *the disposition to think in rigid categories.* [italics ours]

6. *Power and Toughness.* Preoccupation with the dominance-submission, strong-weak, leader-follower dimension; identification with power figures; exaggerated assertions of strength and toughness.

7. *Destructiveness and Cynicism.* Generalized hostility; vilification of the human.

8. *Projectivity.* Disposition to believe that wild and dangerous things go on in the world; the projection outward of unconscious emotional impulses.

9. *Sex.* Ego-alien sexuality; exaggerated concern with sexual "goings on," and punitiveness toward violators of sex mores. (1956, p. 275)

These nine dimensions deal not only with the ways in which authoritarians structure their beliefs and attitudes, but also with their characteristic modes of processing information. Taken together, however, they underscore the authoritarian's low tolerance for ambiguity. Frenkel-Brunswik asserts that for the authoritarian "too much existing emotional ambiguity and ambivalence are counteracted by denial and intolerance of cognitive ambiguity. It is as if everything would go to pieces once the existing discrepancies were faced" (1949, p. 134). In a nutshell, authoritarians organize the world into neatly separated cognitive packages. Moreover, such a cognitive orientation makes it exceedingly difficult to communicate interpersonally, as we shall see later.

Dogmatism

What are the main features of a dogmatic cognitive style; i.e., how do dogmatic persons structure, or organize, their beliefs and attitudes? Rokeach postulates that a highly dogmatic, or closed-minded, belief system has the following characteristics:

1. A rigid cognitive barrier is erected between what one believes and what one does not believe.

2. Differences between what one believes and what one does not believe are sharply defined and highly magnified.

3. There is a tendency to reject all conflicting beliefs, regardless of their ideological distance from the beliefs held. For

example, a dogmatic extreme reactionary will just as quickly reject the views of a moderate conservative as he will the opinions of an extreme left-winger.

4. All conflicting views remain relatively undifferentiated; i.e., every competing position is perceived as unacceptable, and "bad," regardless of its ideological distance from the beliefs held (number 4 is, of course, a corollary of number 3).

5. The world is seen as threatening and hostile.

6. Authority is absolute, and people's acceptance or rejection hinges on their agreement or disagreement with one's authority figures.

7. Dogmatic persons adopt a narrow, future-oriented time perspective. (1960, pp. 55–56, our paraphrase of Rokeach's distinctions.)

These characteristics of a dogmatic cognitive style greatly influence the ways of processing and responding to information.

Comparing authoritarianism and dogmatism

Authoritarianism and dogmatism are cognitive first cousins. Like authoritarians, dogmatic persons have a low tolerance for ambiguity, preferring instead to organize the world into simple, mutually discrete categories. Moreover, both styles place a premium on authority as a basis for belief and both set up clear, unmistakable boundaries between friend and foe. How, then, do the two cognitive styles differ?

Rokeach (1960) refined the concept of dogmatism because he was critical of an apparent bias in the use of the term *authoritarianism*. He felt it had been exclusively applied to people on the extreme right of the political spectrum, whereas extreme left-wingers exhibited cognitive traits strikingly similar to those of their supposed polar opposites: although the political content of the two groups' beliefs was obviously quite different, their way of holding their beliefs was the same. Dogmatism, as Rokeach defines it, refers generally to a kind of cognitive style, independent of content, while authoritarianism refers to a cognitive style characterized by a certain ideology. The two terms are often used interchangeably, however, as indicated even in Rokeach's attempt to distinguish between them.

> If our interest is in the scientific study of authoritarianism, we should proceed from right authoritarianism not to a re-focus on left authoritarianism but to the general properties held in common by all forms of authoritarianism. Authoritarianism can be observed at any one time in history in a variety of human

activities, and we should think that it would have similar properties regardless of whether it is exhibited under Caesar, Napoleon, Hitler, Stalin, Khrushchev, Roosevelt, or Eisenhower. What is needed is therefore a deliberate turning away from a concern with the one or two kinds of authoritarianism that may happen to be predominant at a given time. Instead we should pursue a more theoretical historical analysis of the properties held in common by all forms of authoritarianism regardless of specific ideological, theological, philosophic, or scientific content. (1960, p. 14)

Rokeach is asserting that authoritarian types exist all across the political spectrum. Most of us can probably think of everyday experiences that document his assertion. Recall, for instance, the last time you overheard an argument between a committed revolutionary and a stout reactionary. Does this sound familiar?

REV: What we have to do is overthrow the military industrial complex and establish a new order. All these capitalist warmongers are alike; they think only of their pocketbooks.

REACT: On the contrary, we've got to get back to the solid American values. And a good place to start would be to get rid of all communists and the loafers on welfare who are sapping this country of its economic strength.

REV: All you right wingers think alike. You don't have a damn bit of compassion for all the helpless victims of this evil system. If we listen to people like you, we'll be back in Nazi Germany in no time.

REACT: If by being "back in Nazi Germany" you mean getting tough with all the bums and crooks, in order to protect hard-working, law-abiding citizens, then I say fine! And while we're at it, we might take a second look at all the money we're pouring into schools to produce people like you.

The argument rages, with neither adversary willing to give an inch. A bystander senses that while their ideologies are miles apart, the two adversaries' cognitive styles are like peas in a pod. Both fit Hoffer's description (1951) of the true believer: they have blindly accepted an ideology without carefully scrutinizing its content. Neither sees the other as an individual—the necessary prerequisite for communicating interpersonally—but rather as an envoy of an alien, sinister group. In short, both conform with Rokeach's conception of a highly dogmatic person.

Solving a puzzle

Since we have extensively discussed rigid, simplistic cognitive structuring, you may have become curious about the extent to which you are authoritarian or dogmatic. We will now give you an opportunity to test yourself, using a puzzle actually employed in some of Rokeach's research. Afterward, we will relate the principles embodied in the puzzle to the problem of moving to the interpersonal communication level. But first, the test. Study the "rules" of the situation carefully, for you must understand them to solve the puzzle.

The rules and problem
Picture a small, imaginary insect named "Joe Doodlebug." His ability to move is limited in these ways:

1. Joe can only jump in four different directions: north, south, east, and west. Joe cannot jump diagonally; i.e., southwest, northeast, and so on.

2. Once Joe starts in any one of these four directions, he *must* jump four times in that direction before he can change directions.

3. Joe has a jumping range from very large distances (up to several hundred miles) to very small distances (but not less than six inches).

4. Joe can only jump; he cannot crawl, fly, or walk.

5. Joe cannot turn around or turn sideways.

Joe has been jumping around getting some exercise, when suddenly his master places a pile of food, slightly larger than Joe, three feet directly west of Joe Joe notices the food and stops dead in his tracks, facing north. Since he is quite hungry from exercising, he wants to reach the food as soon as possible. After surveying his situation, Joe says, "I *must* take four jumps to reach the food—no more, no less." (Unlike humans, Joe is a completely logical, rational insect. When he says he *must* take four jumps, he means he is logically constrained to this alternative. If there were any way to make it in less than four jumps, Joe would seize on it.)

Your assignment, should you choose to accept it, is to discover Joe's path to the food; i.e., to figure out Joe's situation when he stopped jumping and to plot his four jumps to the food. In Rokeach's research, thirty minutes is usually allowed for the problem, but you may spend as much time as you wish. Since we will reveal the solution on the next page, do not permit your eyes to stray to it.

Solution and explanation

When Joe stopped after noticing the food, he had just taken one jump east. In order to reach the food, he next takes three short jumps east, which permit him to change direction. He then takes one long jump west, lands on top of the food and eats it. Notice that given the five constraints on Joe's movement, this is the only situation that both compels him to use four jumps and ensures he will not need more than four to reach the food.

What does this little puzzle tell us about dogmatism? In several studies by Rokeach (1960), high dogmatics, as measured by a forty-item questionnaire he developed, usually took somewhat longer to solve the problem. A successful solution hinges upon one's ability to overcome three strongly held beliefs: the facing belief, the direction belief, and the movement belief.

Human beings, as well as most other creatures, face their food while eating; consequently, it is easy to assume unthinkingly that Joe must be positioned to face the food. Actually, of course, Joe can eat from atop the food pile, as can most real insects. If your first reaction was to attempt to move Joe to a position facing the food, and if you continued to cling to this objective, you doubtless found it difficult to plot Joe's four jumps.

Moreover, most animals move in the direction they are facing and can change the direction they are facing at will. Since Joe cannot turn sideways or turn around, he is forever trapped facing north; his facing position in the present situation is a constant, not a variable. To solve the problem, then, one must realize that Joe was not necessarily moving north when he stopped, and that Joe is not only capable of jumping sideways and backward, but that he is compelled to do so.

Also, the ability to change directions at will extends to our own movement. There is nothing to prevent us from taking one step north, turning, and taking two steps west. But Joe is a captive of a restricted movement system; once he has started in one of the four permissible directions, he must make four jumps before changing. Thus, at the time he stopped, he may have been free to move directly west or, as is actually the case, his circumstances may have required him to jump in another direction. Many persons have difficulty with the puzzle because they assume Joe is at the end, rather than possibly the middle, of a sequence of jumps.

Finally, we have added the condition that Joe is totally logical and rational because of our experience with the problem. For some reason, many people respond by saying: "Oh, I've got it! Joe has just finished jumping east (or north). Now he'll jump west four times, land on the food, and eat it." Of course, these circumstances do not compel Joe to expend the energy for four jumps. Since he can jump large distances (we have also added the ceiling of several hundred miles to the problem, because a very open-minded person once suggested Joe could take one more jump east around the world, and land on the food) and since he is completely logical, he would never use four jumps when one will suffice.

Rokeach indicates that when compared to high-dogmatic persons, low-dogmatic individuals are more capable of overcoming these strongly held beliefs, so as to analyze them carefully and to synthesize the new information needed to arrive at the solution.

Rigid, simplistic cognitive styles and interpersonal communication

It is a long jump (no pun intended) from the imaginary universe of Joe Doodlebug to the real world of human communication. But just as we develop strongly held beliefs about movement and direction, we also entertain numerous, seldom-challenged beliefs about people. When we interact with other persons, these beliefs govern our initial perceptions and subsequent predictions. Since the beliefs themselves take the form of cultural or sociological generalizations about groups, the chance to communicate interpersonally depends on our ability to move beyond these generalizations and to identify relevant differences among the individuals with whom we are interacting.

Authoritarianism as a handicap to interpersonal communication
Communicative predictions based on knowledge of one's socioeconomic status are grounded in sociological data. When used intelligently, such data can often aid in accurate prediction, for many (though not all) members of each class share some (but not all) common values and aspirations. For the authoritarian, this aspect of

communication is likely to be seriously affected by his conventionalism, or rigid adherence to middle-class values. For example, most middle-class parents place a premium on their children's formal education, and yet a fair number either do not get highly excited about it or do not feel justified in forcing their children to acquiesce to this value. That this number is apparently increasing is attested to by the tendency of fewer middle-class high school graduates to enroll immediately in college, choosing instead to pursue some issue of social concern to them or just to "cool it" for a while.

This variability is likely to escape the authoritarian. For him, all members of a particular group are characterized by several common attributes; the complexity and uniqueness of each is a phenomenon he cannot, or will not, accept. Thus, when communicating with members of a given group, most of his predictions will be grounded in sociological or cultural generalizations. Should he have occasion to communicate with someone of lower socioeconomic status, he is likely to be guided by an extremely hostile view of his fellow communicator. One can imagine him reasoning along the following lines: "I'd better watch out for this guy. He is one of those worthless misfits who sponge off hard-working people like myself. People like him are all out to get something for nothing. But he won't trick me, because I'm wise to him." Obviously, this kind of thinking destroys any opportunity to move to the interpersonal level and effectively ensures against the growth of individual understanding.

Not only is the authoritarian likely to be interpersonally handicapped in his dealings with out-group members; he will probably find it difficult, if not impossible, to relate to members of his in-group as individuals. Here, too, the authoritarian is trapped by his simplistic cognitive style, which encourages superficial cultural and sociological thinking. Others are either "like him" or "not like him," and if an individual measures up on a few relevant judgmental dimensions, the authoritarian is likely to embrace him uncritically. As a consequence, the authoritarian is robbed of the opportunity to develop rich, meaningful interpersonal relationships; he is imprisoned behind stereotypic, black-and-white, noninterpersonal bars. Moreover, the authoritarian's inability to discriminate, when coupled with his authoritarian submissive tendencies—i.e., his willingness to embrace blindly the dictates of positive authorities—marks him as easy prey for unscrupulous, self-seeking individuals who are able to mask their Machiavellian selves behind the mantle of authority.

Every Saturday evening, millions of Americans are treated to the spectacle of an authoritarian in action. Archie Bunker of "All in the Family" constitutes a walking composite of the nine dimensions summarized by Sanford. On a typical evening, Archie sermonizes on the beauties of middle-class values, admits to a totally uncritical acceptance of authority ("Don't you say anything bad about him; he's the President, ain't he?"), displays a continuing mild paranoia about all the "others" who are out to get him, and slams the door instantly on the forbidden topic of sex ("How many times have I told you not to talk about that in here"). Most important, he is a captive of his rigid categories: blacks, Spanish-speaking Americans, Poles, Jews, Catholics, women, and homosexuals—to name but a few—exist in his mind as precisely defined groups. The individual has no meaning to Archie; instead, he substitutes a tragicomic parody of stereotyped, erroneous cultural and sociological perceptions.

Yet in some ways, Archie elicits viewer sympathy; he is not a totally rejected character. Of course, one would expect other authoritarians to identify with him. But beyond this segment of the audience, we suspect that many persons are drawn to Archie for a simple reason: *Archie would like to communicate interpersonally with others, but he is incapable of doing it.* Occasionally we see a flash of his concern for a person: a tender moment with his wife or daughter conflicts with his typical chauvinistic stance; an expression of fondness for his son-in-law intrudes on his tiresome anti-Polish diatribes; a momentary realization of personal identification with his black neighbors interrupts his bigoted outpourings. During these episodes, we see him struggle to escape his noninterpersonal trap, but he is powerless to do so because of a long history of learning and experience.

In the experimental literature on authoritarianism, we can find support for the notion that certain parental cognitive styles hinder interpersonal communication in families. Byrne (1965) cites a series of studies of family interaction patterns which show that high-authoritarian people tend to assume clearly defined roles of dominance and submission, suppress unacceptable impulses early in life, emphasize the social acceptability of values, stress the importance of duty and obligations, and keep sex roles distinctly separate from each other. Low-authoritarians, however, tend to emphasize obedience less, express emotions more freely, feel less anxiety about conformity, and are more tolerant of socially unacceptable behavior.

Later in this chapter, we will discuss some possible ways to modify an authoritarian cognitive style. For the moment, we will only observe that an authoritarian stance seriously impairs interpersonal communication. Movement to the psychological level can occur only when other communicators are perceived as individuals, rather than as an undifferentiated part of some larger cultural or social grouping.

Dogmatism as a handicap to interpersonal communication
Some research carried out by Gerry (Miller and Bacon, 1971) indicates that dogmatic individuals also have a harder time overcoming strongly held beliefs about other people. This study examined possi-

ble differences in the amount of time required by high-dogmatic and low-dogmatic persons to identify the humorous aspect of a picture when the humor was based on a situation that violated a conventional, seldom-challenged belief. All participants in the study were shown a *Playboy*-type, centerfold picture, taken from the *Harvard Lampoon*'s parody of *Playboy*. The picture's humor lay in the nude girl's tanning pattern: she was tanned where one would normally expect her to be untanned, and untanned where one would expect her to be tanned. As Miller and Bacon predicted, the high-dogmatic persons took significantly longer than their low-dogmatic counterparts to recognize just what was funny about the picture.

Beliefs about tanning patterns may at first seem far removed from the kinds of predictions one makes when communicating with others. Still, such beliefs are grounded in cultural norms, as are many other generalizations about people that are strongly held and go largely unchallenged. One group of erroneous generalizations is the so-called social stereotype: Jews are mercenary and avaricious; blacks are lazy and uneducated; college professors are impractical and soft-headed; politicians are dishonest and self-seeking. Dogmatic persons are not only more likely to accept such stereotypes uncritically, but also to find it more difficult to abandon these cultural and sociological bases of prediction in order to move to the psychological level. Thus, their potential for effective interpersonal communication is severely curtailed.

Summary

We have far from exhausted the theoretical and research undertakings dealing with rigid, simplistic cognitive styles. Gough and Sanford (1952) have investigated a construct labeled *rigidity*, while Budner (1962) has introduced the notion of *tolerance for ambiguity*. Although these cognitive styles can be distinguished from authoritarianism and dogmatism, they share similarities on most of the critical dimensions discussed here. We have attempted to describe the crucial structural and substantive ingredients of these cognitive styles and to show how they inhibit movement to the level of interpersonal communication. It remains for us to discuss some strategies for modifying a rigid, simplistic cognitive style.

Toward a more open belief system: bringing out the shades of gray

In the hit Broadway play *The Music Man*, Professor Harold Hill enjoins the mothers of River City, Iowa, to "watch for the telltale signs of corruption." Perhaps this is the most terse, yet useful, instruction we can give to those interested in modifying a rigid cognitive style. If one is aware of the behaviors that signal rigid, simplistic thinking—and much of the information in this chapter can heighten awareness—he is in a better position to curb such responses, or even to check them before they occur. Still, we realize that our injunction to "watch for them" is somewhat wanting in specificity, and so we endorse the following communicative strategies as beginning steps.

1. Consciously strive to identify significant differences among the people with whom you communicate.

As we have repeatedly stressed, initial predictions about other communicators are necessarily grounded in cultural and sociological data. Moreover, no one is totally immune to the influence of strongly held beliefs grounded in stimulus generalization. Unfortunately, a person who habitually views his world in simplistic, black-and-white terms remains a captive of his generalizations. Acquire the habit of consciously searching for differences, rather than expecting similarities. Instead of declaring, "This person is a _____ and therefore like all other _____ s," ask the question, "How does this particular _____ differ from other _____ s?" Such a question forces you to assume that variation, not constancy, is normal. As with any skill, the ability to spot variation requires practice, especially since many differences are barely noticeable. So do not be discouraged if your first attempts meet with meager success. Just as most musicians must struggle hard to master the nuances of tones and chords, communicators must be constantly alert to the subtle variations in the behaviors of other communicators.

2. Consciously strive to identify similarities between your views and the views of those with whom you communicate.

Although this recommendation may initially seem inconsistent with the preceding strategy, the two are actually harmonious. The first strategy enjoins you to look for ways in which the people with whom you communicate differ, while the second suggests that you look for ways in which they resemble you. Paradoxically, defining common ground is often the first step toward more successful discrimination. When we see another's beliefs as completely alien to our own, we are more likely to succumb to hostile generalizations and injurious stereotypes that indiscriminately lump the individual with the "bad guys," and we are less apt to be on the lookout for meaningful distinctions. The harmful consequences of such thinking are illustrated by a recent incident in which a student confronted Gerry and erroneously predicted his position on a host of political issues, solely on the basis of his knowledge that Gerry opposed faculty unions. Contrary to the student's opinion, however, Gerry supports unionism in general, opposed the Vietnam War, and sees himself as a liberal Democrat. Had the student bothered to explore Gerry's views, he would have discovered not only that Gerry has some particular reasons for opposing unionization of college faculties, but also that Gerry's general political stance is closely akin to his own.

Try to avoid the mistake made by this student. Admittedly, it is easy, particularly during an argument, to interpret mild disagreement on a specific issue as a total rebuff of one's ideological being. Whenever possible, quell this impulse and instead open your mind to areas of agreement. Perhaps communicators must identify the things they share in common before they can successfully discover their differences. We will have more to say about this possibility in the next section of this chapter, when we discuss assumed similarity between opposites.

3. Consciously strive to distinguish between what others say and their motives for saying it.

Think for a moment about some of the cultural and sociological generalizations that we frequently hear: politicians are out to defraud taxpayers; Catholics are trying to take over the country; women seek to dominate and emasculate men; homosexuals want to pervert the youth of America, and so on. Most such statements refer not to behaviors, but to motives or dispositions that underlie them. The simplistic, rigid thinker dismisses a vast array of ideas, many undoubtedly good and many bad, on the grounds that all of them are designed to serve some assumed motive of the proponent. To avoid falling into this trap, attend primarily to the content of a message rather than the motives of its source. Such a cognitive posture assists in discrimination, since many important cues are found in message content. Moreover, careful scrutiny of another's communication aids in the implementation of the previous strategy; i.e., identifying similarities between your views and those of the other communicator.

Again, we do not pretend that it is easy to separate message and motive. All of us tend to speculate about the motives of others. Some psychologists (e.g., Skinner, 1971) argue, however, that the growth of knowledge regarding human behavior has been seriously retarded by a concern with motives rather than with behavior. Although Skinner's arguments are not likely to stop the verbal traffic in motivation, they do underscore a crucial point: the only direct evidence we have about others is their behavior. While it is possible to discriminate among

various behaviors, attempts to differentiate motives are inferential, for we cannot observe a motive.

If we focus on a person's messages instead of his motives, we are less likely to make cultural or sociological generalizations. Since messages are a form of behavior, they constitute a more objective data base: *a man's verbal statements and his nonverbal behaviors can be observed, but his motives must be inferred.* As yet another advantage, concern with a person's communication diverts attention from authority figures who may agree with his views and directs it to the message content itself. Since reliance on authority as a grounds for belief is one of the hallmarks of a rigid, simplistic cognitive style, any strategy minimizing the role of authority is bound to pay interpersonal dividends.

4. Ask someone to monitor your communication behavior and to assess the extent to which you are practicing the preceding three strategies.

Each of these three strategies rests on the assumption that you are capable of spotting instances of rigid, simplistic cognitive structuring and altering your behavior accordingly. Because one's cognitive style is usually firmly ingrained, this assumption is open to question. You may not realize that you have fallen prey to simplistic thinking, and even if you do, your efforts to change may be thwarted by some very stubborn habits. Therefore, any serious attempt to modify your behavior will probably depend on some advice or assistance from others. Acquaint someone else with the details of your program for cognitive fitness. (Obviously, this should be a person close enough to you that you do not rebel at laying your ego on the line; i.e., someone with whom you have developed an interpersonal relationship.) Ask the person to observe your communication behavior and to evaluate your success in using the three strategies. His (or her) feedback should markedly heighten your awareness of how you are communicating and increase your chances of modifying your cognitive style.

Summary

Rigid, simplistic cognitive styles, with their attendant low tolerance for ambiguity, pose a serious obstacle to the development of interpersonal communication. Since a person's cognitive style constitutes an integral part of his or her psychological baggage, it is inherently difficult to modify these deep-seated structural and substantive mainsprings of behavior. Still, we feel that conscientious pursuit of the strategies we have outlined can result in change, and, more important, can increase one's potential for communicating interpersonally. Finally, we are aware that the material regarding strategies is written as if all readers are suffering from impoverished cognitive style. Obviously, this is not the case; nevertheless, we suspect that everyone, including ourselves, can profit from the reminders in our strategies for fostering cognitive change.

Assumed similarity between opposites: with enemies like these, who needs friends?

Thus far, we have focused primarily on discrimination, or differentiation. Our conceptual view of interpersonal communication has stressed the importance of discerning relevant differences between individuals and basing predictions about communicative outcomes on psychological data. Our discussion of authoritarianism and dogmatism dealt with another kind of discrimination process, one involving the division of persons into clearly differentiated cultural and sociological groupings. But might not some people eschew attempts at sharp discrimination, choosing instead to emphasize the similarities of those with whom they come in contact? In this section, we will examine this interesting possibility.

One construct centrally related to this issue, *assumed similarity between opposites*, has been extensively investigated by Fiedler (1960). Perhaps this construct can best be defined by example. Figure 5.1 contains several scales that can be used to measure an individual's perception of another person or persons. Suppose we asked you to rate your best friend on each of these scales. Some of you might check the maximally favorable interval for each scale, while others might select more moderately favorable ratings for some scales. Although we cannot predict exact rating patterns, it seems safe to say that most of you would report generally positive ratings.

FRIENDLY	___:___:___:___:___:___:___	UNFRIENDLY
	7 6 5 4 3 2 1	
SECRETIVE	___:___:___:___:___:___:___	FRANK
	1 2 3 4 5 6 7	
CALM	___:___:___:___:___:___:___	UPSET
	7 6 5 4 3 2 1	
GLOOMY	___:___:___:___:___:___:___	CHEERFUL
	1 2 3 4 5 6 7	
MATURE	___:___:___:___:___:___:___	IMMATURE
	7 6 5 4 3 2 1	

Fig. 5.1 Scales for measuring assumed similarity between opposites

Now suppose we gave you a second sheet containing the same scales and asked you to rate your worst enemy. Once you had completed this task, we could compare your two sets of responses. Moreover, by assigning a number to each interval on the scales (figure 5.1 contains an assignment of numbers), we could determine the distance between the ratings of your best friend and your worst enemy by subtracting the smaller number for each scale from the larger. For convenience, let us assume that the number for your best friend is always larger, though this might not be the case. If you rated your best friend 7 on all scales and your worst enemy 1, there is a large difference between the two, and we can say you have *low assumed similarity between opposites* (Low ASo); i.e., you perceive opposites quite differently. If you rated your best friend 6 and your worst enemy 5, the difference is small, and you have *high assumed similarity between opposites* (High ASo); i.e., you perceive opposites quite similarly. One can use this procedure to gather ratings for a host of opposites: best and worst teacher, most credible and least credible communicator, co-worker easiest and hardest to work with, to name a few.

People do differ in the way they perceive opposites. Some discriminate quite sharply, while others see only modest differences. Furthermore, data we have gathered suggest that these varying perceptual sets are consistent across pairs of opposites. Stated differently, if a person perceives marked differences between his best friend and his worst enemy, he is also likely to discriminate decisively on other pairs of opposites; conversely, if he minimizes the distance between friend and enemy, he is also likely to minimize the distance between other pairs. It is the generality of this phenomenon that qualifies it as an important component of cognitive style, for it seems to reflect a characteristic way of structuring one's beliefs about other people and of processing information pertaining to these beliefs.

Interpersonal communication and assumed similarity between opposites

On the surface, the inference to be drawn seems quite clear: persons with low assumed similarity between opposites should be more effective interpersonal communicators, since they are better able to discriminate differences between individuals. Unfortunately, the issue is not so simple. Let us consider some research findings that complicate the situation.

In an extensive investigation of leadership in task-oriented groups, Fiedler (1960) found that leaders with low assumed similarity between opposites are indeed more effective in stimulating productivity. He attributes this advantage, however, not only to the Low ASo leader's ability to make relevant role discriminations among group members, but also to his tendency to maintain considerable psychological distance from the other members of the group. In several instances, Fiedler refers to the Low ASo leader's "lack of warmth" and to his "remoteness" from the group. By contrast, leaders with high assumed similarity between opposites are pictured as architects of a warm, accepting group climate, even though their charges are not as productive. To the extent that one assumes warm, friendly relationships are a necessity for interpersonal communication, Fiedler's findings cast doubt on the interpersonal superiority of Low ASo persons. We do not believe, however, that psychological closeness, in the sense that Fiedler conceives of it, is a necessary condition for interpersonal communication, and we shall show later how his findings are in harmony with our conceptualization.

A somewhat more disquieting finding emerged from a study by Siegel, Miller, and Wotring (1969). Their study dealt with a construct labeled *credibility proneness*. They reasoned that people who discriminated sharply between their most and least credible communication sources (in other words, Low ASo persons) would be high in credibility proneness; i.e., the credibility of the message source would have a marked influence on the persuasiveness of the message. Conversely, source credibility was expected to have little persuasive impact on individuals with low credibility proneness (in other words, High ASo persons); instead, these people were expected to be more concerned with the content of the message arguments.

The results confirmed the predicted difference in credibility proneness. Low ASo individuals manifested one of the characteristics of the rigid, simplistic cognitive styles discussed earlier in this chapter; they were more concerned with the attractiveness of the communicator than with the content of his message. This preoccupation with the source suggests to us that the ability to discriminate sharply between opposites may not be an unqualified interpersonal blessing. In some instances it may assist a communicator in moving to the interpersonal level, but in others it may lure him into the trap of rigid, simplistic thinking. When one remembers that we are considering only extreme opposites, this possibility is not so surprising. For in communicating interpersonally, we are dealing not with polar extremes, but with communicators all along some continuum of differences.

Perhaps the best way to clarify the role of assumed similarity in interpersonal communication would be to study responses to individuals who are closer together on the continuum. For example, persons might be asked to rate their best friends, their second best friends, their third best friends, and so on. These persons could then be divided into groups on the basis of differences in assumed similarity, and the interpersonal communication effectiveness of the two groups could be compared. We suspect that, if such a study were conducted, the low assumed similarity group would fare better interpersonally.

Let us return to Fiedler's findings and their relationship to our concept of interpersonal communication. As we have repeatedly emphasized, the ability to communicate interpersonally does not necessarily hinge on the development of warm, positive relationships. A salesman may feel very cool toward a customer, but if he can discern significant differences between that customer and other customers, interpersonal communication is possible and the chances for a sale are enhanced. It is even possible that a person who actively hated his fellow communicator but was able to base predictions on psychological data could create a living hell for the other person. While we personally affirm the desirability of warmth and concern in human relationships, we realize that many interpersonal communication situations lack these ingredients.

Most interpersonal relationships flourish best, however, in an atmosphere of mutual friendship and acceptance. Moreover, as we suggested earlier, the identification of common ground may cement these bonds of friendship and acceptance, and heighten the likelihood of subsequent successful discrimination. This fact, however, in no way negates the importance of successful discrimination of individual differences. If one wishes to be an effective interpersonal communicator, he should develop a cognitive style that places a premium on this psychological process.

Summary

Our consideration of cognitive styles underscores two important caveats: first, one should develop some tolerance for ambiguity and avoid rigid, simplistic thinking, which freezes him at the cultural and sociological levels of prediction; second, one should constantly seek to sharpen his ability to discriminate relevant differences among other communicators. Allegiance to these two caveats is one of the keys to effective interpersonal communication.

We shall defer prolonged discussion of the strategies for acquiring discriminative aptitude until the next chapter, which explores the development of empathic skills. Obviously, the secret is largely embodied in one of the strategies introduced earlier; namely, consciously endeavoring to identify relevant differences among the people with whom you communicate. But to succeed in this interpersonal quest, you must know some of the behavioral clues to look for. Most of the remaining chapters are at least partially devoted to spelling out these clues; they seek to make you a sort of Sherlock Holmes—or perhaps more contemporarily, a Columbo—of interpersonal communication.

Probes

1. To what extent, if at all, do you perceive our earlier emphasis on prediction and environmental control as inconsistent with our concern in this chapter for developing tolerance for ambiguity? How would you reconcile the two perspectives? In other words, how can a concern for prediction and control be accommodated within an uncertain, contingent world view?

2. Archie Bunker is mentioned in this chapter as a television character who manifests a rigid, simplistic cognitive style. Can you think of other television characters with authoritarian qualities? Are there contemporary song lyrics that deal with these ideas?

3. In what ways might cognitive style influence initial communication transactions? Who is likely to ask more questions, the open-minded or closed-minded person? In what ways, if any, would you expect the substance of their questions to differ?

4. How would you characterize yourself in terms of assumed similarity between opposites—i.e., do you tend to see opposites as relatively far apart or reasonably close together? In what ways does your orientation toward opposites affect your ability to move to the interpersonal level?

5. Sometimes when you attempt to teach young children the rules of a game, they raise perplexing questions about the rules; e.g., "Why can't a pawn move three spaces?" Are such questions indicative of an open-minded cognitive style, a closed-minded cognitive style, or both? Develop arguments to support your answer.

6. What would you say to a person who asserts, "Tolerance creates uncertainty about the value of various communication strategies and leads to their abandonment"? Does tolerance open or close doors of knowledge about why people act as they do?

6

Commander McHale: Batten down the mainsail;
sweep down the port deck; and all engines full ahead!
Ensign Parker: Gee, I like that kind of talk!!

from the former television series, "McHale's Navy"

Empathic Skills and the Development of Interpersonal Communication Effectiveness

T o communicate interpersonally, one must be able to leave the cultural and sociological levels of prediction and psychically travel to the psychological level. We have already examined some ways in which a communicator's patterns of control, as well as his cognitive style, influence his attempts to reach the interpersonal level. Certainly, the communicator's journey is more likely to be successful if he develops his ability to empathize. In this chapter we will discuss the importance of empathy in interpersonal communication. More specifically, we will develop a definition for empathy, suggest a model for viewing an important dimension of the empathic process, and survey some strategies for improving empathic skills. As the chapter proceeds, it will become apparent that acquiring these skills is crucial to becoming effective in interpersonal communication. In fact, empathic skills and interpersonal communication effectiveness may come to seem almost synonymous.

Toward a definition for empathy

Although the term *empathy* is relatively common, it means many things to many people. After surveying some of the literature in aesthetics and theatre, Gunkle pessimistically concluded that "the term, stretched to mean almost anything, has come to mean nothing" (1963, 15). Katz (1963) devotes a substantial part of his book to examining meanings for *empathy*, as well as distinguishing it from sympathy, projection, and insight. This rich background of meanings can be grouped into two broad categories: psychophysiological response and social perception skill.

Empathy as a psychophysiological response

All of us can probably remember watching someone suck a lemon and feeling the sour taste permeate our mouths. This response is not limited to citrus fruits. When asked her meaning for empathy, a student in one of Gerry's classes replied tersely, "Empathy is when you throw up, I throw up, too!" In a similar vein, we speak of the contagion of laughter, tears, or yawns. Indeed, it is a rare person who has never experienced this sort of psychophysiological identity with another, both in real life and vicariously through the entertainment media.

In its psychophysiological sense, empathy probably occurs most frequently when the empathizer uses multiple sensory channels. While the lemon effect can be produced by mere mention of sucking a lemon, observation of the lemon-sucker heightens it. Still, the auditory channel alone is often sufficient—as it was for listeners to radio soap operas, a vivid childhood remembrance of Gerry's. On weekday visits to his grandparents' home he invariably found people listening to "Valiant Lady," "Lorenzo Jones," "Ma Perkins," "Backstage Wife," ad nauseam. Tears flowed between commercials; joy was eagerly shared, and angry words ("You'll get yours, you _____!") were voiced. The demise of radio in America as a major source of entertainment resulted in more than unemployment for many organists. Today television and films have supplanted this mode of vicarious identification, combining auditory and visual sensations.

So intense is the psychophysiological response and so strong the sense of identity with another that some writers have resorted to rather mystical ways of describing the empathic process.

> When we experience empathy, we feel as if we were experiencing someone else's feelings as our own. We see, we feel, we respond, and we understand as if we were, in fact, the other person. *We stand in his shoes. We get under his skin . . . When we take the position of another person, our imagination projects us out of ourselves and into the other person.* (Katz, 1963, p. 3) [italics ours]

Katz's words are by no means atypical. Empathy is most often defined using phrases akin to "putting yourself in someone else's shoes." Since all of us are forever trapped inside our own skins, however, any judgments we make about the emotional or cognitive states of others must be inferential. The raw materials for our inferences are the actual behaviors of other individuals and our own experiences with similar kinds of behaviors. Thus, when we say we

can identify, or empathize, with someone sucking a lemon, we are saying that we have observed his lemon-sucking behavior and that our own experiences with lemons call forth biochemical changes similar to those occurring in his mouth.

We shall avoid bestowing an aura of mysticism on empathy, preferring to treat it primarily as a behavioral process. Although our approach may lack the imaginative or emotional appeal of the mysterious, we believe it has considerable communicative utility. To tell a prospective empathizer to put himself in another person's shoes or to get inside someone else's skin, is not so helpful as giving him pointers on how to spot behavioral cues presented by others.

A psychophysiological response to someone can express support and understanding, but certainly empathy occurs more often than just when people share the same sensory-emotional reactions. The recipient of such an expression of empathy may or may not consider it to be a desirable response. If, for example, he becomes sick to his stomach, he may well get little relief from an empathic friend who does likewise. The friend is more likely to be perceived as empathically admirable if he tries to help alleviate the sick person's distress. We will have more to say about this later in this chapter when we set forth our transactional definition of empathy.

Empathy as a social perception skill

In the social perception arena, empathy refers to *the accuracy with which an individual predicts the verbal responses of another.* More specifically, empathic ability is concerned primarily with responses reporting the person's emotional states or the way he feels about himself. High accuracy is equated with high empathic skill; low accuracy is taken as evidence of empathic limitations.

Self-other ratings
To illustrate how empathic ability is assessed, we will briefly describe one of the most popular procedures, the self-other rating developed by Dymond (1949). This approach requires two persons (A and B) to provide the following ratings:

For person A:
1. A rates himself (A).
2. A rates B as he (A) sees him.
3. A rates B as he thinks B would rate himself.
4. A rates himself (A) as he thinks B would rate him.

For person B:
1. B rates himself (B).
2. B rates A as he (B) sees him.
3. B rates A as he thinks A would rate himself.
4. B rates himself (B) as he thinks A would rate him.

Typically, the raters use a five-point scale of intensity for rating such personality traits as self-confidence, superiority, unselfishness, friendliness, leadership, and sense of humor. The measure of A's empathic ability, for example, is determined by calculating how closely A's predictions of B's ratings correspond with B's actual ratings.

Suppose two friends, Mary and Ruth, wish to assess their mutual degree of empathy, using the sense of humor trait. On a five-point scale ranging from high to low, Mary would (1) rate her own sense of humor, (2) rate Ruth's sense of humor, (3) provide a rating that *predicts* how Ruth sees her own sense of humor, and (4) provide a rating that *predicts* Ruth's perception of Mary's sense of humor. Ruth would carry out the identical rating procedures. If both predicted the other's responses quite accurately, we would probably conclude that they have established an interpersonal relationship; if one was relatively successful but the other was not, we would say that the relationship reflects a mixed, interpersonal/noninterpersonal level; and if neither was very accurate, we would call the relationship noninterpersonal.

Degrees of empathy and levels of relationship
We see empathy, when viewed as a social perception skill, as closely akin to the predictive process that characterizes interpersonal communication. To some extent, accurate prediction of another's self-perceptions requires the predictor to spot relevant individual differences. Still, we are not willing to view the processes of empathizing and communicating interpersonally as totally synonymous, particularly when research procedures such as the self-other approach are

used as measures of empathy. Examination of some of the character-istics of this research method will reveal why we are reluctant to equate the two processes.

Typically, self-other ratings of empathic ability focus on personality traits. While the ability to make accurate discriminations about others' perceptions of their personalities may frequently aid the interpersonal communicator, his range of concern is naturally much broader. Consider once again our salesman seeking to move to the interpersonal level with a reluctant customer. He is not primarily concerned with predicting the customer's level of self-confidence ac-curately, but with selling his product. On many occasions, the sales-man will achieve greater success by avoiding unnecessary speculation about unobservables, such as personality traits, and by focusing on the ways in which the customer is responding to his messages. In particular, he must ask himself how a customer's response differs from the responses of other customers with whom he has communicated successfully and, given these differences, how he might alter his communicative strategy to increase the likelihood of a sale. Successful discrimination is based on the salesman's skill in spotting subtle behavioral cues and then predicting appropriate message changes. In some instances, prediction may be improved by concern with personality traits, but in many others, the inclusion of personality inferences as part of the predictive equation only confuses and complicates the issue.

Predicting personality traits
from cultural or sociological data

It is often possible to make accurate predictions about others' perceptions of their personality traits solely on the basis of cultural or sociological data, since people do not vary much in their self-ratings on certain personality characteristics. To demonstrate this consistency to yourself, ask several of your friends whether they have a good sense of humor. If more than one or two reply negatively, it will be surprising. By the same token, how many people are likely to see themselves as relatively unfriendly? Since our society assigns a positive value to traits such as having a good sense of humor or being friendly, most people like to believe they possess these personal characteristics.

Graphologists and fortune tellers have long been aware of such invariant areas of self-perception. If you wish to amaze your friends with your psychic powers, try this experiment. Ask several of them for handwriting samples, and tell them you will use the samples to provide them with descriptions of themselves. (If you think friends will feel you based your descriptions on other data, get the samples from relative strangers.) Then for every person, write the same description, including comments such as the following:

> Generally, you are friendly with other people and accept them for what they are. While you trust people most of the time, there are times when you feel others are taking advantage of you and when you believe you have not been given enough credit for things you have done. Occasionally you suffer from feelings of inadequacy. You have a good sense of humor and you are able to laugh at yourself when the occasion warrants.

Return the description to each of your friends and ask them whether it is accurate. Having performed the experiment several times in our classes, we are certain that most of your friends will marvel at the accuracy of your evaluation.

Empathy and stimulus discrimination

This tendency for persons to perceive themselves similarly on certain personality dimensions poses an interesting dilemma for the prospective interpersonal communicator. If such perceptions are accurate—e.g., if almost everyone does have a good sense of humor—these traits are worthless predictive vehicles because variation is a necessary condition for discrimination. If, as is more likely, considerable variability is associated with these traits, many people are victims of their own self-delusions; they do not see themselves as others see them. Since empathic accuracy is defined as the correspondence between the ratings of the empathizer and those of the person with whom he is empathizing, a "good" empathizer accepts self-delusion as a given. By contrast, stimulus discrimination, as we have defined it, deals primarily with the ability to differentiate one person's behavior from another's. Thus, an important distinction can be drawn between the two processes: *when viewed as a social perception skill, empathy involves the ability to predict accurately others' self-perceptions; when conceived of as a crucial determinant of interpersonal communication effectiveness, stimulus discrimination involves the ability to identify ways that the actual behaviors and attitudes of an individual differ from the behaviors and attitudes of others.*

Given this distinction, a social perception skill view of empathy may sometimes actually prevent a communicator from moving to the interpersonal level. How could this apparently contradictory result occur? Assume you are a salesman for a company engaged in manufacturing a new multiple lock system for apartment doors—a flourishing business in this era of high crime rates. During your training period, the sales manager describes some customer problems you are likely to encounter. In particular, he points out that since most people see themselves as friendly and accessible, they are likely to resist the prison-like, inaccessible atmosphere created by an intricate lock system. Consequently, he stresses that your sales pitch should specifically minimize the infringement upon movement and the hostile atmosphere imposed by the adoption of such a system; in fact, he arms you with a particular sales pitch designed to overcome customer resistance on this point.

You successfully use this sales routine with your first three customers. Not only do you accept the manager's dictum concerning people's perceptions of their own friendliness, you detect behavioral cues that these three customers are genuinely reluctant to further isolate themselves from their fellowmen. But now you are face-to-face with customer four. Like the preceding three customers, he probably perceives himself as friendly and outgoing. Still, he is not behaving the same way they behaved. His words, his tone of voice, his reluctance to open the door fully are all cues that he is hostile, suspicious, and prefers to be left alone. Spontaneously, you decide to emphasize, rather than downplay, the increased privacy and inaccessibility offered by the lock system, and you are rewarded with a quick sale.

It is possible, though not probable, that the standard sales pitch would have yielded the same outcome. What is important is that a commitment to basing communicative predictions on empathic grounds, rather than stimulus discrimination, would have resulted in a different message strategy, one less likely to clinch the sale. Had an empathic framework been adopted, you would have been forced to reason as follows: "I know this customer perceives himself as friendly and outgoing, even though his behavior belies this perception. Hence, my messages should minimize the extent to which the new lock system will create a more inaccessible, remote environment." By contrast, a prediction based on stimulus discrimination stems from this line of reasoning: "Even though this customer thinks of himself as friendly and outgoing, his behavior indicates suspicion and hostility. Consequently, I should emphasize the greater privacy and inaccessibility to be gained from the lock system, rather than playing these factors down."

A final deficiency

From a communication standpoint, there is yet another crucial deficiency in the typical definition of empathy as a social perception skill: it is *unidirectional, rather than transactional.* The social perception viewpoint holds that a good empathizer is one who can accurately predict others' responses, particularly in regard to the ways they perceive themselves. From a transactional communication perspective, this definition is inadequate, for when we say that someone is a good empathizer, we mean not only that he can predict how we feel, but also that he communicates with us in ways we find rewarding. We believe a transactional definition of empathy best suits the dynamics of human communication in general and interpersonal communication in particular.

A transactional definition for empathy

Assume you have an acquaintance who is remarkably adept at sensing your current emotional state, even though you may try to conceal it from him. When you are upset or unhappy, he detects your mood unerringly; when you are joyous and happy, this fact never escapes his attention. But despite his sensitivity to your every emotion, you avoid contact with him because he is unable or unwilling to communicate in ways you find satisfying. Rather than reducing your sadness, he heightens or ignores it; rather than rejoicing with you, he discovers a communicative means of transforming your happiness to gloom. In short, you view him as a "bad news" communicator.

Most of you probably know the kind of person we have just described. We doubt that you would characterize him as a good empathizer, even though he is extremely talented at reading your emotional states. Transactionally, empathy embraces two major steps:

1. *The prospective empathizer must be able to discriminate accurately the ways that the individual's motivational and attitudinal posture differs from others.*

2. *Accurate discriminations must be followed by behaviors that are viewed as desirable, or rewarding, by the persons who are the objects of prediction.*

While our hypothetical acquaintance has no trouble accomplishing the first step, he falls short on the second.

Step 1 closely parallels the previously discussed definition of empathy as a social perception skill. Even here it differs in one important respect, placing emphasis on accurate behavioral prediction based on subtle verbal and nonverbal cues, rather than on predictive agreement with the self-perceived attitudes and motives of the other. In drawing this distinction, we are not arguing that there is one correct, preferred

way to gauge motives and attitudes. Sometimes, the best evidence we have is the other person's verbal descriptions of his feelings. At times, however, as we have already indicated, these verbal responses may conflict with other behaviors; e.g., an individual may say that he is friendly and outgoing, and yet he may behave just the opposite. Given such conflicting evidence, predictive accuracy is usually enhanced by relying on behavioral cues other than the individual's verbal report about his usual attitudes toward others.

Step 2 places the definition within the transactional view of communication discussed in chapter 2. Like beauty, empathy is in the eye (or perhaps more descriptively, the perceptions) of the beholder. No matter how accurately someone reads us, we do not bestow the title "good empathizer" upon him unless he also communicates with us in rewarding ways. This fact suggests that the most effective interpersonal communicators not only read cues well, but also select the appropriate communication behaviors implied by the cues.

This transactional definition should not be interpreted as an attempt to impose our values on the communication process. We do not think it necessary to equate "good empathizers" with "nice guys." Still, from a transactional perspective, communicators reserve the accolade "good empathizer" for those who respond to them in rewarding ways. For that matter, an unscrupulous communicator, skilled in exercising effective environmental control, may meet both of our conditions for empathic response and still use his empathic skills to manipulate the other person in devious ways.

An exception

In some instances, a communicator may accurately predict the motivational or attitudinal states of someone else, know how the person would like him to communicate, and still conclude that it would be unwise to do so. Psychiatrists and clinical psychologists are frequently placed in such a situation. They may realize that a client feels persecuted and threatened, and that he would like them to reinforce his perceptions. Still, they may decide that the client's mental health would suffer from such reinforcement. As a result, they may choose to withhold social support on the assumption that any immediate resentment on his part can be eliminated over the longer course of the entire communication transaction. In a similar vein, parents must sometimes deny children certain prerogatives, even though they realize the child wants these behavioral options and would like the parent to agree to them.

A model of the prediction-making process

Although the transactional definition of empathy fits our conceptualization of interpersonal communication, one key question remains: *how does a communicator process data so as to arrive at accurate discriminations and subsequent predictions*? In order to deal with this question, we need to develop a model of the prediction-making process (step 1 in our transactional definition for empathy). Our model of prediction-making is derived from Miller and Dollard's (1941) description of the social learning process. These authors identify four vital elements of social learning: drive, cue, response, and reward.

A *drive* is any strong stimulus that impels action. If a door-to-door salesman were not driven to acquire money and to reap the physical and social rewards associated with financial success, he would not spend hours each day communicating with potential customers. If certain conventiongoers were not driven to realize the social rewards accruing from successful contacts with conventioneers of the opposite sex, they would not squander their energies competing with their peers. If Gerry and Mark were not driven to make money, and/or impress their colleagues, and/or promulgate their viewpoint, they would not devote months to writing this book. Although it is often difficult to specify the precise stimuli that impel a man to action (as we have suggested, by emphasizing the "and/ors" in the last example), we know that without motivation he would not behave.

In social situations, *cues* guide or direct behavior. Cues are distinctive stimuli that impose meaning on the environment. If a male conventiongoer is motivated to establish contact with a female counterpart, his subsequent behaviors are guided by many cues. Some signposts are quite obvious; for instance, he uses gross cultural cues of dress and appearance to identify a female. Even here, however, some females will possess stronger cue properties than others: they may be unusually attractive or striking; they may be clad in eye-catching attire; or they may be exceptionally loud or vivacious. After tentatively selecting a particular woman, the male's eventual response will be determined by still other cues. He will watch to see if she is conscious of his presence; he will catch her eye to obtain a nonverbal emotional barometer. If certain cues are present—or if he perceives they are—the man will eventually approach the woman and initiate conversation. If the cues are absent—or not perceived—he will begin the quest anew.

As we have already indicated, *responses* are the actual behaviors elicited by the cues. Changing one's sales pitch in midstream, ap-

proaching a person of the opposite sex at a cocktail party, or tearing up and rewriting several pages of book manuscript are all complex response sequences occasioned by particular cue patterns. Thus, as we have repeatedly underscored, one's responses are based on predictions arrived at by assessing the cues in a given situation.

Finally, *rewards* are pleasant events that follow a particular response; because they are drive-reducing, they increase the probability that the response will be repeated under similar cue circumstances. If a particular nonverbal behavior (cue) occasions initiation of a conversation (response) and the communication is favorably received (reward), then given a desire to establish contact (drive), a similar nonverbal behavior is more likely to elicit attempted initiation of conversation.

Stimulus generalization and stimulus discrimination in our model

If cue patterns had to be exactly the same to elicit a response, little learning could occur. Stimulus generalization negates this possibility: *reward for making a specific response to a given pattern of cues strengthens not only the tendency for that pattern of cues to elicit the response, but also the tendency for other similar cue patterns to elicit the response.* Generally speaking, the less similar the cue pattern, the less the likelihood of generalization.

This process of stimulus generalization is graphically illustrated in figure 6.1, which displays a typical generalization gradient. A response is learned—i.e., it is rewarded—in association with some original pattern of cues and then generalized to similar cue patterns. The slope of the gradient represents both the degree of similarity to the original cue pattern and the likelihood that the original response will be performed. Thus, the probability of the original response being elicited is high for cue patterns 1 and 2, but relatively low for 7 and 8.

This brings us to a consideration of stimulus discrimination: *by rewarding a response to one pattern of cues and punishing a response to a somewhat different pattern, a discrimination may be gradually established.* Once established, a discrimination increases the specificity of the cue-response connection and corrects inappropriate generalizations.

Applying the model

In chapter 4 we discussed how a small child develops patterns of communicative control. Now suppose the child is frequently driven to seek candy, but his parents, heeding the injunctions of numerous

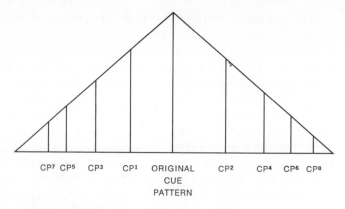

Fig. 6.1 A gradient showing the generalization
of responses from the original pattern of cue stimuli
to other patterns

dental and health authorities, are reluctant to grant his request. One day after a refusal, the child screams, falls on the floor, and kicks his feet. This behavior probably does not represent a conscious strategy, or a deliberately invoked control pattern, for obtaining the candy; instead, it results from frustration induced by parental blockage of a goal. But suppose, after a minute or two, the father exclaims, "Oh, give him the candy! Anything to quiet the racket." The next time the child is refused candy he will probably throw a tantrum again. Moreover, should the response continue to be followed by a reward, a parental refusal to purchase a new toy will likely trigger a tantrum, as will a visiting uncle's unwillingness to cater to the child's sweet tooth. In other words, the child's communication behavior will be based on a process of stimulus generalization similar to that discussed in chapter 1. Having been rewarded for communicating a certain way in one situation, he generalizes this behavior to similar situations. Although the candy was replaced by a toy, the parents still acted as frustrators, and although the parents were replaced by a visiting uncle, the candy remained prominent in the picture. Thus, the cue patterns were rather similar to the original pattern under which the response was learned.

Should the child be refused a pencil by his first-grade teacher, he is less likely to throw a tantrum, since the cue pattern departs more radically from the original. Still, a tantrum may occur, for small children often generalize rather indiscriminately. If our hypothetical child does throw a tantrum following the teacher's refusal of a pencil and the teacher reacts by placing him in the corner or depriving him of recess, the child probably will begin to learn a discrimination. If so, he will continue to throw tantrums when denied candy by his parents, but not when refused a pencil by his teacher. Such a change occurs when the child becomes capable of discriminating between parents and teacher as relevant cue stimuli.

Communication behaviors fit the model nicely; i.e., we learn message strategies that are rewarded in the presence of particular cue patterns, and then generalize these strategies to similar situations. Think back to your first weeks of school when you were learning to communicate with a strange, new person called teacher. For one or more of a variety of reasons, you were driven to seek the teacher's approval: your parents stressed the importance of good grades; you felt your peer status would be enhanced by the teacher's social support; or you were intellectually inquisitive and you realized teacher approval would facilitate learning. As time passed, you learned what responses would be rewarding; furthermore, you discovered that when certain cue patterns were present, some responses would be punished. In short, you acquired numerous cue-response linkages and established certain discriminations.

Even before the year ended, you may have been forced to generalize. Perhaps your teacher was ill, and a substitute took over the class. Certainly, you relied on generalization when you advanced to the next grade. Since the cue patterns were very similar, the best initial predictions you could make about your communication behaviors with the new teacher led you to respond the same way as you had the previous year. At the outset, then, the gradient of generalization from "first-year teacher" to "second-year teacher" was flat.

But teachers, while alike in many regards, differ in numerous crucial respects. Some thrive on controversy and disagreement; others abhor dissent. Some encourage student involvement; others prefer a teacher-centered classroom. Some place great stock in neat, orthodox work; others prefer disheveled creativity. When we ignore these differences, choosing instead to base predictions on perceived similarities, stimulus generalization guides our communication behavior and communication is noninterpersonal. When we seek to identify differences in cue patterns and to alter message strategies accordingly, our predictions are grounded in stimulus discrimination and there exists the possibility for interpersonal communication.

Discriminating cue stimuli

Most cues are much more subtle than those used with our hypothetical child. The trick, of course, is to spot changes in cue patterning. Take the question of reasoned dissent from, or conformity with, a teacher's viewpoint. Since it is educationally desirable to encourage healthy controversy and argument, few (if any) teachers will say, "In this class, I expect every student to agree completely with my views, and I will punish those who do not." Such a statement, while constituting a powerful cue to guide behavior, borders on educational heresy. Still, we have all known teachers who dislike and punish dissent. In order to avoid such punishment, one must be able to discriminate cues and thus to predict whether teacher X prefers conformity or conflict. (Of course, a student might know that he will be punished for dissenting and yet choose to do so; but if avoidance of punishment takes priority over the right to dissent, one must be able to identify teachers who punish dissenting students.) Often, these cues are extremely subtle: a slightly raised eyebrow, a barely perceptible change in intensity or tone of voice, a nervous twitch of the hand, momentary hesitation, or a comment with faint sarcastic overtones.

Accurate prediction hinges on the ability to detect such cues. Some persons are either incapable of making or unwilling to make the needed discriminations. Although motivated by the same drives as more accurate predictors, they see the same cues in every situation. Consequently, they develop habitual modes of response, and their communication behavior often goes unrewarded. Such people begin with a set of predictive generalizations for various types of fellow communicators (e.g., "All teachers expect student conformity"; "All women prefer to be dominated") and tailor their communication to these generalizations. As figure 6.2 depicts, these noninterpersonal types suffer from what can be called a flat generalization gradient. In this figure the dotted slope represents "actual" degree of similarity to the original cue pattern, whereas the solid slope represents the communicator's perceived degree of similarity and therefore the probability of performance of the original response.

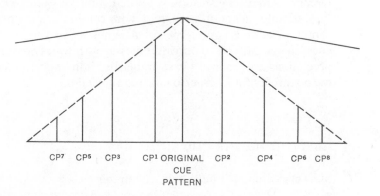

CP7   CP5   CP3   CP1 ORIGINAL   CP2   CP4   CP6   CP8
                        CUE
                        PATTERN

Fig. 6.2   Generalization gradient
of an unskilled discriminator

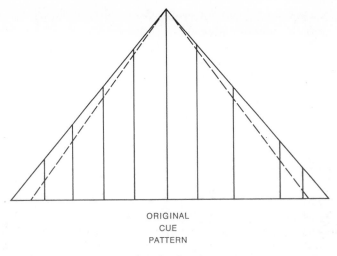

ORIGINAL
CUE
PATTERN

Fig. 6.3   Generalization gradient
of a skilled discriminator

By contrast, a highly skilled predictor can discriminate exceedingly
fine distinctions in cue patterning. As figure 6.3 shows, the generalization gradient for such persons is quite steep. Note also the close
correspondence between "actual" degree of similarity to the original
cue pattern, represented by the dotted slope, and the communicator's
perceived degree of similarity, represented by the solid slope. This
configuration suggests that performance or non-performance of the
original response conforms closely to the relevant cue pattern. Obviously, the skilled predictor has a much greater chance of moving to
the interpersonal level. He may learn a particular response in con-
junction with a pattern of cues associated with a given individual.
When he communicates with another person, many of the same cues
may be present. Nevertheless, because of his finely honed ability to
discriminate, he detects a subtle difference in the pattern and adjusts
his messages accordingly. As a result, he is likely to be much more
successful in controlling the environment than someone with a relatively flat generalization gradient.

What accounts for differences in the ability to discriminate cue
stimuli? In chapter 5 we considered some ways that one's cognitive style can inhibit or facilitate discrimination and subsequent
prediction-making. In addition, physiological factors may sometimes contribute to discriminative difficulties. A person who has poor
eyesight will sometimes fail to observe subtle visual stimuli such as
momentary trembling or a rapid change in facial expression. By the
same token, poor hearing may cause one to miss a subtle auditory cue.

Such physiological differences are themselves enough to ensure variation in discriminative ability.

But to say that not everyone can be an All-American quarterback or an Academy Award winning actress in no way implies that persons cannot improve their forward passing or their stage diction. *Many failures to discriminate cue stimuli stem from careless communication habits.* If a person is easily distracted, inattentive, or self-centered, it is hardly surprising that he misses a myriad of cues and therefore cannot make accurate predictions. The first step to improved discrimination, better prediction, and hence, more effective interpersonal communication lies in monitoring one's own behavior and developing careful communication habits.

Effects of practice on discriminative ability

Research indicates that frequent practice sharpens discriminative skills. Rosenthal and his associates (undated) have developed a test for measuring differential skills in judging nonverbal cues. This Profile of Nonverbal Sensitivity (PONS) consists of a 45-minute movie containing numerous auditory and visual segments. Persons are asked to circle the description of a real-life situation that best suits the segment they have just seen (visual only), heard (auditory only), or seen and heard (both visual and auditory). Every person receives a score for accuracy and subscores for each channel, scene, and scene type.

Several of Rosenthal's findings relate directly to the effects of practice on discriminating nonverbal cues. For example, actors consistently demonstrate unusually good nonverbal skills. A partial explanation for this fact can be found in the amount of time they spend learning and practicing these skills, though it is also possible that people who gravitate toward the stage have more innate nonverbal ability than non-actors. In a similar vein, mothers with toddlers (who, after all, do most of their communicating nonverbally) have better nonverbal abilities than do women without children, who may not have the opportunity for this kind of practice. Finally, Rosenthal's cross-cultural research reveals that greater cultural distance from American cultures leads to less nonverbal accuracy on the PONS test, which deals with American scenes. Since nonverbal behavior is generally thought to be at least partially culture-bound, this finding attests not only to the importance of practice but also to the limitations of noninterpersonal predictions grounded in cultural data.

Some preliminary research we have conducted supports the notion that practice leads to more accurate discrimination of nonverbal cues. The research utilizes a series of slides, each containing three simple cartoon faces. Figure 6.4 depicts the faces on three of the slides. In each case, the face at the left is the stimulus face, and the two others are matching faces. In 6.4a, both faces are identical to the stimulus face. In 6.4b, the face at the far right differs from the stimulus face and the first matching face. Since it differs in several respects, the cue discrimination is relatively easy. Finally, in 6.4c, the first matching face differs from the stimulus face and the matching face at the far right. Moreover, since it departs from the others on only one element, the discrimination is relatively difficult.

Fig. 6.4   Three sets of faces used
to measure discrimination of nonverbal cues

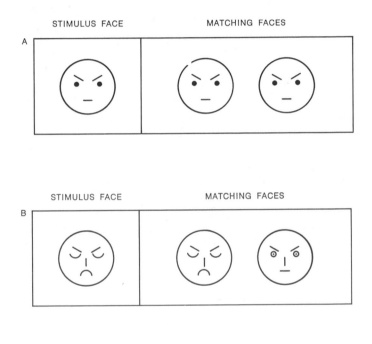

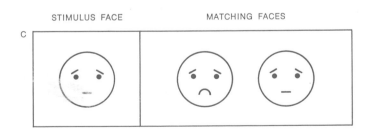

These slides are shown at rapid exposure rates (.5 seconds, 1 second, and 2 seconds have been used). The individual circles either same, if he perceives that both matching faces are identical to the stimulus face, or different, if he perceives that one of the faces is different. Presently the test consists of 35 slides, chosen from an original pool of 102.

Many of our results are hardly surprising. When a group takes the test for the first time, there is wide variance in the number of correct responses: a few people make almost all the judgments accurately; a small percentage err consistently; and the majority cluster around 50 percent accuracy. Difficulty of discrimination and length of exposure have the expected effects: more errors occur on subtle discriminations and at very rapid exposure rates. But even under the most adverse conditions, some persons maintain a high batting average, while others strike out repeatedly.

Some persons have participated in a series of learning trials with the slides. As would be expected, performance improves with practice. Most important, better performance generalizes to slides that have not previously been shown. While persons who initially perform very poorly seldom reach extremely high plateaus of accuracy, they do make steady progress. Presently, we are designing studies to identify some of the traits of extremely good and extremely poor discriminators.

Caution must, of course, be exercised in generalizing these results to real-life communication situations. In fact, we are also planning studies to test the prediction-making effectiveness of high and low scorers in ongoing dyadic conversations. Obviously, the visual stimuli used are tightly controlled, and their simplicity departs markedly from the multiplicity of cues present in actual communication encounters. We are confident, however, that performance on the test will be at least moderately related to predictive effectiveness when communicating with others. If so, practice-related improvement on the test should facilitate prediction-making in actual interactions and, ultimately, increase one's interpersonal communication potential.

Although we are aware of the desirability of an auditory counterpart to our test, we have not as yet developed one. Rogers, Scheerer and Rosenthal (1971) have described a simple system for content filtering human speech. The system renders content unintelligible while retaining such vocal cues as intonation, rhythm, tempo, and continuity. Such a device has promise for testing auditory discriminative ability and could be used in practice sessions to sharpen acuity. Again, questions of generalizability remain to be answered, for in actual communication it is usually impossible to separate content and vocal cues.

Some strategies
for improving discriminative ability

Our strategic injunction to practice, while capturing the essence of discriminative improvement, affords little information about specific steps to take. A fruitful area for investigation lies in the identification of practice techniques that maximize progress. Since we are unaware of such research, we will suggest some admittedly prescriptive strategies, which are supported more by reason and common sense than by research findings.

1. *Practice listening with your eyes, as well as your ears.*
Although there has been considerable interest in the improvement of listening skill, the dominant approach to listening suffers from tunnel vision—or perhaps more appropriately, tunnel hearing. Typically, attention has focused on retention of message content, not ability to discriminate vocal cues. Although message content cues may sometimes assist in prediction-making, cues of intonation, rhythm, and tempo are often better discriminative barometers. Most of us have questioned the sincerity of a remark such as "I'll be happy to discuss your problem with you," because it was uttered with a tinge of sarcasm, exasperation, or frenzy.

Active, successful listening relies on both visual and auditory channels. A rich array of cues may be available to the eyes, but not the ears. One of the first careless communication habits to which we often fall prey is single channel, auditory listening. We assume that we can listen effectively while reading the newspaper, checking out other diners in the restaurant, or completing another memorandum. If one's only concern is comprehension of message content, engaging in perceptual double duty may sometimes work. Certainly, we are seldom as far afield as the typical company of basic trainees who, in the midst of a classroom lecture, stood up when the instructor said, "All right, anyone paying attention to me ignore this next command. ON YOUR FEET!" Still, if we are concerned with the mood of the message source, or with discriminating relevant differences between a source and similar ones, our eyes are invaluable allies.

Practice being an active listener. Focus your eyes, as well as your ears, on the other communicator. In particular, watch for changes in body posture, body tension, body position, facial expression, and gesture. Consciously assess the consistency of what you are perceiving through verbal and nonverbal channels; try to judge whether what a person is saying jibes with his nonverbal behavior. As much as possible, try to compare and contrast the cues you are receiving with those you have received from other communicators. Try particularly to identify conspicuous differences. Enhance the development of active listening by providing verbal and nonverbal feedback; active listeners do not assume a posture of stony silence. Moreover, intelligent use of feedback provides a check on accuracy of discrimination and elicits more cues for processing and evaluation.

2. *Practice screening out distracting situational and environmental stimuli.*

Perhaps very skilled predictors can discriminate relevant cues in crowded subways, noisy offices, raucous stadium crowds, or busy classrooms. Most of us, however, succumb to the countless distracting stimuli in such situations, and the price we pay is a sharply reduced potential for discriminating the cues provided by other communicators. If we want to increase our interpersonal communication potential, we must practice screening out distracting stimuli.

One way, of course, is to avoid serious communicative efforts in inappropriate environments or, stated positively, to arrange the environment so as to minimize distractions. For many years, Gerry kept his office door open constantly, because he thought that doing so would help create a climate of communicative openness and keep people from feeling that he was secretive or remote. Unfortunately, he found that the communicative environment resulting from this policy left much to be desired. When he tried to converse with someone in his office, he was distracted by people talking or laughing outside and even interrupted quite often by someone bursting into the office. These intrusions made it difficult for him to attend to the person he was really trying to talk with, and he sometimes felt he had missed important cues the person was sending. Now, save for the most casual encounters, his door is closed during conversations, with the result that communication fidelity has improved.

Frequently we have options about the environment in which we communicate. When such options exist, try to arrange an environment maximally free of distractions, annoying or pleasant. Turn off the television or radio and tune in to the other person. Find a quiet setting free of other people. If possible, postpone talking about something serious until after the dishes, homework, or other distracting tasks are out of the way. In addition, try to erase as much intrapersonal "noise" as possible: forget problems at the office, midterms, or international crises—unless, of course, these issues are related to the conversation.

Sometimes we have no opportunity to arrange, or rearrange, the environment. Consider the dramatic cliché where a psychiatrist or a policeman tries to convince a disturbed person not to jump from a midtown building or to persuade an armed suspect in a crowded department store to surrender his weapon peacefully. Although the situation calls for unerring accuracy in discriminating cues ("Will he really jump if I take another step?" or "Is he really bent upon pulling the trigger?") the environment is considerably less than ideal. Yet quite frequently, both in fiction and real life, the mission of saving lives or preventing injuries is accomplished.

It may be argued that these situations are atypical, that the cost of communicative failure is so high that every ounce of attention is bound to be riveted on the other communicator, regardless of the number of distracting environmental stimuli. If this is true, and we have no reason to doubt it, an important caveat is implied for anyone wishing to minimize the harmful influence of environmental stimuli on discriminative effectiveness: *the primacy of the communicative transaction must always be accepted.* It is ironic that we accept this proposition for strangers on a building ledge or in a department store, but often reject it for our families or close friends. Perhaps when in more familiar surroundings, we cannot imagine that a communication failure could trigger such catastrophic outcomes. To be sure, no single failure is likely to produce an outcome as dramatic as death, but the cumulative impact of a series of failures may be reflected in a seriously disturbed personality or in the rupture of a potentially rewarding relationship.

To a great extent, the strategic steps for screening out distracting environmental stimuli closely parallel those for active listening. Practice developing a mental set that emphasizes the importance of the communicative venture; become motivated to observe and listen to the other person. If important communication encounters must occur in highly public surroundings, do not fall victim to the conventional wisdom regarding the appropriateness of cool detachment, social reserve, and psychic distance. Obviously, excessive concern with monitoring your own demeanor ensures that many relevant cues will go unnoticed. Students of perception say that the stimuli we select are determined by our needs and motivations. Consequently, if we cultivate a high need to communicate, communication-oriented stimuli will dominate our perceptual field and other irrelevant stimuli will recede.

3. *Observe good and poor discriminators in action.*
Everyone probably knows people who fall at the two ends of the continuum of discriminative skill. One individual is a superlative predictor, capable of spotting the nuances and subtle overtones of every communicative situation; the other is an insensitive communicator, oblivious to even the most blatant, obvious cues.

Much can be gained by observing these two extremes. When one is an outsider looking in, considerable vicarious learning can occur. For one thing, your own ego is not on the line, and since there is less emotional investment, the situation can be viewed more objectively. Moreover, freedom from communicative responsibilities permits you to scrutinize the behavior of both communicators with added care and thoroughness.

Watch the ways that the skilled discriminator alters his ongoing message behaviors. Try to identify the nonverbal or vocal cues that trigger a change in message strategy. Study his methods of relating to the other communicator, and observe how he uses feedback to elicit additional information. In particular, critically analyze your own typical modes of communicating by comparing them with the techniques used by the adept predictor.

Now repeat this process for the unskilled discriminator. See if you can pick up cues that he misses. Note that his message behavior often fails to conform with the empathic demands of the situation, that he often generalizes maladaptively, rather than making relevant discriminations. Reflect upon how you would respond in the ongoing interaction, and identify points at which your behavior departs from the unskilled discriminator's. See if you can recreate the cues that caused you to behave differently. In short, learn as much as you can about how not to communicate and develop an understanding of why it is difficult, if not impossible, for this individual to move to the interpersonal level.

4. *Construct an inventory of the nonverbal and vocal cues you typically present.*
Obviously, it is dangerous to assume that everyone else behaves the same way you do; such an assumption is a prime example of maladaptive generalization. Still, to say that people vary in the kinds of cues they present is not to say they have nothing in common. A study of your own cue repertory, if applied judiciously and intelligently, can provide you with numerous insights into the nonverbal and vocal behaviors of others.

One way to begin your analysis is by role-playing a variety of communicative situations with friends or acquaintances. In our classes we sometimes use a role-play in which one participant plays a student who demands a grade change and another plays a professor reluctant to make the change. Although no role-playing exercise can capture the totality of a real-life communication situation, we find that as the scenario unfolds and the actors become engrossed in their parts, numerous cues begin to surface. The participants may be aware of some of the cues they are presenting, but usually they are not. The outcome of the confrontation varies; sometimes the professor relents and sometimes the student gives up. Frequently, self-analysis by the

two participants, augmented by questions and comments from other class members, unearths many of the cues presented and pinpoints instances when cues were or were not spotted by each communicator. There is often agreement among participants and class members alike that the end result can be explained by the differing cue sensitivity of the two role-players.

Videotaping equipment can help you inventory your cue repertory. Once an interaction has been taped, it can be studied exhaustively and at your convenience. Moreover, after you have catalogued your own cue repertory, you can compare and contrast it with the repertories of other communicators in similar situations. The hard work involved in such analyses should improve your ability to discriminate relevant cue stimuli and thus help you move to the interpersonal level.

Summary

These four strategies, taken singly or together, do not guarantee overnight discriminative success. Even after considerable practice, some careless communication habits may keep you from becoming a highly skilled discriminator. We do believe, however, that most communicators do not normally operate at their maximum discriminative and predictive capacities. Conscientious practice cannot fail to close the gap between present ability and ultimate capacity.

The second step toward empathy: communicating with others in rewarding ways

Relevant cue discrimination and subsequent accurate prediction, while sufficient to move one to the interpersonal level, constitute only the first step in a two-step transactional view of the empathic process. Our second step demands that the prediction culminate in message behavior perceived as rewarding. Only when this occurs is one party to a communication transaction likely to assert that the other party is a good empathizer. Such an assertion is a shorthand way of saying that the person (1) understands, or is capable of predicting, how one feels and, (2) given his understanding, is willing to communicate, and capable of communicating, in ways that are pleasant and rewarding. This complex receiving and transmitting activity captures the essence of our transactional definition of empathy—a definition best suited to the student of the transactional process of communication.

As we have previously indicated, our definition does not seek to impose value constraints on the process of empathy. Indeed, since the parties involved must determine what is rewarding for them, some very bizarre, socially deviant communication behaviors may sometimes be perceived as empathic. George and Martha in *Who's Afraid of Virginia Woolf?*, for example, perceive each other as empathic throughout much of the play; they play their idiosyncratic games according to an agreed-upon rule structure. Only when George departs from the rules and kills their imaginary son does Martha's faith in his empathic skills begin to falter. No longer is he communicating with her in ways she perceives as rewarding, even though he has probably predicted accurately how she will respond to the son's death. It is this two-step, transactional view of the process that distinguishes the communication student's interest in empathy from that of the physiologist or social psychologist.

We have already suggested that professional or parental sanctions may restrain a person from taking the second empathic step. For example, a psychiatrist or a parent may sometimes decide that rewarding certain message behavior would be counterproductive. In some situations, however, taking the second step may be inconsistent with a person's own goals. You may decide against reinforcing someone, not so much out of consideration for his best interests, but to protect yourself. For example, if you recognize that someone is trying to cheat you (step one), you are not likely to play the role of sucker just to make him happy (step two).

Beyond these considerations, it may be difficult to understand why a person would be unwilling to communicate empathically. Quite simply, some people's interpersonal needs may prevent them from extending understanding or sympathy. An individual who is hostile, feels threatened by others, or has deep-seated sadomasochistic needs is more likely to use aggression and punishment than sympathetic understanding in communicating with others. If a person's cognitive style leads him to distrust and suspect members of certain groups, he may communicate belligerently with all of the group's members, even though he can discriminate relevant differences and predict the ways that particular members would like him to communicate.

Summary

Empathy is more than a psychophysiological response, more than a social perception skill. It requires that a person both recognize someone's needs and respond to them. Similar feelings and accurate observation are necessary to empathizing, but our conception of empathy requires that they be accompanied by overt interpersonal involvement.

It is hard to say whether recognition or action is the more demanding step. Together, these two tasks challenge any communicator. To interpret a person's behavior meaningfully and accurately and then translate the interpretation into an appropriate response requires sensitivity, energy, and talent. We hope you agree that the mutual benefits of empathy are more than adequate compensation.

Probes

1. In taking a behavioral approach toward empathy, Gerry and Mark assert that it is impossible to put yourself in someone else's shoes. Develop an argument supporting their position and a second argument attacking it. Do you find it useful to think of empathy as a process of getting into another's head?

2. Study several friends and acquaintances and try to identify the cues you use when communicating with them. Do you find some of your friends easier to "read" than others? How certain are you that you are interpreting their cues accurately? What things about the persons cause you to vary in the degree of certainty you ascribe to your predictions?

3. Try the handwriting analysis experiment described on page 172. What percentage of people agree with your analysis? If you encounter people who disagree, try to develop your own personality description of them. In what ways, if any, do their personalities differ from most persons you know?

4. Are you acquainted with people who seem to have rather flat generalization gradients? How would you characterize their communication transactions with others? Can you see any relationships between the shape of one's generalization gradient and the cognitive styles discussed in chapter 5?

5. Suppose someone consistently responds to you in nonrewarding, or punishing, ways. These responses may occur because the individual is not interpreting cues accurately or because he does not choose to respond in rewarding ways, even though he can read the cues accurately. What evidence would you use to determine which of these reasons more adequately explains his nonrewarding message behavior? How would your conclusion influence your personal judgment of him?

6. In what ways, if any, does our frequent exposure to television and other mass media affect our abilities to make accurate cue discriminations? Consider ways that the media may facilitate this process and ways in which they may hinder it.

7. "Empathy is relatively unimportant in noninterpersonal communication transactions." Attack, defend, or modify this statement.

Communicating
Interpersonally:

Communication
Relationships

Thus far we have dealt with the raw materials of communication relationships: individual communicators. Next we consider individuals in the context of a communication relationship. More specifically, the three chapters in this part address the following key issues:

How do relationships get started? (chapter 7)

What are the principal dynamics of established relationships? (chapter 8)

What are some sources of and solutions to major relational problems? (chapter 9)

There are many kinds of communication relationships. Some are brief and are restricted to the exchange of a few cultural level, noninterpersonal messages. Other noninterpersonal relationships are conducted primarily at a sociological level. They may be either informal (acquaintances, classmates) or formal (colleagues, business associates). Most infrequent are the sustained interpersonal relationships we have with friends, families, and lovers. But even though these are rarer than the others, they are usually most important for us. Consequently, the following three chapters are oriented primarily toward interpersonal relationships.

Relationships must begin somewhere. Chapter 7 identifies the dimensions of social situations that contribute vitally to their establishment and development. Such factors as temporal and spatial proximity and the opportunity for sharing certain kinds of information form part of the noninterpersonal foundation of interpersonal relationships. We discuss some of the influences that abet the "natural" development of interpersonal relationships and some of the message strategies people can use to facilitate relational growth.

Most of the factors that play a role in relational development continue to influence the course of established relationships. Some of these variables, however, assume greater significance than others for long-term harmony. Chapter 8 examines selected characteristics that bear heavily on transaction patterns in ongoing relationships. We begin with one of the most pervasive of all relational dimensions: the degree to which communicators are one-up or one-down in respect to each other. This dimension has a profound relational influence on all phases of message exchange. In addition, we describe communication patterns that produce relational agreement and disagreement, and we identify some of the processes people must understand in order to maintain relational stability. Trust is one characteristic that can be nurtured or destroyed by different kinds of communication behaviors. Our treatment of relational trust is somewhat different from previous discussions, and we think you will find it useful.

Chapter 9 centers on some of the problems faced by communicators in established interpersonal relationships. All relationships run into difficulties, whether serious or trivial. Unfortunately, many people lack either the understanding or the skill needed to minimize the mutual damage these difficulties can cause. We analyze a variety of relational communication problems and suggest some strategies for constructively dealing with them. Two of our major concerns are conflict management and relational termination. Communicators have a great deal to gain from their relational conflicts if they approach conflict situations with open minds and effective communication strategies. Finally, we point out some of the danger signals which may indicate that a relationship's best future is no future at all.

7

The fundamental fact of human existence is man with man.
What is peculiarly characteristic of the human world is above all
that something takes place between one being and another
the like of which can be found nowhere in nature.

Martin Buber, *Between Man and Man*

The Development
of Interpersonal Relationships

ou probably know people who hold views similar to those expressed below (though not necessarily on the subject of communication).

> GERRY: You know, the study of human communication is wildly complex, full of unresolved mysteries, unanswered questions, only fleeting glimpses of certainty. One can observe communication behavior for a lifetime and yet find there are more riddles than reasons.
>
> MARK: What is it you want to know, Gerry? Maybe I can help.

Older, wiser men come to realize the limitations of their knowledge, whereas younger, brasher men tend to roll the universe into a ball, triumphantly but mistakenly exclaiming, "I've got it!" Of course, neither approach to communication is completely right or wrong. Probably a carefully contrived balance, something between mumbled musing and impetuous pronouncement, is best suited to unravelling the mysteries of communication behavior.

Such a balanced position is useful when dealing with the question of how interpersonal relationships develop. Some of us are mystified by this process: "Why did John and I become close friends, but I still can't get along with Harold?" or "She and I have known each other for five years, but I still don't really know her." Others of us seem quite sure of how interpersonal relationships develop: "You got to know John because you like him, and you don't like Harold that much," or "You never really got to know her because you never really talked to her."

While such answers impose a pattern on our social environments and give some certitude to our psyches, they are ultimately about as useful as the trite and not always true proclamations, "Birds of a feather flock together" and "Opposites attract." We still need to know why we like certain people and under what conditions bluebirds will attract bluebirds and not sparrows. Since interpersonal relationships can be scarce and highly valued commodities, most of us want to have some useful, satisfying explanations for how they come about. This chapter rests on the premise that while the scientific community has not yet rolled the universe into a ball, we can tell you a few things about relationship development that we hope you will find interesting and useful.

An overview of
the developmental process

An interpersonal relationship, as defined in chapter 2, is a communication relationship involving mutual predictions based on psychological data. When we talk about the development of interpersonal relationships, we refer to the processes whereby people come into contact with one another, acquire and evaluate information about one another, and come to base predictions about one another's communication behavior primarily on psychological data. Opportunity for contact is clearly a necessary condition for the development of any kind of communication relationship. Beyond this, the duration of the contact, as well as the context in which the contact takes place, has a strong bearing on other relational processes. Information sharing is important because it provides a basis for people to decide what kind of relationship they want to have together: they can take stock of one another and estimate the probability of mutual reward should they decide to venture toward sustained contact. Information is only valuable, of course, when people are able to use it to coordinate effectively their transactions and to elicit further, perhaps interpersonal, information.

Three features of developmental processes should be clarified, since they are often subject to confusion and misunderstanding. First, people sometimes neglect to consider the transactional nature of these processes. Two people, at least, participate in them, and each plays an important part. While it may at times be useful to understand why one person decides to establish a relationship with another, we are more interested in examining how two people establish a mutual relationship with each other. To put it pragmatically, if a person wants to work toward creating an interpersonal relationship with another individual, it is not enough to understand his own gravitation toward that person. It would also be helpful for him to understand what the other party might find appealing about him, so that he can maximize the exchange of relational rewards. In addition, if one of the transactants is unable or unwilling to communicate interpersonally, then no matter how great the other's skill or desire, the relationship is fixed at a noninterpersonal "ceiling."

Second, relational development is notoriously complex. The process cannot be explained by studying one or two variables. Part of the process may be cognitive: people sometimes deliberately decide to establish relationships together. Roommates, for example, may decide even before meeting each other that it would be to their advantage to communicate interpersonally. Emotional processes may also provide the initial impetus, as when people fall in love. Interpersonal communication just seems to "happen" then, without either lover "deciding" anything. But these factors cannot sustain a relationship if the communicators lack understanding, cannot achieve communicative accuracy, or are unable to establish patterns of mutual control. Furthermore, all communication relationships develop in a social environment. It is easy to neglect the influence of other people when charting a relational course and to focus merely on the two principal communicators. However, each person's experiences with other people influence the reasons why he established the relationship, the kinds of rewards he expects from it, and particularly his assessment of the relationship. These influences are important both in the establishment of a relationship and throughout its course.

Third, any approach to relational development should distinguish between interpersonal and noninterpersonal developmental conditions and processes. For example, according to our conception of interpersonal communication, much of what is commonly considered to be interpersonal attraction should be classed as noninterpersonal. To say that liking someone because of his or her physical appearance is an instance of interpersonal attraction seems inconsistent with our conceptualization. Although attraction on the basis of beauty involves discriminating the subjectively beautiful from the subjectively unbeautiful, the basis for attraction often lies in a cultural stereotype: you select the beautiful person from the class of people your culture defines as beautiful. Consider also the case of one student being attracted to another on the basis of the latter's highly rated academic performance. Often such attraction is based on the values of university professors and students who teach incoming group members that superior academic achievement is to be admired. Consequently, the attraction may not be interpersonal but sociological in origin.

We believe that these three considerations contribute to a more enlightening and useful perspective on relational development. We have already discussed other important factors in relational development in preceding chapters: compatibility of patterns of communicative control, flexible and open cognitive styles, and empathic skill. Try to keep these factors in mind as we move ahead.

The noninterpersonal foundations
for the development
of interpersonal relationships

We must first consider the noninterpersonal contexts in which interpersonal relationships are born. *Any kind of communication relationship involves the intersection of two or more individuals in space, in time, and in the context of some information about each other*; that is, a communication relationship involves the sharing of space, time, and information. We will concentrate on these three dimensions in describing the noninterpersonal foundations as factors in the initial formation of relationships, rather than as an influence on relationships already under way.

Space

Disregarding any pen pals we may have, our communication relationships have all depended on some opportunity for face-to-face contact. Sharing a space dimension with other people is important for acquiring the kinds of information about them we need in order to make communicative predictions. But the importance of space goes beyond the opportunity for acquiring information. We should not overlook the simple yet profound assertion that we initiate communication relationships almost exclusively with the people who share space with us (with the exception, of course, of people with whom we come into contact only through the mail or by telephone). There are not an unlimited number of fish in the sea; instead, the relationships in which we might possibly engage are constrained by the species of fish who swim in our waters. Several research studies (for example, Festinger, Schachter, and Back, 1950; Newcomb, 1956; Penny and Robertson, 1962) have centered on the propinquity hypothesis, which states that people communicate more frequently with persons who are nearest to them in space. Findings have shown that tenants of apartment buildings communicate more with their immediate neighbors than with people right around the corner, and that most of us tend to choose marriage partners from among the people who live fairly close to us.

There are several reasons for the importance of spatial relatedness. First, we need to know the people around us. Most of us are uncomfortable living among strangers; to the extent that the cohabitants of our spaces remain strangers, they do not help fulfill our social needs, and we cannot be very sure of our predictions about their behavior. Part of getting to know someone involves certifying that he is "nor-

mal" and that we shall not at some future time be surprised and perhaps adversely affected by some bizarre behavior of his.

Another important factor is energy: it is easier to form a relationship with someone nearer to us than with someone further away. Finally, it is often true that people who share a space also have many other things in common. People sharing an apartment building may have similar incomes and similar tastes in architecture. People going to the same university may have a similar value for the type of education that the university offers. People living in Los Angeles may share a preference for the West Coast or for large cities—maybe both.

These generalizations do not always hold. One can live in Los Angeles and hate large cities, seek new acquaintances outside his neighborhood because he tires of seeing the same faces, or never get to know the people in the house next door. Many of us maintain close ties with friends who live thousands of miles away. Nevertheless, if we define our spatial dimensions as those places where we regularly find ourselves during any given week, we find that most of our communication relationships are with people who inhabit the same space.

An additional factor in space relatedness is territoriality. Anthropologists (see, e.g., Watson, 1970) suggest that people need to stake out some well-defined space which they can call their own and which they will vigorously defend against an intruder. Note how intensely Archie Bunker demands exclusive rights to "his chair," and that in sports the home team usually has the edge even though the two teams are otherwise evenly matched. Our interest in territoriality only marginally involves the notion of defense; rather, our main concern is with the territoriality need as an impetus to relational development. Many territories cannot be mastered or defended alone. When people must associate with others to be at home in or to dominate certain territories, they have a basis for forming communication relationships. For example, when children go to summer camp, when newly recruited marines go to boot camp, when freshmen move into their dormitories, when people move to the big city, and when employees go to work in factories or office buildings, they are entering territories that, socially speaking, no one of them can own. They must turn to other members of the group for mutual assistance in making their environments more secure and comfortable. While there are exceptions to this rule—some people may not want to make certain environments their homes, and some people tend to remain isolates—we often rely on communication relationships to help us with our territorial needs.

In the sense in which we have been discussing it, communication enhances a rather abstract type of defense and ownership of a particular territory. Newman (1972) suggests that communication among neighbors in apartment buildings plays an important part in the concrete defense of their dwelling space. Citing the increase in robberies and personal assaults on urban residents, Newman questions whether the architecture of present apartment buildings does not impede inter-resident communication to the extent that one resident will not even phone the police if a neighbor is being mugged. He proposes a theory of defensible space, which involves a redesign for urban residential centers, one of the effects of which would be to facilitate and encourage closer communication among residents for the common defense of their homes against criminals. He argues that if people know one another they will be more likely to safeguard each other's lives and property.

Time

The length of time we share mutual space with people can be an important factor in relational development. Like space, the time dimension is tied to the information dimension: the longer we associate with people, the more likely we are to acquire information about them pertinent to the development of interpersonal communication relationships. The length of time that we expect to share spatial dimensions with other people can influence our decisions as to what kind of communication, if any, we may want to develop with them. For example, if the length of time we expect to spend with someone is the time it takes to pass him on the sidewalk, we will probably decide against forming any relationship at all. If we anticipate spending a long period of time with someone, however, we are usually quite interested in the communication relationship that will evolve. Furthermore, we may decide that if our association with another person is likely to last a while, it is worth the effort to develop an interpersonal relationship with that person. Conversely, if we anticipate a short, terminal association, we are more likely to disclose information about ourselves we would not disclose to someone who could later use the information against us—witness two strangers on a flight or in the airport cocktail lounge between flights.

We will mention one further aspect of the time dimension that is often overlooked. Toffler (1970) has raised an alarm concerning the increasing rate of change in our society and the effects of these rapid changes on our personal identities. Given accelerated change, persons search more urgently for objects in their environments that have stability and continuity. One source of stability is found in our associations with other people. The notion that old friends are paramount may assume greater relevance as more and more of our surroundings undergo significant change. Time, then, in the sense of relational longevity, may become a factor in and of itself when evaluating communication relationships.

Consider the following two examples. An acquaintance of the authors was looking forward to going home to spend Christmas vacation with his parents. Before he left for home, he mentioned the closeness he felt with his family and how warmly he anticipated the opportunity to associate with relatives during the holidays. His family had traditionally gathered on Christmas Eve for a reunion and an exchange of gifts. This Christmas, however, turned out differently. Our friend's grandfather had died during the previous summer, and, though no one in the family could have guessed this fact, the grandfather had been the focal point of the reunion; everyone had come together for the sake of the family patriarch. Without his unifying presence, the family spent Christmas Eve in their separate homes. For our friend the anticipated season of joy became one of loneliness and depression. The interpersonal relations he had expected with his parents did not materialize; he discovered that the only thing they had in common was the tradition, ritual, and comfort of the Christmas celebration. He had failed to recognize this interpersonal gulf in the glow of previous seasons.

Another acquaintance went home for the same Christmas vacation with different expectations. She had not been home for two years, and was going home this time only at her parents' request. During her college years she had drifted away from the economic, political, and social values of her parents. Since she no longer considered herself a Christian, she saw no point in celebrating a religious holiday. To her surprise, she found herself enjoying immensely the family gatherings of the holiday season. Relatives with whom she might never have been warm or friendly elsewhere seemed like treasured friends.

The experiences of these two people stem from similar factors. Our first friend expected to return to a haven of continuity, sameness, and familiarity, but failed to discover it. Our second friend rediscovered feelings that contrasted sharply to her otherwise constantly fluctuating world. It seems that for young people recently thrust from their home towns, old friends, and families, who have not yet found a new and rewarding pattern in the lives they must make for themselves, reclaiming some sense of continuity in themselves and some history to their existence can be highly gratifying.

Sam Clemens once remarked that when he was sixteen he questioned whether his father had an ounce of sense, but that when he reached age twenty-one he was amazed at how smart the old man had become in just five years. No doubt this change that Clemens perceived can be attributed to an increase in his own wisdom. But a revised explanation of this phenomenon may be more suited to the modern age. Many young people, once away from their families, are shocked at the lack of interpersonal communication they and their families had during their eighteen or twenty years together. We have heard one person remark: "I got to know my roommate better in six months than I did my father in ten years." To the extent that their personal identities are still insecure, people feel a need to return to their families and begin to communicate interpersonally. In this sense, time serves as a strong impetus to interpersonal communication: the longer you know someone, the more he may become a stable fixture of your identity, and the greater need you may have to initiate interpersonal communication with him.

Information

Information influences people's perceptions of others, and, in turn, perceptions influence the ways that people communicate. Therefore, we must take account of the information we acquire about others if we are to understand how communication relationships develop. We do not mean to imply a fixed time order in this process such that people must first acquire information and then form perceptions before they can communicate. Rather, the three activities are interdependent. People's perceptions constrain the type of information they pick up, as well as how they interpret it, and the way they communicate further affects their perceptions and their interpretations of new information. As you can see, it is difficult to make simplistic statements about the role of information in relational development.

As used here, information is any data that indicate (1) the level of reward we are likely to realize from communicating with a given individual (*an evaluative function*), or (2) how we should communicate with a given individual to maximize the probability of eliciting rewarding responses from him (*a pragmatic function*). Information might serve other functions, but we will restrict ourselves to these two. The first provides us with a base-level notion of whether or not we would like to form a relationship with a particular person. If we have little choice in the matter, as with co-workers or fellow classmates, it at least defines the nature of the relationship. Information that serves this function is evaluative. For example, our perceptions of a person's intelligence, sense of humor, or skill in a particular area may serve as evaluative information. Based on our information, we put the person into mental categories such as good/bad, exciting/boring, or potential friend/potential enemy.

Second, information tells us how to control most effectively another's response and how to channel most efficiently our energies toward this end. In this case information serves a pragmatic function.

For example, we might consider a person's need for ego support when deciding upon a particular control procedure to use when communicating with him. We also use pragmatic information to decide whether or not we can ever satisfactorily control an individual's responses.

There is nothing inherent in any item of information that dictates which function, evaluative or pragmatic, it shall serve. All information can serve either or both functions. For example, our information that a certain person is highly compassionate might be evaluative, if we can say we like or dislike compassionate people, and/or pragmatic, if we can make some assessment of our ability to control the responses of compassionate people.

In addition, the two functions are often interdependent. Because we like someone, we may also decide we can elicit fulfilling responses from him; or because we anticipate that we will be able to elicit fulfilling responses from him, we may consequently like him. Of course, the reverse is also true: we may evaluate a person negatively if we do not anticipate eliciting fulfilling responses from him. Some people argue that we examine not only the likelihood of being able to elicit fulfilling responses, but also the probability of being able to provide fulfilling responses for other persons. While there may be some intrinsic satisfaction in helping others, we consider the two as functionally equivalent. The basis for wanting to provide fulfilling responses is the expectation of a thank you, or the recognition of having exerted environmental control, which to us is a fulfilling response.

Research by Byrne (particularly Byrne and Rhamey, 1965; Byrne, 1969) strongly supports the interdependence of the evaluative and pragmatic functions. Byrne has found that people tend to like people who have attitudes similar to their own: that is, information about attitudinal similarity results in a positive evaluation. But what, Byrne asks, is the reason for this? Why should people like each other just because they think alike? Byrne concludes that the basis for attraction is not so much the similarity of attitudes, but that the similarity indicates the likelihood of obtaining rewards from one another. Liking someone, then, seems to be related to pragmatic concerns: the anticipation of being able to exercise control in a relationship with that person.

There are numerous sources of information about other people. We will consider four: the person himself, the extensions of the person, other people, and the social context in which we communicate with the person.

Source 1: The person himself
People provide information about themselves through their physical appearance, the things they say and do, and how they say and do them.

Of course, these modes of transmitting information are interdependent. The statement, "Move over, buddy!" uttered by a strapping person conveys different information than when the statement comes from someone frail. This is not to say that we get the same message from different people but interpret it differently according to certain nonverbal cues. Rather the message is an entity composed of a combination of information sources, verbal and nonverbal; we do not get a verbal message and then interpret it according to nonverbal cues. People, then, can be conceived of as messages, conveying information that we use for evaluative and pragmatic purposes.

Such messages need not be intentional, in the sense of being purposely directed at us for our consumption and assessment. Very often we simply observe people's behavior, although they are not communicating specifically with us. We can observe people communicating with others and infer from their behavior how they might behave toward us or, for that matter, how we might behave toward them. Although we frequently do not get as much information this way as we would like and although we recognize the shortcomings of generalizing from behavior in one situation to behavior in as yet unobserved situations, we sometimes consider information gained about a person through observation of his behavior with others as more valid than information gained through direct contact. When a person is not aware that we are observing him, he is less likely to be trying to create special messages for our benefit. All communicators realize that others are constantly making pragmatic and evaluative assessments of their behavior; after all, they make the same assessments, so why shouldn't everyone else? Part of communicative control involves managing the impressions other people form of us. Therefore, we often view information we get from people when they are not controlling us as a more accurate indication of what they are really like.

In some respects this trust in anonymous observation is misguided. We should be aware that while the people we observe are not directly controlling the impressions we receive, they are, nevertheless, controlling the impressions formed by the persons with whom they are communicating. Therefore, if the people we observe are acting as their own propaganda ministers, even the indirect information we receive is censored, so to speak.

If we take this information as a valid indicator of how the observed person will behave toward us, we are unconsciously and possibly erroneously attributing a particular communication style to the person: *we are assuming that he communicates according to stimulus generalization and that the way he communicates with other people is the way he will communicate with us.* Of course, if he perceives us as different from other people, he may communicate with us differently. To him we are stimuli that evoke certain responses. If one person with whom he communicates evokes trusting behavior, we may evoke deceptive behavior; if he is extroverted in one situation, he may be introverted in another. It is important to remember that our fellow communicators are guided by the same principles as we are.

Much of our information about an individual will be gained by direct contact with the individual himself, through communication situations in which he participates with us. In these cases, when the individual is directing messages to us, he is providing information about himself. Strictly speaking, whenever someone makes a verbal utterance or a nonverbal gesture, he is revealing information about himself. Even a factual statement such as "It's cold outside" discloses information about the speaker. It may tell us that he is interested in the weather. More likely, it is a conversational gesture that signals his desire to communicate and indicates what he perceives to be his relationship with the listener. (This message behavior is different from self-disclosure, which involves the intentional transmission of more private information. We will discuss this process extensively in chapter 10.)

Source 2. Extensions of the person
Intentionally or inadvertently, people convey important information through the material objects with which they surround themselves. Dwellings, clothing, and personal possessions "tell" a lot about their owners. We call such items extensions of the person because people often display objects that give us clues about their particular personality styles. When someone drives a certain kind of car, drinks a certain brand of Scotch, or subscribes to certain magazines, he may be saying, "These things are part of me. If you want to know what kind of person I am, look at the things I own."

A person's clothing is one of his most observable extensions. Even when we have no information about his other extensions, we can see how he dresses. Clothing may range from expensive to cheap, modern to old-fashioned, gaudy to plain, neat to untidy. More subjective judgments about clothing may view it as ranging from liberal to conservative, tasteless to appropriate, pleasant to hideous, all depending on the perceptions of the observer. Besides being highly visible, one's clothing also tends to reflect personal choice; since people usually, though not always, select clothing according to their own preferences, one's apparel can be a valid source of information about the self-image he wishes to convey.

The style and arrangement of a person's home can also convey considerable information and can hamper or encourage the development of interpersonal relationships. Some living rooms are furnished with obviously expensive and delicate objects, which seem to say, "Be

careful in here; these things cost money and break easily; don't get too comfortable." Couches and chairs may be set far apart, increasing personal distance and heightening the formality of communication.

Knapp (1972) cites research dealing with the impact of visual-esthetic surroundings on human interaction. While seated in an ugly room, one group of people were asked to rate a number of photographed faces on several affective dimensions; another group of people rated the same photographs but while seated in a beautiful room. Persons in the ugly room responded very negatively to the faces, while people in the beautiful room reported much more favorable dispositions. This finding, as well as our own common sense, suggests that the information we gain from environmental contexts can significantly affect our evaluations of the people in these contexts. Professional communicators—psychiatrists, lawyers, and insurance salesmen—have long been aware of the importance of environment on the attitudes of their clients, but amateurs are sometimes painfully lacking in this awareness. You have probably been a guest in homes where the decor, color scheme, furnishings, odors, and general cleanliness contributed to an uneasiness and to a desire to quickly end the conversation with your host. Other homes seem to invite you to sit and relax, to continue your conversation, to remain and get to know the people around you.

Other extensions also provide information about fellow communicators. Many people wear buttons or patches on their clothes, place bumper stickers on their cars, and hang inspirational posters in their bedrooms. Such extensions often tell you "where people's heads are at," what ideas are interesting and important to them. Similar information can be obtained from the books they read and even from the movies they see and their reactions to them. From this information you can sometimes evaluate how closely other people resemble you in their orientations toward life and living. This information can be pragmatically important, since it allows you to predict what kinds of communication behaviors certain people will find rewarding. For instance, if you note that a person has a number of posters extolling love and self-awareness (somebody seems to be making a lot of money printing posters with these themes), you are a step ahead in figuring out how to predict his or her behavior.

People also serve as extensions of other people. We are familiar with assertions such as, "He's a friend of Tom's, and Tom is a nice guy, so he can't be all that bad," or, "The people she hangs around with are all pretty freaky, so she must be, too." Whether you like it or not, you are often "known" by the company you keep; many communicators develop impressions of you through generalizations from impressions they have of your friends.

There are two properties of people's extensions that make them useful sources of information. As Harrison (1974) describes them, extensions are "not fast fading." Unlike the verbal sounds and non-verbal gestures presented directly to us by individuals, the extensions of individuals assume greater permanence in time and space. Consequently, we have more time to examine them, to analyze them, and to see how they might provide information about the people with whom they are connected. Harrison further notes that extensions are usually unintentional in that individuals do not specifically use them to transmit information about themselves. However, to the extent that they do reflect on the individual's personal preferences or habits, they may be useful as information that is not especially packaged and transmitted for someone else's consumption. Sometimes people communicate most clearly when they are not aware of communicating.

There is also considerable room for error in trusting the information we receive from the extensions of people. We are forced to make inferences from material objects to the internal states of their owners —or associates, in cases where a person's friends are the objects of concern. We know a young woman, for example, who prefers expensive and fashionable clothes and whose social behavior is similar to a society matron's. For these reasons she has been dubbed "Suzy Sorority," a nickname connoting materialism, light-headedness, and an inability to transact with others on any but the most superficial level. She resents this nickname and its implications, arguing that her taste in clothes has nothing to do with her interpersonal qualities or her intellect—an argument that seems valid in her case. Nevertheless, many people have fallen victim to inaccurate inferences about her character traits because of her sartorial extensions. They reason, "She likes fancy clothes, so she must have all the other traits of a materialistic person," but they do not bother to investigate this assumption. Moreover, no matter how one evaluates this situation, the young lady may find it necessary to alter her style of dress if she wishes to change the general image she projects. Generally, people do select their clothes, posters, and friends according to their own particular needs.

Predictive errors can also arise for a different reason. Goffman (1959) writes that many people work very hard at "impression management," which involves the display of material objects carefully contrived to convey desired information to others. People place avant-garde magazines on their coffee tables and keep their pornography collections in a drawer. They serve premium beer to company but drink a bargain brand when they are alone. Recently a certain premium beer manufacturer has recognized this fact and developed an advertising campaign to change people's beer-drinking behavior; the company's ads imply that the people who really have good taste also drink premium beer when they spend an evening alone. Some people study modern music, not because of its intrinsic satisfaction, but to reach the people who are impressed by an appreciation of modern music. Impression management is common to people of all ages and socioeconomic classes; meaningless facades are not the sole preoccupation of middle-class, middle-Americans. The next time you see someone throw a hamburger wrapper out of his car, check to see whether he has a green ecology flag on his rear window.

Source 3. Other people

Some of our information about individuals comes through other people, who tell us about the individual we are interested in. This source of information strongly influences our predispositions toward people, even though we have had no direct contact with them. If we already have formed some initial impressions, they may be altered or buttressed; if not, new impressions may be created.

When we get information about other people in this indirect fashion, the source of the information is especially important. Since we are allowing other people to act as our eyes and ears, we must rely on the credibility of our information sources. Information from people we trust and respect has more impact than information from low-credible sources. If we like someone, we are at least initially disposed to like the people he likes, and, in turn, to dislike those he dislikes even if we have never met them. These relationships will be explored more fully in the next chapter, when we look at communication relationships from a balance theory perspective.

Source 4. The social context of association

The social contexts in which we communicate with other people are somewhat different sources of information than the three we have thus far discussed. Social contexts influence the kinds of information that may become available about other people and the ways we perceive the information. Certain contexts call for and accentuate particular social behaviors, and we tend to view these behaviors in light of the values germane to these contexts. For example, an automobile accident may call for helping behavior, and we may interpret people's behavior at the scene of an accident according to their selflessness, courage, or level-headedness. Hence, the behavior we see and the way we interpret it are in part artifacts of particular social contexts.

In spite of this, we frequently attribute the behavior we see and our interpretation of it to the people who are behaving, as if they were the only sources of information about themselves and were entirely responsible for the perceptions we have of them. Because social contexts as sources of information about our fellow communicators are relatively implicit, nonobvious influences on relationship development, we should elevate our levels of awareness to these influences to be able to manage more effectively our participation in communication situations.

How do social contexts act as sources of information about people? First, social contexts select particular patterns of behavior from the participants. As we said in our discussion of PCCs, different situations offer different rewards and call for different control strategies. To the extent, then, that people find themselves in different situations, their behavior will appear multidimensional. In a sense people display many different selves, as the demands of various situations pull out one self or another. Of course, a context cannot pull out a pattern of behavior that a person is not prepared to display; there is obviously an interaction between past experience and contextual demands.

Some extreme examples illustrate these points. Recently the major wire services carried the story of an airplane pilot who was injured when his plane went down over the Canadian wilderness, ran out of food supplies, and ultimately resorted to cannibalism to maintain his own life. In Golding's novel *The Lord of the Flies*, the marooned children, isolated from the restraining influence of English society, slowly became cruel and savage in their treatment of one another. Actual and fictional events of this type have raised heated debates among moralists and scientists. What, they ask, is man's fundamental nature? Is man essentially an animal whose bestial instincts are suppressed by the sanctions of civilization but will surface in the absence of social pressure? Is man purely the product of environmental contingencies, or is there a basic human nature that ought to transcend these contingencies?

These questions have an important practical bearing on modern educational and social policy-making; they relate to issues of intelligence, racism, and law and order. The importance of social context for us as communicators is not so far-reaching, but nevertheless still significant. To some extent, what we know of another person (and what he knows of us) depends on what the context of our transaction allows us to know. If we communicate with someone over lunch in a restaurant, we shall learn something about his table manners. On the tennis court we can judge his sportsmanship. In the classroom we may see how good a student he is, but we may learn nothing of his table manners or sportsmanship. Not only do certain contexts call for certain responses, but also they do not call for others. To the extent that a particular context calls for one set of behaviors, it often denies access to other sets of behaviors. Context, therefore, both provides us with information and limits the amount of information available to us.

How can a social context influence the development of interpersonal relationships? Besides pulling out certain kinds of information that may be used for pragmatic and evaluative purposes, the social structure of the context can also increase the probability of certain kinds of relational development. Some social contexts, for instance, are oriented toward competition. In competitive situations—where some scarce and desired resource such as grades, status, money, or love can be attained by only a small number of people—trust, openness, and helpfulness may be minimized. The more prevalent communication behaviors take on a pattern of suspicion, mistrust, and cautiousness. These behaviors are not conducive to the development of close interpersonal relationships.

For example, a friend of Mark's is one of a group of people recently hired by a large corporation as management trainees. The trainees were informed by their supervisors that a small number of them would ultimately be selected for high-level positions, while the rest would be relegated to lower salary and status positions. They were also told that their evaluations would depend considerably on their attitudes: their commitment and loyalty to the corporation, their psycho-emotional stability, and the like. You can imagine the effects of these conditions on the trainees. Already under relatively high pressure in competing for the coveted upper management positions, they were further burdened by the impossibility of receiving socio-emotional support from their fellow trainees. Each person felt constrained to present a self-image to the others of complete satisfaction with corporate objectives and strategies, as well as personal security and happiness, all at a time when they had to work hard, were plagued with doubts as to their futures and values, were experiencing considerable tension, had moved to a new location and needed friends, but could not turn to their fellows because they did not trust them.

However, just as a competitive environment can curtail relational development among competing parties, it can enhance relational development among a group of people who are united in competition against another group of people (see, e.g., Sherif et al., 1954). People who consider themselves as "we" opposed to one or more "theys" often form close bonds with one another. One of the assumptions underlying the concepts of pledging and hell week in fraternities is that, in the context of harassment by the brothers, the pledges become closely united in cooperation and mutual support. Similarly, soldiers in a combat unit, players on an athletic team, and members of extremist organizations seem to find unity in cooperating together in a mutual effort to defend themselves against the enemy, an opposing team, or the policies of the establishment.

We mentioned that social contexts do more than pull out particular behavior patterns. The context of communication also suggests criteria for evaluating these behaviors. The classroom, the restaurant, the athletic field, and the church all provide social contexts maintaining certain value systems. Patterns of behavior deemed praiseworthy or rewarded in one context may be condemned or punished in another. An abstract theoretical discourse on the characteristics of interpersonal relationships may be viewed as intellectual (good) in the classroom and as intellectualizing (bad) in the bedroom. We often evaluate behavior not in any absolute sense but according to its appropriateness for the context in which it occurs.

This is not to say that all evaluations of behavior in a given context will be the same. There are bound to be variations. Two theater critics need not agree on their assessment of a play, nor do boxing referees on the outcome of a match, nor do professors on whether a student should be admitted to graduate school. The main point is that these evaluators base their judgments on criteria supplied by the social context in which the observed behavior occurs. Thus there are usually many possible means of applying a particular context's system of values, as long as there is intra-context agreement by the "judges."

Communication breakdowns arise when behavior in one context is evaluated according to values borrowed from another. That is, the judges do not agree on which value system to use; they suffer from inter-context confusion. This may happen when students judge a professor's academic competence according to his likableness. Or, to suggest a farfetched though poignant example, problems would arise if a football referee borrowed a rule from basketball and penalized a halfback for traveling with the ball.

The developmental process: escalation of interpersonal relationships

At a general level the development of communication relationships involves an association between two or more people in time, space, and an information context. These three dimensions are interrelated and serve as powerful determinants of communication relationships; they provide the basic foundations. But basic foundations are not enough; they leave many relational couplings unexplained. We need to examine some of the conditions and behaviors that seem to have singular importance in escalating levels of communication relationships.

The term *escalation* describes an aspect of the developmental process that has an analogy in quantum physics. When we say that relationships escalate, we mean that they do not develop, or progress, at continuous, steady rates, but that at certain times they leap or jump upward or forward. Successive jumps may occur one after the other or they may be spread out over time. A jump may happen at the outset of a relationship, or only after two people have known each other for a long period. Jumps may be up or down, good or bad, depending on the perspectives of the transactants.

For the notion of escalatory jumps to be meaningful, we need to consider the jumps in quantitative terms. When we say that a relationship has escalated, we mean the participants have more or less of something than they had before. Relational qualities such as trust, liking, jealousy, communicative accuracy, or understanding can all be considered in such more-or-less terms. For instance, two acquaintances who learn that they served in the same battalion in Vietnam experience a sudden increase in their mutual affinity. A professor who discovers that one of his top students has been submitting term papers purchased from a commercial firm experiences a sharp decline in his respect for the student. Of course, not all escalations are as dramatic as these, but in many communication relationships we can isolate particular points at which the communicators undergo noticeable behavioral or emotional shifts.

Let us consider degree of trust as a relational variable that can remain constant, increase, or decrease. In some relationships trust increases at a fairly steady rate: the more time the participants spend together, the more they come to trust one another. (This rate is graphed as the solid line in figure 7.1.) However, it sometimes happens that people experience an especially trying situation in which they discover, "Aha, I can really count on you!" Under these circumstances their mutual trust is likely to escalate (the dotted line in fig. 7.1). Unfortunately, sudden downturns are not unusual either. People can just as easily experience a sudden de-escalation in mutual trust when one person lets the other down in a tight spot. (This situation is graphed as the heavy broken line in figure 7.1.)

We have two reasons for emphasizing the conditions and behaviors that lead to escalation. First, as we mentioned above, they serve as important stimuli to relational development. When conditions are

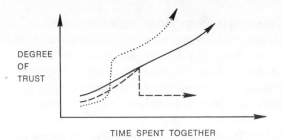

DEGREE
OF
TRUST

TIME SPENT TOGETHER

Fig. 7.1   Escalation of an interpersonal relationship
correlated to degree of trust

ripe—when people experience certain emotional states—they display
and are particularly sensitive to behaviors conducive to escalation.
Second, we hope that, by heightening your awareness of these behaviors, you will increase your control over the course of relationships in
which you wish to be involved.

Before discussing specific factors in relational escalation we should
point out that not all relationships develop in periodic leaps and
bounds; some slowly evolve without noticeable, significant shifts.
Furthermore, many relationships, especially interpersonal ones, frequently evolve through an emotional rather than a deliberate orientation, as our examples suggest. The emotional element of these
relationships contributes to the difficulty of isolating specific escalation
points, particularly if our evidence comes from the communicators
themselves. We cannot always say, "This is what made me like you,"
or, "That was the time I first became attracted to you." Nevertheless,
such events often play a significant role in relational development,
and, because they do, these events warrant discussion.

Relational escalation:
when the time is ripe

At certain times in our lives we are especially susceptible to the
development of interpersonal communication relationships. For
instance, we are sometimes in a state of interpersonal famine; during
these times meaningful relationships with other people are scarce.
Interpersonal deprivation may occur when we move to a new city or
when old friends move to distant locations. At such times we try to get
out to meet people and form new friendships. People require a
relatively stable number of friends, which gives them a sense of
interpersonal equilibrium. When the number of friends is less than
optimal, dissatisfaction results and new friends are sought. Converse-

ly, there is an upper limit on the number of friends we can handle; when the number is too large we have trouble mustering the time and energy to maintain all of our friendships. You can assess your own interpersonal equilibrium by noting the degree to which you actively seek new acquaintances for their potential as friends. If you engage in such searches frequently, chances are you have fewer friends than you would like or you are not completely satisfied with the ones you have.

We also crave interpersonal relationships in times of personal crisis. During crisis periods, when our self-esteem is particularly low or when an intimate relationship with a loved one abruptly terminates, we may escalate relationships with acquaintances or even with strangers, particularly if no close friends are on hand to help out. The classic example here is the person "on the rebound"; a gap has opened in his life, and he seeks to fill it as quickly as possible.

Scarcity and crisis produce general dispositions to escalate interpersonal relationships. But beyond this tendency, certain times create opportune conditions for developing relationships with particular people. The relevant times involve stages of personal development: "where our heads are at" during different times in our lives. People, especially younger ones, undergo growth cycles, intervals when they are particularly interested in learning and experiencing certain things about life, themselves, and other people. During these intervals some people are particularly suited to meeting interpersonal needs, while others are not. Consider this situation in light of a person's PCC hierarchy. If his most salient need at a particular moment involves entering into a long-term, stable relationship with another, he will avoid people whose greater needs are for relational freedom and independence. In a similar vein, a person who fears new and different situations will be painfully incompatible to someone going through a stage of high mobility and adventure.

Relational escalation: when you decide to make it happen

Most people would probably hesitate to say, "Let's you and me become friends," or, "Why don't we develop an interpersonal relationship?" A number of risks are inherent in such statements. The most inhibiting risk is the possibility that the other person will reject your assessment of the relationship. Consequently, when we decide an intensified relationship with another person might be satisfying, we inform him of this assessment in more indirect ways. There are several effective indirect communication strategies for escalating relationships.

One strategy is to shower the individual with attention, to seek him out, show interest in his activities, and solicit his opinions and advice. Naturally, if the individual finds you unattractive, this strategy may backfire; you may only heighten his negative evaluation of you by becoming a pest. Still, when you seek the person out and direct numerous messages at him, you establish a pattern of transaction. Assuming that he does not perceive the pattern as unrewarding, your attention can serve to consolidate the communication link between the two of you, making each successive transaction easier and more predictable.

By showing interest in the person's activities you make yourself more interesting in his eyes. By soliciting his opinions and advice you both flatter the person and raise your own prestige; people respect those who are intelligent enough to recognize they have wise and helpful things to offer.

Relational escalation: when the profit picture is rosy

Underlying all influences on relational development is the prospect of reward. This is especially true of the development of interpersonal relationships, which require an outlay of considerable effort. Two people will decide to embark on an interpersonal journey only if they expect certain rewards for their efforts. Moreover, they will continue the journey only if it is profitable to them. Relational profits are measured by subtracting the costs of obtaining rewards from the absolute values of the rewards. Just as people tend to exchange desirable responses in brief transactions when the exchange is immediately profitable, they tend to develop interpersonal relationships when they predict longer term continual profits.

We will not elaborate on these concepts here because we have already discussed in some detail in chapter 4 how they relate to communicative control. However, we do want to emphasize their relevance to many developmental processes. Consider the information exchange process we described as one of the noninterpersonal foundations of interpersonal relationships. In many respects information exchange involves the communication of reward potentials. Communicators transmit messages that indicate what rewards they have to offer, under what conditions, and to whom. They also try to elicit information that can be used to assess what rewards their fellow communicators want in return: "Can I use my resources in exchange for yours?" If an individual's stock of exchangeable commodities is not in demand, it cannot be used to establish satisfying interpersonal relationships.

Profit is also important in relational escalation. Escalation may be interpreted as the attainment of large profits very quickly. When people suddenly increase their mutual profits, they have something to "invest" back into their relationship in the hope of making further gains. Escalation may also stem from the discovery of an unknown potential for mutual rewards. People will then escalate their relationship to tap this potential. For example, when one "addict" meets another, they may rapidly develop a strong, though sometimes limited, relationship. Their addiction may be to chess, classical music, or horseback riding, but the promise of enjoyable mutual experiences draws them together.

Conversely, de-escalation may often stem from a precipitous decline in profits or from the discovery of a more profitable source of relational rewards. In the former event, individuals find they have lost out on their investments—they have expended their time, energies, and rewards in an unprofitable venture. They are therefore inclined to pull back their investments abruptly and to use caution before trying to continue their relationship. If they lose profits in many areas of their relationship and consequently cease to invest in them, their relationship will rapidly deteriorate and probably terminate. A decline in profits is sometimes slow, however, and may not be calamitous enough to warrant an abrupt retreat from the relationship. But as relational profits decrease, the potential profit of alternative relational liaisons may become greater. The de-escalation may not be noticeable until reward levels dip below the expected reward levels of alternative relationships.

A key distinction in the preconditions for the development of interpersonal and noninterpersonal relationships

It is difficult to draw clear-cut distinctions between the factors that lead to interpersonal, as compared to noninterpersonal, relationships. First, communication relationships do not easily divide according to interpersonal and noninterpersonal dimensions. Interpersonal relationships evolve from noninterpersonal foundations. All interpersonal relationships maintain their noninterpersonal aspects, and few noninterpersonal relationships reflect a complete absence of interpersonal factors. It is a rare individual who bases all of his predictions on either noninterpersonal or interpersonal grounds. Second, the characteristics of individual communicators are often unreliable predictors of the kind of relationship they will develop. Characteristics such as physical attractiveness, intelligence, or even interpersonal sensitivity may or may not be the cornerstones of an interpersonal relationship. Certain combinations of characteristics in a pair of communicators may be necessary for interpersonal development, but they do not guarantee it.

Rather than focusing on observable traits of individuals, or even on how two or more individuals relate to each other, we can use the kind of social transaction in which people are involved to determine the likelihood of a particular kind of relationship developing. Some social transactions require interpersonal communication; if people are going to participate in them, they must base their predictions about other participants on psychological data. An example of a situation requiring interpersonal skill is psychotherapy. In still other social transactions, interpersonal communication is not required but would greatly enhance the successful execution of the transaction. Job-placement interviews and athletic contests exemplify such transactions. A third class of transactional situations neither requires interpersonal communication nor would be much enhanced by it. When ordering ham and eggs in a diner or making an appointment at the doctor's office, a person who attempts interpersonal conversation may even hinder successful completion of the task. We can distinguish these situations by their goals and by the behavior necessary to achieve the goals.

The effect of goals on relational development

Let us reiterate a well-known assertion about human behavior: all social situations involve coordination around some activity for the attainment of a goal. To some extent, the goal of the situation determines the type of coordination necessary for its attainment. We can propose a general rule: *in situations where the goals necessitate stimulus discrimination, interpersonal communication is more likely to come about; conversely, in situations where the goals can be successfully attained through stimulus generalization, noninterpersonal communication is more likely to come about*. Therefore, an essential difference in the preconditions for the development of interpersonal versus noninterpersonal relationships is the nature of the communication most suited to the goals of the relationship.

If a person needs someone to talk to about personal problems, his goal necessitates a move to the interpersonal level. Similarly, when choosing a marriage mate, convincing someone not to commit suicide, selecting jurors for a criminal trial, or hiring someone for an important managerial position, a communicator must be able to elicit a fair amount of psychological level information. In such situations people must be able to deal with one another as individuals, not as role stereotypes. Of course, interpersonal communication will not automatically come about simply because such communication is needed to attain a specific goal. The important point is that when a situation demands effective use of interpersonal skills, lack of such skills dooms the participant to failure.

In many other situations stimulus discrimination is not necessary, but it is helpful. The process of getting a college education is a case in point. Many students quickly become aware that, while they can get good grades by studying hard, their chances for success improve if they can "psych out the prof," and discern his biases and pet peeves.

Finally, the goals of some situations almost preclude the use of interpersonal communication. If, like Carol in the movie *Bob, Carol, Ted, and Alice*, you tried to discover whether your waiter in a restaurant really liked his job or liked you as a customer, you would make it more difficult for him to carry out his job. Few waiters would take your solicitations to heart.

Our society emphasizes noninterpersonal skills

We might take time here for an observation on the nature of our society and its implications for interpersonal communication. The kinds of behavior required to coordinate with others for the attainment of certain goals must almost always be learned. We can infer something of the values of a society by looking at the behavioral skills it teaches its members. Our society educates its members in skills required for coordination around noninterpersonal goals. For example, we are taught how to drive automobiles, cook food, read books, play sports, get a job, and earn money. We are not taught how to make friends, comfort people, or recognize personal problems in our associates. The relative importance of these activities for our culture at large is demonstrated in the great discrepancy of effort, time, and resources devoted to training in these activities. As a culture, we seem to think that learning how to relate to people should come naturally, that it should just develop. When someone gets into an automobile accident, there are people trained to redirect traffic, to tow away and repair the car, to minister to bodily injuries, but no one is trained to provide emotional support (requiring interpersonal communication) to the victims.

A student once told Mark that she saw a bicyclist run into a tree along a crowded sidewalk and that the rider appeared to be uninjured physically but considerably embarrassed. She wanted to say something of sympathy and comfort, but she didn't know how to react. She had no experience or training in dealing with such a situation. Many people have learned how to react to broken bones and cuts, but not to helping someone out of embarrassment. However, it is clear that the general quality of life in any culture would be considerably improved if more people learned to respond effectively to people's interpersonal needs in crisis situations.

Toward a communication-based view of relational development

In this section we will propose that an important basis for the development of interpersonal relationships is whether or not two people can "talk to one another." You will see what we mean by this shortly. The material in this section will be expanded when we discuss verbal message strategies in chapter 10.

You will recall from our discussion of empathy that it is impossible to stand in someone else's shoes, to see the world as he sees it. We cannot know another person's world as he does, nor can he know ours as we do. As Laing (1967) says:

> I see your behavior. You see my behavior. But I do not and never have and never will see your *experience* of me. Just as you cannot 'see' my experience of you . . . I cannot experience your experience. You cannot experience my experience. (p. 18)

Even though we cannot experience another's experience, we still speak of sharing experiences. We also speak of sharing thoughts, values, feelings, perceptions, and the like. When we analyze interpersonal processes, we often propose that interpersonal relationships are largely based on two people's realization that they share certain important qualities such as past experiences, value orientations toward experiences, and feelings about each other. Strictly speaking, such a proposition is nonsense. We cannot share non-mutually experienceable qualities. Furthermore, we do not even know what experiences, values, and feelings are. As usually defined, they are internal to individuals (though fostered and modified in part by external stimuli) and must be inferred. They are abstract, vague, and unknowable.

Yet we persist in thinking that what we cannot observe, let alone share, is a basis for human relationships. We argue that even though we cannot see or share experiences, values, and feelings, we can discover through communication whether or not two or more people have similar experiences, values, and feelings. We look for approximations of complete sharing: "I have a lot in common with Jim, but Carol and I have very little in common." Communication, in this view of interpersonal relationships, plays an intermediary role; it is the

linkage system, or the medium, through which one person's internal states are made known to another.

We want to move beyond this conception of communication and sharing. To say that people share internal states is nonsense; to say that people learn of similarities of internal states, besides being grounded in nonsense, is an unnecessarily cumbersome conception of interpersonal processes. The premise we want to advance is this: an important basis of interpersonal relationships is not that people share similar internal states, but that they can communicate with each other—people tend to develop relationships with people with whom they can communicate.

Let us begin by briefly defining what we mean by "being able to communicate with" another person and then discuss why this can be important to the development of interpersonal relationships. *When we say that we can communicate with someone, we mean that his responses to our messages indicate to us that he understands and supports what we are saying.* For example, if you related an embarrassing experience to another person and he said, "Yes, something similar happened to me once; I know how you feel," you would probably feel both supported and understood. If the person had no idea of what you were talking about or rejected your emotional reaction to the experience, then support and understanding would be lacking; communication with this person might be very difficult.

You can probably think of people you know whom you would describe as easy to talk to. These people seem to know what you mean without your having to go to great lengths relating your thoughts or feelings; you don't have to "make yourself understood" with them. You don't have to expend a great deal of energy to express what you want to say, and you feel not only that what you have said makes sense to them, but that they accept your message without being overly critical.

Such ease of communication can be an important concern for us in developing interpersonal relationships. In chapter 1 we discussed the notion that even though people may undergo objectively similar experiences, each individual interprets his own experience somewhat differently. For example, all people have mothers and fathers. If a person tells you that he has parents, you would probably have little trouble understanding or agreeing with him. However, all of us have our own apparently unique and private experiences with our parents. These experiences may be more difficult to discuss; the meanings we have for them may be less commonly shared.

Precisely because the meanings we have for our personal experiences may be less commonly shared, we need to express them, to communicate them to other people. Whereas experiences we have in common with other people may draw us closer to them, those we feel are unique to us tend to separate us from them. A feeling of separation from other people can be painful, besides giving us cause to question our own identities. We need to communicate these experiences so that we can feel less isolated. That another person understands our statements concerning our personal experiences allows us to feel less alone, to feel more a member of the human race.

Important as this form of communication may be, it is not easy to come by. Most people would acknowledge that they feel understood and supported by a relatively small number of others, at least in regard to the thoughts and feelings that count most for them. This small number of others is usually the group of people with whom we form interpersonal relationships.

Summary

In conclusion, relational beginnings are important, but a communicator who cannot bring skill and understanding to bear on processes of relational maintenance is seriously limited in his capacity to reap satisfaction from his social environment. Some people get off to a fast relational start, but they cannot carry on from there. The skills they use to establish interpersonal relationships are insufficient to ensure long-term stability and harmony. Perhaps these people have not learned that the kinds of sensitivity required for relational development are different from those required for relational maintenance. Communicators expect different things from different stages of their interpersonal relationships and different skills are needed to meet these expectations. Our next two chapters raise several issues regarding relational maintenance.

Probes

1. A recent survey of students at Michigan State University revealed striking differences in the students' criteria for selecting partners for interpersonal relationships. Freshman and sophomore men and women said that physical attractiveness was their most important basis for wanting to establish a relationship with another person, male or female. Juniors, seniors, and graduate students rated intellectual and emotional compatibility as their primary criterion. In addition, underclass women said they would go to local campus bars to meet people, while upperclass women preferred to meet people at small house parties. Do you think these differences are common across college campuses in general? What factors might account for the differences (other than the vague quality of maturity)? In the past few years have your own criteria for initiating interpersonal relationships changed? If so, what kinds of experiences contributed to the change?

2. The propinquity hypothesis states that people tend to communicate and to establish relationships with those who are nearer to them in physical space than with those who are farther away. During an average week in your life (when you aren't on vacation or taking several exams), make a list of everyone you communicate with, the duration of your transactions, and the content of the transactions. Compare these with the distances (in feet or in miles, whichever is more appropriate) your fellow communicators live and/or work from where you live and/or work. Whether or not your own experiences support the propinquity hypothesis, what are the implications of your findings? Is there any correspondence between the distance you typically travel to see someone (how hard you have to work at it) and the degree of satisfaction you expect from the transaction? Are your experiences different from or similar to those of most people you know?

3. Think of the friends you have made in the past year or two. Where have you met them? What were you doing when you met these various people? Did the context of your initial association make any significant contribution to the kind of relationship you developed or to your getting together in the first place? Do you think that the initial context pulled particular information from either of you that increased the probability of your mutual attraction?

4. Of the friends you have made recently, on what communicative level did you first establish a relationship? Were your first experiences together predominantly interpersonal or noninterpersonal; i.e., do your relationships tend to escalate immediately or to develop slowly? What factors might explain different rates of growth?

5. Communicators exchange both evaluative and pragmatic information. Keep track of several conversations in which you participate and try to categorize messages according to each kind of information. Do you transmit one kind of information more often than the other? What kind of information is more often transmitted by the people you commonly associate with? Think about the implications of transmitting either kind of information. When you transmit evaluative information, you may be saying to other people, "I want you to like (or admire, laugh at, or be kind to) me, so I'm telling you some of my personal qualities." When you transmit pragmatic information, you are telling them: "I want desirable responses from you, but I'm not sure you know what to do to provide these responses. So I'm going to tell you what you need to do to provide me with desirable responses. Here is some information you can use to make predictions about me."

6. Sometimes communication is its own reward. At these times you don't communicate to elicit particular responses, nor do you try to impress other people favorably. With what kinds of people can you enjoy communicating in and of itself (or what we called a consummatory activity in chapter 4)? Try to be precise in your characterizations; don't, for example, be content merely to rate "easygoingness" as conducive and "uptightness" as inhibitory. See whether you can discover the elements of these qualities. Are there any people with whom you transact just to engage in communication for its own sake? With how many of your close friends can you not communicate this way? How important is this mutual activity in establishing relationships with boyfriends or girlfriends?

8

Individuals continually
face a three-pronged problem of adaptation.
Each of us must somehow come to terms, simultaneously,
with the other individuals and groups
in our interpersonal environment,
with the world that we have in common
with those persons and groups, and with our own intrapersonal
demands and preferences.

Theodore Newcomb, "Interpersonal Balance"

Some Characteristics of
Communication Relationships

C hapter 7 was primarily concerned with some of the factors that foster interpersonal relationships. In particular, we examined ways in which space, time, and availability of information influence the development of an interpersonal relationship. In this chapter we take the existence of a communication relationship, whether noninterpersonal or interpersonal, as a given, and we focus upon some important characteristics that most, if not all, relationships have in common. As usual, we will also be concerned with how a given characteristic may be affected by the level of the relationship; i.e., we will examine possible differences between noninterpersonal and interpersonal relationships.

We all engage daily in much speculation about communication relationships. We often ask, "Why does Fred allow himself to be dominated by Jack?" or we assert more earthily, "I don't see why Fred takes that garbage from Jack!" We offer judgments about the ways in which a relationship may be influenced by the participants' attitudes toward particular situations or objects; as, for example, when we observe, "Their differing attitudes toward the abortion issue seem to be placing a tremendous strain on their friendship." We scrutinize relationships to determine the relative presence or absence of a given characteristic: "Now there's a couple who really trust each other!" as opposed to, "Their trust of each other extends as far as they can throw each other."

To a large extent, of course, the shape of a relationship is molded by the needs, motives, and attitudes of its participants; they have the capacity to control both the communicative inputs and the subsequent outcomes. Still, inputs and outcomes cannot exist in an individual vacuum. If one wishes to be dominated, there must be someone to dominate him. Similarly, trust is a mutual commodity; although we sometimes speak of trusting or not trusting ourselves, we usually think of trust as something that is shared between two or more persons. Thus, while some reference to individuals is inevitable, we will try to carry out our analysis of relationship characteristics primarily within the transactional perspective of communication that we advocate throughout this book.

Complementarity versus symmetry: who, if anyone, is on top?

In order to differentiate complementary and symmetrical relationships, it may be useful to consider two hypothetical dialogues.

Dialogue 1

HE: I suppose you could say that a lot of things I do are a result of my parents' permissiveness. They always assumed I should be capable of running my own life, and they left me largely on my own from the time I was a teenager.

SHE: I know what you mean. My parents felt pretty much the same way. While a lot of my friends were kept in close check by their parents, mine allowed me a lot of freedom and seemed to figure that I could handle myself in most social situations.

HE: To some extent, though, I always wondered if my parents really cared about me. You know, while most outsiders would probably consider them liberal and enlightened, I often took their permissiveness for indifference or lack of concern.

SHE: Me, too! It's particularly easy for a girl to equate permissiveness with indifference. I always wondered why I never got any of the morality lectures that all my girl friends seemed to be catching at home. It was as if my virginity didn't matter a damn to them. In fact, I remember a couple of times when I rebelled and told them in no uncertain terms that I didn't think they cared an iota for my welfare.

HE: Man, do I remember an explosion at my house! It was after my junior year in high school, and I asked my father what he thought about my hitching out to the West Coast with a couple of friends. Right in character, he said it would be a good experience for me. Well, I got so angry that I told him he probably would sign papers for the Foreign Legion in five seconds if I just laid them on him. That remark started a real hassle.

SHE: I guess those kinds of scenes are inevitable with permissive parents. Why I remember one time . . .

Dialogue 2

HE: Even though we went to the ball game last night, we're still going to the wrestling match tonight. You know I can't stand those damned sorority parties!

SHE: Yes, I suppose the party will be a drag. And I guess it's supposed to be a good match tonight, huh?

HE: Best of the year. Those Iowa Hawkeyes have a good squad. Come here and straighten my shirt collar.

SHE: Does that feel comfortable?

HE: It's OK. While we're on the subject of sorority parties, don't expect me to go to that spring dance this year. I never had a worse time in my life than I did there last year.

SHE: All right. I won't mind missing it this year.

HE: On the way back from class stop by Twitchell Cleaners and pick up my shirts.

SHE: I'll do it. What time will you be back this afternoon?

HE: I may stop by the Airliner for a few beers after my three o'clock class. Start dinner about five-thirty.

SHE: OK, I'll have it ready about six.

Several differences between the two hypothetical dialogues are readily apparent. In dialogue 1, the contributions of the two communicators are roughly equivalent. Moreover, each one's remarks mirror the conversation of the other. The sequence begins with the male's reference to his parents' permissiveness, and the female promptly establishes that her parents also subscribed to a permissive philosophy. What follows is a series of transacts concerning the problems of having permissive parents. To some extent, the dialogue escalates, with each participant attempting to top the other in recalling personal difficulties stemming from parental attitudes. Finally, neither party clearly dominates the transaction; instead, the interchange is characterized by the relative equality of both communicators.

By sharp contrast, dialogue 2 reflects a definite dominant-submissive relationship. Every comment by the male places a demand on the female, and in each instance she complies unquestioningly. While the female in dialogue 1 sought to compete communicatively with her male counterpart, the dialogue 2 female readily acquiesces. Consequently, even the most cursory examination of dialogue 2 reveals that the male holds the upper hand.

Watzlawick, Beavin, and Jackson (1967) have stipulated a conceptual distinction between the two types of communicative transactions exemplified by our hypothetical dialogues. Dialogue 1 illustrates a *symmetrical* relationship, while dialogue 2 captures the essence of a *complementary* transaction. "Symmetrical interaction . . . is character-

ized by equality and the minimization of difference, while complementary interaction is based on the maximization of difference" (pp.
68–69). In a symmetrical relationship, neither participant assumes a
superior position; rather, equality is maintained in the transaction. In
a complementary relationship, however, one participant inevitably
assumes a superior, or one-up, position, with the second participant
placed in a subordinate, one-down posture. This is not to say that a
master-slave relationship is imposed by the dominant member of the
dyad. Instead, as Watzlawick, Beavin, and Jackson point out, "each
behaves in a manner which presupposes, while at the same time
providing reasons for, the behavior of the other: their definitions of the
relationship fit" (p. 69).

Characteristics of complementary relationships

Nothing in dialogue 2 suggests that either party is unhappy with their
complementary relationship. Having assumed the dominant, one-up
position, the male is consistently reinforced in his assertiveness by the
willing submission of the female. At several points in the exchange the
female has the opportunity to rebel; she can refuse to comply with the
male's demands, or she can verbally aggress against the male, attacking him for his domineering behavior. That she does not choose to do
so indicates that the relationship coincides with her expectations, that
the communication transaction fits her definition of the relationship.
Moreover, it would be erroneous to conclude that the male controls
the transaction. As we have indicated, the female's submissiveness
positively reinforces the male's behavior, and by withdrawing reinforcement (i.e., by rebelling or aggressing against him) she could cause
him considerable consternation and mental anguish. In these ways, the
relationship entails elements of mutual control; both parties are successfully controlling a relevant portion of their environments, though
by the use of differing communication strategies. Most important, the
relationship itself permits a sense of mutual control; without the other,
each of the participants would be lost.

This is not to say that all complementary relationships are cheerfully
accepted by the participating parties. The one-down position is often
grudgingly accepted, particularly in noninterpersonal communication
situations. In such situations a complementary relationship is often set
by the social or cultural context in which communication occurs.
When a patient seeks medical advice from a doctor, for example, there
is seldom any question about the doctor's one-up position. Such a
complementary relationship would be ensured under even the most
disarming circumstances, because of the doctor's superior knowledge
and expertise. Unfortunately, the gulf between the two participants is

usually widened, whether intentionally or unintentionally, by numerous things that happen during the patient's visit. Much of his time is spent communicating with a nurse who reassures him that "Doctor will be along in a few minutes." Omission of the article before doctor serves as a double put-down for the patient: first, it removes the doctor in question from the general class of doctors, thereby conferring a god-like, unique status upon him; second, the resultant phrasing closely resembles the style used in conversing with a small child, further assuring that the patient will realize his inferior status. When the doctor does arrive, he is likely to communicate with the patient in a hurried, impatient way, strongly impressing upon the patient's mind that he is a busy man with little time to spend with him. Queries by the patient are frequently met with a string of polysyllabic medical terms or with condescending oversimplification. Small wonder, then, that the patient leaves the office disgruntled, chafing at his one-down bit. So serious has this communication problem become that a number of medical schools are devoting considerable time to improving the dyadic communication skills—in antiquated terminology, the bedside manner—of medical students.

What has been said about doctors and patients is equally true of numerous other noninterpersonal complementary relationships where a wide gap exists between the status and power of the participants. Students must often assume a reluctant one-down position to teachers, clients to attorneys, enlisted men to officers. While the role differentiations implicit in these relationships may be necessary for a smoothly functioning social order, resentment and ruffled egos are frequent by-products of such complementary relationships. Being one-down is no fun unless one willingly chooses his fate.

Many people do indeed seem to choose to be one-down in their relationships with others; they consistently adopt subservient, deferential, or even totally dependent positions. In doing so, they are able to achieve some measure of certainty in their communication transactions. Their consistently one-down behavior tends to elicit predictably one-up kinds of responses from their companions. In this sense, any role is preferable to a variable role, or to no role at all. Ray Birdwhistell (1973) underscores this point when he argues that some people even choose to be ugly. As a longtime student of nonverbal behavior, Birdwhistell has noted that people can dramatically alter their physical attractiveness depending on the role they see themselves playing in relation to others. A person's grooming, diet, posture, and habitual facial expressions can, over a period of time, make him attractive or unattractive, his original appearance notwithstanding. According to Birdwhistell, a person's choice to be beautiful or ugly stems from his family relations. If a person is the third- or fourth-born child in a

family whose parents have dubbed the older children with fixed roles, such as prom queen, star athlete, or "the brain," and if the parents see each role as the sole possession of one child only, the latecomer will have to choose among whatever roles are as yet unclaimed. Choosing to be ugly (or a rebel or a brat) is a means of gaining a role identity. Here, choosing a one-down role at least provides the child with a stable identity.

People choose one-down roles not only for the security that a fixed role provides, but also as a way to achieve control in a relationship. The hypochondriac, for example, uses sickliness and apparent dependence on others to guarantee continued attention and sympathy. Similarly, Mell's comic strip character "Momma" manipulates her children by acting as though without them she could not go on living. You have undoubtedly known people whose basic control strategies involved creating an illusion of dependence and inferiority. The person who says, "I can't live without you," is often more in control than the one to whom the plea is addressed. The strategy is subtle, often indiscernible, and therefore potentially more effective than a blatant and direct effort.

Characteristics of symmetrical relationships

The noninterpersonal arena also contains its share of symmetrical relationships. Chance encounters by travelers often develop into symmetrical transactions. When two individuals converse in an airplane terminal or on a plane, their dialogue frequently assumes a mirror-image quality. On a recent trip to Washington, Gerry began conversing with an elderly gentleman in the next seat. After reviewing the usual biographical information—name, place of residence, and the like—the conversation proceeded along these lines.

JOHN: Well, now that I'm retired, I spend some time consulting. In fact, I'm going to Washington to consult with a control data firm there.

GERRY: I'm on essentially the same mission. I'll be consulting with the United States Information Agency over in Rosslyn. Is this company you're consulting with into information retrieval systems and computer technology?

JOHN: No, it deals with data control systems for machinery—furnaces and things like that.

GERRY: Oh, cybernetic systems, huh? We deal some with cybernetic systems in several of our courses in the Department of Communication at Michigan State.

JOHN: I didn't realize you were in communication. I got my degree in journalism at Iowa State, and I worked for a newspaper for about twenty years. I figure I know the communication business pretty well. As a matter of fact, I'm working on a book with Prentice-Hall now dealing with the control data systems stuff.

GERRY: Well, that's a coincidence. A friend of mine and I are just finishing editing a book of papers on communication and conflict for Prentice-Hall.

No doubt you have been party to many similar conversations. Again, equality is the key term; neither John nor Gerry has clearly seized the one-up position in the transaction. Both are preening their professional feathers, and both are undoubtedly deriving some rewards from the opportunity this relationship affords. While it might appear that their mutual recitation of accomplishments and credentials represents an attempt by each to capture the one-up position, the situational context of the transaction argues against such an interpretation. The encounter lasted only about twenty minutes, and there were no apparent marked differences in status or power between the two participants. In addition, an attempt by either participant to move into a one-up position would probably have been rebuffed by the other. Hence, maintenance of a symmetrical relationship offers both John and Gerry maximum environmental control as well as maximum rewards from the transaction.

Still, one must be careful to avoid bestowing an unqualified communicative blessing on symmetrical relationships; for, under certain circumstances, such relationships can escalate into quarrels or even open warfare. As Watzlawick, Beavin, and Jackson point out:

> In a symmetrical relationship there is an ever-present danger of competitiveness. As can be observed both in individuals and in nations, equality seems to be most reassuring if one manages to be just a little "more equal" than others, to use Orwell's famous phrase. This tendency accounts for the typical escalating quality of symmetrical interaction once its stability is lost and a so-called runaway occurs, e.g., quarrels and fights between individuals or wars between nations. In marital conflicts, for instance, it is easy to observe how the spouses go through an escalating pattern of frustration until they eventually stop from sheer physical or emotional exhaustion and maintain an uneasy truce until they have recovered enough for the next round. (pp. 107–108)

The element of competitiveness in a symmetrical relationship can be particularly destructive when public commitment is involved. What frequently evolves is an "If you do this, I'll do that" transaction, a tit-for-tat strategy in which specifying one's response constitutes a public commitment. Such transactions sometimes culminate in the severing of a relationship, as when a marriage partner threatens to move out or to see a divorce attorney. If the other partner ignores the warning and carries out the unacceptable action, the threatened response is likely to be performed since failure to act places the threatening party in an unfavorable, one-down position.

Complementarity and symmetry in interpersonal relationships

As we have indicated, the social or cultural context in which communication occurs often fixes the shape of a noninterpersonal relationship. Upon moving to the interpersonal level, however, the situation becomes considerably more complicated. For one thing, it seems likely that the needs, motives, and characteristic control patterns of the communicators will have much to do with whether a relationship moves from the noninterpersonal to the interpersonal level. Winch (1958) has argued for the importance of need complementarity in the selection of marriage partners. Such an "opposites attract" hypothesis recognizes the importance of the participants' agreeing on their definition of the relationship. If one has a high need to dominate, he is more likely to feel comfortable entering into a complementary relationship with a highly submissive partner. Given that both participants can perceive definitional harmony early in the transaction, the relationship has a good chance of moving from the noninterpersonal to the interpersonal level. By contrast, noninterpersonal encounters by two highly dominant individuals are likely to follow the pattern of symmetrical escalation discussed above, and since such encounters generally lack reward value, the relationship will usually be nipped in the noninterpersonal bud.

Errors of relational judgment can and do, of course, occur. In particular, the inability of one of the participants to move from the cultural or sociological to the psychological level of prediction may create serious relational hazards. Rigid, simplistic thinking of the kind discussed in chapter 5 may cause a person to accept the veracity of such generalizations as, "All women crave domination." Even so distinguished a thinker as Friedrich Nietzsche demonstrated his vulnerability to cultural and sociological oversimplification with his famous injunction, "Thou goest to a woman? Do not forget thy whip!"—an injunction implying that all women have masochistic needs and crave complementary relationships that place the male in a sadistic, one-up position. That most women do not thirst for such relationships is attested to by the current vigor of the feminist movement, which seeks to extricate women from the one-down position to which they have been so frequently relegated by society. Again, however, these kinds of predictive errors effectively ensure that communicative transactions will remain noninterpersonal, even though the participants may wish to move to the interpersonal level.

In a healthy, ongoing interpersonal relationship, shifts between complementarity and symmetry are almost inevitable. Stated differently, few, if any, long-term interpersonal transactions are completely complementary or solely symmetrical. Instead, the participants in the transaction mutually define a set of rules that govern the shape taken by the relationship. Typically, shifts occur: the relationship may be characterized by symmetry in certain situational contexts and by complementarity in others. Moreover, the participants may also agree to share the one-up and one-down positions, again depending upon the context in which communication occurs.

Consider the following hypothetical interpersonal relationship between two marriage partners. Some of their shared communication is devoted to making personal and professional plans, and in this area their relationship is primarily symmetrical. They discuss economic and social alternatives as equals, contributing their own ideas and seeking to arrive at mutually satisfactory solutions. When the scene shifts to social activities with the husband's professional associates, the wife assumes the submissive, one-down position. She realizes that when her husband is in this environment he feels, rightly or wrongly, that a good deal of his ego is on the line, and she is willing to accommodate his dominant needs. He, in turn, refrains from exploiting the situation; he does not become unduly dominant or unreasonable in his demands, for he knows that at a certain point his wife will be forced to defect from her one-down position. Finally, in social situations involving relatives and family members, the husband usually slips into the one-down position, since he is aware that his wife has always resented her father's domineering approach to family affairs and has a strong need to demonstrate her independence to family members.

Even the preceding example oversimplifies the dynamic changes in relational shape that accompany ongoing communication transactions. Obviously, there will be evenings when the wife is unwilling to accept her one-down role at a business cocktail party, and unless the husband is able to make the necessary discriminations, conflict will probably result. By the same token, certain decisions may require that one of the partners move into a one-up position, while the other accepts a submissive, one-down posture. *Seldom are the rules governing the relationship formally articulated by the participants.* Their evolution demands a rather long, complex series of communication transactions. As with any other communication situation, predictions regarding relational preferences can be based on noninterpersonal considerations (i.e., cultural or sociological generalizations) or they can be arrived at primarily by using psychological data (i.e., by making accurate discriminations) about the other party, or parties, in the relationship. The latter strategy, of course, sharply reduces the possibility of error. Finally, if shared definitions cannot be established, conflict is inevitable, and at some point the relationship is likely to disintegrate. Two persons with highly dominant needs may find it impossible to agree on the appropriate shape of their relationship, since each will strive for complementarity with himself in the dominant, one-up position. Conversely, two highly submissive people may also encounter relational difficulties, for neither may be willing to seize the initiative and provide the leadership needed to sustain the relationship.

A final caveat seems warranted: *when agreement upon the shape of a particular communication relationship is vital, every effort should be made to move to the interpersonal level.* To base predictions about the relational preferences of another on cultural or sociological generalizations is risky; while such data may permit us to be accurate most of the time, the margin for error is still substantial. Furthermore, since the pattern of a relationship usually evolves, rather than being sharply defined at the outset, cultural and sociological generalizations are of limited value. Instead, attention must be focused on the cues presented by the other participant, so as to determine how situational factors influence his preference for a symmetrical or complementary relationship.

Defining and sharing perceptions of others: balanced and unbalanced relationships

Thus far we have been concerned primarily with the ways people mutually define their relationships with each other. Relationships, however, do not exist in a social vacuum. Consequently, the participants' perceptions of, and attitudes toward, a host of objects, acts, and situations can exert a powerful impact on their relationship. In this section we briefly examine the dynamic process of evaluating others, and we consider how differing evaluational perspectives can affect the stability of noninterpersonal and interpersonal relationships.

Effects of attitudinal similarity or discrepancy on the development of a relationship

A certain amount of attitudinal similarity usually constitutes a necessary condition for the development of a viable relationship. Think of the people with whom you have formed relational bonds. Undoubtedly, most of them share many of your attitudes toward the world and toward people. Often when you converse with them about social, political, and economic issues, you find that your views coincide with theirs; moreover, this attitudinal correspondence is comforting, since it furnishes a set of common assumptions from which communication can flow comfortably and uninhibitedly.

Conversely, when a great deal of attitudinal discrepancy exists between yourself and the other communicator, you are likely to feel defensive and ill-at-ease. As the transaction progresses, you may find yourself seizing upon the faults of the other party and magnifying them. Not only do the two of you disagree on the merits of abortion reform (or establishing diplomatic relations with communist countries, or long hair and beards, or *The Exorcist*, or some other subject), but also you begin to perceive him as loud, crude, uneducated, and intolerant. Nor does his affective machinery stand idle during the transaction; rather, he is likely to be attributing similar negative characteristics to you. As a result, interaction usually is terminated quickly and by mutual consent—unless, of course, there are other rewards to be gained from continued disagreement and controversy; e.g., you may perceive that you are enhancing your credibility with onlookers by giving your antagonist a sound argumentative thrashing. Furthermore, the probability of subsequent communication is also minimal; unless circumstances demand interaction, the two of you will henceforth avoid each other.

This is not to say that we form relationships only with those who are ideological carbon copies of ourselves. If this were so, we would all be guilty of the rigid, simplistic thinking that we have consistently indicted. Still, without areas of shared attitudinal agreement, attempts to form relationships will usually fail. Of central concern to us here is the assumption that once a relationship has been formed, its stability hinges upon the perceived agreement, or attitudinal coorientation of the participants toward particular objects, acts, or situations that intrude upon the relationship.

When is attitudinal agreement necessary for relational harmony, and when is it not? It seems that one important factor is the degree to which attitudinal similarity is necessary for two people to coordinate their mutual behaviors. Any task that requires coordination requires agreement on the nature of the task and on each person's role in completing it. The more salient the task, the more important it is that the communicators reach agreement. For example, a man and a woman may meet at a party and begin a conversation about child-rearing practices. If one is a strict disciplinarian, while the other opts for relative permissiveness, they may engage in a small-scale debate, and each may try to win the other to his or her point of view, but neither is likely to feel very threatened or upset by the disparity in their attitudes. However, should they fall in love and talk of marriage, this disparity will assume greater significance. They are now faced with the prospect of being unable to coordinate their prospective roles as parents. Similarly, it probably would not bother you that a friend was a sloppy housekeeper until he approached you with the suggestion that you share an apartment together. When two people decide to venture on some joint enterprise—marriage, sharing an apartment, a business partnership, or even a golf match—their attitudes relevant to the mutual transaction of the enterprise become highly important. You probably don't care much if someone you know likes anchovies, doesn't pay his debts, or chain-smokes, until you want to split a pizza, he wants to borrow twenty dollars from you, or you have to share a room together.

The changing balance in a relationship

Figure 8.1, based primarily on Newcomb's (1953) theory of interpersonal balance, depicts a balanced, stable relationship. Assume that *A* and *B* are the two participants in the relationship, while *X* represents some object or situation toward which both participants are oriented. Keep in mind that *X* can be an animate object (e.g., a person, a dog, or a snake), an inanimate object (e.g., a gothic-styled cathedral, a sports car, or a chocolate ice cream cone), an act (e.g., executing convicted murderers, bombing targets in Cambodia, or admitting a specific quota of minority group students to universities), or a situation (e.g., a cocktail party, a football game, or a ballet). At a more abstract level, *X* can even represent a process or a relationship. For example, we will shortly consider the possibility that *X* represents the quality of the relationship between *A* and *B*, as each of them perceives it.

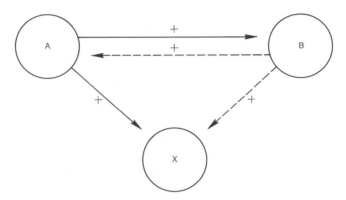

Fig. 8.1   A balanced relationship

Note that four cognitions of the two participants, *A* and *B*, are relevant to the state of the relationship. Looking at the situation through *A*'s eyes we see that *A* has a favorable attitude (+) toward both *B* and *X*. In addition, *A* perceives that *B* is favorable (+) toward himself and toward *X*. From *A*'s perspective, then, the relationship is balanced: his positive attitude toward *B* is reciprocated by *B*, and his positive attitude toward *X* is shared by *B*. Furthermore, by examining *B*'s perceptions of the relationship, we see that *A*'s judgment is accurate; i.e., all four of *B*'s cognitions are also positive.

Figure 8.2 demonstrates how a change in cognition transforms a balanced, stable relationship into an imbalanced, unstable one. Again, *A* and *B* are positively oriented toward each other; but unlike the previous situation, both are not positively oriented toward *X*. Instead, *A* has a positive attitude toward *X*, while *B* responds toward *X* negatively. In addition, both *A* and *B* are aware of the discrepancy between their attitudes toward *X*. Assuming that *X* represents a third party with whom they are both acquainted, the situation can be translated as follows: *A* (Louie) likes both *B* (Patricia) and *X* (Bart), while Patricia likes Louie, but cannot stand Bart. Since the inconsistency in their attitudes toward Bart adds a note of instability to their relationship, Louie and Patricia will be motivated to behave in some way calculated to restore stability. What are some of the avenues open to them?

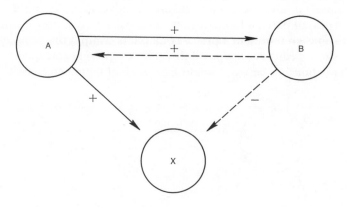

Fig. 8.2   An unbalanced relationship

First, one of them may undergo a change of attitude toward Bart. If his relationship with Patricia is extremely important to Louie and if he feels that his friendship with Bart is totally unacceptable to her, he may decide that Bart is an unsavory character unworthy of his friendship. Such a change of attitude restores balance to Louie and Patricia's relationship, since both are now negatively oriented toward Bart. Of course, given other situational constraints, Patricia may be the one to experience a change of heart; under such circumstances the relationship would also be balanced, but both parties' orientations toward Bart would be positive.

Second, balance may be restored by mutually modifying the intensity of the relevant attitudes. That is to say, Patricia may become less intensely negative toward Bart and less intensely positive toward Louie, with Louie's attitudes toward Bart and Patricia manifesting a similar change. Note that this method of restoring balance has a detrimental effect on Louie and Patricia's relationship: mutual attitudinal accommodation of Bart reduces the intensity of their positive orientation toward each other. We would expect that if such disagreements occur frequently, the relationship will suffer severe strain, with Louie asking, "How can I continue a relationship with someone who doesn't like my friends?" and Patricia querying, "How can I go on associating with someone who surrounds himself with such unsavory people?"

Another means of restoring balance—or at least of minimizing the imbalance—is to de-emphasize the importance of the particular X to the relationship. Returning to our hypothetical example, Patricia might reason that since Louie sees Bart only infrequently, their friendship is relatively insignificant and should not weigh heavily on her relationship with Louie. Here again, this method of dealing with the problem is not entirely satisfactory. As long as Bart does appear on the horizon only rarely, Patricia will be able to handle the situation; however, if Louie begins to spend more and more time with him, it will soon become next to impossible to discount Bart's importance. Furthermore, this particular technique loses effectiveness rapidly if more and more Barts arrive on the scene; i.e., if Patricia and Louie keep discovering other Xs toward whom their orientations differ. Although it may be possible to discount the importance of two or three such disagreements, a critical mass will be reached quickly, and once reached, Patricia and Louie may begin to question their compatability or the compatability of their life styles.

Of course, an imbalanced relationship can be avoided, at least temporarily, by erroneously interpreting the other party's orientation toward X. Patricia may conclude that Louie does not really like Bart, or conversely, Louie may surmise that Patricia does not actually object to the friendship. When invoked frequently to deal with relational difficulties, this approach resembles the fairyland methods of control discussed in chapter 4: to deny the existence of an unstable relationship may on occasion suffice, but to fall back on this defense habitually is to bury one's head ostrich-like in the relational sands.

Orienting toward the relationship itself

As we have already indicated, the X toward which the two participants in a relationship orient need not be a person. On certain occasions, X may be the relationship itself; in such cases, we have the interesting situation of a relationship being imbalanced because of differences in the way the participants think the relationship should be defined. Thus, Patricia and Louie may be positively oriented toward each other, but they may manifest sharply divergent attitudes toward the nature of their present relationship. Suppose, for example, that at some earlier time they mutually agreed that both of them were free to date other persons. At the time of their pact, both had positive attitudes toward this dimension of their relationship. As time passes, however, Louie grows dissatisfied with this arrangement, while Patricia continues to view it positively. Since imbalance has been generated, conflict is almost certain to ensue with Louie arguing for a change in X (the definition of the relationship) and Patricia advocating continuance of the present understanding. Unless a satisfactory compromise can be reached, Louie's and Patricia's orientations toward each other will become less positive; in fact, the relationship itself is likely to be terminated. Thus, *the characteristics of a relationship itself often constitute relevant Xs toward which the two parties must share similar orientations.*

The preceding analysis indicates why the classic triangle, immortalized by poets, playwrights, novelists, and contributors to pulp love story magazines, invariably contains the seeds for a relational explosion. When a third person intrudes on a relationship, the other two involved parties often spend most of their time arguing about the merits of the intruder. For example, if Louie and Patricia do redefine their relationship and then Louie enters into a relationship with another woman, it is almost inevitable that the following exchange with Patricia will take place.

PATRICIA: I can't see what you see in her! She's the most selfish, grasping person I've ever known.

LOUIE: You're obviously overlooking a lot of her good points. Once you get to know her, she's a very warm and understanding person. In fact, you could do with a little of her understanding yourself.

PATRICIA: Don't presume to lecture me about understanding. If you weren't totally blind, you'd be able to see through her the way everyone else does.

Further eavesdropping is unnecessary, for the course of the dialogue is highly predictable. Note, however, that heated controversy about the characteristics of the third person is largely irrelevant to the real conflict, which actually centers on a relational disagreement. Probably Patricia would react similarly to any other woman, no matter what her qualities. What enrages Patricia is Louie's perceived violation of their defined relationship, not his particular feminine companion. By the same token, Louie seeks to assert his assumed prerogative to redefine his relationship with Patricia; while he may indeed have affectionate feelings for the third party, his major concern is maintenance of his relational freedom. Unless their relationship can be satisfactorily redefined, Patricia and Louie will remain at communicative loggerheads, and eventually their relationship will end.

Comparing balance in interpersonal and noninterpersonal relationships

The preceding discussion points to an important generalization concerning the role of balance in noninterpersonal and interpersonal relationships: *usually, the number of Xs demanding balanced orienta-*

tions by the two parties will be greater in interpersonal than in noninterpersonal relationships. For most noninterpersonal transactions, only a single X is relevant. Consider, for instance, a customer's typical relationship with his milkman. Over the course of several years of doing business, the two may develop a casual friendship; noninterpersonal pleasantries and remarks about the weather may be exchanged when deliveries are made. Foremost in the customer's mind, however, is a positive orientation toward the concept of service: he expects fresh dairy products to be delivered regularly and punctually to his door. As long as the milkman's behavior suggests a similar positive orientation toward service—i.e., as long as deliveries are regular and punctual—the customer is unlikely to be concerned with the extent to which the milkman's political leanings, social habits, or religious beliefs correspond with his own. Conversely, if service declines sharply, the customer will perceive imbalance between his milkman and himself in their orientations toward the only X directly relevant to their relationship. Should he have some concern for the milkman's feelings, he may seek an explanation for the deteriorating service; more likely, however, he will find a new milkman.

But suppose that, atypically, the customer and the milkman are motivated to move to the interpersonal level. Perhaps an early conversation reveals a strong mutual interest in hunting and fishing, and they begin to engage in these activities regularly. Weekend hunting and fishing trips give rise to more intensive interaction; exchanges that result in mutual revelation of their attitudes toward numerous social, economic, and political issues. As their relationship develops, they not only become aware of each other's orientation toward more and more Xs, but in addition, achieving mutual balance in these orientations assumes more importance. When an imbalance is perceived, there is strong potential for tension, causing both parties to seek ways of restoring equilibrium.

To a large extent, the preceding situation captures the meaning of the frequently uttered assertion that interpersonal relationships are somehow richer than their noninterpersonal counterparts. As the parties to the transaction move from the cultural and sociological levels to the psychological level of prediction, they acquire more information about each other. This information not only fixes perceptions of their mutual orientations toward previously discussed Xs; it also enables more accurate prediction about each one's probable orientations toward Xs that have never been specifically discussed. Thus, each party to the transaction can justifiably assert that he "knows" the other person, and this feeling of shared knowledge adds a richness to the relationship not normally present in transitory, limited noninterpersonal encounters.

Relative importance of sources of imbalance

Obviously, it is next to impossible for two persons to be harmoniously oriented toward every X they experience. As a result, various Xs differ in their importance to the stability of the relationship. A husband and wife can disagree on the merits of pistachio nut ice cream, be cognizant of their disagreement, and still carry on a close, rewarding interpersonal relationship. In fact, absence of common orientation toward certain Xs may add excitement and interest to the relationship. Some couples enjoy arguing about the quality of a movie, the literary merits of a book, or the wisdom of an Academy Awards selection.

One reason that such arguments seldom threaten an interpersonal relationship—and in fact, as we have indicated, may enliven it—can be found in the likelihood that the two parties share a balanced orientation toward a higher level, more important X. Thus, if the persons involved are both positively oriented toward freedom of intellectual and aesthetic expression, they can argue about a host of specific Xs while maintaining a balanced orientation toward this more general relational dimension of their transaction. In other words, controversy is a good thing; it even contributes to their intellectual and aesthetic freedom. What would place a severe strain on the relationship would be insistence by one of the parties that the other consistently orient in a balanced way toward each specific X that they discuss. Such insistence would cause the acquiescing party to perceive that the other person no longer shares his positive orientation toward freedom of intellectual and aesthetic expression. Again, the dispute centers on a basic disparity in the way the relationship is defined, suggesting that satisfactory resolution of such disputes is essential to the continuing health of any interpersonal relationship.

This is not to say, of course, that all severe threats to the stability of a relationship are strictly relational in origin. Disagreements about financial matters, religious values, or appropriate sexual conduct—to name but a few sensitive areas—can place the closest of relationships in serious jeopardy. How two people manage the family budget is considerably more important than their taste in ice cream; if one of them orients positively toward the concept of fiscal conservatism, while the other does not, the interpersonal sparks are certain to fly. Such basic disparities manifest themselves in heated arguments about numerous specific Xs: immediate purchase of a new car or major appliance, the merits of buying on credit, the importance of savings, and the meat cuts to be served at dinner, to mention only a few. Unless the warring parties can achieve a balanced orientation in their financial outlook, the relationship will grow increasingly tempestuous and in time may become mutually unbearable.

What we are proposing, then, is a hierarchical ordering of Xs, with some assuming greater importance than others in determining the stability of an interpersonal relationship. When imbalance exists about either the defining characteristics of the relationship itself or about the basic economic, political, or human values of the parties involved, considerable tension is inevitable and both transactants will be strongly motivated to seek means of restoring equilibrium. Conversely, apparent imbalance over specific Xs may, at worst, create only mild tension and, at best, may actually be consistent with a balanced orientation toward higher level, more important Xs.

Balance and control

Two additional points concerning the balance mechanism deserve mention. First, one party to a relationship may sometimes systematically manipulate balance to control the behavior of the other participant. Such a technique, while often of dubious ethical merit, can be quite effective, particularly when used against highly dependent persons who are especially susceptible to threat. Suppose, for example, that in a particular marriage relationship the husband feels very dependent upon his wife and that he places a high value on the maintenance of their relationship. By threatening to orient negatively toward relational maintenance, the wife may extract numerous concessions from her husband; she may, in fact, make him a slave to her every whim. Such threats may be communicated quite explicitly, as when the wife threatens to leave the husband or to enter into a relationship with another man, or they may be expressed subtly, by means of nonverbal flirting behaviors or casual comments about the attractiveness of another man. In terms of our earlier discussion, the wife maintains a consistent one-up position; the complementary nature of the transaction is fixed by her husband's dependency.

This particular example relates closely to our second point: *many relationships persist in the face of numerous imbalancing elements.* All of us know of relationships in which the parties apparently have little in common; their orientations toward many Xs differ sharply. Why are these relationships not dissolved? Thibaut and Kelley (1959) have underscored the importance of the construct *comparison level for alternatives* in any attempt to determine whether or not a relationship will be maintained. Succinctly stated, they argue that many less than optimally satisfactory relationships are maintained because the cost of ending the relationship is too great. Thus, the dependent husband may endure considerable misery with his manipulative wife on the grounds that a breakdown of the marriage would not only isolate him interpersonally, but also would be injurious to the couple's children.

Summary

Overall, the value of the balance construct lies in its potential utility as a tool for analyzing communication relationships. We have attempted to demonstrate how the balance mechanism functions, and we have argued that this mechanism increases in both importance and complexity as communicators move from the noninterpersonal to the interpersonal level. To a large extent, the possibility of maintaining relational stability hinges upon the sensitivity of the transactants. In particular, psychological level predictions may often represent a necessary prerequisite for establishing a balanced orientation, a consideration that points yet again to the importance of interpersonal communication.

Trust: an elusive ingredient
in communication relationships

With the possible exception of the word *love*, the term *trust* is probably used more frequently than any other in conversations about communication relationships. People worry considerably about whether to trust other persons; individuals are categorized by their degree of trustworthiness; relationships are characterized by the relative presence or absence of trust. Our concern with trust extends all the way from the President of our country to a brief contact with a television repairman. "We're working to earn your trust," trumpets a major oil company, and by its choice of words acknowledges the importance of this intangible commodity to commercial success.

Still, while we frequently speak of the need for trust, the concept itself is a slippery one to define. For some, the meaning of trust is closely akin to Louis Armstrong's famous rejoinder when asked for his definition of jazz: "Man, if you don't know what it is, I can't tell you." Hence, the title of this section refers to the elusiveness of trust in communication relationships, not because we are cynics who feel that trust is usually absent in dealing with our fellowmen, but because we realize the difficulty in defining exactly what we mean by *trust*.

Motivational aspects of trust

People often use the term *trust* to refer to the motives or intentions of another. When viewed in this light, questions about trust are not so much concerned with the ways in which someone is behaving but rather his reasons for behaving as he does. Moreover, the more difficult it is to discover possible ulterior motives for an individual's be-

havior, the more likely it is that he will be deemed trustworthy. If a relative takes up residence with a wealthy maiden aunt and ministers to the aunt's needs during her declining years, the relative's protestations of love for the aunt are likely to fall on skeptical ears; but if the aunt is penniless, others will probably laud the relative for making unselfish, altruistic sacrifices. The difference for the aunt herself could be largely academic, since she may be primarily interested in companionship and comfort, and, if so, the behaviors of her relative are more important to her than the motives for the behavior.

Frequently, of course, the motives for present behavior assume significance because of their implications for future actions. Suppose two persons are contemplating embarking on the long-term relationship of marriage. In such a situation, assessment of the other's motives may pose a crucial problem for one of the parties. For example, if the potential wife is wealthy or possesses considerable social stature, she may agonize endlessly over whether she can believe her suitor's vows of love. Perhaps he wishes to marry her because of economic or social benefits. Implicit in such agonizing is the assumption that if her suitor is untrustworthy (i.e., if he is motivated by the marketplace values of money or fame, rather than by his love for her), the long-term relationship between the two will be less satisfying, primarily because the husband will at some point begin to behave differently toward her.

In some cases, this assumption may be warranted. We suspect, however, that excessive worry about the motivational aspects of trust often results in the deterioration or destruction of promising human relationships. As we have previously indicated, one can never be certain of another person's motives—in fact, if psychoanalytic theorists are at all correct, the person himself may not be certain of them. To allow a communication relationship to be dominated by questions regarding the reasons for another's behavior is to risk continuous anxiety, an emotional state that hampers relational development and growth.

Behavioral aspects of trust

Trust can also be grounded in a behavioral foundation: when viewed from this context, we say that *we trust someone when we believe there is a high probability that he will perform promised, trustworthy behaviors.* If a father promises to leave work early to play ball with his young son, the son will probably place considerable trust in his father's word, but if the father fails to arrive home early, the son's confidence will be reduced. Similarly, if someone says, "I trust Barb to be discreet," he is asserting that Barb can be depended upon to refrain from certain communication behaviors. In these cases, behavior, rather than reasons for behavior, is the key consideration. Upon arriving home late, the father may give his son numerous reasons for his failure to perform the promised behavior: an emergency at the office, an unexpected traffic snarl, and so on. None of these reasons is likely to carry much weight with the child, since for him the presence or absence of certain behaviors is the major criterion for assessing his father's trustworthiness. By the same token, one's reasons for trusting Barb to be discreet may range from a belief that she is an honorable person who treats others' confidences with integrity to an expectation that she will be afraid to talk because of embarrassing information that could subsequently be revealed about her. While these two motives for Barb's discreetness differ radically, each is secondary to the acid behavioral question of whether or not Barb will remain prudently silent.

Trust in interpersonal and noninterpersonal relationships

Both motivational and behavioral aspects of trust are relevant to the development of communication relationships. Whether for better or worse, we suspect that motives become more important as the relationship moves from the noninterpersonal to the interpersonal level. In most noninterpersonal transactions we have little reason to dwell on the motives of the other party; instead, our primary concern rests with his fulfillment of certain behavioral commitments. To trust one's insurance agent is to believe that he will settle claims fully and promptly, regardless of his motives for doing so.

At the interpersonal level, mere behavior is often not sufficient; in addition, it must be performed for the "right" reasons. For a wife to assert that she trusts her husband to remember their anniversary usually means not only that he will give her a gift, but also that he will do so because of his love and affection for her. As we have repeatedly stressed, her conclusion about the second factor must, of necessity, be inferred. As a result, we would anticipate that disagreement over the motivational dimension of trust would occur more frequently in interpersonal relationships, while controversies about the behavioral manifestations of trust would take place more readily in noninterpersonal settings.

Summary

We have completed our brief inventory of some of the relevant characteristics of communication relationships. Once again, we should underscore the crucial point that constructs such as symmetry and complementarity, balance, and trus are *relational*; they transcend the traits and habits of individual communicators and focus instead on the relationships between two or more transactants. Since most of us are not used to talking in transactional terms, such concepts may seem somewhat unusual. Consequently, chapter 9 provides some examples of how these concepts may be applied to the analysis of various kinds of communication relationships. As you read that chapter, the relevance of these relational constructs to both noninterpersonal and interpersonal settings should emerge more clearly.

Probes

1. Think about some of the communication relationships with which you are acquainted. Do you know people who assume a one-down position in order to exert relational control? Do you think this is a wise strategy? An ethically defensible one?

2. "It would be impossible to maintain a symmetrical relationship for an extended time period." Attack or defend this statement, taking into account our discussion of the possibility of escalation in a symmetrical relationship.

3. What do you think of Winch's notion that mate selection is based on need complementarity? Do you know married couples who seem to conform to the maxim, "Opposites attract"? Do you know any who seem to conform to the maxim, "Birds of a feather flock together"? If so, how would you reconcile this apparent contradiction?

4. We have mentioned the relationship between George and Martha in *Who's Afraid of Virginia Woolf?* on several occasions. Would you characterize their relationship as complementary or symmetrical? After you have reached a conclusion, take a look at Watzlawick's, Beavin's and Jackson's analysis of the relationship in *Pragmatics of Human Communications*.

5. Can you see any relation between the aspects of cognitive style discussed in chapter 5 and a person's responses to imbalanced communication situations? In particular, would individuals with rigid, simplistic cognitive styles be likely to use different means of restoring balance than would people with open, flexible styles?

6. Can you apply the balance model to some of your own communication relationships? Does it seem to work in some of the ways described in this chapter? Do you see any differences in the way balance functions in your noninterpersonal and your interpersonal relationships?

7. Analyze some of your relational disputes with friends and acquaintances. Are there times when an ostensible argument over another individual or a particular activity actually reflects a dispute over a definition of your relationship? How might you improve your chances of resolving such disputes?

8. Can you construct a hierarchical ordering of importance for the various Xs that enter into your relationships with others? What kinds of disagreements cause you little stress or discomfort? What kinds of disagreements place a serious strain on the relationship? Have you ever actually terminated an interpersonal relationship because of serious disagreement about a particular X, or Xs?

9. Gerry and Mark argue that people often overestimate the importance of the motivational dimension of trust. Do you agree with their position? If so, why? If not, develop an argument attacking it.

10. Given Gerry's and Mark's conceptualization of interpersonal communication, would it be possible for two people who do not trust each other to have an interpersonal relationship? Develop arguments supporting your answer.

9 There are no problems, only poorly defined opportunities.

Francis Byrnes

A Selected Inventory
of Communication Problems
in Interpersonal Relationships

nyone who reads "Dear Abby" or "Ann Landers" will recognize that the following fictional letter is only a slight exaggeration of the ones sometimes printed in their columns.

> Dear Gabby:
>   My husband is an alcoholic who beats me every day. I have to work two jobs to support me and our five children because he spends all of his welfare check on booze and barflies. We have been married eight years, and in all that time he has never said one kind word to me. I am dictating this letter to a nurse in the hospital because the last time he got drunk he beat me and broke both my arms. The trouble is, Gabby, I still love him very much, and I couldn't bear to live without him. What do you think I should do? Sign me,
>
> Black and Blue but not Through in Waterloo

Although, thankfully, few people could write such a letter from direct personal experience, many couples remain together for years with few obvious sources of marital satisfaction. As we suggested in chapter 1, George and Martha in *Who's Afraid of Virginia Woolf?* typify this kind of relationship. They seem to be united in a mutual torture society. But just as there are people who actually seem to enjoy systematic punishment, there are those with relatively low tolerances.

> Dear Gabby:
>   I never thought I'd write to you, but I can't stand it any longer. I've been going with this girl for six months. She's a fine girl in most respects, but she has one habit that's just driving me crazy. Whenever we eat dinner together, she eats her dessert before she eats the main dish. She lets me eat my dessert last, but Gabby, it just isn't right to have cake and ice cream before salad and

casserole. If this continues, I'm going to leave her. Is there anything I can do to change her disgusting behavior? Sign me,

Reeling but not Unfeeling in Wheeling

The writer of the first letter might wish her problems were all this small. But different people see different things as problems, and the same problem will assume varying importance in different relationships. People have a wide variety of needs, peeves, problem-solving capabilities, and sensitivities to others. For these reasons it is sometimes difficult to answer the question:

What factors contribute to the development of a bad interpersonal relationship?

It may be even more difficult to answer the related question:

What factors enhance the development of a good interpersonal relationship?

Before reading further, it might be helpful if you tried to answer these two questions for yourself. Make up a list of factors that you believe contribute to the development of a bad interpersonal relationship. Make the list as personal as possible. For instance, you may feel that alcoholism generally has a detrimental effect on the quality of a relationship, but include it in your list only if it has some salience for you. Develop a similar list of the factors that enhance the possibilities of a good interpersonal relationship, again keeping in mind those that are most relevant to you. (*Good* and *bad*, of course, must also be interpreted personally here.) As you continue to read this chapter, compare our descriptions of factors that engender good and bad relationships with your own.

Our perspective on the sources of relational problems

Despite the fact that different folks go for different strokes—that one person's nightmare may be another's delight—our selection of some relational communication problems and not others reflects our own perspective on relational assets and liabilities. We should clarify this perspective at the outset. We feel that relational problems generally stem from three sources:

1. *Fearfulness.* Many relationships suffer considerable difficulty due to the fearfulness of one or both members. Fear leads to concealment of information, inaccurate communication, and sometimes a tendency to try to maintain a relationship long after it has "died."

2. *Thoughtlessness.* Many relational problems could be avoided if the members took time to recognize the consequences of their communication behaviors, to consider the needs of others, and to manage the course of their relationships more prudently and effectively.

3. *Lack of experience.* Experience provides people with an information space: a means of putting relational events into perspective. Numerous problems arise because people have not yet learned to anticipate them. People may overreact to certain problems because they have not yet learned that these problems may be trivial from the perspective of a wider time frame.

An overview of this chapter

This chapter centers on problems facing communicators in relatively sustained interpersonal relationships. While the problems considered are relevant to any relatively long-term interpersonal relationship, much of our discussion focuses on relationships between boyfriends and girlfriends or husbands and wives. When examining transactions between members of the opposite sex, we limit ourselves to relationships that have reached the "post-romantic" stage. The romantic stage of a relationship is the period of high excitement and getting-to-know-one-another, when just the thought of your new love sends pleasant chills along your spine, when you see each other day and night if you can, when . . . well, you know the feeling.

Perhaps much of the excitement of a new relationship can be attributed to the novelty of the situation, or to the amount of information one gets in interacting with a new and different person. There is a high degree of uncertainty about the other's personal history, behavior patterns, and relational dispositions. The value in reducing this initial uncertainty is, of course, related to the extent of physical attractiveness between the two people. We would speculate that the reduction of this uncertainty (accompanied by the establishment of predictable transactional patterns) is at least partially responsible for the decline of many romances. (For readers who have some background or interest in information theory, figure 9.1 presents an information theoretic perspective on romance.)

The romantic stage can be contrasted with the stage when the newness wears off, when your emotions reach an equilibrium, when you begin to get used to each other. Except for the fact that you may not get much homework done or that your friends wonder why you walk around with a silly grin on your face, we cannot see any serious problems with romantic episodes. For most couples problems arise when the momentum of their romance produces relational escalation, when they decide to go steady or even to get married. We would hardly suggest, however, that people avoid sustained, post-romantic relationships. They necessarily involve greater communication problems than do most other kinds of interpersonal relationships, and are common and important enough to warrant specific discussion here.

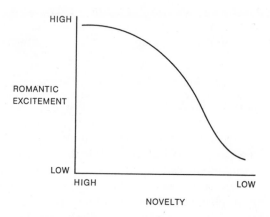

Fig. 9.1   Romance from an information theory perspective

We will discuss several kinds of problems in the remainder of this chapter. Our first topic is relational conflict. We discuss some common forms of conflict and some methods for resolving and dissolving conflict. Second, we examine relational legislation, the set of mutual agreements that a couple develops to avoid conflict in, and give structure to, their relationship. Finally, we consider three danger signals in interpersonal relationships. If people learn to recognize these signals, they may be able to avoid significant relational hardships.

Relational conflict

People who want to minimize the negative consequences of conflict and to maximize the value of conflict in their interpersonal relationships will find it useful to make three assumptions about relational conflict.

> 1. *Conflict is inevitable.* No relationship can hope for a conflict-free existence. Conflict is a natural outcome of the interdependence of two people.

2. *Conflict is not a dirty word.* The presence of conflict in a relationship is not a sign that its participants are feeble or that the relationship is headed for ruin; as a matter of fact, when the participants deal effectively with it, conflict can often be highly beneficial to their relationship.

3. *Conflict arises for many reasons and takes many forms.* No single approach to dealing with conflict can succeed all of the time. The effectiveness with which one handles conflict situations is related to one's ability to see differences across a variety of conflict situations.

Keeping these assumptions in mind constitutes a first step toward keeping conflict from becoming a major relational menace. Our focus here is not on how to eliminate conflict, but on how to confront it and manage it.

Negative and positive aspects of conflict

Everyone is familiar with the negative aspects of conflict in interpersonal relationships. Often conflict hampers efficiency of coordination. To the extent that there is friction in the relational machinery, the machinery cannot run smoothly. Sometimes it even grinds to a halt when major repairs become necessary. Furthermore, inefficiency usually requires the expenditure of considerable communication energy, which can be taxing for the people involved. But perhaps the most serious consequence of conflict is the weakening of people's self-concepts. When someone is consistently unable to manage conflict situations, his perception of his ability to control his environment is likely to suffer: "What is wrong with me that I am so often embroiled in conflicts and that I cannot easily put an end to them?" In addition, when conflict gets out of hand, people frequently begin to attack one another's self-concepts: "If you can't see my side of it, you must be pretty stupid!" Such statements uttered hastily in the heat of battle can have long-lasting effects on relational solidarity.

When people know how to manage conflict, it need not be destructive. And when people are not apprehensive or afraid of conflict, they can learn from it. Some have argued that learning cannot take place in the absence of conflict. Certainly, the conflict of people's attitudes, values, and general behavior patterns can highlight and sharpen their perspectives. The strengths and weaknesses of an individual's viewpoints can be more adequately tested in conflict with alternative viewpoints than in isolation.

Conflict can also provide an impetus for learning about the material world. Suppose a husband and wife have conflicting positions on household finances; they cannot agree on mutually acceptable budgetary practices or investment policies. Of course, they could each accuse the other of fiscal idiocy and irresponsibility, embarking on bruising personal attacks. Or they could sit down and each could present the facts that support his or her position. If both adopt a nonthreatening posture, they might expose the fallacies and point up the strengths in each position, thereby obtaining new and useful information about household economic systems. They may discover that neither can marshall sufficient evidence for his own position and turn to a financial expert for additional guidance, increasing even further their store of knowledge.

Coser (1956) and Simons (1974) have written in detail about the beneficial by-products of relational conflict. They argue that the suppression of conflict can cause severe relational and personal damage, and that cooperative communication about conflicting perspectives and feelings can actually strengthen relational bonds. Many of the strategies of conflict management we will suggest are based on the assumption that the presence of conflict in a relationship can be as much an opportunity as a threat.

Conflict management

If we assume—not pessimistically but realistically—that conflict is inevitable, then the term *conflict prevention* has little meaning. It makes more sense to talk of *conflict management*. Managing conflict involves reducing the frequency of destructive responses to conflict and guiding people's post-conflict communication toward constructive ends. Conflict management is a form of communication that tries to replace dysfunctional, maladaptive arguments with productive agreements.

We will shortly discuss three forms of conflict, and for each we will specify some management strategies. But here we want to emphasize one overarching skill that is essential for effective conflict management: *the ability to make psychological-level discriminations in conflict situations*. There are many forms of conflict, and there are many alternative responses to it, some more effective than others. One task of the conflict manager, then, is to determine the nature of the conflict in which he is involved and then to select an appropriate response to deal with it. For example, a conflict manager must decide whether to focus on the issue over which a conflict arises or on the way people are communicating about the issue. As we have said so often, different people react differently to different situations. Conflict situations are no exception. Therefore, a conflict manager has the task of eliciting the most constructive and cooperative responses from the individuals with whom he is involved. We will discuss interpersonal strategies for assessing people's perceptions of conflict situations and for reducing barriers to amiable termination of conflicts. (The term *conflict manager* does not denote a special role performed by a few people. Like *interpersonal communicator*, it implies an activity that any of us can perform from time to time, and that all of us should be familiar with.)

Some possible outcomes of conflict management
Conflicts come in different forms, require different management strategies, and have several possible outcomes. Here are five possible outcomes of conflict.

1. People may decide they cannot deal with the conflicts in their relationship and terminate it. For the time being, we will assume that the termination of an interpersonal relationship is an undesirable outcome of conflict. Later in this chapter we will discuss conditions under which termination might be advantageous.
2. People may be unable to deal effectively with the conflict but decide to suffer through it, as did the woman who wrote the letter about her aggressive, alcoholic husband. People who cannot cope with a particular set of conflicts may see no alternatives to their present situation, or they may feel that other aspects of their relationship are valuable enough to warrant continuation.
3. People may be able to dampen the conflict, i.e., to reduce the negative dimensions of a continual conflict. For example, if a friend tends to break dates at the last minute, you may be able to arrange alternative plans for the evening. The conflict still exists, but you are not permitting it to affect you as much.
4. People may be able to resolve their conflicts, i.e., to quell a recurrent conflict with a minimum of effort and emotional cost,

even though they are unable to keep the conflict from arising. Many conflicts that stem from faulty communication are readily amenable to resolution. People can remain alert to the possibility that their conflict may be caused by unshared meanings for behaviors. Whenever conflict arises, they check immediately to see whether they have understood one another. Another means of resolving conflict is to flip a coin whenever you fail to reach an agreeable decision in any other way. The conflict may crop up again, but by the same means you can dispense with it quickly.

As we suggested in chapter 3, the difference between conflict dampening and conflict resolution is the degree of relational strain that remains after the outcome. A dampened conflict is bearable, but still intrudes on the relationship. A resolved conflict is completely and agreeably terminated, even though the same conflict may surface repeatedly.

5. People may be able to attain the ultimate in conflict management, conflict dissolution, the mutually satisfying and permanent removal of a conflict. Nobody can dissolve all of their conflicts, but certainly some conflicts are amenable to this outcome. For example, in relationships where one person smokes and the other does not, the nonsmoker may be concerned about pollution in his own environment, as well as the long-term effects of smoking on the other's health. Conflict may be permanently avoided if the smoker is willing to quit and if he does not replace smoking with habits that the nonsmoker finds equally upsetting.

Consider the conflicts to which you have recently been a party. What was the outcome of each? Let us assume that the five outcomes we listed are arranged in order of increasing desirability, relational termination being the least desirable and conflict dissolution the most desirable. Could you have done anything to produce a more desirable outcome for any of your conflicts? How much did your own or another's stubbornness contribute to a failure to achieve a more desirable outcome? Did ignorance of the issues involved in the conflict or of one another's point of view prevent you from resolving or dissolving a conflict? Or if you were able to arrive at a mutually satisfactory outcome, how did you do it? What strategies did you use?

Three forms of relational conflict

The three most common and potentially troublesome forms of relational conflict are simple conflict, pseudo-conflict, and ego-conflict. Simple conflict involves one person saying, "I want to do X," and another saying, "I want to do Y," when X and Y are incompatible forms of behavior. Although this form of conflict lacks certain elements that complicate the other forms, it is not always "simple." Pseudo-conflict results from misunderstanding; inaccurate communication gives rise to false perceptions that simple conflict exists. Ego-conflict may embrace both simple and pseudo-conflict, but the key element is that people's needs to defend their egos stand in the way of effective settlement of disputes.

Our suggestions for strategies of conflict management will not propose specific solutions to specific conflicts. Rather, we will suggest general principles that should be useful in a variety of situations. To paraphrase an old proverb, knowing how to cope with a particular conflict will provide relational harmony for a little while; knowing general principles of conflict management can abet relational harmony for a lifetime.

Simple conflict
This form of conflict is probably the easiest to understand but not always the easiest to manage. It arises when two people know what each of them wants, but neither can get it without preventing the other from realizing his goals. For example, two people may have saved a certain amount of money, and one wishes to buy a new car while the other desires to make a down payment on a new house. Or one person may want to watch a particular television program, while the other prefers to watch a different show being aired at the same time. Or one person may hope to ask a particular individual to join himself and a third person on a vacation, while the third person objects to the prospective interloper. The kinds of situations that give rise to simple conflict are almost endless.

Each of the five outcomes of conflict is possible with simple conflict. But the cardinal rule in achieving a desirable outcome of the conflict is: *keep it simple and try to avoid complicating the issue with pseudo-conflict or ego-conflict.* If you can prevent misunderstandings and assaults on one another's pride, a speedy and harmonious outcome is much more likely. Therefore, propose a straightforward statement of the problem; e.g., "Let's get it clear. You want me to invite your brother to the football game and I don't want to. Is that the issue?" Avoid using emotional language or implying that you have already evaluated the merits of the other's position; e.g., "Let's get it clear. For some stupid reason you want me to invite your lousy brother to the football game, and he's a jerk." (Warning: you can say the words contained in the former statement but actually "say" the latter with your tone of voice. Learn to keep value judgments out of the way you speak.)

Beyond keeping the conflict simple, there are other effective strategies for managing simple conflict. If you are not pressed for an

immediate decision, try waiting awhile—a few minutes or a few months. Let tensions subside. Think about possible solutions. Something may happen to eliminate the source of the conflict, and perhaps a solution neither of you had thought of will materialize.

Of course, the luxury of waiting is not always possible. When a conflict seems to demand immediate attention, you should first clarify the issue and then get all the relevant facts. Returning to our example, you might ask: "Why would you like me to invite your brother to the game? Is there anything else I can do that would be equally satisfactory?" You may find that your friend's brother has been particularly depressed for some reason, and that your humanitarian instincts override your dislike for the fellow. Or you may find that you do not necessarily have to invite him to a football game (which you might find intolerable) but that any attention you can give him would be fine (leaving you an opportunity to come up with a more bearable alternative).

Try to cast the conflict in a mutual frame. Make it something you have to face together, rather than as two individuals competing for the most personally favorable outcome. Emphasize the mutual nature of the causes and results of the conflict. Using words like *we* and *our* instead of *I* and *me* can help maintain harmony in your approach to the conflict, and it can also increase the probability of a creative response to the conflict. For many conflicts there are no readily apparent means of resolution or dissolution. Creativity must be brought to bear on the problem. Nothing stifles creativity like dictatorial methods of controlling the problem-solving process. In an atmosphere of cooperation and mutual respect, a solution you'd never thought of can be found more readily.

Pseudo-conflict

"Now I see what you were saying. There was actually nothing to fight about in the first place." When people actually agree on something, but because of inaccurate communication perceive themselves to be in disagreement, they are faced with a pseudo-conflict. Though pseudo-conflicts can be no less damaging or manageable than other forms of conflict, the management strategy rests upon eliminating distortion rather than reaching agreement on some course of action. Here is an example of pseudo-conflict.

MARY: Are you coming over tonight?

JACK: Not tonight. I'm going out with some of the guys.

MARY (thinking): I thought we had agreed that he wouldn't go out and pick up girls anymore.

JACK (thinking): I assume she knows that "out with the guys" means "out with the guys."

If Mary fails to verify her interpretation of "out with the guys," she is likely to believe that she and Jack are in conflict over living up to relational agreements. No real conflict exists, but if Mary believes that one does, the impact on Mary and Jack's relationship will likely be the same.

Pseudo-conflicts are, in one respect, very easy to avoid. Generally, the initial step in managing simple conflict—asking for clarification of the issue—is all that is necessary for resolving a pseudo-conflict. If Mary simply asks Jack for a clarification of his plans for the evening, the appearance of conflict can be avoided. A straightforward question like "What do you mean by that?" often prevents needless friction.

In another respect, however, psuedo-conflicts are quite difficult to manage effectively. People frequently jump to conclusions about the reality of the perceived conflict and never think to verify their perceptions. What would happen, for instance, if Mary says nothing to Jack about his apparent breach of faith but proceeds to give him the cold shoulder? How many people turn erroneous perceptions into relational battles because they are unaware of the possibility of pseudo-conflict?

There are, then, two basic steps in managing pseudo-conflict: first, remember to verify your perceptions of the existence of relational conflict; and second, actually verify your perceptions via direct communication. You should also recognize the possibility that someone else may perceive a conflict where you do not. If you suspect that something you said is open to misinterpretation, then offer clarification of your own messages. It is just as important to make sure your messages are clear as it is to verify the messages others send to you. Moreover, as you will see momentarily, pseudo-conflict can sometimes be linked with ego-conflict. Thus, Mary may find it ego-threatening to ask Jack to clarify his plans. If Jack senses this reluctance on Mary's part, he should seize the initiative and explain that he is not violating a relational understanding.

Ego-conflict

"Take that, you #$%¢@#!!" Perhaps the most devastating and complicated conflicts are those caused by people burying their egos too deeply in relational transactions. When people feel they have to save face or put another person down, ego-conflicts become a problem. In the following example two people are turning a simple conflict over television viewing preferences into an ego-conflict.

> HARRY: I'll be darned if I'm going to watch the shows you want to watch all the time.
>
> JANE: What do you mean, "the shows *I* want to watch"? You get your way in practically everything we do. I'm getting a little tired of your selfishness.

HARRY: Selfishness? Are you so weak you can never give in? Besides, I remember the time you spoiled my birthday because you wanted to go to a lousy party.

JANE: Oh yeah, well why don't you just shut up. Your voice is starting to make me sick.

We would like to think that dialogues like this are rare, but that seems a bit too optimistic. What typically happens in situations like this one? Both parties become defensive and attack each other's self-esteem, thereby closing off rational communication channels. Insult begets insult, each successive assault becoming more intense than the preceding one. Soon the initial issue is completely forgotten as each person reaches into the past to resurrect a wide assortment of the other's shortcomings and sins. Before you know it, both are shouting, maybe even slugging, until tears flow; tempers are so far lost that no one even knows where to begin looking for them; doors slam; and emotional scars are cut deep enough to require major restorative surgery. In this respect, Irving Rein (1969) recalls an oft-ignored warning: "Sticks and stones can break my bones, but words can REALLY hurt me."

Strategies are available to detect high ego-involvement in conflict situations and to minimize the potential for damage. Approaches that are effective in coping with other forms of conflict may not work here, however; for when people put their egos on the line, they erect barriers to cooperative communication. These barriers must be lowered before anything else can be accomplished. Therefore, the first step in managing ego-conflict is to *give people a chance to bring out relevant concerns and then stop.* The parties should not be prevented from expressing primary concerns, even if they are highly emotional, but they should be discouraged from escalating the conflict into violent personal attacks and counterattacks. When an ego-conflict looms stormily on the horizon, take control of the communication situation and let each person have his say, but do not allow either one to carry on too far.

What does this tactic accomplish? Primarily, it gives each person "formal recognition." It is an acknowledgment of mutual concern and respect. When a person has a fair opportunity to express himself, and particularly when he feels the other person is listening to him, he usually feels less need to rant and rave, to attack the other person, or to defend himself. Of course, the effective use of this strategy requires some detachment on the part of conflict managers; they must say to themselves, "I see what's happening here, and I'm not going to let my own ego get so embroiled that I can't pull us out of this mess."

Sometimes, however, you may discover this emotional detachment too late. If so, you may want to suggest an emotional cooling off period, an opportunity for both people to come to their senses. Never try to force a settlement or even a discussion when you have already gone too far in diminishing one another's self-esteem. You may be waiting for a chance to get even, or your adrenalin may be flowing too strongly for calm, reasonable discourse.

When it is time to discuss the conflict, would-be conflict managers often make the mistake of beginning the discussion by saying, "Okay, why don't you tell me why you said what you said, and then I'll tell you why I said what I said." This approach can add to the fires already burning. People are likely to explain their own outbursts by referring to some prior "criminal" behavior on the part of the other person. Such explanations are composed of a personal defense of the speaker and an implied attack on the listener. Instead of developing a mutual, cooperative perspective on the conflict, people develop an individual-istic, competitive point of view. *Rather than explaining the conflict, merely describe it; ask what happened, not why it happened.* A simple, relatively unbiased account of the events related to the conflict marks the beginning of the conflict's desirable outcome.

When you reach an agreement about what actually happened in the conflict, then begin to look for its sources. Many ego-conflicts arise from disputes over relational control. Who is going to make the de-cisions? Whose interpretation of relational transactions is going to be adopted by both parties? In most interpersonal relationships there is some conflict over who will occupy the power position in the rela-tionship. If you are trying to settle a dispute over which movie to see and you are getting nowhere with a discussion of the relative merits of the movies themselves, you might well suspect that the conflict in-volves determining the process by which movies are selected. There is nothing wrong with wanting to control some relational decision-making; rather, the error comes in not recognizing other people's needs for environmental control as a factor in relational conflict.

Few conflicts that stem from needs for control can be dissolved; you cannot permanently eliminate disagreement over who shall run the show. Resolution of such conflicts is a more reasonable goal. In our next topic of discussion—relational legislation—we suggest a strategy for resolving power-based conflicts in interpersonal relationships.

Relational legislation: "In order to form a more perfect union, we hereby resolve that. . . ."

As soon as a relationship begins to emerge from the romantic stage, the members suddenly realize that relational harmony does not happen all by itself. Conflicts arise. Grievances come to the surface. Personal differences cause misunderstandings and arguments. That these things occur should come as no surprise. Any time people form an interpersonal relationship there are bound to be difficulties. Once a couple realizes, however, that their relationship is not destined to be perfectly harmonious, they have to learn to deal with the problems that arise. We suggest that couples learn to devise, enact, and enforce a set of legislative measures to maximize relational harmony.

What is relational legislation and why do we advocate it? *Relational legislation involves a series of agreements in which each party promises to behave in a certain manner, given certain circumstances.* A couple agrees, in effect, that when circumstance X occurs, one or both of them will respond in a predetermined manner Y, and not in manner Z. This approach sounds fairly simple, and in practice it usually is. Some common examples of relational legislation are: "Whenever we have an appointment and you know you're going to be late, call and tell me" (a piece of communicative legislation); "The first one up in the morning will feed the dog"; or "When we go to a party, one of us will stay sober enough to drive home."

There are two reasons for the importance of relational legislation.

First, no matter how compatible a couple may be, the individual characteristics of the members are bound to cause conflict. One person may have a penchant for neatness, while the other is more casual about the placement of his personal belongings. One person may like to vacation in the mountains, while the other prefers the seashore. Or both people may like to wash dishes but hate to dry them. If people are to maintain some degree of harmony in their relationship, they must devise means for coping with conflicts that arise from their own idiosyncracies. Can you see how relational legislation could be enacted to minimize conflict in each of the three examples cited above and how communication plays an integral role in legislating against conflict?

Second, when people form a sustained interpersonal relationship, they become interdependent. Each person's behavior has some influence on the other. The degree of a couple's interdependence may be relatively trivial (as when they have to decide on what flavor of ice cream to buy) or consequential (as when they consider whether or not to get married). Whenever two people are mutually dependent, they need to systematically coordinate their behavior. This means that they must agree upon the whats, whens, hows, whos, and wheres of their mutual activities. Perhaps even more important, coordinating their behavior also means agreeing upon the processes by which these agreements are to be made. In the absence of such agreements relational chaos is inevitable.

Relational legislation helps structure a couple's mutual expectations and helps ensure that these expectations will be met. For example, two people may enjoy eating dinner together regularly, and have no particular preferences as to the best time for dinner (i.e., no conflict is likely over a choice of dinner time). It is obvious, however, that they must agree beforehand on a dinner time, or one person may prepare to eat at 5:00 and the other at 7:00. Therefore, they enact some relational legislation: "We'll agree to eat dinner at 6:30." Or they may agree to "set a time for dinner each day, depending on our schedules."

Relational legislation is important, then, in preventing conflicts and in providing a basis for relational coordination. Some relational laws are implicit, as when a couple adopt some regular behavior pattern but do not directly discuss it. For example, two people may attend church services every Sunday, but never actually say, "We agree to attend church services every Sunday." They just do it and, in so doing, create mutual expectations. Other laws are explicit: the two people verbally agree to follow some guideline for mutual behavior. As a general rule, *relational legislation should be made explicit whenever there is some conflict in the performance of mutual activities and whenever there is some doubt as to whether mutual expectations are sufficiently structured for maximal relational harmony.*

Problems associated with relational legislation

We have isolated three kinds of problems associated with relational legislation. The first problem is underlegislation, when people fail to recognize the importance of instituting relational laws. The second problem is overlegislation, when people assume they can solve all their problems by passing laws. And the third problem is irrelevant legislation, when people try to govern an interpersonal relationship by non-interpersonal laws. We will discuss each of these problems in turn.

Underlegislation

There is a popular story about a husband and wife who owned an electric blanket with dual controls. Each had a separate dial to regulate the temperature for his or her half of the blanket. One night they accidentally switched dials, and so the husband had the dial for his wife's side while she had the dial for his side. The husband, feeling a little too warm, lowered the temperature setting on "his" dial. The wife, suddenly feeling cooler, dialed "her" half of the blanket to a higher temperature. The consequences of this move were soon felt by the husband, who lowered his dial even further, prompting his wife to dial hers even higher, and so on until they discovered the reason for their discomfort.

People in an interpersonal relationship may "burn" or "freeze" one another if they fail to enact even minimal legislation. They may step on one another's toes, offend each other's sensibilities, or otherwise cause needless aggravation simply because they are unable or unwilling to say, "Here is a matter on which we need to reach agreement."

Recently Mark went to dinner at the home of a newly married couple. Before dinner the husband put a record on the stereo, turned the volume up, and proceeded to "get into" the music. After a few minutes his wife rushed over to the stereo, pushed the reject button, and shouted loudly, "Turn that record off!" It immediately became clear that the wife had been silently suffering for a week while her mate played his favorite record over and over again. It seems they had decided that in their marriage both could do as they pleased. But because they were unwilling to set down some basic guidelines for the use of the stereo when both were at home, the wife was hardly able to do as she pleased. In the long run the husband's freedom also would have been restricted. His behavior was having certain negative consequences for his wife, and he was bound to feel the repercussions sooner or later.

This example points out an important by-product of the legislation process: increased communication and understanding. When two

people begin to lay out the rules by which they intend to govern their relationship, they must exchange considerable information about their personal preferences and pet peeves regarding numerous relational activities. This information can be useful to each person in attempting to maximize both his own and the other's satisfaction. In addition, by developing mutual legislation they can avoid one of the more serious problems a relationship can face: hidden legislation.

Hidden legislation is legislation privately adopted by one member of a relationship. The obvious drawback to this kind of legislation is that the uninformed person may unknowingly be judged guilty of "criminal conduct," and having had no reasonable opportunity to follow the "law," must suffer whatever penalty the legislator has in store. One of the basic principles of our government is that all citizens shall be free to learn what laws govern their conduct, so that no court can arbitrarily or capriciously punish them for violating a law that the judge has just pulled out from under his robe. But many interpersonal relationships have no such safeguard.

A friend of ours once had a roommate who passed hidden legislation. Every evening the roommate talked on the phone with his girlfriend. The roommate decided that during these phone conversations our friend was supposed to leave the room so his girl and he could chat privately. But since he never informed our friend of his wishes, our friend frequently remained in the room, unintentionally irritating his roommate. Apparently there were several other similarly hidden laws that our friend unknowingly violated, and one day the roommate abruptly announced that he was moving out, saying he had never known such an inconsiderate person in all his life.

Problems of underlegislation, and the related problems of hidden legislation, are relatively easy to avoid. Given good will and a cooperative spirit on the parts of both people, reasonable and effective legislation can be developed for any relationship.

Overlegislation

The question is, how much is enough? How many laws does a relationship need? Certainly some relationships pass the point of no return in constructing systems of laws. The laws may be too pervasive and extensive, or they may become more important to the relationship than the people forming it. Although we feel that the problems arising from underlegislation are more common and more severe than those arising from overlegislation (problems of underlegislation stem from a lack of information, which makes them harder to solve), the causes of overlegislation are significant sources of relational difficulty.

One cause of overlegislation is tyranny by one member of a relationship. When a tyrannical party is able to force adoption of one piece of legislation after another, because of either weak opposition or default by the other party, the result is overlegislation. One obvious drawback to overly extensive and nonmutual legislation is that the weaker party may eventually become dissatisfied and, at first opportunity, rebel or quit the relationship. But there is a more subtle and perhaps more serious drawback associated with tyrannical overlegislation. When one member of a relationship is routinely deprived of the opportunity to make relational inputs, the relationship as a whole may become impoverished. Just as political and military power tends to corrupt, so can relational power corrupt the person who totally dominates the legislative process. Furthermore, the self-esteem of the powerless member may diminish significantly. Unless legislative control is more evenly divided, neither member of the relationship may be able to provide much satisfaction for the other.

Another source of relational overlegislation is fear on the part of one or both members of the relationship. Any relationship inevitably results in some degree of uncertainty. At an elementary level, there may be uncertainty about simple matters of coordination: housekeeping chores (whose responsibility is it to clean the bathroom), finances

(figuring out who owes what on the phone bill), or love-making (should one person wait for the other to initiate it). At a different level, there may be uncertainty as to the faithfulness or reliability of each party ("Will you always tell me the truth?" or "Is there anyone else but me?") or about the permanence of the relationship ("Will you love me tomorrow? A year from now? Forever and always?"). Some people have learned to tolerate more uncertainty than others. People who can live with relational uncertainty recognize that some future events cannot be reliably controlled and that, therefore, any attempt at control is foolish and doomed to ineffectiveness.

Other people fear that relational events will somehow slip from their grasp. They cannot abide much uncertainty and often try to "legislate out" the possibility of unpredictable or undesirable events. They seem to need to place extra-relational restrictions on themselves or their counterparts, ostensibly to assure themselves that they will not have to deal with unpleasantries at some future time. Perhaps the archetypal overlegislator in this regard is the person who, fearing abandonment or rejection by his or her lover, urges marriage. The marriage ceremony institutes, in effect, a set of laws by which the parties promise to love and cherish one another forever. We are not, of course, saying that all people who get married do so out of fear, but the marriage vows do offer convenient (though usually short-lived) solace for those who cannot tolerate the uncertainty of an unbound relationship.

Irrelevant legislation

If you are an automobile driver, at least once in your life you have probably found yourself in this dilemma: you are driving home at three in the morning; the streets are deserted, and you come to a red light at an intersection. You stop and note that there are no cars approaching from either direction. Do you wait for the light to turn green or do you drive on? You may wonder if maybe, just maybe, there is a policeman parked on a nearby sidestreet waiting for you to violate the law, and this possibility keeps you on the straight and narrow. Nevertheless, you may be irritated that your behavior must be regulated by a law meant for other people at other times of the day under different conditions. If you are philosophically inclined, you may speculate on the necessity for uniform laws covering diverse circumstances for a heterogeneous population, on the matter of the greatest good for the greatest number, and so on—as you wait to shift into first gear, and be on your way.

Such cultural-level legislation can be contrasted with psychological-level legislation. Participants in an interpersonal relationship have the opportunity to design legislation to suit the needs of their own relationship. They do not need to govern themselves as they would govern the whole of society. In other words, they can avoid tying each other up at traffic lights with laws that are unnecessary or inappropriate for themselves.

Noninterpersonal legislation is fairly common. The man who says, "My wife will have dinner ready at five, do the laundry, and clean the house," is disposed to noninterpersonal legislation. (Recall from chapter 1 our acquaintance who divorced his wife because he felt she did things for him out of enjoyment rather than wifely duty.) Similarly, the woman who arbitrarily decides it is not her role to mow the lawn, take the car in for tune-ups, or empty the garbage is prone to design irrelevant legislation for her relationships. When people fail to base their legislative decisions on information concerning their mutual needs, capacities, and expectations, their legislation is likely to be irrelevant for their relationship and possibly dysfunctional for governing their mutual transactions.

An example of the intricacies of relational legislation: communicating about sex-related problems

Often in sustained interpersonal relationships, problems arise about sexually-oriented matters. This is hardly surprising since most people have difficulty talking about such matters. They feel that sex is a crucial element of their self-concepts: our culture teaches the importance of "being a man" and "being a woman." It is not surprising, therefore, that even people who can openly discuss general sexual topics hesitate to say anything about their own problems. Since there is a chance that the information could be used against them, with strong negative consequences, they classify this information as very private and resist sharing it with their relational counterparts.

Frequently, problems of sexual communication are compounded by relational underlegislation. Even though one or both of the parties manifest attitudes or engage in behaviors that are annoying, or even traumatic, to the other, the issues remain buried because of reluctance to suggest legislation. For example, one participant in the relationship may see nothing wrong with talking about sexual hangups or disclosing sexual experiences to friends and acquaintances. If the other participant regards such information as relationally sacred and confidential, he or she is likely to be embarrassed, hurt, or angered by these perceived communicative indiscretions. Or one party (usually the male) may apparently delight in telling off-color jokes, reading "adult" books, or attending X-rated movies, much to the mortification and resentment of his mate. Although she does not explicitly express her distaste, it is, nevertheless, communicated subtly to him, and he begins to resent what is perceived as her puritanical bent.

If neither seeks recourse in relational legislation, the seeds of conflict are sown. Many aspects of the relationship are detrimentally influenced: the couple find that their own sexual encounters are less frequent and less satisfying; they begin to argue about other previously harmonious dimensions of their relationship; they grow suspicious of each other's mental health and moral fiber. Perhaps they are driven to seek companionship with a third party to compensate for the developing void in their own relationship. By this time attempts at relational legislation are probably doomed, for egos are squarely on the line and the participants are almost certain to perceive the attempts as threats to relational freedom.

Of course, overlegislation about sexual communication is also a distinct possibility. If a couple seeks to formally legislate every sexual message, attitude, and behavior, much of the freedom and spontaneity disappears from their relationship. In the case of relational tyranny, the power figure may enact sweeping legislation, to the psychic detriment of the other participant, or participants, in the relationship. Thus, in the Archie Bunker household there is one overriding "law": sexually-oriented communication is forbidden. Although Edith bears up surprisingly well under this sanction, she sometimes appears frustrated or stifled (to use Archie's own terminology) by the oppressive atmosphere concerning matters sexual.

Finally, probably no other area suffers so much from irrelevant legislation as sexual communication. Because of its powerful personal impact, sex is strongly influenced by cultural and sociological norms; this is as true of what we say about sex as what we do about it. Consequently, there is a strong tendency to try to legislate sexual communication noninterpersonally. Keeping up with the Joneses—or perhaps more accurately, remaining as repressed as the Joneses—has been the traditional order of the day. Recently, of course, there has been considerable emphasis on becoming sexually liberated. Ironically, however, this quest for individual freedom has been largely predicated on cultural and sociological generalizations about "proper, healthy" sexual attitudes, rather than on allowing the participants in a relationship to define the sexual parameters of their relationship according to their preferences and demands. Paradoxically, *Playboy* and *Ms.*, not individual choice and stimulus discrimination, dictate our attitudes about sexual "freedom."

We believe that most potentially long-term relationships would profit from the prudent use of interpersonal relational legislation in regard to sexual problems. Couples should agree on the conduct of their sexually-oriented transactions: they should spurn the hazards of under-, over-, or irrelevant legislation. How they agree to communicate about sexual matters is infinitely more important than how most others deal with such problems. To ignore, dictate, or depersonalize this important relational matter is to court disaster.

When the going gets rough

Thus far our discussion of relational problems has rested on the assumption that interpersonal relationships should be maintained, that people should try to stay together in the face of difficulties. For example, in our listing of the outcomes of conflict management, we indicated that the least desirable outcome was the termination of an interpersonal relationship. Nevertheless, we do not believe that it is always in people's best interests to sustain their interpersonal relationships through a storm of problems. Sometimes people just seem to be incompatible: no matter how hard they try, they are unable to get along together. Occasionally, one or both persons demonstrate a striking lack of interpersonal skill, whether it manifests itself in obsessive jealousy, overbearing selfishness, insensitivity to the needs of others, or extreme hostility. Such ineptness may make the maintenance of a relationship very difficult, if not dysfunctional, for the people involved.

Danger signals in interpersonal relationships

Several danger signals can usually be observed if an interpersonal relationship is in serious trouble. For some people a danger signal may mean that they should reevaluate their relationship. Often major restructuring of the relationship is necessary; sometimes termination is the only reasonable way out.

People are frequently unsure as to what constitutes good grounds for terminating an interpersonal relationship. They note that they are generally bored with the relationship or that it has ceased to grow. Often they are simply tired of continually coping with relational conflict. But to the extent that people do not know what to expect from an interpersonal relationship or have no basis for comparing their present relationship with others, they may either terminate a relationship too abruptly or try to sustain a relationship that has little chance for improvement. We suggest the following danger signals as general guidelines for evaluating the success of relational efforts.

Danger signal 1
A relationship is likely to be in trouble when 50 percent or more of the communication is devoted to conflict management. This point is so obvious that it is often overlooked: when people spend a majority of their time talking about conflicts, it is a good indication that they are having a lot of conflicts. Communication that is oriented toward avoiding or patching up disputes, soothing hurt feelings, or restoring communication channels after severe breakdowns is often accompanied by considerable stress. Some people seem to expend much energy in relational fire-fighting, but the frequency and intensity of the fires do not diminish.

When conflict is a consistent, integral aspect of a relationship, the participants may legitimately ask where the relationship is getting them. To be sure, there are some important benefits to be gained from conflict situations: increasing your understanding of yourself and other people and using this increased understanding for improved environmental control. When it appears that all you have to show for your efforts is a relational holding pattern—when you can see no improvement in understanding or control—you should probably question the long-range value of your relationship.

To say that 50 percent is a danger point is, of course, somewhat arbitrary. We derive this estimate from the basic proposition that with relationships as with other spheres of life, you should get as much out of them as you put into them. Although this may not always be possible in the short run—some periods are more loaded with problems than others—we believe that it is a good long-run measure of the success of a relationship.

Danger signal 2
A relationship is likely to be in trouble when relational escalation is not congruent with relational satisfaction. You will recall our discussion of relational escalation in chapter 7. A relationship escalates when a certain dimension of it significantly increases in intensity. Our interest here is in escalations having to do with the expected permanence

of a relationship. We can isolate four such escalation points typical in our culture:

1. When two people consider themselves as going together rather than merely dating
2. When they decide to become engaged
3. When they decide to get married
4. When they decide to have children

Certainly, the pattern is not always so highly formalized, nor do the steps always occur in the order we listed. But the pattern is general enough to be representative of a large number of people.

At each of these four escalation points people are deciding, in effect, to increase their interdependence and to extend their relationship further into the future. One would hope that the progress of a relationship could be charted as the solid line in figure 9.2. People should decide to escalate their relationship as their happiness with the relationship increases. Escalation should result from satisfaction. However, it seems that the progress of many relationships is more accurately reflected by the broken line in figure 9.2.

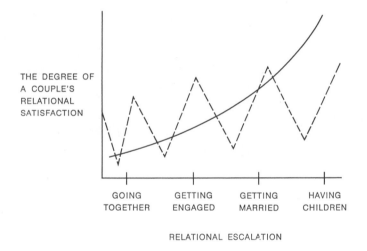

THE DEGREE OF A COUPLE'S RELATIONAL SATISFACTION

GOING TOGETHER   GETTING ENGAGED   GETTING MARRIED   HAVING CHILDREN

RELATIONAL ESCALATION

Fig. 9.2   Desirable and undesirable progression of relational escalation and relational satisfaction

Some couples seem to view continuance of their relationship as their number one goal. When their mutual happiness begins to flag, they attempt to revive it by digging in deeper—by escalating their relationship. Perhaps they believe that, by defining themselves as more interdependent and more permanent, their dissatisfaction will dissipate or that, as a consequence of greater commitment, they will be motivated to work harder for the success of the relationship. In addition, they may recognize that escalation can act as a temporary rejuvenator: their new relational status gives people something to talk about; it puts them in a novel situation.

Both members of a relationship may not be equally convinced of the restorative powers of escalation. Perhaps more often than not, one member is more threatened than the other by a possible breakup of the relationship and undertakes to persuade the other of the merits of escalation. This move can place considerable pressure on the skeptical party; it may also bring the two people into direct confrontation over their estimates of the probable success of escalation.

A third general pattern of escalation seems noteworthy. Sometimes people decide to escalate when they reach what might be called a "critical limit" in their relationship. Suppose a couple has been going together for six months. Friends and relatives may begin to say, "When are you going to get engaged (or married)?" Similarly, if two people have been married for some time they may be questioned as to when they will have children, especially by people who already have children. There seem to be certain cultural expectations about how long a couple should remain at one stage of relational escalation before moving on to another. Moreover, the members of the relationship may have similar expectations. They may say, "Well, we seem to be doing pretty well, but how long can we continue to go together without formally getting more serious? There doesn't seem to be any future in that. Maybe we should begin to talk about getting married. Isn't that the inevitable result, anyway?" People are especially prone to this form of decision-making when one person is about to graduate from college or take a job in another city. If the separation brought about by such an event seems likely to result in termination of the relationship, they may escalate to higher levels of relational permanence, not so much out of a desire for permanence as out of a fear of termination.

People escalate their relationships, then, when they are particularly satisfied with them, when they are afraid of losing them, or when it seems as if no other suitable alternative is available. The latter two bases for escalation are negative; they stem not from a positive desire for escalation but from a desire to avoid the consequences of not escalating. Considerable internal or external pressure may result in escalation for reasons apart from relational satisfaction. The consequences can be long-term misery. For a relationship to survive and thrive, there must be an active desire for what the relationship has to offer rather than an active escape from the drawbacks of not sustaining the relationship.

Danger signal 3

A relationship is likely to be in trouble when the participants no longer feel like taking part in it. This danger signal is rather subtle, and yet can be a highly useful indicator of trouble in an interpersonal relationship. A relationship tends to have an existence that is directly tied to, but somehow separated from, the individuals who comprise it. This distinct existence consists of the mutual behavior patterns of the members, their set of legislative agreements, their expectations for the relationship, and their attempts to maintain it. When someone refers to "the relationship I have with John" or to "Margie and me," they are referring to something that is almost a living and breathing entity, something that exists apart from the speaker and his or her relational partner. A person can be sensitive and open-minded; a relationship can be insensitive and restrictive. Someone can wish you the best for your future, but a relationship can narrow your horizons and stifle your growth.

Because a relationship can be conceived of as a separate entity, we can talk of "taking part in a relationship." Even though you have participated in the creation and structuring of the relationship, it becomes more than your individual input, more than the input of any single person. A relationship has a past and a future, a set of values and attitudes, and predictable patterns of behavior. You can see the future course of a relationship as consistent or inconsistent with your own future. You can see its values and attitudes as congruent or incongruent with your own. You can prefer its predominant behavior patterns, or some other set of patterns. To the extent that you no longer feel like participating in, and contributing to, the relationship, you should question the appropriateness of continuing it.

When you feel that an interpersonal relationship is not progressing smoothly, focus upon the relationship as an entity as well as upon the individuals (yourself included) who form the relationship. Because the relationship is the product of the combined inputs of the two people but yet is different than either person, your examination is likely to yield different results than if you examined John-as-John or Margie-as-Margie. John-and-Margie-as-they-are-together should be the subject of your analysis. If the results of your examination are negative, it does not necessarily imply an indictment of either individual in the relationship. Some people can get along fine as friends, but when they become intimates, their relationship is doomed. Termination of an interpersonal relationship may sometimes be the only answer for preserving the integrity of the parties involved.

Finally, it should be stressed that any decision to maintain or terminate an interpersonal relationship is inevitably rooted in a subjective estimate of the reward/cost ratios associated with the alternative choices. A person may have a generally satisfactory relationship with someone else and yet choose to terminate it because the rewards of an alternative relationship are perceived even more positively—reasonably happy people sometimes dissolve a marriage. Conversely, an individual may be relatively disenchanted with a relationship and yet remain in it because the alternatives are perceived as even more costly—reasonably miserable people sometimes continue to endure a marriage. This is not to say that these subjective estimates are always accurate: the reasonably happy person may rue the day he chose to strike out anew and the reasonably miserable person may eventually regret a life of unhappiness.

People's relational problems are always relative; they are heightened or diminished by a feast or famine of other potentially attractive interpersonal relationships. This fact suggests a final rule of thumb when deciding whether or not to continue a relationship: *as much as possible, try to determine the relative merits of sustaining or terminating a relationship apart from the considerations of potential relational alternatives.* Although we suspect it often happens, the best time to terminate a marriage probably is not when one of the partners is involved romantically with a third party. Even though it is admittedly difficult for the scorned partner to adopt a forgiving stance or for the smitten one to behave with relational rationality, there may be times when both stand to gain more relationally by avoiding hasty termination than they stand to profit individually by agreeing on a swift dissolution. Such are the intricacies of a relational viewpoint.

Summary

What kinds of relational situations are problematic? How serious are they? Why do they arise? What strategies should be used in dealing with them? Although similar enough to warrant general answers to questions like these, patterns of human communication vary so much that general answers are bound to be inadequate for specific individuals.

Our intent in this chapter has not been to supply answers, even general ones, to questions about relational problems. Instead, we have tried to suggest a broad approach based on concern for a communication relationship. Most approaches with which we are familiar focus almost exclusively on the individuals having difficulties with one another. Our suggestions concerning relational conflict, legislation, and danger signals derive from a holistic conception of communication. Coupled with sensitivity to individual differences and skill in interpersonal communication, they can serve as a basis for your own personally tailored approach to relational problems.

Probes

1. Try to identify instances of the three types of conflict in your own relationships or those of your friends and acquaintances. What communication strategies would you use to deal with each? What strategies seem ineffective to you?

2. Gerry and Mark point out that pseudo-conflict often evolves into ego-conflict. How does this occur? What communication strategies can minimize the likelihood of this occurrence?

3. "Conflict dissolution seldom, if ever, occurs." Attack, defend, or modify this statement. Have you ever been a party to successful conflict dissolution? If so, explain how this result came about.

4. Write a paper speculating how a person's cognitive style (chapter 5) may be related to his approach to relational legislation. Are highly dogmatic people likely to be especially susceptible to underlegislation, overlegislation, or irrelevant legislation? What about low-dogmatic people?

5. Examine several of your interpersonal relationships for relational legislation. Does your approach to legislation differ from relationship to relationship? What factors about the relationship and/or the other party determine your approach?

6. Gerry and Mark mention three relational danger signals. Can you add to their list? What criteria do you use to assess the quality of your interpersonal relationships?

7. Locate a record of John Prine's song "Dear Abby." (It's in the album *Sweet Revenge.*) Listen to the relational problems detailed by the "letter writers" and select several that reflect concepts discussed in this chapter. Use the concepts in a paper analyzing the problems.

Communicating Interpersonally:

Making Messages

This part contains a single chapter, but each of its four major sections could be a chapter in itself. We chose to group them in one chapter to maintain their internal consistency and to emphasize the interrelatedness of their topic areas. Each topic deals with an important facet of making messages: message-making energy, self-disclosure, making conversation, and some limitations of language.

The term "message-making energy" refers to the effort people expend when encoding and decoding information in symbolic transactions. The amount of energy demanded for effective communication depends on message complexity, communicative skill, as well as situational and relational uncertainty. Our discussion centers on methods for reducing energy expenditure and catalogues some of the effects brought about by high energy demands.

Self-disclosure involves the revelation of personally private information. The message strategy of self-disclosure can foster personal and relational development and maintenance, but it can also be used to create illusions of openness and honesty. We treat self-disclosure as an important interpersonal skill often essential to the exchange of valuable relational information. But we do not believe it is a panacea for all relational problems. Self-disclosure can be used for selfish purposes, and unskilled self-disclosure has great potential for individual and mutual damage.

You may be surprised that we have included a discussion of making conversation in this chapter. Many conversations seem limited to noninterpersonal exchanges. The importance of conversation lies partly in its facilitation of relational escalation. Conversation is often the starting point for more intimate interchanges. Furthermore, conversation commonly provides us with casual social contacts that most individuals need. For these reasons, conversational skills are highly useful weapons in interpersonal arsenals.

The final section of chapter 10 details several of the limitations imposed by language on our communicative transactions. Sometimes the encoding methods available do not permit us to say precisely what we mean. Sometimes the things people say seem more important than the things they do. And sometimes the communication media we use lack the capacity to convey all the information we want to convey. When people are faced with one or more of these language-related limitations, they have to compensate in some way to avoid communication breakdowns and relational strains.

10

Man is a communicator, . . . and his survival, as well as the quality of his survival, depends upon communication.

William Brooks, *Speech Communication*

For each of us life begins in communication.

R. Wayne Pace and Robert Boren, *The Human Transaction: Facets, Functions, and Forms of Interpersonal Communication*

Man is a communicating animal.

James McCroskey, Carl Larson, and Mark Knapp, *An Introduction to Interpersonal Communication*

Communication, like breathing, is necessary to our continued existence.

Gerald Miller and Mark Steinberg, *Between People: A New Analysis of Interpersonal Communication*

Interpersonal Messages: Problems and Strategies

Few would quarrel with the opening quotes for this chapter, taken from the beginning pages of several recent texts on human communication. We interpret such assertions to mean that human beings are strongly disposed to communicate with each other, and that communication is an exceedingly important aspect of social behavior. Sometimes, however, we interpret such statements to mean that we have a natural ability to communicate—and to communicate well. If man really is a communicating animal, what ails those of us who feel we often have trouble communicating? After all, we also describe man as a warm-blooded animal, and when his body is unable to maintain the temperature at about 98.6 degrees, we know he is ailing. But we are often unable to maintain an appropriate level of communication, to keep our communication functioning well, and to sustain it against various dangers.

Perhaps when you were a teenager, someone told you that your high school years would be the best in your life. If, as with many people, these years proved to be miserable, you may be able to understand people's feelings about communication ineffectiveness—whether or not you have since revised your estimation of those years. Sometimes we get the impression we are supposed to be good at communication, but often we wind up utter failures. Others do not always understand us. We have difficulty saying what we mean. Our messages get distorted, and we in turn distort the messages of others. Should we feel less than human because man is a communicator and we are so often very poor communicators?

Those of us who have difficulty communicating can take heart from Berlo's (1971) assertion that "the probability of perfect communication is zero" (p. 7). He implies that, with the many barriers to successful communication, people should be more surprised when their communication transactions go well than when they do not. Still, although statements like "Man is a communicating animal" do not mean that man has an innate capacity for trouble-free communication, neither does the assertion that "the probability of perfect communication is zero" mean that we cannot improve our communicative abilities.

Our perspective on making messages

We view message-making as a transactional process. When people communicate, there is considerable simultaneous sending and receiving; the communicators transact messages. For instance, when Jill talks to Jack, not only can he see and hear (and perhaps smell and touch) her, but also she can see him. Both of them send nonverbal messages that offer clues to the ways they are reacting to each other. Also, when people communicate, they are interdependent since each one's messages are influenced by the other's behavior. Jill, for example, may alter her message in midstream because of messages from Jack.

There is no good language for talking about simultaneous activity by two or more communicators. If we believed that message transmission is sequential and linear, we would not object to saying that first Mark sends, then Gerry receives, then Gerry sends, then Mark receives, and so on. Observe two people communicating and try to tell someone else about the simultaneous behaviors of both. Undoubtedly you will have to resort to some sort of sequential strategy, though you may be able to reduce linearity by using such words and phrases as "while" or "at the same time as." You might say, for example, "While Jill was shouting and waving her hands angrily, Jack seemed detached and preoccupied" or "Jill was trying to clean a stain off her skirt at the same time as Jack was explaining his problem."

Since we know of no good, analytic way to totally avoid linear sequencing, we sometimes divide the topics discussed in this chapter into sending and receiving, or encoding and decoding. Obviously, when two or more persons engage in a communication transaction, simultaneous expenditure of encoding and decoding energy occurs; nevertheless, to analyze the situation carefully, some separation of the two activities is demanded.

There is a second justification, besides pure necessity, for examining separately the component parts of some message-making processes. To say that both encoding and decoding energy are expended simultaneously should not be taken to mean that the energy levels are identical for both communicators. One participant may be burning up considerable encoding energy, while the other devotes minimum effort to decoding. In fact, one typical way of dealing with low perceived

expenditure of decoding energy is to accelerate encoding efforts. Should a communicator seek to cultivate a favorable impression and a subsequent positive response (e.g., when striving to land a very desirable professional position or to arrange a social engagement with a highly attractive partner) and should the other party seem disinterested or aloof, the communicator is likely to work harder at message encoding: to weigh more carefully his content options and to talk more loudly or emphatically.

The state of a relationship or transaction can be partially assessed by analyzing similarities or differences in the energy outputs of the participants. When neither party expends much communication energy, the relationship is usually unimportant to both. (There may be some long-term interpersonal relationships where the participants know each other so well that high levels of energy expenditure are unnecessary.) When both parties exert themselves strenuously at message-making, the relationship is perceived as mutually important. When two parties differ in energy output, their perceptions of the importance of the relationship also vary. Thus, at the noninterpersonal level, it is hardly surprising that low status persons devote considerable effort to communication attempts with high status counterparts even when faced with a continuing absence of reciprocity (Kelley, 1951). For the former, the relationship is perceived as quite important; while for the latter, the rewards to be gained from the relationship are generally perceived as minimal.

An overview of the chapter

In this chapter we examine some message strategies that may enhance communicative capacity. More specifically, we discuss some of the difficulties people experience in dealing with messages, both noninterpersonal and interpersonal, and we suggest some methods for either avoiding or overcoming these difficulties. Moreover, as we have tried to do throughout this book, we consider some of the differences in making noninterpersonal as opposed to interpersonal messages and examine some of the ways in which skillful use of message strategies can aid a communicator in moving from the noninterpersonal to the interpersonal level.

Rather than surveying a wide spectrum of possible variables, we shall focus on four aspects of message-making that cause difficulty for many communicators. We have already mentioned the first area, *communication energy*, or the amount of energy a person needs to expend in transmitting and receiving messages. Then we move to a topic that has generated considerable research and controversy in recent years, *self-disclosure*. We seek to clarify some of the issues involved in self-disclosure and to highlight some advantages and disadvantages resulting from the use of self-disclosing message strategies. Our next topic, *making conversation*, we view as one of the most troublesome yet important aspects of human communication. Finally, we consider some of the *limitations on our use of verbal language*: some of the problems people encounter because of overreliance on verbal as opposed to nonverbal messages.

Our perspective on making messages has caused us to depart from the approach typically used in dealing with message transmission. This approach usually results in two chapters on the subject: one dealing with senders and one with receivers or, alternatively, one focusing on encoding and one on decoding. To maintain our transactional perspective, we have combined these two topics into a discussion of communication energy. We also treat the other three topics mentioned above as related aspects of message-making. Each one of these four topics, however, can be considered independently if such an approach seems preferable.

Communication energy: encoding and decoding

"Man, I really had to work to get through to him!"

"It took all the energy I had to stay awake and pay attention to that lecture."

"Wow, after a discussion like that I feel totally drained!"

How often have you heard people use these kinds of statements to describe a particular communication transaction? The first assertion focuses on encoding energy, the second on decoding effort, and the third on a subtle blend of both aspects of message-making. Naturally, we sometimes encounter the antithetical counterparts of these utterances; e.g., "I wasn't even thinking about what I said" or "My mind was a thousand miles away while she was talking." Attention to one's communication transactions demands energy.

We feel that the notion of communication energy, both when encoding and decoding, is an important—and as yet barely explored—aspect of communication transactions. This notion involves such questions as:

> In general, how hard do you have to work to communicate?

> How much energy do you have to expend to initiate, maintain, or conclude a transaction?

> How much effort does it take to achieve a particular communication goal?

Near the end of chapter 7 we noted that in certain situations, or with certain people, we may find it more or less easy to communicate. We argued that the ease with which you and another person can communicate in part determines whether the two of you will develop an interpersonal relationship. The degree to which people find it easy or difficult to communicate can be measured in part by the amount of energy they expend in encoding and decoding messages.

High energy situations

If you have visited a non-English-speaking country or studied a foreign language, you are keenly aware of the high level of energy needed to communicate in these situations. To put your thoughts into words you have to think very carefully. You have to organize your thoughts, translate them into the other language, take care to speak with the proper pronunciation, and closely observe your receiver to make sure he has interpreted your message as you intended. Each of these steps, save possibly the final one, requires much more energy than when you communicate in English—and even interpreting cues is likely to be more taxing, since you are less certain about how to interpret the other person's feedback. You are aware of the high probability of error in your communication. You may want to say "Come!" but in fact you say "Go!" You may want to speak politely, but the words you say may convey rudeness to the native speaker. Incorrect verb tense, word choice, or pronunciation can all grossly distort your intended meaning. Encoding messages in a foreign language can be exhausting if you are not very fluent.

By the same token, decoding the messages of your foreign acquaintance demands considerable effort. While he may be speaking at a normal conversational rate for a native user of the language, the words sound to you as if they were coming with lightning speed. You strain to pick up key verbal cues and fill in the missing spaces by educated, but sometimes erroneous, guesswork. Some words and idioms do not register, and you find yourself searching frantically for their probable meanings. Moreover, you become aware of a tendency to respond to his messages and then immediately to doubt that you understood them correctly. (Much the same phenomenon occurs when we do not hear the words of a speaker of our native language; but being unwilling to admit it, we reply, "Yes," "Right," or "Um-Hmm," only to be plagued by the thought that the speaker may have said something like, "Boy, I'm really a stupid oaf!") In short, a continued serious attempt to receive messages rather than to drop out of the communicative transaction is certain to take a heavy toll in decoding energy.

Can you recognize similar difficulties in any relatively common communication transactions that are carried out in your own language? Have you ever tried to console a bereaved friend, searching for the right words to convey your sympathy? Have you ever attempted to patch up a strained interpersonal relationship after a highly emotional misunderstanding? Have you ever told a series of lies and then had to be very careful of what you said to particular people for fear of tripping yourself up? Perhaps you have been obliged to carry on a conversation with someone with whom you have little in common. Or you may have had to explain some complicated and touchy personal feelings to someone, and you wanted to be very sure that he or she clearly understood what you were trying to say. Think about these situations and you will quickly conclude that they usually demand considerable encoding and decoding energy.

Three forms of encoding energy

One form of encoding energy involves deciding what to say, how to say it, or even whether to say anything at all. The thinking and choosing inherent in these decision-making processes can require a great deal of energy. A second form comes after you have said something, when you try to determine whether your receiver has understood your message. You may have to reiterate, elaborate, clarify, or even recant the message you have sent. Finally, you may expend a great deal of energy just worrying about real or imagined communication transactions. The tension produced by worry is often a significant energy drain.

Several factors are related to the amount of energy it takes to send messages. One factor is the amount of choice you have in a given communication situation. If you can think of several messages to send, or several ways to send one message, and you are unsure which is most likely to elicit the response you desire from your receiver, then the resulting decision process can take considerable energy. For example, chess—similar in many ways to a complex communication transaction—demands considerable energy. Players are often mentally exhausted by the end of a game. Similarly, courtroom lawyers questioning witnesses during a criminal trial may exert a great deal of effort deciding which questions will elicit the information they want. You may have experienced the energy drain associated with taking an oral or written examination, trying to sell something to a hesitant buyer, or attempting to teach something to a slow learner. The more you have to think of what to say and how to say it, the more you have to expend encoding energy.

Sometimes you may have to decide whether to say anything at all. Suppose a friend and you are taking a course from a certain professor and one day the professor tells you that he thinks your friend is not bright enough to stay in college. Should you relay this information to your friend? Whether the professor's opinion is valid or not, will the information be helpful to your friend? How will your friend react to you for telling him? In a similar vein, many husbands and wives or boyfriends and girlfriends devote considerable energy to deliberating whether to tell their mates of some indiscretion. To disclose or not to disclose is the question they must answer. Whatever their decision, they will have to make the effort either to conceal their errant behavior or deal with the consequences of disclosing it.

The notion of encoding energy should not be confused with Homans's (1961) notion of cost. For him, cost is always related to choosing between two or more behavioral alternatives. If you choose alternative A—with which you associate, say, ten units of reward —instead of alternative B, which is valued at six units of reward, then the cost of choosing A is six: the amount of reward you would have gotten had you chosen B. Cost, then, is relative. The amount of energy expended in a communication situation, however, can be measured apart from considerations of the amount of energy dissipated in any other situation.

Decoding energy

Just as one has to make decisions about the kinds of messages to send, he must also determine what messages to receive. Sometimes the selection of messages requires minimal expenditure of energy; for example, we have already discussed the ways in which prior experience and learning influence the messages a person focuses upon and the ones he ignores. These principles of selective exposure, perception, and retention are graphically illustrated in an old film titled *Eye of the Beholder*. In the movie we see an individual, Mike Gerard, through the eyes of five other persons. Not surprisingly, the visions differ dramatically: a lecherous waiter sees him as a ladies' man, his loving mother as a good boy, a suspicious cab driver as a hoodlum, a literal-minded landlord as a maniac, and a timid, frightened cleaning lady as a murderer. Taken as a whole, these five accounts tell us very little about Mike, but a great deal about the persons decoding messages from and about him.

When decoding is based on strong attitudinal predispositions or firmly embedded stereotypes, little decoding energy is demanded. In fact, if *choice* is taken to mean the conscious weighing of alternatives, such habitual response tendencies do not require decision-making; rather, the filtering of messages occurs at an unconscious level. Suppose, however, that the lecherous waiter were asked to identify messages indicating that Mike is a happily married, faithful husband. Or suppose the waiter's daughter was firmly committed to marrying Mike. The waiter could go on attending only to the verbal and non-verbal messages from Mike that fit his stereotype of Mike as a ladies' man, or he could begin to seek out and choose messages that suggest Mike's potential good qualities as a husband. The former course would require little decoding energy; the latter would probably be quite demanding.

Although the situation just described may seem far-fetched, there are times when self-interest dictates the need to choose another subset of messages. For instance, when an individual has a strong negative stereotype of a particular minority group he can usually filter out and interpret negative messages with little decoding effort. Suddenly, however, he is placed in close professional proximity with a new colleague who is a member of that group. Quite likely he will be motivated to choose positive messages about his new colleague (assuming, of course, that he does not enjoy working in a hostile atmosphere or having negative feelings about his work). Here greater decoding energy must be expended, at least initially, if for no other reason than that our stereotyper is conditioned to attend to negative messages.

There is a second sense in which receivers must expend decoding energy making decisions between alternative messages. Almost everyone has experienced situations involving two or more attractive messages transmitted simultaneously. Suppose, for example, that you are at a party and you are exchanging potentially useful information with a classmate about an upcoming examination. At the same time, two persons within earshot are sharing some juicy gossip about one of your friends. Although there are a few people who can comprehend simultaneously transmitted messages (usually, however, at a high cost in decoding energy), you know that you lack this ability. Hence, you are likely to expend considerable decoding energy on two counts: first, you must choose which of the two attractive messages merits priority; second, even after choosing you will probably have to work hard to tune out the competing message because of its reward value to you. Of course, there are times when choice can be avoided by postponing one of the messages (e.g., you might have asked your classmate to excuse you for a few minutes). But often this request itself involves energy expenditure because it is difficult or awkward. In the hypothetical situation described, your conversation provided the best cover for lurking in the vicinity of the gossipers, and should you terminate it, you might put yourself in the awkward social situation of being perceived as an eavesdropper.

Not only do communicators expend energy attempting to determine whether they have been understood, they also fret about whether they understand the messages of others: this concern for understanding is the decoding analogue to the second form of encoding energy discussed earlier. There is a cartoon showing two psychiatrists exchanging the commonplace greeting hello. As they proceed down the street, the cartoon shows that both have the same thought in mind: "I wonder what he meant by that?" The two psychiatrists are expending decoding energy. In a less whimsical vein, a married friend of ours recently worried for several days about a possible misunderstanding of the messages of some educational testing specialists who were interviewing her son. Although the specialists never asked her to leave the room, she later became concerned that they had been giving her subtle cues to depart, cues that she had not picked up. Both of us sought to reassure her that in this noninterpersonal communication situation it was the responsibility of the interviewers to make instructions, if any, specific. Still, we suspect that if a "decodometer" were available to measure decoding energy expenditure, our friend would have gone clear off the scale.

How much a person worries about decoding accuracy depends, of course, on the importance he attaches to understanding a message "correctly." Perceived importance can be a function of one, or all, of at least three factors: the attractiveness or power of the person transmitting the message, the importance of the message content (usually as it relates to some potential reward for the receiver), and certain communicative characteristics of the receiver himself.

Naturally, if a man is attracted to a woman and would like to develop a relationship with her, he may make a sincere effort to understand her messages and may spend considerable time reflecting about whether he is "reading" her accurately. Since her opinion of him is important, he ponders her messages, attempting to assess what she thinks of him (though at times he may fall prey to some distortion resulting from his need to be accepted by her); since her opinion is at least partially a function of his communication with her, accurate decoding increases the likelihood of an appropriate response. By the same token, if a communicator has considerable control over our rewards and punishments, we worry a great deal about decoding accuracy, regardless of the person's relative attractiveness. Fortunately, both of us like our department chairman, but even if we did not, we would strive to decode his messages accurately, since he exercises considerable control over such rewards as raises, promotions, teaching schedules, and travel funds.

Importance of message content is also a crucial determinant of decoding energy expenditure. Assume two situations with identical message content: directions on how to get from Madison Square Garden to the Statue of Liberty. In the first situation, the communicator says only, "Let me tell you how to get from Madison Square Garden to the Statue of Liberty," while in the second he adds, "and when you get to the Statue of Liberty you will discover at the base of the stairwell an envelope containing $10,000, which will be yours to keep." Can there be any question about which situation will result in the greater drain on decoding energy?

Recently we illustrated this point on a more modest scale with an informal experiment. At two successive graduate student parties, largely attended by the same people, sides were chosen and charades were played for an hour. At the first party prizes were not mentioned and the players were not timed. We noticed that for the first fifteen minutes the players attended fairly closely and manifested concern about decoding messages accurately. For the rest of the hour attention progressively lessened, with some players becoming totally passive and others actually striking up side conversations about other topics. At the second party we offered small prizes to the winning team and indicated that we would time each team's performances carefully. Even these relatively meager rewards produced decided increments in decoding energy; most players were highly active throughout the entire hour and several commented on their fatigue at the game's end.

Finally, receivers differ in their willingness to expend energy in concern over accurate decoding. Each of us knows persons whom we would classify as sympathetic, attentive listeners and others whom we would not. In some cases, these differences may be due to the degree to which we are perceived as attractive or powerful or to the perceived importance of our message content. But even when we take these factors into account, it seems likely that some communicators are just generally more concerned than others with accurate message decoding. We will have more to say about individual communicator differences in communication energy expenditure later in this section.

Laying aside considerations of accuracy and understanding, we suspect that, as with message encoding, some communicators suffer from generalized worry about message decoding. We have known students who seem to manifest a chronic fear of note-taking. Eysenck (1958) has argued that introverted individuals are oversensitive to external social cues; since a message constitutes such a cue, the introvert might be expected to dissipate considerable energy worrying about its implications. While the line between specific concern for decoding accuracy and generalized anxiety about message decoding may be difficult to draw behaviorally, both are probably significant determinants of energy expenditure.

Situational determinants of message-making energy expenditure

We have explicated the concepts of decoding and encoding energy in some detail, for we feel they are important dimensions of the message-making process. Obviously, some communication situations place greater energy demands on the participants than others. We will next examine some of the situational factors that influence the amount of communication energy expended by communicators.

Uncertainty and unfamiliarity
When a communicator is uncertain about the relevant factors in a given situation—e.g., when he is relatively unfamiliar with the other communicators or with the topic of interest—he will work hard to ascertain these factors both prior to and during encoding and decoding of messages. Obviously, this kind of scrutiny requires energy.

A related factor is the degree to which a communicator is practiced or skilled in a given communication situation. If he is unfamiliar with the "rules of the game," or the likely outcomes of a particular situation, he may have to work to learn the rules and to predict outcomes. For example, recall your own experience as a college freshman, entering the strange campus environment. You may have wondered about how to talk to people: How does one talk to a dorm resident advisor? With deference or as a peer? What information does he have about campus life? How does he see his role toward me? How does one talk to professors? What kind of people are they? Do they expect me to know a lot?

The same process occurs when people take new jobs or move to strange cities. They must learn how to communicate. In addition, many specific situations require substantial energy output until you become skilled at them. Asking a professor for an incomplete in his course, applying for a loan, conversing at a formal cocktail party, or trying to run a successful bluff in poker all demand high encoding energy until you have mastered the rules and have become familiar with the outcomes.

Formality

Highly formal situations offer little communicative leeway, since only a few communication behaviors are acceptable and appropriate. Formality affects energy expenditure in two ways. First, the rules for formal situations are often arbitrary and differ widely from rules learned in informal situations. Therefore, there is no choice but to learn the rules from scratch. Second, even after rules have been learned, energy must be directed toward channeling, or restricting, transmitted messages, since there is a narrow range of appropriate communication behaviors. Young children in church expend energy keeping themselves from talking and from running around. During a formal meeting businessmen sometimes have to work to keep their messages on business, rather than social topics. When communicators feel restricted from saying and doing what comes naturally, they have to exert some energy to keep their communication within acceptable bounds.

Complexity and vagueness

Complex or vague situations usually do not make immediate sense. Communicators must work to figure them out, to impose some sort of pattern on them. Choice situations, uncertainty situations, and formal situations all demand more energy when they are complex and vague. For example, if a person works for a company in which he is in daily contact with twenty people, all with different role positions, he will have to exert more effort to ascertain his appropriate communication relationships than if his job entails contact with only three people at his own level.

Vague situations demand more energy because of the multiple meanings they often evoke. A relatively commonplace example involves a bumper sticker often seen on automobiles in the area of Michigan State University. The sticker reads, "I'm a Spartan lover." This statement can have at least three meanings. Since the MSU football team is nicknamed Spartans, one possible meaning is, "I'm an MSU football fan." A second meaning is, "I'm a lover as well as a football fan"; finally, the statement could also mean, "I make love in the manner of the Spartans."

Vagueness often results from a lack of feedback from co-workers, professors, or friends concerning ways they are reacting to incoming communication. How should communicators interpret such a lack of feedback? Are people totally satisfied with them? Have people forgotten them? Are they being purposely ignored? Are others dissatisfied but unwilling to be critical? Each of these interpretations may be legitimate, but it takes work to determine which one is accurate.

Four communicative implications of communication energy expenditure

1. People sometimes evaluate a particular situation or person negatively simply because of high communication energy demands.
Such persons seem to feel there is something inherently wrong with the situation or person because of their vague feelings of discomfort or dissatisfaction. In reality their problem stems from the fact that they have to work hard to communicate. For instance, a friend of ours habitually stands up and paces about whenever he engages in conversation. He may even leave the room for a few seconds, return, and momentarily leave again. Some of his companions react quite negatively to his unconventional communication style, for it makes them exert more energy in adapting their own behavior to his movements. While they do have to work harder to communicate with him, he does not necessarily deserve their enmity.

Many people react negatively to groups advocating reform, whether in regard to civil rights for blacks, equal rights for women, or environmental protection. At least some of their negative responses might be accounted for by the fact that reform groups make strong demands on encoding and decoding energy. Broad-scale social reforms often involve changing ingrained, comfortable patterns of social transaction. People may be unwilling to change these patterns in part because learning new patterns can be highly taxing. The women's liberation movement, for example, has called for major changes in the ways men and women communicate with each other, ranging from general injunctions about role relationships to specific criticisms of words like *chick* and *babe*. We suspect that although both men and women may object to such changes for fear of losing what they perceive as comfortable role relationships, much of the hostility of the counterrevolutionaries stems from their not caring to devote the energy in their daily lives to accomplish these changes.

2. You can decrease energy expenditure in certain communication situations through experience and practice.
Complex situations become simpler, formal situations more natural, and choice situations more habitual once you become familiar with them. Even if a communication situation initially demands considerable encoding energy, you need not permanently steer clear of it. Increased understanding of the situation can result in a significant reduction in your energy expenditure. For example, we mentioned earlier the extreme demands placed on students when they first arrive at an unfamiliar college or university. Can you contrast your present campus experiences with your first days on the scene? You can probably think of many communication situations where increased familiarity has led to a sharp reduction in the effort required to communicate.

3. If you know that you are soon to undergo a taxing communication experience, you should literally rest up for it.
Does it sound strange to say you should take a nap before you talk to someone? People feel quite natural resting up for an athletic event, an examination (which does, of course, drain communication energy), or a cross-country auto trip. They know there will be high energy demands on them for these events; they know that if they want to perform at peak efficiency and effectiveness they must be well prepared. The same thing goes for trying communication events. When you are tired, you are more likely to fall victim to error and breakdown; consequently, you must exert additional energy to rectify your errors. You also want to terminate interaction sooner than when rested, and thus run the risk of hard feelings or further breakdown. In short, you have less patience and less stamina for communicating.

4. As a general rule, the greater your communicative skill, the less energy you need to devote to communication.
Skillful application of communication principles is often useful in coping with situations that demand high energy output. Skilled communicators know how to prevent, recognize, and solve energy-draining problems. They are attuned to the ways in which symbolic subtleties affect energy levels. However, their greater sensitivity to

these subtleties, especially in interpersonal contexts, can sometimes cause them to use up more energy in the short run than would less skilled communicators.

Communication energy expenditure and levels of communication

It would perhaps be comforting if we could make some simple, sovereign generalizations about the relationship of energy expenditure and levels of communication; e.g., it requires more communication energy to communicate interpersonally than to communicate noninterpersonally. Unfortunately, the issue is not this cut and dried. What we will do instead is set forth some general statements that hold most of the time and consider some important exceptions to each of them.

Assertion 1: When compared with interpersonal communication, noninterpersonal communication imposes lower communication energy demands on the communicators.
Given our conceptual framework for distinguishing the two levels of communication, this assertion makes sense, both intuitively and behaviorally. We have repeatedly stressed that when persons base predictions about communication outcomes on cultural or sociological data (the noninterpersonal level), they are expecting a particular communicator to share a few similarities with other members of his culture or of a social group. Assuming they have some information about the culture or relevant social group—and this assumption itself illustrates one restriction we must place on our original generalization—the message-making process should not be too taxing.

In the realm of encoding, cultural or sociological data help to restrict the choice of available messages. Moreover, if the communicator is quite confident of the accuracy of his cultural or sociological level predictions, he need not attend closely to the behaviors of the other transactant. In a sense, message transmission is almost preprogrammed, with certain messages fitted to cultural or sociological expectations. Finally, when it comes to decoding, we have already stressed earlier in this section that cultural or sociological predictions minimize receiver energy expenditure, since they predispose him to look for and to hear certain messages.

Still, we can easily demonstrate that some instances of noninterpersonal communication can be quite taxing. Take the phatic ritual of exchanging greetings; for most of us a casual hello or "How are you?" requires little energy expenditure. Consider, however, a shy person who is somewhat threatened by any human contact. For such a person, even this brief noninterpersonal transaction may be quite demanding.

In a related vein, there are times when a person may want to establish contact with someone especially attractive or powerful. Since an exchange of greetings often constitutes a first step in this process, considerable energy may be expended in planning the transaction and in screwing up courage to make the contact.

Many readers may recall the trauma experienced by Charlie Brown in his efforts to get acquainted with an attractive new girl in his class. Charlie suffers from numerous hangups in his human relationships; he is a retiring person for whom most contacts, no matter how transitory, are difficult. Moreover, he perceives the girl as highly attractive and wants to establish a relationship with her. Consequently, Charlie's days are taxing: he resolves that today will be the day he will say hello, only to renege at the last moment; he speculates endlessly about the way the girl will respond to his greeting; he watches the girl's every movement and attempts to analyze the extent of her awareness, if any, of him. In short, Charlie expends an enormous amount of communication energy worrying about the probable outcomes of a brief, noninterpersonal encounter. In our efforts to establish human contact, most of us have, on occasion, been afflicted by this syndrome.

Noninterpersonal communication can also extract considerable energy when the outcomes are perceived as both important and relatively unpredictable. In most of our daily noninterpersonal transactions, the outcomes are highly predictable; hence, communication energy demands are minimized. If we wish to buy a sirloin steak or a pair of shoes, we have learned where to go to make our purchase, and, assuming the commodities are available, we know the sequence of role behaviors that guide the communication transaction with the butcher or the shoe salesman. Moreover, the price is fixed and usually displayed, and so we know the cost of the product.

But suppose that we are about to purchase a new car. Here the outcomes are both important (if we buy a tough cut of steak for $3 we are unhappy, but we can adjust to the loss; if we buy a lemon for $3,000 we have made a serious financial blunder) and relatively unpredictable (while the price of the steak is fixed at $2.79 a pound, the price of the car is variable, and haggling or bartering is an expected dimension of the transaction). As a consequence, noninterpersonal transactions with car salesmen usually involve a tremendous energy investment; in fact, some people find them so unpleasant that they seek to avoid such encounters. When making a major purchase that requires bargaining, one of our acquaintances takes along a friend who enjoys this game-playing process. While the friend negotiates with the salesman, our acquaintance leaves for a while and returns only to pay the agreed-upon price for the commodity. In a sense he avoids the high energy cost by employing a surrogate communicator.

Similar energy demands are often exacted by a crucial job or placement interview. Again, outcomes are both important and relatively unpredictable, and initial predictions must be based on cultural or sociological data. Despite the resulting noninterpersonal atmosphere, the interviewee is likely to expend considerable communication energy. He may lie awake a long time the night before the interview, planning his responses; the next day have difficulty digesting his breakfast; and enter the interview situation in a highly anxious state. Recently, for instance, our department decided that a personal interview would constitute one data point for determining whether a student should be admitted to graduate study. Since, for some unfathomable reason, most applicants keenly wish to pursue graduate work, the outcome of the interview is important to them; since only a limited number of applicants can be accepted, the interview outcome is relatively unpredictable; and since the faculty interviewers and the potential student interviewees are seldom acquainted, the communication transaction is noninterpersonal. We have ample testimony to indicate that energy expenditure is high; not only are potential students anxious when they enter, they are emotionally and physically drained when they depart.

Thus, while the majority of noninterpersonal communication transactions probably require relatively low levels of communication energy expenditure, there are some obvious exceptions. Significantly, one major source of energy drain in most of the exceptions noted lies in the communicator's motivation to move from the noninterpersonal to the interpersonal level. Questions such as the following are often of crucial import: given that I have several firmly established cultural and sociological generalizations about car salesmen, how does this particular salesman conform to these generalizations and in what ways does he depart from them? How do the faculty members conducting this interview differ from other faculty I have known? What characteristics of this job interviewer set him apart from job interviewers in general? In other words, how can I relate to this communicator as an individual, rather than as a set of cultural expectations or a bundle of sociological roles?

Assertion 2: Attempts to move from the noninterpersonal to the interpersonal level of communication place high energy demands on the communicators.
As we have already indicated, accurate stimulus discrimination (the first step of the empathic process) is a necessary condition for reaching the interpersonal level, and accurate discrimination is hard work. In most cases, then, a communicator must be prepared to offer heavy

payments in energy to achieve the goal of moving to the interpersonal level.

This is not to say that the energy demands on all communicators are equally onerous, nor does it imply that for a given communicator, all attempts to move from the noninterpersonal to the interpersonal level will be equally trying. We have already noted the likelihood that people differ in the degree to which they posess the communicative skills needed to bridge the gap between noninterpersonal and interpersonal communication. Moreover, every person has encountered people with whom communication comes easy, and others who pose a formidable communicative challenge. When the energy drain for initial, noninterpersonal transactions is not excessive, the chances for movement to the interpersonal level are better—given, of course, that the communicator wants to develop an interpersonal relationship.

One word of caution is in order. When we first encounter others who are quite similar to us, we should be careful not to fall prey to the illusion of interpersonal communication. Upon discovering that another individual shares many of our values, attitudes, and personal tastes, it is easy to proclaim, "Oh yes, I understand this person!" Unfortunately, our proclamation may reflect a self-delusion; what we actually understand (or think we understand) is not this person but a set of cultural or sociological generalizations that describe persons who are similar to us. Unless this distinction is kept clearly in mind, it is easy to fall into a comfortable, noninterpersonal relationship that places minimal energy demands on us; while this may be affectively comforting, it is likely to engender unfortunate behavioral consequences. Relevant differences are overlooked and the opportunity for interpersonal communication is aborted. Hence, even when conditions are ripe for the development of interpersonal communication, the communicators must be willing to pay a price in communication energy expenditure.

Assertion 3: During the initial stages of an interpersonal relationship, communication energy demands on the communicators are high; as the relationship matures, communication energy demands decrease. This assertion squares with what we know about human learning. At the outset of a relationship, learning appropriate discriminations requires considerable effort; subtle verbal and nonverbal cues will not be picked up unless close attention is directed to the communication behaviors of the other party. As the parties continue to interact, accurate predictions can be made with greater ease, for the communicators learn the kinds of cues that signal expected communication behavior.

Consider, for example, the development of idiosyncratic rules governing the kind of communication activity commonly labeled *arguing*. In most interpersonal relationships the participants impose boundaries on permissible arguing behaviors; in a sense, each attempts to communicate to the other that you may go this far for this long, but no further and no longer. During the first few arguments the verbal and nonverbal cues denoting the breaching of permissible boundaries are often hard to sort out. But as the parties acquire greater experience in arguing transactions, they usually become more sensitive to these cues, permitting them to spot any interpersonal storm clouds on the horizon.

Again, a precautionary note. In long-standing interpersonal relationships communicators may be lured into underestimating the required amount of communication energy expenditure. To become too confident about your understanding of another person renders you particularly vulnerable to this communicative pitfall. We are all familiar with relationships where one party asserts confidently, "I know him backwards and forwards," while the other laments plaintively, "He takes me for granted." Although the "taking for granted" phenomenon undoubtedly springs from diverse roots, one of its origins can be the interpersonal overconfidence that sometimes develops in a party, or parties, to a long-term relationship.

Summary

Since the amount of communication energy expended can be consciously controlled, at least within certain limits, we conceive of decisions regarding the expenditure of communication energy as part of a communicator's strategic arsenal. We recognize that many noninterpersonal transactions go forward effectively with minimal energy expenditure, but that others impose a great energy drain on at least one of the communicators. Transitions from noninterpersonal to interpersonal communication relationships usually exact a heavy energy toll from the participants, if the transition is to take place successfully. Finally, the amount of energy devoted to sustaining an interpersonal communication relationship somewhat depends on the duration of the relationship and the motivation of the communicators.

You are at least partially the master of your own communicative ship: *you can decide how much communication energy should be invested in particular communication transactions*. Wise investment of this psychic and physical resource is sure to pay communicative dividends, both at the noninterpersonal and interpersonal levels of communication.

Self-disclosure as a message strategy

SELF-DISCLOSER: There are some things on my mind I need to talk about, Fred. I've been feeling really bummed out lately. Nothing seems to be going right for me. I'm close to flunking out of school. I just can't seem to get it together. My roommate has been avoiding me lately. As a matter of fact, all my friends have been avoiding me. I just feel lonely, left out, depressed, and washed up.

FRED: A lot of people feel that way. I've felt like that myself.

SELF-DISCLOSER: Really, Fred? Oh, man, I feel a lot better now that I've gotten those things off my chest.

FRED: Why? You're still lonely, left out, depressed, and washed up.

Earlier we talked about god words and devil words. God words, such as *progress*, *love*, and *mother*, trigger positive emotional responses. By contrast, *Watergate*, *pollution*, and *chauvinism* have become devil words, capable of generating negative responses among many people. Judging from comments by numerous students in our classes and from the contents of recent books on interpersonal behavior, *self-disclosure* has apparently achieved god word status in our society, while its antonym, *self-concealment*, has become a devil word. It is generally considered "good" to self-disclose and "bad" to be unable or unwilling to self-disclose—i.e., to self-conceal. The two terms seem to have acquired the following associations:

People who self-disclose are open, honest, authentic, warm, friendly, free, together, strong, trusting and to be trusted, and maturing personally and interpersonally.

People who self-conceal are phony, dishonest, unauthentic, hung up, fearful, manipulative, distrustful and not to be trusted, cold, and stunted personally and interpersonally.

For the moment, we leave it to you to pass on the accuracy of these associations.

Most discussions of self-disclosure seem to start with the axiom that self-disclosure is a fundamentally powerful aid in establishing closeness and trust, that it is essential to relational escalation and personal growth. Most advocates of self-disclosure do append caveats to their admonitions that people practice self-disclosure. Jourard (1971) writes that too much self-disclosure indicates a disturbed orientation to communication situations. Egan (1970) lists several "possible dangers associated with self-disclosure," though all the dangers involve improper approaches to disclosure. Wenburg and Wilmot (1973), along with Jourard and Egan, do not seem to question the utility of self-disclosure, but do warn their readers of some possible risks in disclosing potentially self-incriminating information.

We agree that self-disclosure can be important to both personal and relational growth. Still, even after heeding the cautions of the preceding authors, we have observed that *self-disclosure is not a sufficient condition for relational development,* nor is it always effective in producing positively valued results for communicators. We contend that self-disclosure is a useful message strategy for personal and relational development only when certain other conditions also exist. Although this position may appear self-evident, self-disclosure has not always been treated within the context of greater relational processes, but rather as a thing-in-itself.

Any relatively thorough discussion of self-disclosure should involve at least two topics: the conditions that surround self-disclosing acts and the consequences that follow from self-disclosure—for the discloser, for the receiver, and for their relationship. Furthermore, the intentions and goals underlying acts of self-disclosure are vitally important. Our discussion departs from the predominantly source-oriented treatments of self-disclosure that have been popular and seeks to examine this phenomenon from within a relational context.

What do we mean by "self-disclosure"?

One of the more practical definitions of self-disclosure has been developed by Culbert (1967).

> Self-disclosure refers to an individual's explicitly communicating to one or more others some personal information that *he believes these others would be unlikely to acquire unless he himself discloses it.* Moreover, this information must be "personally private"; that is, it must be of such a nature that it is *not something the individual would disclose to everyone who might inquire about it.* (p. 2 [italics ours])

Culbert also distinguishes between self-disclosure and self-description.

> Self-description designates self-data that an individual is likely to feel comfortable in revealing to most others. Additionally, self-description includes information that an individual knows about himself, that is readily perceivable by most others, and by which he agrees to be known. Self-description is likely to include an individual's physical characteristics, his occupation, marital status, and so on. However, both self-disclosure and self-

description, as defined here, contain many *relative* aspects. Self-information that is "personally private" for one individual may not, for whatever reason, be personally private for another. Self-information that one individual believes most others have about him may be the guarded secret of another. Self-information that one individual acknowledges others have, and thus faces up to, may be vigorously denied by another, lest he be flooded by feelings of embarrassment. (p. 2)

To be sure, as we shall indicate later, there are some cultural and sociological generalizations about intimate and non-intimate topics: in our society an exchange about sexual preferences is usually thought of as more intimate than an exchange of biographical information. But this does not alter the fact that some people speak freely about their sexual episodes while others are mortified by their place of birth.

Two conditions relevant to self-disclosing transactions
Culbert directly asserts that *a self-disclosing message must be intentionally encoded*, rather than accidentally or unconsciously transmitted. If we see someone slip on an icy sidewalk, we do not say that he "disclosed" a temporary inability to maintain his balance. However, the statement "sometimes I feel clumsy" might be regarded as self-disclosing. Second, Culbert indirectly implies that *self-disclosure often involves some degree of risk* for the discloser. Since the discloser is revealing "private" information, he cannot always be sure how others will react. Since the information concerns himself, he may be particularly vulnerable to undesirable responses.

There is some ambiguity associated with Culbert's concept of "personally private" information, and we think the reduction of this ambiguity is fundamental to clarifying the notion of self-disclosure. Culbert's ambiguity may have been purposeful to allow for wide flexibility of interpretation; for, as he says, people have widely differing conceptions of what kinds of information are personal and private. Nevertheless, we can be somewhat more precise about the concept of personally private information without unduly decreasing the generality of the term. It is possible to gain some understanding as to why people tend to conceal certain information and as to the effects of self-disclosure by stipulating that *people define certain information as personally private when they want to avoid the consequences of revealing that information.*

Consequences of self-disclosure
The consequences of revealing personally private information may be personal or relational. Some of these consequences are as follows.

1. *Being forced to publicly acknowledge and to deal with certain facts about yourself.* Saying often is believing; that is, putting something into words often creates a reality not always associated with mere thinking. To verbalize personally private information is also to see it reflected off one or more other people, giving it an explicit social reality in addition to a personal reality.

2. *Having to expend energy in meeting the response obligations you have incurred toward the other party or parties.* Most recipients of self-disclosing messages are aware of the special role in which they have been placed and do their best to respond in an appropriate manner. Their responses may involve reciprocal self-disclosure or attempts to give support or reinforcement or even useful advice. Whatever the response, they have usually invested some energy in sensitively encoding and decoding. This puts you, as the discloser, in a position of obligation: you must respond to their responses.

3. *Taking the chance of engendering feelings of hurt, anger, and discomfort or affection, affinity and trust in the other party or parties.* In addition to short-term response obligations, you should anticipate emotional responses from your receivers, especially if the disclosed information directly concerns them. They may interpret the information negatively. Or they may interpret it as a basis for relational escalation, even though you did not intend it as such. For example, they may now feel they have greater access to your time, energy, and feelings. Self-disclosure can arouse both negative and positive emotions, neither of which may be expected or desired.

4. *Risking rejection or abuse by the other person or persons.* Your listeners may refuse, blatantly or through lack of attentiveness, to participate in the self-disclosure situation. This refusal is likely to be devastating. In offering to share personally private information with someone, you place him in a position of trust, intimacy, and very often respect offered to few others. In refusing to accept your offer, he communicates a lack of regard for one of the most precious commodities you have to exchange. Of course, he may listen to you and still do you harm. He may deny the validity of your messages or ridicule them, probably not in your presence, but to third parties. (Recall our discussion in chapter 3 of bartering gossip and rumor in return for environmental control.)

5. As a result of either (3) or (4) or both, *generating some undesirable change in your relationship with the other party or*

parties. Self-disclosure does not always promote relational betterment. It can lead to a weakening of stability, a decrease in harmony, or a less favorable definition of a relationship. Since your initial offer is highly valuable, you stand to lose a lot if your listener replies with an offer of much less or of negative value.

This list, of course, is only partial. There are numerous other possible negative consequences of self-disclosing messages. The essential element of personally private information, however, is that its revelation often produces uncertainty and change in a person's self-concept, in his relationship with other persons, or in both. Uncertainty results from not knowing exactly what change, or changes, will come about. These changes may result in an increase or a decrease of self-esteem; a feeling of greater or lesser contact with reality; feelings of closeness to, or estrangement from, other people; a decrease or an increase in personal or relational tension; or a greater or lesser capacity for controlling a relevant part of the environment. Because the information disclosed is likely to be salient to one or both of the communicators and because the very act of self-disclosure indicates that at least one of the parties defines the relationship as one in which such information can be exchanged—with all the relational implications associated with this definition—some change will almost undoubtedly come about.

Paradoxically (at least in terms of the way self-disclosure is usually viewed), it may often be easier, and more functional, to self-disclose in a casual, transitory relationship than in a long-term, close association. Persons who converse fleetingly in a bar or occupy adjacent seats on a two-hour airline flight may share more personally private information than a couple who have dated for several months. When one recalls the consequences that may result from self-disclosure, this fact is hardly surprising, for such consequences are more likely to come to fruition in long-term relationships. Obligations usually do not develop on a single flight from Chicago to Los Angeles, nor are the parties likely to be overly concerned about the positive or negative emotions that may result from their conversation. Most important, future revelation of personally private information is cloaked in anonymity; contrast, "Boy, you think you've got problems, I met a guy on the plane . . ." with "Man, I thought I'd heard hangups, but my girlfriend, Joan . . . ."

An example of self-disclosure

Despite the many potentially negative personal and relational consequences of indiscriminate self-disclosure, the prevailing societal view appears to be, "The more shared, the better," particularly if the relationship is ostensibly important to the parties. Typical of this viewpoint is the response of one of the syndicated advice columnists to a recent letter. The letter writer stated that he was about to marry a girl whom he loved deeply. During adolescence he had engaged in several homosexual experiences (of an unspecified nature). The question: should he reveal these homosexual episodes to his fiancee? The answer: by all means, the relationship demands honesty and straightforwardness on his part.

We consider this type of superficial advice to be as potentially dangerous as a column providing instruction for the manufacture of cheap, do-it-yourself nuclear weapons. Mind you, we do not suggest that self-concealment is the preferred alternative; rather, given the limited information available, we would be unwilling to offer advice and we feel the columnist should have exercised similar caution. Before attempting to resolve the self-disclosure/self-concealment dilemma in this case, numerous questions merit exploration. Here are just a few of them.

1. How is the potential husband's act of self-disclosure likely to affect the relationship between his fiancee and himself? The

letter provides no information about the personality characteristics, the prior learning experiences, or the attitudes concerning homosexuality of the second party to the relationship, the writer's fiancee. This paucity of data does not disturb our intrepid columnist; armed with the relational bromide, "It's always good to be honest and open," she unhesitatingly and unreservedly counsels self-disclosure. We do not share her universal enthusiasm for this bromide, any more than we unreservedly endorse its antithesis, "What someone doesn't know doesn't hurt him." When applied to all communicative decisions, the latter maxim serves the liar and the unscrupulous manipulator, while the former identifies the thoughtless, egocentric individual who is blissfully ignorant of the differences that exist among other communicators. In short, both bits of advice are source-oriented; they serve the needs and motives of the communicator without taking into account the other party, or parties, to the transaction or the possible relational impact of self-concealment or self-disclosure.

If our letter writer really cares about his fiancee and his relationship with her, any revelation of personally private information must be preceded by a careful analysis of its probable effects on her and on their relationship. Moreover, if his motive is primarily therapeutic—i.e., if he is troubled by the source-oriented need to purge himself of guilt feelings—he would be well-advised to seek thorough professional counseling (not two column inches of lovelorn advice), disclose the information to the counselor, and carefully weigh the relational consequences of disclosing or not disclosing the information.

2. What was the nature of the homosexual experiences? As we have indicated, the letter does not specify the behaviors labeled as homosexual experiences. Since certain types of homosexual activities are fairly common among adolescent boys, the issue of whether or not to self-disclose could be analyzed more meaningfully if we knew just what the writer means by "homosexual experiences." Suppose we find that the activities that concern the writer are reasonably commonplace. Now we can offer him one of two kinds of advice, depending upon our expectations about his fiancee's probable reaction: "Don't worry about it; the sort of things you describe are common to many young boys," or "Go ahead and tell her; it's so commonplace she isn't likely to think much about it." Note that once again the proffered advice hinges upon a consideration of the other person's probable response and its effects on the relationship between the two parties.

3. Are these homosexual activities likely to occur again? It is one thing to call explicit attention to a persistent tendency that may drastically affect a relationship and quite another to unearth all the old bones from the past on the assumption that everything that ever happened must be disclosed to the other party. Certainly, if the letter writer presently harbors strong homosexual inclinations and feels he may be motivated to seek out future homosexual relationships, a strong case can be made for self-disclosure, for this dimension of his behavior is likely to exert a strong impact on the ongoing relationship between his fiancee and himself. Conversely, if he is dwelling only on a few isolated childhood incidents, it may indeed be better to let sleeping dogs lie.

Note that the three questions we have raised gain their primary significance from their implications for the relationship between the letter writer and his fiancee. We believe that the question of whether to disclose personally private information can be examined most meaningfully from within a relational context, at least if one is primarily interested in the communicative implications of self-disclosure. Granted, it may often be therapeutically useful for a person to share personally private information. Some clinical psychologists contend that many people are overly repressed, too unwilling to share their innermost feelings with others. They also maintain that self-disclosure is necessary for healthy personal growth and that the release of certain kinds of information leads to insights and changes not otherwise possible.

Our approach to interpersonal communication emphasizes the importance of individual freedom of expression, of not being bound by cultural and sociological conventions that are irrelevant to interpersonal communication. Are we consistent, then, in advocating strict precautions in regard to self-disclosure? The issues here are profound. They involve the thin lines between freedom and license, between responsibility for the needs of others and slavery to them. People can be just as stifled and repressed in an interpersonal dyad as in a formal organization if fear of making waves becomes a dominant motive for their behavior.

We believe that the structure of an interpersonal relationship allows its members individual freedom. Indiscriminate or purely selfish self-disclosure can have a searingly destructive impact on this structure, inhibiting both personal and relational freedom for growth and expressiveness. If one's primary concern is the development of rewarding communication relationships, self-disclosures should be made selectively, not indiscriminately.

Decoding self-disclosing messages

There is no shortage of injunctions about the importance of being a good listener or a faithful guardian of confidences, but the relational complexities of self-disclosure often transcend these well-meaning words of advice. We suspect, for example, that in their zeal for maximum openness and honesty, some persons seek to extricate personally private information from others without carefully weighing the possible relational consequences for the discloser, the disclosee, or both. The following dialogue (typical of conversations sometimes encountered in books, movies, and real life) illustrates some of these consequences.

HUSBAND: Something I've always wondered about is your relationship with Ken. Did the two of you have something going before we started seeing each other?

WIFE: I don't know what difference that makes.

HUSBAND: Oh, it's nothing important; I've just always been curious. Don't worry, you can confide in me.

WIFE: Well, yes, we were pretty close at one time.

HUSBAND: I knew there was some reason for all the knowing looks he throws me at parties. Just how close were you, anyway?

Rather than spelling out the relational consequences of this brief exchange, we will pose several questions for you to ponder. How will the husband's behavior affect his wife's subsequent willingness to self-disclose? How will the husband's future perceptions of the relationship be influenced by his wife's response? In terms of the balance notions discussed in chapter 8, what changes are likely to occur in the relationships between the husband, the wife, and Ken, the third party? While far from complete, these questions underscore the relational intricacy of self-disclosing transactions.

Many, of course, would argue that this short conversation is merely a manifestation of a deep-seated relational problem, the husband's jealousy and suspicion about a prior relationship between Ken and his wife. One can grant this point and remain skeptical about the husband's wisdom in dealing with the problem. If a warm, close relationship with his wife is of crucial importance, he might have concluded that the personal gains afforded by probing would be more than offset by the relational losses—in other words, he might have chosen to remain ignorant of the exact status of his wife and Ken's relationship. Given the impossibility of this psychological alternative, he could have at least cast himself as encoder rather than decoder—i.e., he could have chosen to self-disclose to his wife instead of attempting to pry personally private information from her. Had he done so, the dialogue might have followed this more harmonious course.

HUSBAND: You know, I feel almost silly saying this but there's something that's been bugging me for quite a while. I think I'm jealous of Ken and you.

WIFE: Really? I never realized that you felt like that.

HUSBAND: Yeah, I guess I do. I keep having the feeling that the two of you had something going at one time and that the fire hasn't quite died out yet.

WIFE: Well, it's true we did see each other some before I met you, but you can be sure there's nothing romantic there now. Still, if it's bothering you I think we ought to talk about it. You see. . . .

This approach has several communicative advantages. First, by disclosing his own feelings, the husband makes it clear that the matter is important to him, that it is not trivial as he tried to imply in the first conversation. Second, his own self-disclosure takes his wife off the defensive, enabling her to speak more frankly with him. Finally, there is a subtle change in the direction of the second dialogue, with the emphasis placed upon the relationship between husband and wife, rather than the two parties' relationship with someone else. Although one can never predict outcomes with certainty, it seems more probable that the participants will be able to reduce relational tension while at the same time remaining on good terms with Ken.

We suspect this probing technique is frequently employed in touchy relational situations, even though its effectiveness is questionable. After all, self-disclosure increases one's vulnerability and, if relational one-upmanship is of concern, it is much safer to maneuver the situation so that the other party is cast in the self-disclosing role. But if continued relational harmony (not relational dominance) is the primary goal, a straightforward, declarative strategy (rather than an interrogative subterfuge) will usually pay dividends.

Self-disclosing transactions impose other responsibilities on message decoders. What appear to be soul-searching, revealing exchanges may sometimes constitute only need fulfillment on the receiver's part. Such a situation arises when the receiver, consciously or unconsciously, controls the content of messages by the kinds of feedback he presents. *If this happens, the ostensible self-discloser often ends up concentrating upon what the receiver wants to hear, not the things that are really bothering the sender.*

This problem may occur even in professional settings such as therapeutic transactions. Some people have argued that the theoretical preferences of psychiatrists or psychologists frequently determine what the client self-discloses. For example, if a therapist subscribes to neo-Freudian views, he may lead the client into an almost exclusive discussion of sexual anxieties and problems. This leading or shaping process does not occur consciously; rather, the subtle verbal and nonverbal cues provided by the therapist point the client in a particular direction.

Functions of self-disclosure

An additional set of relational issues involves roles that specific listeners play in regard to the functions of self-disclosure. Some disclosures serve cathartic purposes: getting something "off one's chest." A cathartic disclosure may be directed at a particular listener, as when someone needs to confess a crime to his victim or, as happens quite often, to almost any receptive person. At other times self-disclosure can function to clarify situations that an individual finds especially confusing or upsetting. When a communicator feels alienated, or somehow out of touch with his social environment, he may try to convey these feelings to someone who can help him overcome these difficulties. If self-disclosure is to serve a clarification function, then the discloser is likely to select a listener who is particularly skillful at listening, clarifying, and perhaps at offering useful advice.

A third important function of self-disclosure is relational escalation. When people share personally private information they tend to feel closer to one another, and to see their relationship in a more interpersonal light. But it is interesting to note that communicators do not go about randomly self-disclosing in efforts to achieve relational escalation: they usually select as their listeners people with whom they already have some desire to become more intimate. This suggests that interpersonal attraction is a key variable. Two people who are attracted to each other may enter into self-disclosure very soon in their relationship to pave the way to relational intimacy. People who see self-disclosure as a thing-in-itself often neglect these relational considerations.

Nowhere are the relational complexities of self-disclosure more clearly illustrated than in transactions involving two parties who vary markedly in their values for self-disclosure or their willingness to self-disclose. Obviously, people differ both in their propensity to self-disclose and their desire to be privy to the personally private information of others. Often these differences place serious stresses on a relationship. One party may perceive the other as too open and too eager to share private information; in turn, the second party may see the other as overly suspicious and reluctant to open up. In particular, the person with a high value for self-disclosure may sense a lack of reciprocity in the relationship; after all, he has exposed some of his psyche while the second party has remained in psychic hiding.

Self-disclosure and levels of communication

Just as a gun can be used either to destroy life or to help preserve it, self-disclosure can be used either to enhance the quality of a communication relationship or to serve the purposes of a skilled con artist. We realize that since many people are inclined to think of self-disclosure (or apparent self-disclosure) as an unqualifiedly "good" thing, this statement is likely to strike a discordant note. In considering the role of self-disclosure in noninterpersonal and interpersonal settings, we will attempt to clarify our reservations about this message strategy.

Distinguishing genuine from apparent self-disclosure
Initially it may seem strange to link self-disclosure with noninterpersonal communication settings; instead, it may appear that self-disclosure can occur only when the parties are communicating interpersonally or, at a minimum, making a sincere effort to move to the interpersonal level. Here, however, an important distinction must be made between genuine and apparent acts of self-disclosure, a distinction related to Culbert's earlier quoted assertion that "self information that is 'personally private' for one individual may not, for whatever reason, be personally private for another" (1967, p. 2).

Suppose you asked twenty friends to write down the one item they deem most personally private, i.e., the item they would be most reluctant or embarrassed to discuss with other persons. Assuming that they responded candidly, you would expect considerable variance in their choices: some would mention an economic matter; others would suggest a real or imagined physical defect; still others would identify a sexual hangup. Moreover, you would probably encounter some very unique and unexpected responses; for example, you might discover that one of your friends has a deathly fear of electric mixers or that another frequently steals money out of church collection plates.

In a sense, you have approached the problem of self-disclosure interpersonally; i.e., you have sought to identify differences in the ways your friends define personally private information. When we want to talk about self-disclosure in general terms, however, we are forced to rely on noninterpersonal tactics; i.e., we formulate cultural or sociological generalizations concerning definitional similarities. Thus, we resort to saying that most people in a particular society or group would regard certain kinds of economic and sexual information as personally private, realizing that the phrase "most people" introduces an element of error.

By now many of you have probably arrived at the difference between genuine and apparent self-disclosure as we view it. When a communicator engages in an act of genuine self-disclosure, he is sharing information that he regards as personally private and is reluctant or embarrassed to share with most people. By contrast, an act of apparent self-disclosure involves transmission of information that most people would be reluctant or embarrassed to share, but that the communicator himself does not define as personally private. Stated differently, the communicator is disclosing information that he is willing to disclose to almost anyone; hence, he is not subject to most of the undesirable consequences that can result from genuine self-disclosure.

A second distinction between apparent and genuine self-disclosure lies in the function the discloser sees his messages as having. People can impart information that is truly personal and private for purposes other than personal or relational growth. A revelation may be intended to shock, embarrass, or hurt, or to secure an advantage in a communicative control enterprise. For example, an individual may reveal a highly traumatic and very personal experience to shame a listener who strongly resembles some party to the experience. An individual may also self-disclose to elicit personal information from another person, intending to use it for manipulative purposes. In both cases, the initial disclosure does entail a risk, but only at the greater expense of someone else.

The rub, of course, comes in determining whether a particular communicative transaction represents an instance of genuine or apparent self-disclosure. It is precisely this ambiguity that permits individuals to use the strategy of apparent self-disclosure to their advantage in noninterpersonal settings. We have emphasized the obligations imposed on receivers by an act of self-disclosure; since self-disclosure is widely thought of as a courageous, potentially humbling undertaking, the receiver is expected to treat personally private information with respect and respond to it sympathetically. Once these expectations are understood, the potential for exploitation becomes obvious. Next time a relative stranger or a casual acquaintance begins to recount intimate details of his financial problems, his marital difficulties, or his deep-seated fears, ask yourself the following question: is this individual disclosing information that is embarrassing and difficult to reveal (genuine self-disclosure) or is he merely sharing information that he would have few qualms about revealing to many others (apparent self-disclosure)? If you conclude that you have been party to an act of apparent self-disclosure, it would not be unduly cynical for you to ponder carefully the communicator's motives in sharing this information with you.

Examples of apparent self-disclosure
Consider the following rather bald exploitative use of apparent self-disclosure in a noninterpersonal setting.

SELLER: "Hi there, my name is Fred Smith and I have a problem I think you can help me with."

BUYER: "Oh, what is it?"

SELLER: "Well, you see I'm working so I can go to college. I come from a very poor family [apparent self-disclosure], and they can't afford to help me with my expenses. But for every magazine subscription I sell I get 10 points toward a college scholarship, and I only need 150 more points."

BUYER: "That's certainly a good cause. What magazines are you selling?"

SELLER: "I knew you were the kind of person who'd understand! I've got. . . ."

Since most persons are reluctant to share information about their economic privations (in general, we have found that while it may indeed be no disgrace to be poor, most people refrain from admitting it), the seller's admission that he comes from a poor family is an act of apparent self-disclosure calculated to obligate the buyer, particularly when the admission is paired with a professed belief in the Puritan ethic of industry and hard work. At worst, the "disclosure" is an outright lie; at best, it represents information that the seller will "disclose" to any potential customer. That it works is attested to by newspaper accounts of outlandish selling successes; e.g., one unwary person actually bought more than $60,000 worth of magazine subscriptions.

An excellent example of the use of apparent self-disclosure in noninterpersonal settings occurs in a circle game called "Honesty." Each player says something he has done or something that has happened to him. All other players who have the same experience raise their hands, and each receives one point. The player who scores a specified number of points first wins. The name of the game results from the rule (probably oft-violated) that the initial statement must be true and that the other players must be honest when raising their hands.

Invariably, the game degenerates to a self-disclosing "can-you-top-this." Astounding sexual exploits, bizarre sexual experiences, unique fears and anxieties, unsavory acts of bigotry: these are the communicative staples of the game. A friend of ours, disenchanted by the entire undertaking, once related the following experience to the group: "For the last thirty minutes I've been sitting here feeling embarrassed because I feel the need to think up these weird episodes to tell you." Interestingly, none of the other players raised his hand to indicate that this had happened to him.

Ritual self-sacrifice
At certain times, communicators are placed in uncomfortable or embarrassing positions, having for one reason or another strained their relations with powerful others (the "angry gods"). On these occasions they will sometimes resort to disclosing what appears to be personally private information in an effort to placate those who are angry with them. Children use this tactic with their parents. If a child has misbehaved around his mother, he might rush to his father the moment he arrives home to confess his misdeed. Of course, the child is aware that if his father does not presently know this information, he soon will. The self-disclosure, then, even though it may reveal personally private information, is only apparent—for the information will shortly become public. However, the child is hoping that his virtue in being honest will mitigate his father's wrath: "But, Dad, didn't I tell you the truth? How can you get mad at me if I was honest? Don't you want me to be honest anymore?"

This strategy (which has been enshrined in American culture ever since George Washington admitted to cutting down the cherry tree) puts the father in a bind: how can he demonstrate displeasure with his son's misbehavior while still encouraging him to be honest? Richard Nixon may have attempted this strategy in "revealing" the content of his White House tapes, perhaps hoping to elicit a favorable public reaction by so humbling himself. We might add that this strategy is quite similar to one frequently used by certain animals: when attacked by more powerful foes, they roll onto their backs so as to expose their vulnerable bellies. People no longer perform this same activity, but they can try to achieve the same effects by transmitting apparently self-disclosing messages.

Genuine self-disclosure in noninterpersonal settings
We have already suggested that when the situational context precludes the occurrence of undesirable consequences (i.e., when encounters are transitory and relatively anonymous), people often choose to engage in noninterpersonal self-disclosure. More to the point, perhaps, are instances when communicators self-disclose in noninterpersonal situations to enhance the possibility of moving to the interpersonal level.

Genuine self-disclosure increases the number of cues available to the other party, cues that enable him to distinguish the individual self-discloser from other similar persons. Armed with this additional information, communicators are more likely to base predictions on psychological considerations, rather than on cultural or sociological generalizations. For instance, a mutual acquaintance of ours maintained a casual, noninterpersonal level friendship with a black student for several months. One day the black student engaged in what appeared to be an act of genuine self-disclosure: he confided that despite all of the emphasis on black pride he was ashamed of his racial origins. Immediately, our acquaintance altered a number of his predictions about his black friend's probable responses to certain message inputs. Moreover, both participants in the relationship agree that the friendship has since moved from the noninterpersonal to the interpersonal level. Obviously, no one communicative act precipitated this relational change; nevertheless, this initial act of self-disclosure undoubtedly contributed to the development of a climate conducive to an enriched relationship.

The preceding example underscores a second way that self-disclosure may assist communicators in bridging the gap between noninterpersonal and interpersonal communication. *If an act is perceived as genuinely self-disclosing it creates, or strengthens, a bond of trust between the transactants.* Such an improved emotional climate has strong relational consequences. For one thing, it increases the probability of reciprocal self-disclosure, thus ensuring that each of the parties will have more information for making predictions. Furthermore, reciprocal self-disclosure results in shared obligations; both parties are now privy to potentially embarrassing information about the other. To the extent that confidences are honored, mutual trust increases.

Self-disclosure in interpersonal relationships

Typically, of course, people think of self-disclosure as a strategy aimed at relational enrichment, as a technique for improving the quality of an interpersonal relationship. For most instances we are willing to accept this viewpoint. But if discord develops within the relationship, the self-disclosing acts of one party can be used as a weapon by the other. Potentially embarrassing information becomes embarrassing information when confidences are violated and secrets revealed to others. Nor is it always necessary that the information be shared with outsiders; in some cases, its mere reintroduction within the confines of the dyad may satisfy a destructive impulse. A common manifestation of the injury that can be caused by such relational betrayal is captured by the plaintive query, "Why did you have to bring that up again?"

Still, if we wish to communicate interpersonally, we must be willing to take this gamble, for without genuine self-disclosure most relationships would forever remain at the noninterpersonal level. What we advocate, then, is a discriminating approach to self-disclosure. At times the potential relational rewards justify the risks; on other occasions it is best to be wary of removing our noninterpersonal masks and exposing our psychic vitals. For just as self-disclosure and openness can often enhance the quality of a relationship, defense mechanisms and relational caution sometimes provide the most functional means of coping with our environments. While some may label this a pessimistic position, we consider it a realistic one.

Making conversation

We were recently asked to speak to students in three undergraduate classes on the subject of interpersonal communication. Rather than deciding what we would talk about, we asked the students ahead of time what topics they would most like to discuss. We expected that they would want to talk about how to develop honesty and trust in interpersonal relationships, how to avoid being overly manipulative, or some similar "heavy" topic. Instead, the students' predominant request was for information on "how to talk to people I've just met" —in short, how to converse. In this section we consider some strategies for enhancing conversational ability.

> "Nice day, isn't it."
> "Yeah, if it doesn't rain."
> "Well, the weather report said there's only a 10 percent chance."
> "Yeah, but they're wrong half the time."
> "Yeah."

On the face of it, making conversation should be an easy task. Yet for many people, chit-chat is an excruciating venture. They are unable to think of anything to say. They find periodic "dead spots" in the conversation unbearable. Even if they are not bothered by these things, they tire of the weather, news, and sports routine in conversation after conversation. College students are said to begin every conversation with such questions as: What's your major? Where are you from? Where do you live on campus? Got a job yet? Older people ask: Where do you work? Got any kids? Can you believe the price of beef these days?

At Michigan State University instructors in the basic communication course frequently begin the first day of classes with an exercise called the "Introduction Game." They ask individual students to introduce themselves to the class in such a way that the rest of the students will remember what they said. Even with these instructions, the students almost invariably recite their class standings, majors, and so on. After several students have introduced themselves the instructors ask another student to re-introduce them. Almost always he cannot; he has forgotten everything the students said. When asked to explain his failure he often says, "I wasn't paying attention. Besides, they didn't say anything important. And heck, I didn't know you were going to call on me." Many students argue that this exercise demonstrates the trivial nature of introductions in particular and conversation in general: "If nobody remembers what you said, and you didn't say anything important, why do it?"

The importance of conversational ability

For better or worse, most people are inhibited about beginning transactions on a highly interpersonal level. Even if you are able to smash boldly through the cultural and sociological preliminaries, the majority of people whom you meet are likely to find them necessary. These initial stages in conversation-making have been studied by Berger (1973). Unacquainted students were paired and asked to carry on short conversations. Their conversations were unobtrusively recorded and the content analyzed. Invariably, the first several minutes were devoted to exchanging standard biographical information: name, major, class standing, favorite subjects, and the like. To determine the pervasiveness of this approach to initial interaction, Berger instructed some pairs of students to skip the preliminaries and get right into heavy topics. In almost all cases, the result was the same: there was a period of increasingly strained silence, terminated by one of the students blurting out something such as, "Boy, the weather has been really lousy lately, hasn't it?" Finally, in a later study, students were explicitly forbidden to exchange biographical and demographic information. Almost without exception, the students reported great difficulty in starting a conversation without access to this information.

We think that this research, rather than demonstrating that initial conversations are trivial, makes a different point: people do begin their transactions at cultural and sociological levels. Moreover, given our view that all communication transactions involve prediction-making, this fact is hardly surprising. The kinds of information gleaned in the beginning stages of conversation provide the data for making cultural and sociological predictions about the other conversant. Furthermore, the decision to ask certain initial questions is partially based on sociological level predictions about the roles of the participants. Thus, instead of belittling small talk, we should recognize it as a common, necessary occurrence and become proficient at it.

We feel that the ability to make conversation is an important communication skill, in both the interpersonal and the noninterpersonal arenas. An introductory conversation can pave the way to more meaningful transactions, even if the communicators initially confine it to cultural and sociological information. Many communication situations are not conducive to the exchange of personal information—there may be other people present, or time may be short. Small talk can set the stage for more intimate interchanges at another place and time. Some people prefer to shorten these preliminary stages as much as possible. We know a girl who came to a party with a sign around her neck. It stated her name, age, hometown, major, and grade point average. At the bottom of the sign she had written: "Now that I've told you all this, let's talk about something important."

If you are a good conversationalist, you can smooth the transition from making introductions to making friends. Conversely, inability to engage in small talk limits your chances to move to the interpersonal level of communication. Most initial transactions are likely to be largely noninterpersonal in nature. On these occasions people make decisions as to whether or not it would be worthwhile to make the effort to move to the interpersonal level.

Most opportunities for small talk occur during relaxation, not work. Small talk takes place between classes, at parties, during coffee breaks, on dates, in bars, and at other times when the pressures of school or work are supposedly off. Since small talk is often fundamental to these occasions, it stands to reason that you cannot readily relax if you cannot easily engage in small talk. You probably know people who avoid these situations simply because they feel awkward or uncomfortable because of their inability to converse freely. If you are unable to relax in situations where relaxation is the major objective, you may want to improve your skill as a conversationalist.

Developing your conversational ability

Several articles in popular magazines and books have instructed people on how to be better conversationalists, often in the context of "winning friends and influencing people" or "attracting members of the opposite sex." One frequent bit of advice is: "Become an interesting, informed person: read books and magazines, go to plays and lectures, travel." Though there are advantages to heeding this advice, we feel that it misses the point of what most conversations are all about. You do not have to be a profound, witty information source with an encyclopedic memory to be a good conversationalist. You may know people who come to parties with "fun facts to know and tell" from the Sunday comics section of the newspaper, and who tell you the average circumference of a centipede's legs or the record number of eggs laid by a sunfish in Lake Champlain in the month of October. We leave it to you to judge whether these people are usually interesting conversationalists.

A second bit of advice commonly offered is: "Just be yourself. Let your own true beauty shine through, and the rest will flow from there." While there may be some wisdom in this advice, it often is of little help. How does one go about being oneself? What behaviors are self-like and which ones are not? Even if it is possible to define oneself, people who are especially sadistic, shy, or given to vulgar language probably ought not follow this advice too frequently.

People who are interested in changing their behavior have two broad avenues open to them. The first may be called consciousness raising, or gaining insight into the sources of problems and the ways to overcome them. In terms of becoming a better conversationalist, you can think about your personal barriers to heightened conversational skill, and you can think of things to do that might help you improve. This is the "inside-out" approach to changing behavior: thinking precedes overt behavior. The other avenue has been called behavior modification; you do things in an improved manner, and then internalize the correct procedures. This is the "try it, you'll like it" approach. Although a combination of consciousness raising and behavior modification is desirable, we are limited here in what we can do with the latter approach. Nevertheless, we do feel that many people's conversational skills suffer because of common misconceptions about the nature of conversation. Let us briefly consider several of these misconceptions.

Misconception 1: "Most conversations are boring.
I never learn anything, and nobody ever says anything interesting."
This statement reflects one of the most widely shared misconceptions about the nature of conversation. Many people believe that the function of conversation is to convey information, i.e., that the content of the messages is of primary import. They feel that their role in a conversation is to say interesting, witty things. They believe that simple chit-chat is trivial and boring, and that people who engage in it are "surface-level," phony, or simpleminded. While such beliefs may sometimes be true, this attitude toward conversation, as well as the advice that the best road to becoming a good conversationalist is to become an information repository, ignores the primary function of conversation: to make contact with other people. This point is well made by Bateson:

> When *A* communicates with *B*, the mere act of communicating can carry the implicit statement "we are communicating." In fact, this may be the most important message that is sent and received. The wisecracks of American adolescents and the smoother but no less stylized conversation of adults are only occasionally concerned with the giving and receiving of objective information; mostly, the conversations of leisure hours exist because people need to know they are in touch with one another. They may ask questions which superficially seem to be about matters of impersonal fact—"Will it rain?" "What is in today's war news?"—but the speaker's interest is focused on the fact of communication with another human being. With comparative strangers, we "make conversation" rather than accept the message which would be implicit in silence—the message, "We are *not* communicating." It seems that this message would provoke anxiety because it implies rejection; perhaps also because the message itself is explosive with paradox. If two persons exchange this message, are they communicating? (1951, p. 213)

What implications for improving your conversational skills do you see in Bateson's comments? An important point he makes is that contact is often preferable to no contact; to talk of trivial matters is better than not to talk at all. As Bateson says, failure to engage in conversation implies a rejection of the people around you. On the positive side, conversation enables you to convey information about yourself and about your conception of your co-transactants. The way you communicate—more than what you say—can pave the way for continued contact or erect barriers to further relationships with other people. This is the interpersonal dimension to making conversation. When people converse, then, the underlying topic of conversation is the people themselves, in the ways they make contact with one another.

Misconception 2: Each conversationalist has unilateral responsibility for maintaining the conversation.
When the familiar "dead spot" in the conversation occurs, have you ever said to yourself, "I'd better say something?" If so, you have probably felt that the burden of the conversation was on you, that the other participants were sitting comfortably waiting for you to pick up the ball. If you ask other people how often they have felt under the same gun, you will probably find that each conversationalist feels solely responsible for the success of the conversation. It should be clear that all participants share a mutual responsibility for maintaining the transaction.

People who harbor the misconception of unilateral responsibility take on an unnecessary and dysfunctional conversational burden. Has anyone ever said to you, "Quick, be funny, tell a joke," or "Quick, be creative, come up with a unique idea"? Most people respond to such unexpected demands by becoming tongue-tied and self-conscious. Similarly, if you believe you have sole responsibility for the success of a conversation, your fellow conversationalists seem to be demanding of you, "Communicate! Make contact with us." It is difficult to respond easily or successfully in such situations. The pressure is too great, the spotlight is too bright. We advocate, therefore, that you recognize the mutuality of conversational responsibility. The reduction you then may feel in the demand to perform should allow you to participate more effectively in the transaction.

Misconception 3: Good communicators are born, not made.
People who fall prey to this misconception are likely to believe that whatever level of conversational skill they possess right now is the highest level they can ever attain. While it is true that some exceptionally skilled conversationalists seem to and probably do in fact have some degree of natural ability, most of us can profit from basic training in talking with people.

In many respects, the conversationalist who harbors the natural ability misconception is similar to the tennis player who refuses to take lessons. Both cling to their given levels of skill, continually relying upon and thereby reinforcing their bad habits. Both seem to be afraid to try anything different, i.e., to give up familiar techniques in order to learn new and better techniques. They are aware that it will take some time to perfect the new techniques, and that during this training period they are not going to perform as well as before. But they are trapped in a limited time frame: they are unwilling to undergo the temporary awkwardness and uncertainty of learning new techniques, even though eventually their performances may be significantly improved.

The converse of the natural ability position for the conversationalist would be: "I am, in a sense, a 'conversational baby.' I will not expect myself to be highly skilled at the start. I know I need practice and training. I am willing to relinquish dysfunctional habits and attitudes in order to replace them with more effective habits and attitudes." Returning to our comparison with tennis, "I am willing to 'lose a few games' while I learn new skills." This point is particularly important. Both communicators and tennis players, if they seek to improve their skills, must keep their egos from getting in the way of improvement.

Summary

Skill at making conversation is an important ingredient of general communication effectiveness. Initial small talk bridges the barrier between persons; it provides a starting point for all relationships. During the beginning stages of an association, it permits mutual data-gathering by the transactants, who use the information to formulate the cultural and sociological generalizations necessary for preliminary prediction-making. Finally, and of crucial importance, continued conversation increases the amount of information available to the transactants. Thus, if they are so motivated, their chances of moving to the interpersonal level are vastly improved. Conversation is a major source of the raw materials for initial generalizations and subsequent discriminations; hence, it is a powerful ally in both noninterpersonal and interpersonal relationships. Wise communicators make good use of this relational resource.

Some problems in our use of language

Thus far we have stressed the centrality of communication energy to effective message-making, considered some potential assets and liabilities of using the message strategy of self-disclosure, and illustrated how conversational skills affect the quality of both noninterpersonal and interpersonal relationships. One additional caution merits emphasis. To be an effective interpersonal communicator, you should be aware that words alone are often a poor means of transmitting a message.

Codification: translating an experience into words

DOCTOR: What seems to be the trouble, Mr. Brown?

PATIENT: Well, I've got this pain in my stomach.

DOCTOR: What kind of pain do you have?

PATIENT: It hurts kinda bad, right down there in my stomach.

DOCTOR: Is the pain sharp, or throbbing, or just a dull ache?

PATIENT: Boy, you said it, Doc.

DOCTOR: Well, you know, Mr. Brown, if I'm going to be able to prescribe some treatment, I've got to have more specific information about what's ailing you.

PATIENT: How can I describe it any better than that? My stomach hurts. . . . Do you think it's serious, Doc?

You can codify the experience of physical pain by saying, "Ouch"; or your reaction to a painting by saying, "It's beautiful"; or your intentions by saying, "I want to do that!" Many experiences—especially emotional experiences—are difficult to codify. It can be irksome to translate some nonlinguistic experiences into words. You have probably felt the frustration of not being able to find the "right words" to verbalize your feelings about someone, or about some communication situation in which you have participated.

As long as all you want to do is express yourself, the only consequence likely to result from difficulty in codification is temporary frustration. But when the statements you make in reference to your feelings have some bearing on your communication relationships, more serious problems can arise. Our patient in the doctor's office was unable to find words the doctor could use to do his job effectively; Mr. Brown could not adequately codify his experience of physical distress. Consequently, the doctor-patient relationship could not progress smoothly. Similar problems can arise in interpersonal relationships, with inaccurate codification of feelings bringing about serious breakdowns in relationships.

Sometimes when two people are together one of them feels a vague uneasiness, perhaps accompanied by a tightening of the facial and stomach muscles. The feeling may be no more specific than that. If you have ever felt this way, how have you labeled the feeling? Have you called it "anxiety," or "threat," or "dislike for the other person," or

"anger"? Numerous emotion-word labels can be attached to such vague feelings, but the way you actually codify both your feeling and its perceived source can be very important. The codification statement indicates whether you believe the other person is the source of your discomfort, and it indicates the kind of discomfort you think the other person is causing.

What are the differences, for example, among these codification statements: "You're irritating me"; "I feel irritated"; and "I feel tense"? The first codification can be roughly translated, "I am experiencing a specific negative emotion, namely irritation, and you are the cause of it." Your choice of labels indicates that you have come to a conclusion about what you feel and why. When you accuse another person of causing you discomfort, he has only a limited range of response alternatives. Most people respond either apologetically or defensively; they either accept your statement as valid or deny its validity—"Oh, I'm sorry," or "You're nuts!" The issue has become one of who is right and who is wrong. You have implied that the only sources of your discomfort are external stimuli (recall our discussion of external and internal stimuli in chapter 2).

By contrast, the codification "I feel irritated," while still implying a conclusion about the kind of emotion you are experiencing, leaves open the question of its cause. As a result, you increase your companion's possible range of responses. Because he has no reason to feel attacked, he may be more willing to help you figure out why you are feeling irritated. Perhaps he has caused your irritation (though he is not necessarily under attack for it); maybe he has done nothing wrong, but you are particularly sensitive to something he said; or your feeling of irritation may be left over from some earlier experience.

Finally, consider the codification, "I feel tense." Here you make no explicit assumption about the exact nature of your feeling or its cause. While tension may be the result of irritation, it also can result from anger, uncertainty, insecurity, guilt, and a wide range of other negative or even positive emotions. Each of these emotions, while often manifested quite similarly in tension, can have different antecedents (causes) and different consequences (ways of dealing with them). Sometimes an emotional state arises largely from internal stimuli, at other times as a result of external stimuli, and yet at other times because of a combination of both. Since there is so much room for error, you may want to delay precise codification until you have investigated the nature of your emotion and its causes.

Most people are poor codifiers of their emotions. They have not learned how to judge the reasons behind a particular feeling before labeling it. Feelings of threat, dislike, anger, and even indigestion can all result in similar physiological reactions. To be unable to codify feelings accurately is often also to misread the state of your interpersonal relationships. The people you are with will respond to the labels you use to refer to your feelings—and, more importantly, they have no very good way to check the accuracy of your report. You are the only one who has direct access to your emotional state. Those around you can only infer what is going on inside you.

Reification: when words become more real
than the objects or events they supposedly represent

> BOY: You know, Karen, you don't seem to love me as much as you used to.
> GIRL: Come on, Charley, you know I do.
> BOY: But you act differently lately.
> GIRL: Oh, Charley, but I *told* you I love you.
> BOY: Well. . . . Okay, if you say so.

The Soviet Union is called a "communist" nation. This label has helped obscure from people the fact that the Soviet Union has actually adopted many capitalist economic practices. Because they are communists, the Russians are therefore expected to act like communists, whether they do or not all the time. Similar inaccuracies can occur in interpersonal relationships. Did Charley, in our introductory dialogue, fall victim to reification when Karen told him she loved him, though her behavior "told" him otherwise?

When people become involved in a reification problem, they focus on the words rather than on the specific sense in which they are used, the context that generated them, or whether they are used validly. For example, people may begin an interpersonal relationship because the words "I love you" are spoken in a moment of passion; the words assume greater force than the feelings that inspired them. Or at a party a friend may introduce you and a person you have dated once or twice as "boyfriend and girlfriend," a label neither of you would have used to describe your relationship. However, the label may establish certain expectations for your relationship. You may actually begin to act like boyfriend and girlfriend because the label takes on more significance than your own feelings. It also frequently happens that people continue acting like boyfriend and girlfriend or husband and wife long after their mutual affection has diminished, largely because the title for their relationship overshadows their current attitudes.

Many communication errors stemming from reification reflect a common process. A word or statement stimulates the formation of an image in a person's mind. For instance, someone tells Joe that "Cathy has a lot of personal problems," and he forms an image of Cathy as someone who has personal problems. Subsequent messages Joe sends to Cathy are shaped by this image, and he interprets her messages to him in a corresponding fashion. Problems arise if Cathy's problems subside but Joe's image of her—and his communication relationship with her—does not take account of the change. Obviously, the consequences of his fixed image of Cathy are unfortunate for both of them. The accuracy of Joe's communication predictions about Cathy's behavior is likely to suffer (since his image does not correspond to her reality), and he is clearly not helping Cathy when he treats her as if she were still burdened by personal problems.

What can be done to avoid reification problems? Probably the best protection is simply to be aware of them. Reification problems afflict primarily the unwary. More specifically, two things should be kept in mind. First, especially in the context of significant interpersonal relationships, it is important to check occasionally to determine how the things people say correspond to reality as you perceive it. In other words, do not buy someone else's (or your own) faulty verbal representation. This advice may sound about as basic as "Don't drink from a bottle marked 'poison'." Nevertheless, the frequency with which communicators commit reification errors indicates that it is worth repeating. Second, recall our discussion of process in chapter 2. Human behavior changes. Even if you initially arrive at a valid image, the behavior that first justified the image may disappear. Remember to look occasionally for evidence of changes in people so that you have the opportunity to modify your images of them if need be.

Restricted information

> BOY (calling on the telephone): Hello, Jane, this is Ken. How are you?
> GIRL: I'm fine, how are things with you?
> BOY: Not bad. Hey, are you busy tonight?
> GIRL: Oh, gee, Ken, yes I am. I'm really disappointed you didn't call sooner. I already have a date.
> BOY: Well, have a good time. I'll probably call you next week.
> GIRL: I hope you do.

There are three primary modes by which one human being can communicate with another: *language, paralanguage,* and *kinesics.* Language consists of the words we use when we communicate. Paralanguage involves such things as voice inflection, punctuation, and emphasis to give special meaning to words when we speak them. Kinesics involves our body language: how we use our face, hands, and posture when we communicate.

Paralanguage adds considerable meaning to our messages. The way you say something gives your receiver instructions on how to interpret your message. Through paralanguage—your voice tone—you can emphasize certain words in a message, tell your receiver how you feel about the message, and indicate how you want your receiver to respond to your message. For instance, consider the statement, "I think you're smart." If you vocally emphasize one or more words in this statement, how might you change its meaning? What are the differences between, "*I* think you're smart," and "I *think* you're smart," and so on? Furthermore, by subtly modifying your tone of voice, you can instruct your receiver to interpret your message as serious, sympathetic, sarcastic, amusing, or doubtful. Stop and think how much of the meaning of a message is conveyed in the speaker's tone of voice as compared to the actual words he uses.

Considerable meaning is also conveyed by kinesics, or body language. Through smiles and frowns, hand gestures and finger pointing, leaning toward or away from your receiver, you can add to your verbal message in the same ways as you can with paralanguage. Many nonverbal behaviors can even cancel out a verbal message. Have you ever conversed with someone who said, "We've got all the time in the world," and then looked at his watch while he tapped a finger impatiently on his desk?

People rely a great deal on paralanguage and kinesics when they communicate, often without fully realizing the importance of these two message elements. They are trapped into thinking that words alone are the primary conveyers of meaning. This misconception can lead to trouble when a communication channel that blocks paralanguage and/or kinesics (e.g., the mail or the telephone) is used. Have you ever experienced communication difficulties when your only communication channel with someone for a long time consisted of letters? People forget that without paralanguage or kinesics the bare words of a letter can be vague, misleading, and oftentimes cold substitutes for face-to-face contact.

For example, when you are separated from a loved one, do you take account of the restrictedness of the information in the letters you write? When you want to write "I miss you" or "I love you," are you aware that the normal modes of emphasis, feeling, and sincerity are absent, and that you must add these features mechanically to your letter? You must underline words, be redundant, or use alien phraseology to compensate for the loss of the vocal intonations that usually carry these meanings. To make up for the absence of kinesics, you may even draw a smiling face or hearts or some other symbol. If you want to tell someone you miss them you may have to write, "I really, really miss you very, very much" and underline each word. Is it possible that the famous love letters of Lord Byron or Keats were inspired, not by strong sentiment or poetic greatness alone, but by the writers' awareness of the necessity to compensate for the lack of paralinguistic and kinesic cues?

Of course, another major limitation of letter writing is the impossibility of immediate feedback. This restriction can be serious when lovers are separated for any length of time, especially if one or both are not sufficiently sure of the other's continuing affection. In face-to-face situations it is often easy to predict another's response to your statements, or at least to get feedback on how your messages are received; but matters are not so simple when few opportunities for feedback are available. This may explain why it is not uncommon for lovers' letters to become decreasingly affectionate over time, and why few people put much stock in the old adage, "Absence makes the heart grow fonder."

Have you ever spent a small fortune on telephone calls to a friend or a loved one because it was taxing to communicate by mail? A telephone conversation provides the added element of paralanguage. But while communication by telephone clearly has advantages over communication by mail, the lack of kinesics still generates problems. Particularly when people are dealing with interpersonal matters, it may be necessary to compensate for such restrictions on the mutual flow of information. Continual verbal reinforcement of the other communicator is demanded when he talks at length, for unless you say something, he may think you have gone for a walk. Consider what might happen if one of the parties to a telephone conversation responded with nods of the head. Furthermore, when you do want to let him know you are still with him, you may have to exaggerate vocal emphasis. After all, if your voice fails to tell him how you are feeling, he will probably remain in the dark about your feelings.

Problems of language usage versus problems of language

In discussing the problems of codification, reification, and restricted information, we have implicitly taken the position that many common communication problems are related to the ways people use language, rather than to limitations inherent in language itself. People can increase the probability of accurate and effective communication if they learn to avoid certain errors in the ways they use language to communicate.

Some people, however, argue that language should not be used at all as a communication medium. Their position is well stated by a musician we know who said, "You should use words only when you're having trouble communicating." Probably most people would not go so far as to totally denounce language as a communication medium, but they might say, borrowing from political rhetoric, "The system is so corrupt that we have to either vastly rework it or trash it altogether and create a new system." B. L. Whorf (1956) and his followers have argued that any language provides an inherently limited view of the world, and that people's thoughts are highly constrained by the particular language they use. From Whorf's principle of linguistic relativity, referring to language differences across cultures, others have derived the often-quoted aphorism "Meanings are in people," referring to language differences across individuals. While neither the cultural relativists nor the individual relativists claim that the nature of language makes communication impossible, they do emphasize the communication barriers imposed by language.

Another group of people go a step further than the relativists, from describing language-related communication problems to evaluating particular languages. Here we are referring to Korzybski and those he has influenced. Korzybski argued that the English language provides a distorted, inaccurate view of reality. In *Science and Sanity* (1933) he catalogues numerous errors in scientific disciplines, such as biology and psychiatry, as well as in day-to-day discourse, which he sees as inherently related to linguistic structure.

In this book we have chosen to focus on communication problems that most communicators have the ability, time, and energy to overcome. While Whorf, Korzybski, and a host of others after them have offered many provocative, if not always provable, insights into the relationship between language and communication, the complexity and subtlety of their insights place them beyond the usefulness of most communicators. Few of us have the motivation to rework the English language so that it has maximal utility as a communication tool. Rather, we are content to accept its limitations while trying to achieve a satisfactory level of error reduction in our communication with others.

Summary

As we stressed at the beginning of this chapter, we have chosen to focus on four problem areas related to making interpersonal messages. We have chosen depth over breadth, particularly since we believe the four sections of this chapter deal with message-making strategies and problems that are particularly relevant to our conceptualization of interpersonal communication.

As far as we know, our notion of communication energy is a relatively new addition to the list of processes relevant to the study of interpersonal communication. To the extent that satisfaction with and willingness to engage in communication are related to the amount of energy expended, the notion merits further investigation. A good place to begin is the research literature on human information processing. This research has shown that, as people work harder to process more and more complex information, they experience greater stress and the probability increases that they will make errors in processing the information.

Our comments on self-disclosure underline its relationship to the concept of communication energy. We noted that under certain conditions the disclosure of personally private information can result in heavy demands: after such information is revealed, the disclosing party must deal with its effects. We also highlighted several of the relational aspects of self-disclosure: conditions under which self-disclosure can lead to greater intimacy, response obligations incurred in self-disclosing situations, and the utility of self-disclosure in enhancing communicative accuracy. We have deliberately avoided labelling self-disclosure as good or bad. Such labels merely cloud people's perspectives of transactional processes. Instead, we have taken a functional approach to self-disclosure, focusing on when and how it may be useful in achieving particular noninterpersonal and interpersonal communicative goals.

Were you surprised to find in this book a section on making conversation? Normally textbooks do not grant this topic a high priority. Nevertheless, we believe that conversation is important as a bridge to interpersonal relationships and as a method of making human contact. Many people have asserted that one of the great problems of our age is our inability to relate to other people. We hope our discussion of conversation will help you avoid the perils of such loneliness and move from the noninterpersonal to the interpersonal level of communication.

Finally, we reviewed three pitfalls to communicative accuracy that result primarily from limitations in our use of language. Codification, reification, and restricted information cause some relatively common problems that can be exasperating. Even so, they can be avoided fairly easily once they are understood. Codification problems can be reduced by examining the sources of feelings before labeling them. Reification problems arise when words become more important than the nonsymbolic activities they represent. Keeping an eye open for inconsistencies between labels and activities prevents the development of faulty perceptions of oneself and of other people. When a restricted information situation arises, it is usually wise to postpone consequential interpersonal judgments until more information becomes available.

Probes

1. Analyze some of your own communication transactions. Can you identify differences in the amount of communication energy you expend? What factors seem to determine your expenditure of communication energy? Are there factors operating that were not discussed in this chapter? If so, what are they?

2. "The more energy you expend encoding messages, the less you will expend decoding them." To what extent do you agree with this statement? Suggest some conditions under which the statement would probably hold and some conditions under which it would not.

3. What kinds of information are you reluctant to disclose? How many of your sensitive areas are consistent with cultural and sociological generalizations about touchy topics? How many seem relatively unique to you?

4. Think about some of your friends and acquaintances and rank them in terms of your willingness to divulge personally private information to them. What characteristics of these persons influence your choices; i.e., what are the traits you consider in reaching decisions about whether to self-disclose?

5. Observe some of the conversations that occur in your daily activities. To what extent do the misconceptions about conversation discussed in this chapter influence these conversations? How do you react to the idea that the major function of conversation is to establish human contact? Develop an argument for or against this idea.

6. Try to initiate a conversation with a relative stranger but bypass the exchange of biographical and demographic information. How would you characterize the outcome of the conversation? How effectively were you able to make predictions about appropriate message strategies? How did you feel while conversing?

7. Do you see yourself primarily as a verbal or a nonverbal type; i.e., do you get most of your information from verbal or nonverbal channels? How might you increase your sensitivity to your less-preferred channel of information?

To like you, to be involved with you,
to be your friend, I must know who you are.

David Johnson, *Reaching Out: Interpersonal Effectiveness
and Self-Disclosure*

Hello darkness my old friend; I've come to talk to you again.

Paul Simon, "The Sounds of Silence"

This is the age of appearances, when the wrapping
seems more important than the contents.

Eric Sevareid, *Candidates 1960*

Interpersonal Communication in Today's Society

I n the preceding chapters we have developed a conceptual framework designed to distinguish between noninterpersonal and interpersonal communication transactions; we have considered the functions served by human communication; we have delineated some important characteristics of individuals that influence their ability to communicate interpersonally; we have stressed the importance of viewing communication transactionally, or relationally; and we have examined some message strategies that can be used at both the noninterpersonal and the interpersonal levels. Not surprisingly, we believe our approach has utility for those who wish to improve their interpersonal communication skills. Furthermore, although we chose not to emphasize research undertakings in this volume, we also feel that our conceptualization suggests promising avenues for future inquiry.

It has been tempting to stop here. Concluding or "wrap-up" chapters are a ritual of textbook writing, at least within the domain of communication. Still, we believe some of our earlier observations about the role of communication in contemporary society merit reinforcement, particularly since our position departs from most of the currently popular conceptions. We view our position as both realistic and optimistic. To support this claim, we will briefly consider what we perceive to be three contemporary views of the role of communication in our society, and compare and contrast our position with each of them.

Three viewpoints on communication that we reject

In chapter 1 we associated the teleological view of interpersonal communication with the notion of "togetherness." The togetherness position holds that society's ills result largely from people's inability to relate interpersonally: each of us should strive to "know" others as individuals and to communicate with them on an individual basis. Encounter groups and sensitivity training sessions are examples of communicative activities that attempt to implement this concept of togetherness.

The anomie position and the togetherness position share one common denominator: both seem to stem from a sincere concern for the plight of the individual in a large, depersonalized, technological society. Here, however, the similarities cease. For rather than calling for a united effort to obliterate all noninterpersonal barriers, the anomie position reflects a resigned acceptance of the individual's solitary loneliness. People enter and leave the world alone, counsel the proponents of the anomie position, and, during their brief tenure on earth, they are doomed to a life of solitude. The establishment of interpersonal communication bonds with fellow travelers is viewed as an impossibility; a kind of pessimistic existentialism and a belief in the absurdity of human existence are the hallmarks of this viewpoint.

Although the veneer position is in some ways an offshoot of the anomie position, we see it as sufficiently different to merit separate consideration. Whereas the anomie viewpoint is characterized by the notion that solitary loneliness is inevitable, the veneer position emphasizes the selfish superficiality of communication exchanges. The phrase "grey flannel mouth," which most people are acquainted with, nicely characterizes the veneer position. For proponents of the veneer position, communication is almost always confined to the noninterpersonal realm and consists largely of attempts to feather one's economic or social nest. Phrases such as "impression management" and "image building" are the stock-in-trade of veneerists; in fact, our term *veneer* connotes a concern for noninterpersonal frills and packaging along with a disinterest in interpersonal substance. Thus, unlike the anomie position, the veneer position does not necessarily hold that interpersonal relationships are impossible; rather, it purposefully relegates communication to the noninterpersonal level.

Our objections to the togetherness position

Our reservations about the togetherness position are threefold. First, as we have previously emphasized, the transition from noninterpersonal to interpersonal communication seldom occurs without substantial effort. If everyone were to attempt to establish an interpersonal relationship with everyone else, literally all available time would be devoted to exploring relational avenues for moving to the interpersonal level. Even then, it is doubtful that such efforts would bear

fruit; there are simply not enough hours in the day for people to relate with all of their acquaintances at the interpersonal level. Thus, persons are compelled to make choices, to decide which relationships are sufficiently important to warrant the costs involved in communicating interpersonally. Such trade-offs are neither pessimistic nor cynical; they merely reflect the realities of available communicative time and space.

Still, it may be argued that the preceding objection does not militate against the desirability of a universal brotherhood of interpersonal relationships; all it does is underscore the impossibility of such a situation. Consequently, we will go a step further: not only is it impossible for people to operate exclusively within the interpersonal domain, but also it would be undesirable for them to do so. Just as the world is not entirely threatening and foreboding, neither is it totally benign and supportive. Given this state of affairs, we hark back to an assertion made in the previous chapter: defense mechanisms are often useful and functional. Discriminating adventures in openness and self-disclosure can yield rich, rewarding interpersonal relationships; indiscriminate attempts to move to the interpersonal level in all situations can result in considerable psychic trauma and mental anguish. Thus, an implied social caveat emptor accompanies every decision to seek the interpersonal level, and only the most foolhardy or masochistic communicators strike out in search of interpersonal treasures without carefully weighing the risks.

Finally, it is important to remember that judgments about the quality of any particular relationship are, of necessity, comparative and relative. Think about highly significant, landmark relationships in your own life. Why do they stand out in your mind? Partially, at least, because you have experienced numerous less significant relationships that provide yardsticks for comparison. In other words, much of the richness of an interpersonal relationship lies in its uniqueness. Lovers, for instance, always feel that theirs is a unique relationship. Yet a cynical acquaintance of ours, upon observing two lovers deeply engrossed in each other's company, once remarked: "Look at those people. They think they are the only ones in the world who ever felt that way. But actually, there are millions of other people going around with the same feelings, and all of them think they are the only ones who have ever experienced such ecstasy."

In the sense in which it was offered, our cynical acquaintance's remark hit the psychological nail on the head. Objectively speaking, the feelings that accompany an intense interpersonal relationship are probably common social currency; they are feelings that many others have experienced upon becoming party to such a relationship. Subjectively, however, these feelings are very unique to the concerned parties, largely because such relationships occur relatively infrequently in their lives. The togetherness position risks the transformation of a relational rare event to a commonplace; it represents a reverse alchemy that would transform interpersonally precious ore to social fool's gold. The fabric of one's life is woven most skillfully and pleasingly by a judicious mixture of noninterpersonal and interpersonal communication relationships, not by slavish commitment to the impossible and, in our opinion, misguided objective of establishing interpersonal communication relationships with everyone.

One further point merits emphasis. As we have previously suggested, there is nothing inherently demeaning or patronizing about noninterpersonal relationships. All of us have a host of casual friends and acquaintances with whom we enjoy noninterpersonal exchanges. These exchanges can themselves be satisfying and rewarding for the parties involved, even though predictions are based largely on cultural or sociological data, rather than on psychological considerations. Paradoxically, in fact, many cordial noninterpersonal relationships would probably suffer from concerted efforts by one or more of the participants to move to the interpersonal level. It is doubtful that these relationships could withstand the stresses imposed by the quest for interpersonal grounds. As with most cliches, the assertion "Familiarity breeds contempt," while not universally valid, contains an element of truth. And above all else, familiarity is the rallying call for proponents of the togetherness position.

Our objections to the anomie position

We emphatically reject the premise that man must remain a communicative alien from his fellowmen. To be sure, there are limits to what we may hope to know about other people. As we have previously stated, it is literally impossible to "get inside" another's head; each individual's mental states are his or her private property. Nevertheless, communication enables us to make inferences about the thoughts and feelings of others. Even more important, it permits us to share our perceptions of these thoughts and feelings with one another. Through such sharing we develop not only self-knowledge but also knowledge about our fellowmen, or about a particular person. To say that such knowledge can never be foolproof, or in some sense "perfect," does not negate the possibility of establishing interpersonal bonds with others and reducing the sense of anomie that accompanies a solitary existence.

To subscribe to the anomie position is to engage in what the sociologist Robert Merton (1957) has called the "self-fulfilling prophecy." As we have repeatedly stressed, interpersonal communication demands hard work, both physically and psychically. If one starts with the premise that each man is an island—an island rendered completely inaccessible by the rocky shoals and giant waves that surround it—the probability of exerting the necessary effort to reach the friendly shores is indeed slight. Thus, the self-fulfilling prophecy operates in the following manner: the person begins with the premise that interpersonal communication with others is an impossibility; consequently, when he encounters others, his attempts to establish communicative links are minimal to nonexistent; not surprisingly, he fails to communicate, and each failure further reinforces his belief in the hopelessness of the communicative enterprise. Everyone occasionally falls prey to the self-fulfilling prophecy, but to allow such reasoning to influence all of our relationships (or perhaps more accurately, our non-relationships) with others strikes us as a tremendous waste of human resources and as a denial of man's individual and collective potential.

Moreover, just a bit of introspection underscores the implausibility of the anomie position, at least for most people. Few of us feel that our communicative efforts have been totally discordant; we know that we have achieved relational harmony on at least some occasions. For the most part, serious subscribers to the anomie position are those unfortunate few who have not met with such successes. Rather than entertain the ego-threatening possibility that their failures to establish interpersonal contact can be laid at their own behavioral doorsteps, they choose to posit a hostile, alien world where attempts to relate to others are destined to fail. The bitter charge "No one cares and no one understands!" usually tells us more about the individual uttering the statement than about the external circumstances the statement supposedly describes. This is not to say that people are never thoughtless or cruel, but only to suggest that things are seldom as interpersonally desperate as the proponents of the anomie position would have us believe.

Our objections to the veneer position

We do not deny the utility of the veneer position for certain kinds of communication transactions. What we do denounce is the implication that veneerist transactions are the sum and substance (or at least the significant sum and substance) of human communication. Throughout this volume we have stressed the distinction between noninterpersonal and interpersonal communication transactions. Moreover, we have argued that even when transactions focus on marketplace concerns —e.g., job interviews or seller-client exchanges—successful efforts to move to the interpersonal level may often result in higher payoffs.

Finally, while we have stressed the centrality of environmental control, our conception of control extends far beyond the crassly materialistic domain of the veneerists. In short, the veneer position grossly underestimates man's communicative potential; it manifests a callous disregard for man's ethical responsibilities to his fellowmen; and, from a pragmatic perspective, it imposes a set of communicative blinders that reduce the likelihood of optimum payoffs in the most commercial of communicative situations.

Summary

We have examined three contemporary views of the role of communication in our society and have found all three wanting: the togetherness position suffers from a misguided, muddleheaded optimism about the universality of interpersonal communication; the anomie position is born of unwarranted pessimism about the communicative condition of man; and the veneer position reflects a slick, cynical view of communication as superficial image building. How, then, does the position we have espoused in the preceding chapters differ from these three viewpoints and why do we find it preferable?

Some characteristics of our position

Unlike the three positions already discussed, the viewpoint we advance places a premium on choice. Rather than relying upon simple, sovereign generalizations about the universality or the impossibility of interpersonal communication, we contend that the participant, or participants, in a communication transaction have the power to define the nature of that relationship. In some instances, reason may dictate that the relationship remain at the noninterpersonal level; in others, conditions may warrant the costs involved in attempting to move to the interpersonal level. Thus, any communication relationship requires assessment by the participants. Rather than being guided by preconceived notions about the limits, or lack of limits, of communication relationships in general, the communicators assess the importance, or potential importance, of the particular relationship; estimate the likelihood that greater communication fidelity could be achieved by striving to move to the interpersonal level; weigh the probable costs involved in attempting to communicate interpersonally; and, on the basis of all these considerations, choose either to remain at the noninterpersonal level or to move to the interpersonal level.

As we have already stressed, all of these decisional elements need not be weighed at a highly conscious, cognitive level. At times, choices may be made and predictions arrived at with very little conscious stocktaking. Still, regardless of the extent of their obtrusiveness, we contend that communicators can and do choose whether or not to communicate interpersonally in particular situations. Furthermore, if a decision to try to move to the interpersonal level bears fruit, highly rewarding communication relationships are often established.

A second basic ingredient of our position is the broad conception of control that we have espoused. Although we have argued that a concern for environmental control pervades all communication transactions, we do not believe that the meaning of *control* should be restricted to marketplace exchanges rooted solely in the quest for economic or social currency. As we have underscored in chapter 3, any effort to realize one communicative outcome rather than another entails considerations of control; hence, any indictment of this broad conception of control hinges on the presumption that it is somehow unethical, or undemocratic, for persons to prefer one outcome over another. By contrast, the veneer position often seems to conceive of control in a narrow sense that we ourselves find repugnant: it views communication largely as a tool for improving one's financial standing or enhancing one's social status.

Finally, we believe that, when contrasted with the other three positions outlined in this chapter, our position concerning the role of interpersonal communication most closely conforms with sound principles of a contemporary democratic society. We have already underscored the centrality of choice to our conception, and choice remains a staple commodity of a democratic system. In addition, our view of interpersonal communication is firmly grounded in a value for individual responsibility. Each person, in his role as individual communicator, must assume the responsibility for determining when to seek the interpersonal level. Furthermore, every communicator has the responsibility of dealing with the how question, of exerting the physical and psychic effort that the transition from noninterpersonal to interpersonal communication demands.

Although simple generalizations and preconceptions about the nature and limits of interpersonal communication may relieve communicators of their individual responsibilities, we do not believe that reliance upon such generalizations squares with man's communicative potential, at least as that potential is reflected by democratic institutions and practices. This is why we are convinced that our position is both realistic and optimistic. At best, our ideas and arguments have also convinced you; at worst, you have weighed the merits of our position and found it wanting. In either case, the choice and the responsibility are yours. We would not want it any other way.

Probes

1. Try to discover instances in your daily experience that reflect the various approaches to the role of communication in our society discussed in this chapter. Can you identify popular song lyrics that mirror each of the approaches? Television, motion picture, or popular fiction plots?

2. "Each of the approaches to the role of communication in our society is separate and distinct from the others." Attack or defend this assertion.

3. Some social commentators have argued that many of our current political and social problems can be traced to the dominance of the veneer approach to communication among contemporary leaders. How would you evaluate this argument?

4. Gerry and Mark deny the possibility of a universal brotherhood of interpersonal relationships. Do you agree, or do you think such a goal is attainable? Develop arguments supporting your position.

5. "Whereas the three other approaches to the role of communication in our society are themselves based on noninterpersonal considerations, Gerry and Mark's position rests on an interpersonal foundation." Attack, defend, or modify this statement.

6. Can you think of another position concerning the role of communication in our society not developed in this chapter? If so, write a short paper spelling out this position.

References

Adorno, T. W.; Frenkel-Brunswik, Else; Levinson, Daniel J.; and Sanford, Nevitt R. *The Authoritarian Personality*. New York: Harper & Row, 1950.

Albee, Edward. *Who's Afraid of Virginia Woolf?* New York: Atheneum, 1962.

Anderson, Kenneth E. "An Experimental Study of the Interaction of Artistic and Nonartistic Ethos in Persuasion." Unpublished doctoral dissertation, University of Wisconsin, 1961.

Barnlund, Dean C. *Interpersonal Communication: Survey and Studies*. New York: Houghton Mifflin, 1968.

Bateson, Gregory. "Conventions of Communication: Where Validity Depends upon Belief." In Jurgen Ruesch and Gregory Bateson, *Communication: The Social Matrix of Psychiatry*. New York: Norton, 1951.

Bem, Daryl J. "An Experimental Analysis of Self-Persuasion." *Journal of Experimental Psychology* 1 (1965): 199–218.

Berger, Charles. "The Acquaintance Process Revisited." Paper presented at the Annual Convention of the Speech Communication Association, New York, December 1973.

Berlo, David K. "Human Communication: The Basic Proposition." *Essays on Communication*. East Lansing: Department of Communication, 1971.

_____. *The Process of Communication*. New York: Holt, Rinehart & Winston, 1960.

Berlo, David K.; Lemert, James B.; and Mertz, Robert J. "Dimensions for Evaluating the Acceptability of Message Sources." *Public Opinion Quarterly* 33 (1970): 563–76.

Birdwhistell, Ray L. "Dimensions of Nonverbal Behavior." Lecture presented to the Departments of Communication and Sociology, Michigan State University, April, 1973.

Brooks, William D. *Speech Communication*. Dubuque: Wm. C. Brown, 1971.

Buber, Martin, *Between Man and Man*. Boston: Beacon, 1955.

Budner, Stanley. "Intolerance of Ambiguity as a Personality Variable." *Journal of Personality* 30 (1962): 29–50.

Byrne, Donn. "Parental Antecedents of Authoritarianism." *Journal of Personality and Social Psychology* 1 (1965): 369–73.

_____. "Attitudes and Attraction." In Leonard Berkowitz (ed.), *Advances in Experimental Social Psychology*, vol. 4. New York: Academic Press, 1969, pp. 35–90.

Byrne, Donn, and Rhamey, R. "Magnitude of Positive and Negative Reinforcement as a Determinant of Attraction." *Journal of Personality and Social Psychology* 2 (1965): 884–89.

Caplan, Nathan, and Nelson, Stephen D. "On Being Useful: The Nature and Uses of Psychological Research on Social Problems." Ann Arbor: Center for Research on Utilization of Scientific Knowledge, 1972. (mimeo report)
Coser, Lewis A. *The Functions of Social Conflict*. New York: Free Press, 1956.
Culbert, Samuel A. *Interpersonal Process of Self-Disclosure: It Takes Two to See One*. Washington: N.T.L. Institute for Applied Behavioral Science, 1967.

D'Amato, Michael R. "Instrumental Conditioning." In Melvin H. Marx (ed.), *Learning: Processes*. London: Macmillan, 1969, pp. 35–118.
Dance, Frank E. X., and Larson, Carl E. *Speech Communication: Concepts and Behavior*. New York: Holt, Rinehart & Winston, 1972.
Dymond, Rosalind F. "A Scale for the Measurement of Empathic Ability." *Journal of Consulting Psychology* 8 (1949): 127–33.

Egan, Gerard. *Encounter: Group Processes for Interpersonal Growth*. Belmont, Calif.: Brooks/Cole, 1970.
Eysenck, H. J. *Sense and Nonsense in Psychology*. Baltimore: Penguin, 1958.

Festinger, Leon; Schachter, Stanley; and Back, Kurt. *Social Pressures in Informal Groups*. New York: Harper, 1950.
Fiedler, Fred E. "The Leader's Psychological Distance and Group Effectiveness." In Dorwin Cartwright and Alvin Zander (eds.), *Group Dynamics*, 2 ed. Evanston, Ill.: Row, Peterson, 1960, pp. 586–606.
Frenkel-Brunswik, Else. "Intolerance of Ambiguity as an Emotional and Perceptual Personality Variable." In Jerome S. Bruner and David Krech (eds.), *Perception and Personality: A Symposium*. Durham: Duke University Press, 1949, pp. 108–43.

Gamson, W. A. "Experimental Studies in Coalition Formation." In Leonard Berkowitz (ed.), *Advances in Experimental Social Psychology*, vol. I: New York: Academic Press, 1969, pp. 82–110.
Giffin, Kim, and Patton, Bobby R. *Fundamentals of Interpersonal Communication*. New York: Harper & Row, 1971.
Goffman, Erving. *The Presentation of Self in Everyday Life*. Garden City, N.J.: Doubleday, 1959.
————. *Behavior in Public Places*. New York: Free Press, 1963.
Gough, Harrison G., and Sanford, Nevitt R. Rigidity as a Psychological Variable. Unpublished manuscript, University of California, 1952.
Gover, Robert. *One Hundred Dollar Misunderstanding*. New York: Ballantine, 1961.
Gunkle, George. "Empathy: Implications for Theatre Research." *Educational Theatre Journal* 15 (1963), 15–23.

Harrison, Randall. *Beyond Words: An Introduction to Nonverbal Communication*. Englewood Cliffs, N.J.: Prentice-Hall, 1974.
Herbert, Frank. "Listening to the Left Hand." *Harper's Magazine* 247 (1973): 92–100.

Hoffer, Eric. *The True Believer*. New York: Harper & Row, 1951.
Homans, George C. *Social Behavior: Its Elementary Forms*. New York: Harcourt, Brace & World, 1961.

Johnson, David W. *Reaching Out: Interpersonal Effectiveness and Self-Actualization*. Englewood Cliffs, N.J.: Prentice-Hall, 1972.
Jones, J. Charles. *Learning*. New York: Harcourt, Brace & World, 1967.
Jourard, Sidney M. *The Transparent Self*. rev. ed. New York: Van Nostrand, 1971.

Katz, Elihu, and Lazarsfeld, Paul F. *Personal Influence*, New York: Free Press, 1955.
Katz, Robert L. *Empathy: Its Nature and Uses*. New York: Free Press, 1963.
Kelley, Harold H. "Communication in Experimentally Created Hierarchies." *Human Relations* 4 (1951): 39–56.
Kelman, Herbert C. "Processes of Opinion Change." *Public Opinion Quarterly* 25 (1961): 57–78.
Keltner, John W. *Interpersonal Speech-Communication: Elements and Structures*. Belmont, Calif.: Wadsworth, 1970.
Knapp, Mark. *Nonverbal Communication in Human Interaction*. New York: Holt, Rinehart & Winston, 1972.
Korzybski, Alfred. *Science and Sanity: An Introduction to Non-Aristotelian Systems and General Semantics*. Lancaster, Pa.: Science Press, 1933.

Laing, R. D. *The Politics of Experience*. New York: Ballantine, 1967.

McCroskey, James C. "Scales for the Measurement of Ethos." *Speech Monographs* 33 (1966): 65–72.
McCroskey, James C.; Larson, Carl; and Knapp, Mark L. *An Introduction to Interpersonal Communication*. Englewood Cliffs, N.J.: Prentice-Hall, 1971.
Merton, Robert K. *Social Theory and Social Structure*. New York: Free Press, 1957, esp. pp. 421–36.
Miller, Gerald R. "On Defining Communication: Another Stab." *Journal of Communication* 16 (1966): 88–98.
_____. *Speech Communication: A Behavioral Approach*. Indianapolis: Bobbs-Merrill, 1966.
Miller, Gerald R., and Bacon, Paula. "Open- and Closed-Mindedness and Recognition of Visual Humor." *Journal of Communication* 21 (1971): 150–59.
Miller, Neal E., and Dollard, John. *Social Learning and Imitation*. New Haven: Yale University Press, 1941.
Mortensen, C. David. *Communication: The Study of Human Interaction*. New York: McGraw-Hill, 1972.

Newcomb, Theodore M. "An Approach to the Study of Communicative Acts." *Psychological Review* 60 (1953): 393–404.
_____. "Interpersonal Balance." In Robert P. Abelson, Elliot Aronson, William J. McGuire, Theodore M. Newcomb, Milton J. Rosenberg, and Percy H. Tannenbaum (eds.), *Theories of Cognitive Consistency: A Source Book*. Chicago: Rand McNally, 1968, pp. 28–51.

Newman, John B. "A Rationale for a Definition of Communication." *Journal of Communication* 10 (1960): 115–24.

Newman, Oscar. *Defensible Space: Crime Prevention through Urban Design*. New York: Macmillan, 1972.

Pace, R. Wayne, and Boren, Robert R. *The Human Transaction: Facets, Functions, and Forms of Interpersonal Communication*. Glenview, Ill.: Scott, Foresman, 1973.

Packard, Vance. *The Hidden Persuaders*. New York: McKay, 1957.

Penny, R., and Robertson, L. "The Homans Sentiment/Interaction Hypothesis." *Psychological Reports* 11 (1962): 257–58.

Pieper, Walter A., and Marx, Melvin H. "Effects of Within-Session Incentive Contrast on Instrumental Acquisition and Performance." *Journal of Experimental Psychology* 65 (1963): 568–71.

Rein, Irving. *Rudy's Red Wagon*. Glenview, Ill.: Scott, Foresman, 1969.

Rogers, Peter L.; Scheerer, Klaus, R.; and Rosenthal, Robert. "Content Filtering Human Speech: A Simple Electronic System." *Behavioral Research Methods and Instruments* 3 (1971): 16–18.

Rokeach, Milton. *The Open and Closed Mind*. New York: Basic Books, 1960.

Rosenthal, Robert; Archer, Dane; Kiovumaki, Judy; and Rogers, Peter. "Task Group on Development of the Profile of Nonverbal Sensitivity (PONS)." Interim progress report to the National Science Foundation, undated.

Sanford, Nevitt. "The Approach of the Authoritarian Personality." In James L. McCary (ed.), *Psychology of Personality: Six Modern Approaches*. New York: Logos Press, 1956, pp. 253–319.

Scheff, Thomas J. *Being Mentally Ill*. Chicago: Aldine, 1966.

Sevareid, Eric (ed.). *Candidates 1960*. New York: Basic Books, 1959.

Sherif, Muzafer; Harvey, O. J.; White, B. Jack; Hood, W. R.; and Sherif, Carolyn. *Experimental Study of Positive and Negative Intergroup Attitudes between Experimentally Produced Groups. Robbers' Cave Study*. Norman, Okla.: University of Oklahoma, 1954. (Multilithed)

Siegel, Elliot R.; Miller, Gerald R.; and Wotring, C. Edward. "Source Credibility and Credibility Proneness: A New Relationship." *Speech Monographs* 36 (1969): 118–25.

Simons, Herbert W. "Prologue," and "The Carrot and Stick as Handmaidens of Persuasion in Conflict Situations." In Gerald R. Miller and Herbert W. Simons (eds.), *Perspectives on Communication in Social Conflict*. Englewood Cliffs, N.J.: Prentice-Hall, 1974, pp. 1–13, 172–205.

Skinner, B. F. *Beyond Freedom and Dignity*. New York: Knopf, 1971.

Stevens, S. S. "Introduction: A Definition of Communication." *Journal of the Acoustical Society of America* 22 (1950): 689.

Thibaut, John W., and Kelley, Harold H. *The Social Psychology of Groups*. New York: Wiley, 1959.

Toffler, Alvin. *Future Shock*. New York: Bantam, 1970.

Watson, O. Michael. *Proxemic Behavior*. The Hague: Mouton, 1970.

Watzlawick, Paul; Beavin, Janet H.; and Jackson, Don D. *Pragmatics of Human Communication*. New York: Norton, 1967.

Weaver, Richard M. "Ultimate Terms in Contemporary Rhetoric." In Richard M. Weaver, *The Ethics of Rhetoric*. Chicago: Regnery, 1953, pp. 211–32.

Wenburg, John R., and Wilmot, William W. *The Personal Communication Process*. New York: Wiley, 1973.

Whorf, Benjamin L. *Language, Thought, and Reality*. New York: Wiley and M.I.T. Press, 1956.

Winch, Robert F. *Mate Selection: A Study of Complementary Needs*. New York: Harper, 1958.

Index

Budner, Stanley, 156
Bunker, Archie, 154–55, 165, 204, 278
Bunker, Edith, 278
Byrne, Donn, 155, 208
Byrnes, Francis, 256

C

Caesar, Julius, 138
Candidates 1960, 342
Caplan, Nathan, 48
Catalyst control strategies, 125–28
Category systems, 26, 96, 208
Catharsis, and self-disclosure, 319
Change
  and prediction, 9–10
  and process, 41
Choice
  and energy, 295, 296
  freedom of in interpersonal relation-
    ships, 35, 56–57, 316, 349
Clarification, and self-disclosure, 319
Clemens, Samuel Langhorne (Mark
  Twain), 206
Codification, 332–35, 341
Cognitive style, 195, 239
  and ambiguity vs. clarity, 144–53
  bringing out the shades of gray, 156–61
  and complementarity vs. symmetry of
    relationships, 239
  defined, 143–44
  and interpersonal communication, 29,
    144, 146–47, 148, 153–56, 162–64
  and relational development, 201
  and relational legislation, 285
Commander McHale, 166
Communication, 5, 15, 31, 59
  and control, 35, 63, 64, 66
  defining, 33–46, 59
  functions of, 61–64
  importance of, 5–6, 288–89
  and information, 15, 30
  and intentionality, 35–37
  and prediction, 7–12
  and process, 40–43

relational approach to, 48–52
and self-identity, 83–84
social nature of, 5, 44
and symbols, 43–46
transactional approach to, 37–40
Communication breakdown, 15–16,
  18–19, 58, 216, 280
Communication relationships, 46–58,
  90, 91
  and Siamese twin strategies, 130–31
  and territoriality, 204
Communication rules, 21, 35, 49
Communication skill, 41–42, 74, 137–38
Communication strategies, 7–9, 10,
  31, 59, 72
Communicative angel, 134–35, 138
Communicative basis for relational development, 224–26, 229
Communicative control; *see* Control
Communicative energy; *see* Energy
Communicative gangster, 134, 138
Communist Manifesto, 74
Comparison level for alternatives, 249
Competition
  and complementarity vs. symmetry, 238
  and compliance, 70
  and conflict, 270
  and relational development, 215–16
Complementarity, 232–41, 254
  and interpersonal relationships, 238–41
Complexity, and energy, 300–301
Compliance, 66, 68–73, 84
  interpersonal approach, 71–72
  noninterpersonal approach, 69–71
Conditional prediction, 117, 124
Conflict, 61–62
  assumptions about, 260–61
  forms of, 264–70, 285
  management of, 73–74, 262
  outcomes of, 262–63
  positive and negative aspects of, 261–62
  and relational legislation, 271–72
  sources of, 74–75
Consummatory activity, 121–22, 229
Control, 64–86, 91–92, 165, 351
  and attitudinal similarity, 208, 254
  and balance, 249

Control (cont.)
  and communication, 35, 62
  and complementarity vs. symmetry, 238
  and conflict, 261, 270
  consciousness of, 103, 136–38, 140
  and energy, 291
  functions of, 63
  and information, 77–80, 87, 207–208
  interpersonal, 63–64, 86, 92
  levels of, 66, 68
  measuring effectiveness of, 66, 101–108, 132–33, 140
  moral implications of, 64–65, 87, 93, 133–38, 254, 351
  noninterpersonal, 63–64
  relational view of, 52, 120–21, 124, 140
  and self-disclosure, 312, 313, 321
  and self-identity, 63, 80–86, 87
  and social norms, 84–85
  transactional view of, 66, 87
Control strategies, 92, 103, 108–33, 140
Conversation, 324–31, 341
  interpersonal dimension of, 330
  misconceptions about, 329–31
  conversational skill, 326–31
Coordination of behavior, 51
  and attitudes, 242
  and information, 200
  and relational legislation, 272
Cory, Richard, 85
Coser, Lewis, 262
Cost, 90, 220–21, 295
  and control, 104, 118–19, 124
Creativity, and communication, 100
  and conflict management, 208
Credibility, 77
Credibility proneness, 163
Crisis, and relational escalation, 218–19
Critical limit in relationships, 282
Cue, 111, 177–79, 181–84, 195
Culbert, Samuel, 310–11, 320
Cultural control, 13
Cultural level of analysis, 12–17, 20, 22, 30, 31, 44, 52, 110–11
  and conversation, 326
  data gathering, 15
  errors in prediction, 15–16
  and information, 30
  and prediction, 172

  and stimulus generalization, 311
Cultural level relationships, 53
Cultural norms, 12–14, 26, 105
Cultural values, 12–13, 125, 127–28
Culture, 12–13, 17

D

D'Amato, Michael R., 119
Dampening conflict, 73, 75, 263
Dance, Frank E. X., 46
Danger signals in relationships, 279–84, 285
Dangerfield, Rodney, 83–84
Dangling carrot control strategies, 108–17, 122, 123–24, 126, 128
  goals of, 109–10
  procedures, 110–13
  skills, 113–17
Dear Abby, 257
Decoding, and energy, 295–99, 341
  and self-disclosure, 317–19
Defense mechanisms, 25, 28
Definition of relationships, 238–39, 240–41, 254, 281–82, 349
  interpersonal vs. noninterpersonal, 56
  and self-disclosure, 313–14
Desirable response, 103–104
Desired response, 103–104
Deviation amplification, 120, 122–23
Devil words, 15, 309
Direction of behavior, 109–10
Dispositional factors in prediction, 11–12
Dissolution of conflict, 264, 270, 285
Dogmatism, 148–49, 285
  and interpersonal communication, 29, 155–56
  vs. authoritarianism, 149–50
Dollard, John, 177
Drive, 177
Dymond, Rosalind, 170

E

Egan, Gerard, 309–10
Ego-conflict, 268–70, 285

Emotional content of interpersonal relationships, 201

Empathy
  defining, 167–74
  and cognitive style, 195
  and interpersonal communication, 101, 170, 173–74, 183, 306
  and predictions, 101
  as psychophysiological response, 168–69
  and relational development, 201
  as social perception skill, 169–74
  and stimulus discrimination, 172–74, 192
  transactional view of, 174–76

Encoding, and energy, 294–95, 341

Encounter groups, 28, 344

Energy, 292–308, 341
  communicative implications of, 301–304
  and conflict, 261
  and control, 137–38
  forms of, 294–95
  and level of communication, 26, 53, 304–308
  and relational development, 204
  and self-disclosure, 312

Ensign Parker, 166

Environmental control; see Control

Escalation, 216–24, 260
  and danger signals, 280–82
  and self-disclosure, 312, 319

Evaluative function of information, 207–208, 215, 229

Extensions of persons, 210–13

External stimuli, 38, 334

Eysenck, Hans J., 299

F

Fairyland control strategies, 85, 131–33, 245

Fearfulness, 258, 275–76

Feedback, 6, 48, 49, 338
  and cognitive style, 160
  and measuring control effectiveness, 108

Festinger, Leon, 202

Fiedler, Fred E., 161, 162–63, 164

Forced compliance, 69, 74

Formal sociological relationships, 53–54

Formality, and energy, 300

Frenkel-Brunswick, Else, 147, 148

Future Shock, 4, 28

G

Gamson, W. A., 116

General systems theory, 51

Genuine self-disclosure, 320–22, 323–24

George and Martha, 21–22, 28, 84–85, 193, 257

Gerard, Mike, 296

Giffin, Kim, 6, 63

Goals
  and measuring control effectiveness, 102, 103–104
  and relational development, 222–23

God words, 15, 309

Goffman, Erving, 71, 213

Golding, William, 214

Gough, Harrison G., 156

Gover, Robert, 18, 31

Groups, 17–19, 25

Gunkle, George, 167

H

Hanging sword control strategies, 117–24, 126, 128
  effects of, 119–20
  and egocentrism, 123
  kinds of, 117–19
  procedures, 120–24
  vs. dangling carrot strategies, 123–24

Harper's Magazine, 42, 60

Harrison, Randall, 212

Harvard Lampoon, 156

Hedonism, 135

Herbert, Frank, 42

Heterogeneity
  of cultures, 13
  of groups, 17

and self-disclosure, 316, 324–25
transactional nature of, 200
and trust, 252–53
Interpersonal relationship vs. noninterpersonal relationships, 28, 55–57, 201
and balance, 246–47, 248–49
and choice, 56–57
and criteria for defining, 56
preconditions, 221–23
and rule generation, 21–22, 55–56
Intrapersonal communication, 44–46
Introversion, and energy, 299
Irrelevant legislation, 276–77, 278

Learning
and communication, 20, 44
and conflict, 261
and control, 91–92
and PCC, 97–101
Lemert, James B., 77
Level of analysis, 12–22
Linearity of message transmission, 290
Linguistic relativity, 339
Logical connection between rewards,
114–16
Lord Byron, 338
Lord of the Flies, 214

J

Jackson, Don D., 22, 32, 35, 233–34, 238
Joe Doodlebug, 151–53
Johnson, David, 342
Jones, J. Charles, 122
Jourard, Sidney, 309–10, 341

K

Katz, Elihu, 6
Katz, Robert, L., 167, 168
Keats, John, 338
Kelley, Harold H., 90, 249, 291
Kelman, Herbert, 68–69
Keltner, John, 6
Kinesics, 336, 337, 338
Knapp, Mark, 6, 211, 288
Korzybski, Alfred, 339

L

Lack of experience and relational prob-
lems, 259
Laing, R. D., 224
Landers, Ann, 257
Language, limits on the use of, 331–39
Larson, Carl, 6, 46, 288
Lazarsfeld, Paul, 6

M

Management of conflict, 73–74, 262–64
Marx, Karl, 74
Marx, Melvin H., 117
Mass media, 69–70, 195
McCroskey, James, 6, 77, 288
Measurement of control effectiveness,
101–108, 140
desirability of response, 103–104, 107
eliciting a response, 102
and fairyland control, 132–33
replicability of responses, 106–107
responsibility for responses, 104–106,
107
Mell, 236
Mentalist school, 38
Merton, Robert K., 347
Mertz, Robert J., 77
Messages, 35
and linearity of transmission, 290
and relational development, 210
sequential approach to, 48, 290
transactional nature of, 290–91
Miller, Gerald R., 36, 40, 155, 163
Miller, Neal, 177
Mitty, Walter, 131
Mixed levels problem, 57–58, 170
"Momma," 236
Mortensen, C. David, 64
Motivation, and trust, 250–52
Motives, 158–59
Ms, 279

The Music Man, 156
Mutual system, and communication
  relationships, 48–58

N

Need fulfillment, 98
Nelson, Stephen D., 48
Newcomb, Theodore, 202, 230, 242
Newman, John B., 34
Newman, Oscar, 204
Nietzsche, Friedrich, 239
Nixon, Richard, 223
Noninterpersonal communication, 22–29,
  79–80, 182, 195, 234–35, 237
  and compliance, 69–71
  and conflict resolution, 75–76
  and control, 63–64, 101
  and conversation, 326–28
  and energy, 304–308
  and self-disclosure, 323–24
Noninterpersonal foundations of relational development, 202–16
Noninterpersonal relationships, 28, 44,
  52–54, 170, 347
  and balance, 246–47
  and energy, 204
  and trust, 252–53
Noninterpersonal to interpersonal (transition), 70, 78, 144, 173, 238–39, 252, 306,
  327

O

One Hundred Dollar Misunderstanding,
  18, 31
The Open and Closed Mind, 142
Overlegislation, 275–76, 278

P

Pace, R. Wayne, 288
Packard, Vance, 70

Paralanguage, 336, 337, 338
Parity principle, 116, 124
Parts and wholes, 46–52
Pattern of communicative control (PCC),
  92, 93, 94, 108, 124, 140
  fixed and variable elements, 99–101
  and interpersonal communication, 101
  learning of, 97–101
  and relational development, 201, 214,
    219
  and social context, 214
Patton, Bobby R., 6, 63
Penny, R., 202
Perceptions, 9, 21, 38, 95
Person, as a source of information in rela-
  tional development, 208–10
Personal identity, and time, 205–206
Personality, 97, 170, 172
Personally private information, 310–11,
  341
Pieper, Walter A., 117
Playboy, 15, 156, 279
Profile of Nonverbal Sensitivity (PONS),
  184
Post-romantic stage of relational develop-
  ment, 259–60
Power, 68–69, 73–74
Pragmatic function of information,
  207–208, 215, 229
Pragmatic view of interpersonal com-
  munication, 28, 31
Pragmatics of Human Communication, 32
Preconditions for interpersonal vs. nonin-
  terpersonal relationships, 221–23
Predictability-as-desirability, 104
Predictability of stimulus-response-reward
  sequence, 111–12
Prediction, 7–22, 31, 110–11, 165, 341
  accuracy of, 14, 15–16, 19, 22,
    24–25, 37, 41
  and category systems, 96
  and cognitive style, 165
  and communication, 7–12
  consciousness and unconsciousness of,
    9–12, 103
  cultural level, 12–17, 110–11, 113,
    326–27
  and empathy, 169–70, 173–74

errors in, 15–16, 19, 24, 41, 213
errors related to level of analysis, 15–16, 24–25
and ideology, 14–15
and information, 15–16, 19
and level of analysis, 12–22, 22–29, 240
and psychological level, 19–22, 111, 113
and reification, 335–36
and sanity, 11
situational and dispositional factors, 11–12
sociological level, 17–19, 111, 113, 326–27
Prediction-making model, 177–81
Prine, John, 285
Process, 40–43, 59
The Process of Communication, 40
Professor Harold Hill, 156
Profit, 116–17, 122–23
and escalation, 220–21
loss of, 118–19
and self-disclosure, 312, 318
and termination of relationships, 284
Propinquity hypothesis, 202, 228
Pseudo-conflict, 267–68, 285
Psychological level of analysis, 12, 19–22, 33, 69–70, 262
and complementarity vs. symmetry, 238–41
and control, 111, 122, 126
and prediction, 22, 30
and relational development, 200–201

R

Rate of behavior, 109–10
Reaching Out, 342
Rein, Irving, 269
Reification, 335–36, 341
Reinforcement of behavior, 109–10, 234
Relational development
and attitudes, 208, 241–42
and communication, 224–26
and conversation, 327–28
and self-disclosure, 310
Relational legislation, 270–79, 285

and communication, 273–74
and conflict, 272
Relational view
of balance, 253
of communication, 48–52
of complementarity and symmetry, 253
of control, 52, 120–21, 124, 140
of self-disclosure, 310, 314–16
of trust, 253
Relationship as an entity, 51–52
and balance, 245–46
and danger signals, 283–84
Replicability of responses, 106–107
Resolution of conflict, 61, 73–77, 87, 263–64, 270
interpersonal approach, 76–77
noninterpersonal approach, 75–76
Response, 177–78
and control, 102
desirability, 103–104, 107
Response obligations, and self-disclosure, 312
Responsibility for responses, 104–106, 107
Restricted information, 336–38, 341
Revere, Paul, 35
Reward, 90, 200, 208
and control, 65–66, 87, 108–109, 110–11, 112, 114–16, 117, 123
definitional problems, 113–14
and empathy, 179, 192–93, 195
and energy, 297
and escalation, 220–21
magnitude of, 115–16
and social context, 214
Reward/cost ratio, 283–84
Rhamey, R., 208
Risk, and self-disclosure, 311, 312–14
Ritual self-sacrifice, 323
Robertson, L. 202
Robinson, E. A., 85
Rogers, Peter L. 186
Rogers, Will, 138
Rokeach, Milton, 142, 148–53
Roles, 18, 21, 27, 70
Role theory, 48
Romantic stage of relationships, 259–60, 270
Rosenthal, Robert, 184, 186

Rules
  articulation of, 241
  communicative, 21–22, 49
  generation of, 21–22, 55–56
  cultural, 53
  interpersonal, 21–22, 35, 51

S

Sanford, Nevitt, 147, 154, 156
Sanity, 11
Schachter, Stanley, 202
Scheerer, Klaus, R., 186
Scheff, Thomas J., 122
Science and Sanity, 339
Scientific American, 34
Security, 107
Self-concealment, 309
Self-concept, 51, 261, 275
  and self-disclosure, 313
Self-concept development, and control, 63, 80–86, 87
Self-description, 310
Self-disclosure, 309–25
  consequences of, 311–14
  decoding, 317–19
  functions of, 319–20, 321
  and intentionality, 311
  and level of communication, 26, 341
  and relational development, 310
  and risk, 311, 312–14
  and time, 205
  interpersonal vs. noninterpersonal, 320–25
Self-other ratings, 170, 171
Self-fulfilling prophecy, 347
Self-perception theory, 95
Sensitivity training, 26, 28
Sensory deprivation, 6
Sequential concept of communication, 48, 290
Sevareid, Eric, 342
Sex-related communication problems, 277–79

Sherif, Muzafer, 215
Siamese twin control strategies, 128–31
Siegel, Elliot, R., 163
Simon, Paul, 342
Simons, Herbert, 262
Simple conflict, 265–66
Simultaneity of message-making, 290
Situational factors and prediction, 11
Skinner, B. F., 65, 85, 158
Social context of association, 201, 213–16, 228
The Social Psychology of Groups, 90
Sociological generalizations, 240, 307, 311
Sociological level of analysis, 12, 17–19, 20, 22, 30, 31, 44, 52, 69, 111
  and accuracy of prediction, 19, 72, 172
  and group norms and values, 17–19, 20, 84–85, 105, 125
  and cognitive style, 153–56
Sociological relationships, 53–54
"The Sounds of Silence," 342
Space, and relational development, 202–205
Spassky, Boris, 60
Speech Communication, 288
Speech Communication: A Behavioral Approach, 40
Stereotype, 16, 31, 70, 154, 201, 296
Stevens, S. S., 34, 35
Stimulus discrimination, 22–25, 29, 240
  and cognitive style, 146–47
  and empathy, 170–71, 172–74, 179
  and practice, 184–86
Stimulus generalization, 22–25, 29
  and cognitive style, 157
  and compliance, 72
  and empathy, 179
  and relational development, 209–10
Stimulus-response-reward sequence, 110–11, 112
Strategy of control; *see* Control strategies
Substance of behavior, 109, 110
"Sweet Revenge," 285
Symbols, 5, 35, 43–46
Symmetry, 232–41, 254
System of communication, 48–52

366

Gerald R. Miller

received his Ph.D. at the University of Iowa in 1961 and is presently a Distinguished Professor of Communication at Michigan State University. He has authored six books and many articles dealing with communication theory, interpersonal communication, and persuasion. Among his honors are the Distinguished Faculty Award and the *Centennial Review* Lectureship at Michigan State University, a Golden Anniversary Award for outstanding scholarly publication from the Speech Communication Association, and a concurrent resolution of tribute from the Michigan Legislature for his research dealing with the use of videotape in courtroom trials.

Mark Steinberg

was born twenty-six years ago in Connecticut. He is currently trying to apply many of the techniques discussed in this book to finishing requirements for his Ph.D., improving the quality of his interpersonal relationships, and improving his poker playing.

This book was set in 10-point Times Roman
by Dharma Press, Emeryville, California.
It was printed by the Printing Division
of the American Can Company,
Indianapolis, Indiana.

Project Editor	Gretchen Hargis
Designer	Bruce Kortebein
Illustrator	Victor Moscoso
Sponsoring Editors	Karl Schmidt, Frank Geddes